Boundaries and Belonging

States and Societies in the Struggle to Shape Identities and Local Practices

This interdisciplinary volume maintains the importance of a spatial understanding of society and history, but it suggests a way of conceiving of borders and space that goes beyond a school map of states. Its subject is the struggle among differing spatial logics, or mental maps. It is concerned with the meaning that state borders hold for people but recognizes that such meaning varies and is contested by other social formations. The authors here ask, To what degree do state borders encase the mechanisms that make the decisive rules governing people's lives and to what extent do they give way to other rulemakers? To what extent do states circumscribe the communities to which people feel attached and to what extent do they intersect with other communities of belonging? The essays in this book home in on the struggles and conflicting demands on people, given that state borders are not automatically preeminent and that other spatial logics demand attention.

Joel S. Migdal is author of many works of comparative state-society relations and the politics of Israel and the Palestinians. His books include *The Palestinian People: A History* (with Baruch Kimmerling, 2003), *Through the Lens of Israel: Explorations in State and Society* (2001), *State-in-Society: Studying How States and Societies Transform and Constitute One Another* (2001), *State Power and Social Forces: Domination and Transformation in the Third World* (with co-editors Atul Kohli and Vivienne Shue, 1994), *Palestinians: The Making of a People* (with Baruch Kimmerling, 1993), and *Strong Societies and Weak States: State-Society Relations and State Capabilities in the Third World* (1988). He has taught at Tel Aviv University and Harvard University and has been a visiting professor at the Hebrew University of Jerusalem, the Institut d'Etudes Politiques de Paris, and the School of Oriental and African Studies in London. He has been a Fulbright-Hayes Fellow and a Lady Davis Fellow. For most of the 1990s he was chair of the Social Science Research Council's Committee on the Near and Middle East. He is currently president of the Association for Israel Studies. He was the founding chair of the International Studies Program at the University of Washington.

Boundaries and Belonging

States and Societies in the Struggle to Shape Identities and Local Practices

Edited by
JOEL S. MIGDAL
University of Washington, Seattle

CAMBRIDGE
UNIVERSITY PRESS

CAMBRIDGE UNIVERSITY PRESS
Cambridge, New York, Melbourne, Madrid, Cape Town, Singapore, São Paulo

Cambridge University Press
The Edinburgh Building, Cambridge CB2 8RU, UK

Published in the United States of America by Cambridge University Press, New York

www.cambridge.org
Information on this title: www.cambridge.org/9780521835664

First published 2004
This digitally printed version 2008

A catalogue record for this publication is available from the British Library

Library of Congress Cataloguing in Publication data

Boundaries and belonging : states and societies in the struggle to shape identities and local practices / edited by Joel S. Migdal.
p. cm.
ISBN 0-521-83566-6
1. Boundaries. 2. Allegiance. 3. Group identity. I. Migdal, Joel S.

JC323.B677 2004
320.1′2 – dc22 2003061210

ISBN 978-0-521-83566-4 hardback
ISBN 978-0-521-06849-9 paperback

Contents

Contributors

Yeşim Arat is a professor in the Department of Political Science and International Relations, Boğaziçi University, Istanbul. She has worked on women's political participation, and her latest research is on Islamist women activists in Turkish politics.

Lauren Basson is a Kreitman Post-Doctoral Fellow in the Department of Politics and Government at Ben Gurion University in Beer Sheva, Israel. Her research focuses on citizenship, national membership, and ethnicity in comparative perspective.

Mary P. Callahan is an assistant professor in the Jackson School of International Studies at the University of Washington. She teaches classes on human rights, civil-military relations, and international studies. She is the author of *Making Enemies: War and State Building in Burma* (2003).

Lisa Conant is an assistant professor of Political Science at the University of Denver and author of *Justice Contained: Law and Politics in the European Union*. She wrote "Contested Boundaries" as a Jean Monnet Fellow at the European University Institute.

Neil J. Diamant is Associate Professor of Asian Law and Culture at Dickinson College in Carlisle, Pennsylvania. He is the author of *Revolutionalizing the Family: Politics, Love and Divorce in Urban and Rural China, 1949–1968* (2000).

Béatrice Hibou is a researcher at the CNRS-CERI and has been a member of the editorial board of *Critique Internationale* (1998 to 2003). She is now studying the transformation of economic regulation in North Africa and in Southern Europe. Her recent publications include *The Criminalization of the State in Africa* (with J. F. Bayart and S. Ellis, 1998), and she has edited *Privatizing the State* (2003).

Reşat Kasaba is Professor of International Studies at the University of Washington and an adjunct professor in the Departments of Sociology and

Political Science. He is the author of *The Ottoman Empire and the World-Economy: The Nineteenth Century* (1988) and co-editor with Sibel Bozdoğan of *Rethinking Modernity and National Identity in Turkey* (1997).

Adriana Kemp is a lecturer in the Department of Sociology and Anthropology, Tel Aviv University. Her fields of research are labor migration, citizenship, identity and borders, boundaries, and nationalism. She has published numerous articles on these subjects in journals such as *Political Geography, Ethnic and Racial Studies, Gender and Society*, and *Identities*.

Kenneth G. Lawson is a professor of Political Science and International Studies at Shoreline Community College in Seattle, Washington. His research focuses on the issues of nationalism, civil society, globalization, and U.S. foreign policy. He is working on a study that compares the civic effects of the First World War in small communities in the United States and Ireland.

Joel S. Migdal is the Robert F. Philip Professor of International Studies at the University of Washington. He has written widely on state-society relations. His most recent book on that topic is *State in Society: Studying How States and Societies Transform and Constitute One Another* (2001). He also writes on Israelis and Palestinians in the Middle East. Recently, he published *The Palestinian People: A History* (2003) with co-author Baruch Kimmerling.

Matthew Sparke is an associate professor of Geography in the Jackson School of International Studies at the University of Washington. He is the author of *Hyphen-Nation-States: Critical Geographies of Displacement and Disjuncture* (2004), and is currently writing a textbook on globalization. His research on cross-border regions and the transnational development of civil society is sponsored by a National Science Foundation CAREER grant.

Sarah Abrevaya Stein is an assistant professor in the History Department and the Henry M. Jackson School of International Studies at the University of Washington and author of *Making Jews Modern: Yiddish and Ladino Press in the Russian and Ottoman Empire* (2003). Her articles have appeared in *Slavic Review, Jewish History, Jewish Social Studies, The Oxford Handbook of Jewish Studies*, and numerous edited volumes.

Nicole F. Watts is Assistant Professor of Political Science at San Francisco State University. She has published articles on Kurdish ethnic politics in the *International Journal of Middle East Studies* and *New Perspectives on Turkey*. She is currently working on a book manuscript, tentatively entitled *Routes to Ethnic Resistance: Kurdish Politics in the Turkish Republic*.

Patricia J. Woods is Assistant Professor of Political Science and Jewish Studies at the University of Florida and Visiting Scholar at the Center for Middle Eastern Studies at Harvard University. She is completing a book on the role of socio-professional ties linking high court justices and social movement lawyers in the religious-secular conflict in Israel.

Preface and Acknowledgments

This book began to take shape in two workshops that were held at the University of Washington in July 1999 and September 2000. For me and, I think, for the others who attended, those workshops were extremely exciting. They played with and integrated some of the most compelling current topics in the social sciences: issues of borders, multiple and changing identities, differing vectors and senses of belonging, states, the lines between public and private space, and more. Perhaps what made them so exciting to me was that they brought new voices to some of the old questions in comparative studies. In this volume, all the contributors except Yeşim Arat, Reşat Kasaba, and me received their Ph.D.s after 1995.

It is not simply that this volume introduces bright new minds. These scholars bring a new sensibility to the study of comparative politics and society. All are area experts with deep knowledge of one or more parts of the globe, but they have used their immersion in a place as a way of seeing how old boundaries have been transgressed, even obliterated. They have used their area knowledge to bypass old binaries, such as between migration and stasis, state and society, public and private, national and transnational. Their methodological orientation is to look beyond the lines dividing these supposed opposites to their ongoing interplay, leading to unexpected processes and results. All take culture very seriously but flesh it out in ways that go beyond the tired analysis of attitudes, values, norms, and beliefs. For them, culture is manifest in key practices and is shaped and reshaped in the critical survival choices people make day in and day out.

Part of their new sensibility that I think infuses this volume comes from their interdisciplinarity. Trained as political scientists, sociologists, geographers, and historians, they all have worked in interdisciplinary settings and have gone beyond the limits of their own disciplines. Working with others outside their regions has also contributed to the originality of their outlooks. Cases here come from North America, East Asia, Southeast Asia, the Middle East, and Europe, and Hibou's conclusion throws in a strong dose of Africa as well. I believe the breadth of cases attests to the wide applicability of the ideas here. The disproportionate number of chapters dealing with the Middle East probably reflects my own selection bias but also stems from the complex notions of boundaries and belonging that came out of the Ottoman Empire and its demise. The Middle East gives insight into worldwide contemporary struggles over identity in a way that primary reliance on European experience and thought would not.

The book starts with a chapter by me laying out the key issues and explicating an approach that grew out of the discussions at the two workshops. This is followed by four substantive sections. Part II, with chapters by Reşat Kasaba and Sarah Abrevaya Stein, examines issues of movement, stasis, and identity in the Ottoman Empire, before the construction of modern states in the territories it ruled. Next are two sections focusing on modern states and their often tense relationship with other boundary-creating entities and processes inside (and spilling over) their borders. Part III has chapters by Adriana Kemp on Israel, Mary Callahan on Burma, and Nicole Watts on Turkey and Virtual Kurdistan, which examine the states' difficult relations with groups that fall outside the accepted definition of the nation. In Part IV, chapters by Lauren Basson (on the United States), Kenneth Lawson (Canada), Neil Diamant (China), and Patricia Woods (Israel) explore the unexpected and dynamic results of states' attempting to inscribe social boundaries on their populations. The chapters by Matthew Sparke (on Cascadia), Lisa Conant (European Union), and Yeşim Arat (Turkey and the larger Islamic world) explore the tensions between states and transnational spatial configurations challenging conventional notions of state and citizens, nation and nationals. Finally, Béatrice Hibou draws from all of these to offer analytic and theoretical conclusions.

The ideas coming out of the workshops were immeasurably enriched by participants who have not contributed to this volume. I express my deep appreciation to Uri Ben-Eliezer, Madeleine Dong, Leila Fawaz, Kathie Friedman, Edward Gross, Steven Heydemann, Christine Ingebritsen, David Newman, and Jonathan Warren. Michael McCann was both an intellectual inspiration and, through his role as the head of the newly formed Comparative Law and Society Studies (CLASS) program at the University of Washington, a major provider of material support. Invaluable assistance for the workshops and volume was given by Chandni Gupta, Laura Korey, Jarod Krissman, Tamara Leonard, Jane Meyerding, Brian Peters, Kammerle Schneider, Zoë Stemm, Cathy Vuong, and Wanli Yuan. I also thank those who funded the project, including the University of Washington's Tools for Transformation Program; the CLASS program; the International Studies Center, administered by Reşat Kasaba; the Middle East Center, administered by Ellis Goldberg with the aid of Felicia Hecker; the Robert F. Philip Professorship in International Studies; and the Crossing-Borders Ford Foundation grant, administered by Gary Hamilton and, later, Laurie Sears.

PART I

INTRODUCTION

1

Mental Maps and Virtual Checkpoints

Struggles to Construct and Maintain State and Social Boundaries

Joel S. Migdal

In the period from the end of the Cold War, at the beginning of the 1990s, to the present, academics and laymen alike have moved away from a view of borders as fixed and hard features of international life. Today, borders are much more commonly understood as contingent, porous, and in flux. The Cold War, especially its last two decades, had managed to make the lines dividing countries on world maps seem to be permanent parts of the landscape, like rivers and mountains. Those years had eclipsed the memories of the dissolution of huge empires in World War I, the creation of new states and mandates after that war, and the occurrence of massive territorial changes during World War II. Indeed, once the old European empires finally faded away in Africa and Asia and decolonization drew to an end, mostly by the mid-1960s, remarkably few countries disappeared or even had significant border changes. One could cite a few cases – the transformation of East Pakistan into Bangladesh, the appearance and disappearance of Biafra, the cease-fire lines after the 1967 war in the Middle East – but they were the limited exceptions to a period of extraordinary state-border stability.

Not surprisingly, then, outside an interest in decolonization, few books and articles by political scientists and sociologists dealt with the question of borders in the postwar period and, especially, in the generation from the mid-1960s to the early 1990s.[1] And consequently, I think, few works addressed larger political and cultural meaning attached to borders: questions of the essence of sovereignty and the degree to which borders served as frames for actual human communities. There was little interest in what kind of

[1] William J. Foltz, "Modernization and Nation-Building: The Social Mobilization Model Reconsidered," in *From National Development to Global Community*, ed. Richard L. Merritt and Bruce Russett (London: George Allen & Unwin, 1981); Saadia Touval, *The Boundary Politics of Independent Africa* (Cambridge, Mass.: Harvard University Press, 1972). Geographers were much more likely to deal with boundaries. See, e.g., Peter Gould and Rodney White, *Mental Maps*, 2nd ed. (London: Harmondsworth, Penguin, 1986), who coined the term "mental maps" used in my title.

meaning, or sense of belonging, borders created for people, as they tried to place themselves socially in the world.

In the 1990s, though, events brought the issues of territory and borders back into the popular and academic imagination.[2] Old states vanished and new ones appeared. The Soviet Union splintered into fifteen new states; Yugoslavia, into five; Czechoslovakia and Ethiopia, into two each. Namibia (1990) and the Palestine Authority (1993) appeared. The European Union replaced the European Community, grew larger, moved toward a single currency, and appropriated functions from its member states. The flow of capital and communications across borders, which appeared increasingly porous, went off the charts. These changes and more created cottage industries in the social sciences and humanities examining the implications of border changes, including numerous studies of sovereignty,[3] transnationalism,[4] globalization,[5] European integration,[6] and territorialization.[7] Some went so far

[2] Jeffrey Herbst, *States and Power in Africa: Comparative Lessons in Authority and Control*, Princeton Series in International History and Politics, ed. Jack L. Snyder, Marc Trachtenberg, and Fareed Zakaria (Princeton, N.J.: Princeton University Press, 2000), John G. Ruggie, "Territoriality and Beyond," *International Organization* 47, no. 1 (1993): 139–67.

[3] Joseph A. Camilleri and Jim Falk, *The End of Sovereignty?: The Politics of a Shrinking and Fragmenting World* (Brookefield, Vt.: Edward Edgar, 1992); Julie A. Erfani, *The Paradox of the Mexican State: Rereading Sovereignty From Independence to NAFTA* (Boulder, Colo.: Lynne Rienner, 1995); Edmond J. Keller and Donald Rothchild, *Africa in the New International Order: Rethinking State Sovereignty and Regional Security* (Boulder, Colo.: Lynne Rienner, 1996); Gene M. Lyons and Michael Mastanduno, eds., *Beyond Westphalia? State Sovereignty and International Intervention* (Baltimore, Md.: Johns Hopkins University Press, 1995).

[4] Stephen Castles, "Studying Social Transformation," *International Political Science Review* 22, no. 1 (2001): 13–32, Ivo D. Duchacek, Daniel Latouche, and Garth Stevenson, *Perforated Sovereignties and International Relations: Transsovereign Contacts of Subnational Governments* (New York: Greenwood Press, 1988).

[5] Stephen Castles and Alastair Davidson, *Citizenship and Migration: Globalization and the Politics of Belonging* (New York: Routledge, 2000); Frederic Jameson and Masao Miyoshi, eds., *The Cultures of Globalization, Post-Contemporary Interventions* (Durham, N.C.: Duke University Press, 1998), Anthony D. King, ed., *Culture, Globalization and the World System: Contemporary Conditions for the Representation of Identity* (Binghamton: Department of Art and History, State University of New York at Binghamton, 1991); James H. Mittelman, ed., *Globalization: Critical Reflections* (Boulder, Colo.: Lynne Rienner, 1996); Proshanta K. Nandi and Shahid M. Shahidullah, eds., *Globalization and the Evolving World Society* (Boston: Brill, 1998); Nicanor Perlas, *Shaping Globalization: Civil Society, Cultural Power, and Threefolding* (Quezon City, Philippines: Center for Alternative Development Initiatives, 1999).

[6] Michael Calingaert, *European Integration Revisited* (Boulder, Colo.: Westview Press, 1996); Jytte Klausen and Louise A. Tilly, eds., *European Integration in Social and Historical Perspective* (Lanham, Md.: Rowman & Littlefield, 1997); George A. Kourvetaris and Andreas Moschonas, eds., *The Impact of European Integration: Political, Sociological, and Economic Changes* (Westport, Conn.: Praeger, 1996); James B. Steinberg, *"An Ever Closer Union": European Integration and Its Implications for the Future of U.S.-European Relations* (Santa Monica, Calif.: RAND, 1993).

[7] David J. Elkins, *Beyond Sovereignty: Territory and Political Economy in the Twenty-First Century* (Toronto: University of Toronto Press, 1995); Thom Kuehls, *Beyond Sovereign*

as to reject "the nationally-constituted society as the appropriate object of discourse."[8]

All these subfields suggest that borders are impermanent features of social life, dependent on particular circumstances rather than being permanent fixtures of human society. The status of borders has been contingent on varying historical circumstances, rather than being immutably rock-like. Borders shift; they leak; and they hold varying sorts of meaning for different people. No one could simply assume that any person's primary identity is necessarily rooted in the people within his or her state's borders, whether that state is the Congo or even France.

Yet even in the new streams of social science, many studies, wittingly or unwittingly, continue to "remain fixed and thematized at the level of the spatial and the geopolitical" associated with the nation-state.[9] This volume maintains the importance of a spatial understanding of society and history, but it suggests a way of conceiving of borders and space that goes beyond a school map of states. Its subject is the struggle among differing spatial logics, or mental maps. It is concerned with the meanings that state borders hold for people but recognizes that such meanings vary and are contested by other social formations. The authors here ask, To what degree do state borders encase the mechanisms that make the decisive rules governing people's lives, and to what extent do they give way to other rule makers? To what extent do states circumscribe the communities to which people feel attached, and to what extent do they intersect with other communities of belonging? The chapters in this book home in on the struggles and conflicting demands on people, given that state borders are not automatically preeminent and that other spatial logics demand attention.

Boundaries

I use the term "boundaries" here to convey more than simple borders, lines dividing spaces as represented on maps; boundaries signify the point at which something becomes something else, at which the way things are done changes, at which "we" end and "they" begin, at which certain rules for behavior no longer obtain and others take hold. That is, boundaries include symbolic and social dimensions associated with the border divisions that appear on maps or, for that matter, other dividing lines that cannot be found

Territory (Minneapolis: University of Minnesota Press, 1986); Warren Magnusson, *The Search for Political Space: Globalization, Social Movements and the Urban Political Experience* (Toronto: University of Toronto Press, 1996); Steven R. Ratner, "Drawing a Better Line: *Uti Possidetis* and the Borders of New States," *American Journal of International Law* 90 (1996): 590–624; Michael J. Shapiro and Hayward R. Alker, *Changing Boundaries: Global Flows, Territorial Identities* (Minneapolis: University of Minnesota Press, 1996).

[8] King, ed., *Culture, Globalization and the World System.*

[9] Jameson and Miyoshi, eds., *Cultures of Globalization.*

on any map at all. Because boundaries connote the site at which things are done differently or the limits to where things are done in one way, they are social constructions. And as the site where different ways of doing things meet, they are likely to be replete with tension and conflict. People thus create barriers through accepting common manners of acting and rejecting – even fighting off – other ways of acting. One may think of people's acting according to a set of laws on one side of a state boundary, for example, and others acting on the basis of a different code on the other side of the boundary. Boundaries are barriers that people establish, but by no means are they airtight.

Deborah S. Bernstein demonstrates this point nicely for a boundary between not two states but two social groups: Jewish and Arab workers in Palestine in the early stages of their century-long bitter conflict. In the critical interwar years, she writes, the pattern that emerged in the town "of Haifa's labor market was the overall, pervasive separation and boundary construction between Jews and Arabs which was pushed through by organized Jewish labor. The essence of the construction of boundaries in the economic sphere was to close the Jewish economy to Arab labor so as to protect Jewish workers from the competition of much cheaper Arab workers."[10] Nonetheless, she argues, the two communities cannot be understood as "secured within clear-cut, impenetrable and unrefuted boundaries.... Such a focus did not lead to sufficient understanding of the formation of boundaries. It could not shed light on the controversies and conflicts concerning boundary formation, as the boundaries themselves were taken for granted.... They were conveyed as part of the basic order rather than as a negotiated and dynamic social construct."[11]

Boundaries, to my mind, incorporate two elements beyond serving as simple separators: *checkpoints* and *mental maps*. Boundaries are constructed through the practical monitoring devices that groups use at actual and virtual checkpoints to divide one space from another. Checkpoints refer to the sites and practices that groups use to differentiate members from others and to enforce separation. Monitoring at actual checkpoints includes a variety of surveillance techniques, from checking visas and passports to insidious practices such as racial profiling. At virtual checkpoints, practices go from scrutiny of modes of dress to detection of language and accent differences. Dress and language, along with other daily practices, then, not only are accepted ways of doing things among certain people; they also serve as signifiers at virtual checkpoints, as separators, marking who is included in a group and who is not.

[10] Deborah S. Bernstein, *Constructing Boundaries: Jewish and Arab Workers in Mandatory Palestine*, ed. Russell Stone, SUNY Series in Israel Studies (Albany: State University of New York Press, 2000).

[11] Ibid.

All sorts of practices, both obvious and subtle, act as boundary markers, which tip people off as to whether someone is a member of their group or not. Monitoring devices at checkpoints are among the numerous ways of scrutinizing and interrogating people so as to determine into which social space they fall or to which group they belong. They are also the ways of enforcing the categorizations of space by using various sanctions and rewards. Enforcement devices can include something as innocent as giving someone the cold shoulder as well as a practice as horrible as ethnic cleansing. As Adriana Kemp's chapter notes, the construction of Israel's new boundaries after the state was created in 1948 included not only the physical patrolling of the armistice lines but devices designating certain citizens, the Palestinian Arabs, as a dangerous population. What the actual monitoring devices should be and who the guardians of the checkpoints should be can be intensely contested questions. In Israel, as Patricia Woods notes in her chapter, even among the privileged Jewish population, secular and religious agencies and courts within the state itself have battled over boundary questions, including the all-important one of who is a Jew.

Besides monitoring practices at actual and virtual checkpoints, boundaries also are constructed and maintained by people's mental maps, which divide home from alien territory, the included from the excluded, the familiar from the other. Mental maps incorporate elements of the meaning people attach to spatial configurations, the loyalties they hold, the emotions and passions that groupings evoke, and their cognitive ideas about how the world is constructed. All these act to establish and maintain the attachment of people to one another, but in so doing, they also mark the separation between groups.

If one indeed believes that boundaries have been built and maintained by what people do and think, both through the practices at virtual checkpoints and through mental maps, then one can imagine boundaries to be more than simply dividers of spaces occupied by states. Multiple sets of boundaries can exist, beyond those associated with state borders. Social groupings have their own boundaries, virtual checkpoints, and mental maps marking them off from other groupings. The boundaries of social groupings have their own spatial logic. That is, social groups, too, have territorial dimensions (usually physical, sometimes virtual), quite apart from state borders. A smuggling ring, to take an extreme example, may have all sorts of monitoring devices marking it off, such as code words, secret names, signals, established routes for travel, and sanctions for breaking the rules of the ring. And the mental map of its boundaries, including its territorial reach as well as who is in the group and who is outside, can be firmly embedded in its members' imagination and in the minds of border guards, customers, competitors, and others.

The boundaries constructed by the smuggling ring's monitoring devices and mental maps certainly do not appear on any school map and are very different from those of the state; indeed, they are meant to diminish – bypass, erase, neutralize – those of the state. Other social groupings, such as an extended family with members on two or three continents, may have no such overt intentions, but they, too, have their own spatial logic and share a mental map of the limits of their clan and its ways of doing things – language and acts of familiarity, forms of material exchange, and more – that establish spatial boundaries different from those of the state. The space of a group, such as a multicontinental clan, might differ from that of a state in that it may be discontinuous (although, it should be noted, that a few states are discontinuous, too). Jews, as a people, for example, maintained clear social boundaries through history without having a continuous space. Daniel S. Milo put it this way: "The Jewish perception of space is marked by two unique characteristics: it comprises a notion of multiple spaces, rather than one of a single space; and between these spaces – a void. In other words, the Jewish spatial experience is *differential* and *discontinuous*."[12] Space may also be deconcretized, as with a family in which concrete space is far less important than the boundaries created by the social relations themselves.[13]

All people face multiple social groupings, including the state, in their daily lives that offer differing divisions of space, that is, differing mental maps of how their world is constructed and laid out and different monitoring devices marking the boundaries of that world. People thus encounter multiple sets of boundaries, which configure space differently and which have various sets of meaning as well as checkpoints with scrutinizing and enforcing devices attached to them. Individuals, in short, daily confront radically divergent mental maps of how the world is configured. Sometimes, perhaps most times, multiple social groupings and the maps they project coexist harmoniously, causing minimal dissonance. But at other times they clash, using sanctions and rewards to demand contradictory ways of doing things and loyalty from people.

One example of such conflict that received much publicity came out in the tense days immediately after the infamous 2000 presidential election in the United States, when neither George W. Bush nor Al Gore could claim victory. John Ellis had served as election day vote analyst for the Fox network, the first of the national news associations to call the election (prematurely) for Bush that night. All the networks understood the enormous significance of their casting Bush as the presumptive winner at a moment when the outcome was still very much in doubt. Most of them later undertook internal inquiries as to what had spurred them to jump the gun. Fox's call for Bush pushed the others into following suit and was thus extremely important. Fox officials later found out that Ellis, a cousin of Bush, traded information with

[12] Daniel S. Milo, "Introduction I: The Perception of Space," in *A Historical Atlas of the Jewish People*, ed. Eli Barnavi (New York: Schocken Books, 1992), vi–ix.

[13] Judith Baskin, "Strategic Alliances and the Human Factor: Migration for Marriage in Two Medieval Jewish Societies, lecture, Seattle, 2000.

Bush throughout election night, actions that threatened the independence and integrity of Fox, possibly leading it to call the election before there was any real certainty over the actual outcome. As one Fox executive said after the election, the network hired him "because of his ability, not his bloodline."[14] Fox had one set of rules and demands that it made on its employees; the "bloodline," another. Fox's transnational boundaries suggested one mental map of where boundaries lay and which social grouping's code should take precedence over others. It had checkpoints with monitoring devices, ranging from subtle ways of affecting professional reputation to censure, to enforce that representation. The Bush "bloodline" suggested quite another set of boundaries, with their own map and checkpoints (Bush jokingly suggested excluding members from the Thanksgiving dinner table who did not hold up their ends for the bloodline during the election).

Social groupings, such as news networks and extended families, or even states themselves, may seem to be inviolable social formations, with firm boundaries. They appear to enter the fray of conflicting boundaries as wholly formed institutions, with their checkpoints and monitoring devices to maintain their boundaries, such as professional censure, family ostracism, or imprisonment, in hand. In cases of severe conflict, the state itself, often through its judicial system, presents itself as the final arbiter of which rules of conduct should take precedence, but in so doing, courts rarely challenge the legitimacy of particular social institutions to exist; the "hardness" of social organizations and the permanence of their boundaries remain unquestioned.

The idea of the hardness of social groupings is frequently reinforced by the virtual checkpoints, boundary markers, and monitoring devices that their members employ in order to project the essentiality and primacy of the group's own boundaries. The fact that people use an attribute, such as skin color, unthinkingly as the default indicator separating "us" from "them" makes the categories of black and white and the divider between them seem natural and permanent. Lauren Basson's chapter notes how key social actors and state officials in the late nineteenth- and early twentieth-century United States used a variety of means, including pseudoscience, to make racial categories and the dividers between them seem hard and fast in the country.

In short, people depend on those checkpoints and markers, such as skin color, to navigate daily life, and in accepting those signposts to guide them, people lend an additional feeling of hardness to the boundaries of existing social groupings. Marking off social groups in this way is tremendously important, especially where those social groups are large and impersonal. People encounter others every day whom they have never met or barely know as acquaintances. This is a terrifying prospect. What kind of confidence can

[14] "Election Furor Prompts Fox to Review Role of Bush Cousin," *New York Times*, November 14, 2000, p. A22.

they have that strangers and near-strangers will act civilly and not stab them in the back, figuratively or literally? Routine practices – those boundary checkpoints, markers, and monitoring devices – help to separate those with whom one feels safe, for whom one has clear expectations for how they will behave, from others. The monitoring of boundaries, then, alerts them to who falls within one's group and who remains outside.

People's feelings of security rest on a sense that checkpoints and markers separate the familiar – those who share language, dress, skin color, mannerisms, citizenship, or other identifiable attributes – from the unfamiliar. Sometimes the markers are quickly identifiable, as when African Americans greet each other as "brother," even when they are not acquainted. At other times, the markers might be very subtle, as when Jews in Nazi-occupied Europe, fearing that any overt sign of their being Jews could doom them, murmured various words or phrases, including the word "*amhaw*" ("[I am one of] your people"), as codes to identify possible coreligionists. In short, the ability to identify boundaries of social groups is tremendously important for people simply to make out the lay of the land – where they believe that threats lurk and where security resides.

People draw their mental maps by configuring the world as familiar and unfamiliar spaces. They are thus constantly navigating, searching for those "manners of acting"[15] that can delineate configurations of spaces where they feel that they are, or should be, relatively safe, places that somehow feel familiar and different from the chaotic sense of the totally unfamiliar. As much as high crime rates, the unfamiliarity with how things are done and how strangers behave is what makes a particular neighborhood feel "dangerous." In contrast, the reassuring message people take with them on their forays into meetings with strangers in familiar places, such as a city bus, is that by knowing the markers and checkpoints they can minimize risk and know what to expect from others. They feel, within the parameters of mingling with strangers, who by definition represent the unknown, that they still can have a sense of what to expect and how to behave. This cognitive element, the mental map, helps construct and maintain boundaries, even if those boundaries are somewhat arbitrary and fluid.[16]

Regular checkpoints and habitual monitoring devices serve to naturalize a state or social group, creating a reassuring mental image of it as permanent and unchanging and a mental map that sets it off from other social groups. The perception that the groups are rock-hard diminishes the terror of vulnerable people in their dealings with strangers. Any feeling of threat is mitigated by the unquestioned assumption that the person one is encountering is a "brother" or "*amhaw*." And the perception acts, in turn, to validate

[15] Peter J. Steinberger, "Public and Private," *Political Studies* 47 (1999): 294.

[16] Carol J. Greenhouse, Barbara Yngvesson, and David M. Engel, *Law and Community in Three American Towns* (Ithaca, N.Y.: Cornell University Press, 1994).

the checkpoints for scrutinizing boundaries, even when the practices associated with those checkpoints are demanding and costly, such as having to purchase a passport and spend endless hours in line going through customs. The mental map and the checkpoints seem to be in a virtuous cycle feeding off one another to make the state's or social grouping's boundaries appear to be inviolable. It is easy to understand how laypeople and academics alike could slip into seeing states in the Cold War era as givens and the particular division of boundaries on maps as a depiction of the permanent configuration of the social and political landscape.

But the virtuous cycle of mental maps and checkpoints does not exist in a vacuum. Other forces intervene to change and challenge boundaries and highlight the impermanence of social groupings, as the 1990s made clear for some states. Perhaps this notion of the mutability of boundaries, their malleability in the face of human events, was portrayed most vividly in a statement attributed to Louis XIV. When his grandson became king of Spain, Louis is purported to have said, "There are no more Pyrenees." For all the efforts to maintain hard racial boundaries in the United States of a century ago, Basson demonstrates how those classifications were confounded by the challenges of racially mixed people who did not fit into any of the categories, for whom the mental map of space made no sense and for whom the normal checkpoints raised more questions than they answered.

No matter how much people like to think of their mental maps as permanent, they must be very sensitive to changing and uncertain boundaries. Those on the lowest social rungs, especially, need to be prepared at a moment's notice to remake their map of the social terrain. They must face the fact that today's boundaries are not static. Different social groups make contradictory demands on them and, in so doing, complicate both the placement of the boundary and the question of which boundary should take precedence in a given social situation. Is security in a difficult situation to be found in citizenship, gender, religion, ethnicity, kinship, or perhaps some other social formation, such as gangs or social clubs? These are not idle questions nor do they have an invariable answer; indeed, being sensitive to necessary changes in the answer may determine a person's very survival. Navigating the boundaries of these social formations, knowing which boundaries will provide maximum security, and patrolling those boundaries so as to ally with those who will be most helpful are important skills, particularly when exogenous factors undermine old mental maps and checkpoints.

For social scientists, it is probably preferable to think of the normal state of boundaries as in flux, rather than as permanent or semi-permanent, when trying to understand the configuration of human space. To be sure, the rate of flux will vary in different circumstances. The dynamics of social life come when competing boundaries, demanding different, even contradictory practices and mental images, bump up against one another. They put varying demands on people in terms of behavior, emotions, and cognition, causing no small amount of distress and dissonance for people. After all, these conflicting boundaries are asking people to assign very different sorts of meaning to the world, events, and people that they encounter. And as boundaries do clash and people encapsulated by them make choices about which demands to follow and which to ignore, those boundaries change. That means that dividing lines, the scrutinizing practices that maintain them, loyalty, and the like change in an ongoing process. Mental maps and virtual checkpoints are constantly being contested and transformed.

All the chapters in this book focus on such processes. They all examine struggles over the construction of groups at moments when old boundaries, mental maps, and virtual checkpoints are being challenged: Which groups will succeed in demanding membership? Which will command people's loyalties and personal identities? Which will make rules for behavior that will displace other rules or impulses? All the authors here ask about the construction and maintenance of boundaries between groups. What are the sites and practices that constitute people's virtual checkpoints? What sorts of boundary markers are used to identify members (e.g., language, race, or personal presentation such as clothes or food)? How do boundaries include and exclude particular people? What kinds of monitoring devices are used to interrogate people about their membership?

Each of the social entities discussed in the following chapters is constructed and reconstructed in ongoing struggles and negotiations with other groups. Each has a spatial logic associated with it, and these logics, too, are often at odds. That means that people face tough choices about where to throw their lot, which boundaries to accept for determining how they act and to whom they are loyal. All the chapters stress that the configuration of social space is contested.

The assumed spatial logic in so much of the historical and social science literature, of course, has been the territory of the state (the school map, again), and the primary social group has been its associated nation. Of course, one cannot ignore the notion of the nation-state. But what the chapters that follow demonstrate is that these entities – state and nation – have been constantly defined and reconstructed by the other spatial logics put forth by the groups that they claim or with which they interact. School maps have been challenged by other mental maps. Those other groups may be fully contained within the boundaries of individual states; they may traverse the boundaries of two or more states; or they may subsume multiple states within their own boundaries. Not only have the boundaries of states been reconstructed continually, they also have varied in importance in people's lives.

The contestation of state boundaries, at first glance, may seem to be a fairly obvious phenomenon: You will know it when you see it. One can immediately think of the disintegration of Yugoslavia's boundaries in the early 1990s. It was perfectly clear that the old boundaries were dissolving and that this dissolution was unleashing the most vicious sort of contestation: the

Balkan Wars that consumed Croatia, Bosnia, and Serbia, including Kosovo, for the better part of the decade. But, in fact, the contestation of boundaries can be much more subtle and less immediately obvious. One way to think about these less obvious, but still insidious challenges to state boundaries is through a central institution of the state, the law. For states, probably nothing constitutes them more than law, the rules of conduct that prescribe proper behavior of its members and the control implied by the enforcement of the codes. Not only does law set out the ways of doing things, it also projects an essential part of the image of the state, as when it denotes the whole body of rules, institutions (such as courts) associated with them, and their affective component (as in "respect for the law"). People are classified by whether they stay within state laws (law-abiding) or step outside them (lawbreakers). State law, then, both prescribes behavior within the boundaries of the state and symbolically demarks those boundaries by signifying the realm and limits of the state's law.

When others put forward an alternative code to state law – let's say, that of a street gang – they contest not only the code itself but the realm and its limits suggested by the law. That challenge puts forward an alternative spatial logic to that offered by the state's borders; in the case of a gang, perhaps a streetcorner or neighborhood. Lisa Conant's chapter, in a case seemingly far from street gangs, suggests that the European Union, with its own spatial logic, has contested state laws that determine whether such people as long-term resident migrant workers from other member states or from third countries are entitled to certain social rights that local citizens have. And in response to clear and supposedly binding decisions by the European Court of Justice, member states have ignored, evaded, and flouted those judgments. "As the European Court of Justice attempts to blur national boundaries by creating transnational European rights and obligations," Conant concludes, "member states actively maintain and reconstruct territorial and national borders through their law, policy, and practice." This is every much a contestation over the binding codes associated with different boundaries as the battle between street gangs and local police. In another case of transnational boundaries, Yeşim Arat demonstrates how, from within the structures of the Turkish state, onetime prime minister Necmettin Erbakan and his Welfare Party similarly set out a transnational set of boundaries, in this case based on Islamic unity, as an alternative to the territorial construction of the state. Erbakan eventually was sentenced to a year in prison for his advocacy. No contending spatial logic today is more powerful than yet another transnational force, neoliberal capitalism, as discussed by Matthew Sparke in his chapter on the PACE lane intersecting the U.S.-Canadian border. He argues that the implications for state boundaries and the concept of citizenship are stark with "neoliberalism beginning to operate as a fundamentally unaccountable political rhetoric at the same time as it legally straitjackets democratic governance in practice."

In the European context, Conant begins to make sense of a contest over which body properly has the final say on law, the member states or the European Union. In that case, there is a guiding set of precepts on how to resolve such questions, although Conant demonstrates that, even then, there is tremendous ambiguity and decisions made on the fly that complicate the process. For people such as migrant workers and state welfare bureaus, this ambiguity confounds attempts to figure out which are really the key boundaries. It raises the question of whether migrants from outside Europe can somehow work their way into social boundaries in Europe or will forever remain outside them. For Europeans generally, the struggle is over which law will trump and, ultimately, with which boundaries, national or pan-European, people will identify. The battle is over which mental map will take precedence in Europeans' minds and which boundary checkpoints will prevail in determining who is an insider and who an outsider.[17]

In other cases of the contestation over law, the kinds of formal institutions and constitutional principles that putatively referee battles between member states and the European Court of Justice have not existed at all. Often, challenges to or flouting of law has been dismissed as plain old criminality or corruption. That is, collective lawbreaking has been seen as simple deviance from the established norm – state law – rather than the proffering of an alternative law. I think this is a mistake. Collective efforts of lawbreaking, in fact, have presented spatial logics different from the state's, suggesting alternative mental maps and varying notions of which checkpoints are in effect; that is, the question for individuals becomes which groups with whom one is most closely allied should take precedence. In brief, behaving according to nonstate rules of conduct challenges the most fundamental claim of states, that they appropriately make or delegate the right to make the rules that guide even the minute details of people lives.

Belonging

The challenge goes beyond a calculated decision of with whom one allies, say, the members of a smuggling ring or the members of the state. Because people find the essential security that they need for their survival in social groupings – whether the state or some other group with a different spatial logic – they invest tremendous emotional capital in the group. That is one reason it is so important to have all sorts of virtual checkpoints and

[17] Robert Picht, "Disturbed Identities: Social and Cultural Mutations in Contemporary Europe," in *European Identity and the Search for Legitimacy*, ed. García Soledad (New York: Pinter, 1993); García Soledad, "Europe's Fragmented Identities and the Frontiers of Citizenship," in *European Identity and the Search for Legitimacy*, ed. García Soledad (New York: Pinter, 1993).

markers delineating who is inside and who is outside. Their personal investments generate a transcendental process, transforming instrumental alliances into communities of belonging with deep affective ties.[18] People thus invest meaning in this process of selecting social groupings and their rules of conduct and in protecting and policing the group's boundaries. The emotional ties prompt people to acts of personal sacrifice that cannot simply be explained by their instrumental considerations. Belonging, then, has both a formal, instrumental sense attached to it – that is, one's status – and an informal, affective component – that is, one's sense of identity. Communities of belonging thus designate one's external standing, one's status, for others to see. But these communities of belonging gain succor from the affective elements associated with identity that bind people together in ways transcending their material and instrumental interests, inducing them to sacrifice for the group. For states, the status of individuals is that of citizen, and the identity is the sense of being part of the nation.

In short, the struggles over the construction of boundaries – which mental maps and checkpoints will prevail, which will take precedence – involve the most fundamental personal and social processes. These processes construct a personal sense of belonging and identity, and they provide cement to social groups by binding their members in communities of belonging, which hold together beyond people's momentary considerations of their personal interests. Such struggles are complex affairs. No one has just one set of operative boundaries; people operate according to multiple social logics simultaneously, but they face difficult questions on the ordering of these logics and how to respond when they encounter contradictory demands. These sorts of questions cut to the heart of their *status* – who they are to others and where they stand in one group or another – and to their *identity* – whom they understand their essential selves to be, especially in terms of the others to whom they liken themselves.[19] The chapters that follow cut into these struggles. While not at all assuming that the state simply triumphs, they do place the state in the midst of these struggles everywhere. These battles complicate the most fundamental categories of status and identity beyond kinship in today's world: those of citizen and member of the nation.

French sociologist Dominique Schnapper, a staunch defender of the community of belonging created by state borders (i.e., the nation), captured the link between citizenship and status in the modern state: "Citizenship was not only a juridical and political attribute in the narrow sense of the term. It was certain means of acquiring social status, the necessary – even if not

18 Edward Shils, *Center and Periphery: Essays in Macrosociology* (Chicago: University of Chicago Press, 1975).

19 Dahlia Moore and Baruch Kimmerling, "Individual Strategies of Adopting Collective Identities: The Israeli Case," *International Sociology* 10 (1995): 387–408.

always the sufficient condition – for the individual to be fully recognized as an actor in collective life."[20] In a world of strangers, states represent an institutional complex aiming to provide a basis for personal safety and, by means of that sense of safety, the most meaningful social boundaries in people's lives.[21] "Citizenship laws," writes Jeffrey Herbst, "...explicitly tie populations to unique, territorially defined polities."[22] Through citizenship, states provide a status packaged with common legal standing, rights, and responsibilities designed to insure one's security and to maintain the state's ability to continue providing a secure environment. Beyond this legal dimension and the instrumental contract-like relationship between state and subject that it implies, citizenship provides the basis for a stronger sense of belonging, conveying loyalty to the social group represented by the state and its particular boundaries, the nation. Rogers Brubaker put it this way: "Debates about citizenship, in the age of the nation-state, are debates about nationhood – about what it means, and what it ought to mean, to belong to a nation-state."[23] State borders thus are intended to mark both the limits of the state as an institutional complex and the limits of the primary community of belonging, the nation. In Sparke's words in his chapter on the PACE lane, "Borders, then, are hybrid sites where the reciprocal ties between the social and cultural definition of belonging to a nation and the bureaucratic regulation of belonging to a state – ties that form the very basis of modern citizenship – are worked out and written out in space."

Mazzini, the great Italian nationalist of the nineteenth century, sought to capture the connection between citizen (status) and nation (identity). "A nation," he stated, "is the universality of citizens speaking the same tongue."[24] But that connection between citizenship and member of the nation, mediated by a common language, has never been easily achieved.[25] Mary Callahan's chapter in this volume demonstrates the explosive relationship between language and citizenship in contemporary Burma. Imposition of a single language, Burmese, on a multilingual population lay at the center of the military regime's ambitions to "create new boundaries that would define the terms under which the population throughout the country could belong, be left alone, or be heard. At the heart of the regime's reconstruction process was

[20] Dominique Schnapper, *Community of Citizens: On the Modern Idea of Nationality*, trans. Séverine Rosée (New Brunswick: Transaction, 1998).

[21] Norbert Elias, *The Civilizing Process: The History of Manners and State Formation and Civilization*, trans. Edmund Jephcott (Cambridge, Mass.: Blackwell, 1994).

[22] Herbst, *States and Power in Africa*.

[23] Rogers Brubaker, "Immigration, Citizenship, and the Nation-State in France and Germany," in *The Citizenship Debates: A Reader*, ed. Gershon Shafir (Minneapolis: University of Minnesota Press, 1998), 131–64.

[24] *Encarta Book of Quotations* (Microsoft Corporation, 1999).

[25] Eugen Weber, *Peasants into Frenchmen: The Modernization of Rural France, 1870–1914* (Stanford, Calif.: Stanford University Press, 1976), makes that abundantly clear.

its attempt to create, to deploy, and to animate a new racialized definition of citizenship."

Even beyond the specific issue of language homogeneity, if one does not take the phrase "speaking the same tongue" literally, Mazzini's intent is clear in connecting the formality of the status of citizenship to the intangibles of commonality in the nation. For Schnapper, the connection comes in transcending the notion of a mere collection of citizens by the state's making the nation "a concrete reality, inscribed in time and space and capable of mobilizing populations."[26] The jump from the legal status of citizen to the emotionally laden identity of member of the nation is not an easy one to negotiate, for Italy, Burma, or other countries. The new Turkish state, for example, gained control of Anatolia after World War I and established the status of citizen for all the inhabitants of the territory. But the connections needed to extend the status of citizen to universal Turkish identity were far more problematic. The new Republic reacted to the Kurdish revolt of 1925 by redefining Kurds as ethnically Turkish, as part of the state's single nation. This move, as Nicole Watts makes clear in her chapter, did little to meld status and identity, Turkish citizen and member of the Turkish nation. Similarly, as Arat shows in her chapter, the Turkish state wasted no time after its founding to undercut Islam as a principle for political legitimacy, attempting to replace it with the concept of sovereignty within the new Turkish borders. Again, success in this realm was hard to come by. The state elites, she writes, were "reluctant to divorce themselves from the attractiveness of religious ties to reinforce national solidarity.... Religion crept into the secular nationalist constructions of citizenship." Once the door was open, "Islamists in Turkey were ready to offer an alternative bond of allegiance cross-cutting territorial boundaries and competing with secular ties of citizenship."

What becomes clear from the cases in this book is that the status of citizenship and the identity of member of the nation have been contested on multiple fronts around the globe. The spatial logic associated with the state and its relationship to its subjects has faced challenges at every turn. Even though it is usually the wealthiest and most complex of all social formations that people encounter, the state within its defining borders is not simply the monolith suggested by popular views and academic definitions. The common image portrays the state across the globe as an integrated, autonomous organization with clear social and territorial boundaries, whose parts work together in a fairly coherent manner. In this image, state rules – represented singularly as the Law – demand primacy over any other precepts, and if they are challenged, the state uses violence or the threat of it to insure conformity. Indeed, to the degree that other social groups can make their own rules, they are sanctioned to do so by the state.

[26] Schnapper, *Community of Citizens.*

This common image of the state implies two boundaries that set it off from those it rules: its territorial borders separating its space and population from those of other states and the social-political boundary between the state and those it rules. The territorial border demarks the state and separates it from other states (the internationally recognized boundary, marking the territory itself). It also defines those subject to its rule (i.e., for the most part, those physically within that space). Herbst has analyzed the deep importance that territorial boundaries and what he calls "boundary systems" with their buffer institutions (the actual and virtual checkpoints associated with state boundaries) has had for states in Africa:

> African state boundaries have been perhaps the critical foundation upon which leaders have built their states. In addition, the territorial boundaries help shape other buffer institutions that also insulate polities from international pressures. These other buffer institutions vary considerably but include currency exchange mechanisms (which define the means of conversion between domestic and international units of money) and citizenship rules (which determine the difference between citizens and foreigners).[27]

The status of citizenship points to and helps maintain, first and foremost, the boundary separating the state from the international arena. But citizenship also implies a social-political boundary between the two parties to the contract-like relationship: the citizens with their rights insuring their security and the state that provides such security and demands resources so that it can keep offering it. Not only is the state set off from its subjects by this boundary; as the ultimate rule maker it also is marked off from all other social formations of these subjects, who, in this common image, can make rules only if sanctioned to do so by the state. This boundary is the state-society divide.

While the territorial boundary is intuitively grasped and through its checkpoints quite evident to the casual observer, the social-political boundary is not always obvious. This phenomenon of now-you-see-it-now-you-don't comes from a basic paradox in the state-nation relationship. John Breuilly contends that at the same time that there exists a "distinction, peculiar to the modern world, between state and society," state leaders have sought to abolish in people's minds that very distinction through nationalism.[28] I have referred to this as the paradox of the state's being simultaneously *a part* of society and *apart* from society.[29] That is, state officials sometimes act to blend the state into society – for the state to appear as nothing more than the representation of society – and other times act to mark the state clearly as different, as the ultimate source of authority standing above its subjects. The

[27] Herbst, *States and Power in Africa.*

[28] John Breuilly, *Nationalism and the State* (Chicago: University of Chicago Press, 1994).

[29] Joel S. Migdal, *State in Society: Studying How States and Societies Transform and Constitute One Another* (New York: Cambridge University Press, 2001).

strengthening of subjects' loyalty to the state comes through efforts by state leaders to merge status (citizen) and identity (national). These state leaders have aimed to eliminate the perception that the state stands above society and to foster an alternative view, that the state and the society are indistinguishable in purpose, if not in form. Governing rests on a fiction, as Edmund S. Morgan notes. For the last two centuries, that fiction has centered on the belief that sovereignty resides in "flesh-and-blood people," that states are "inferior in power to the people themselves, that the people possessed 'real majesty.'"[30]

The attempts by states to merge the status of citizen and the identity of the national – to make the political boundary correspond to the social-psychological boundary – explain states' preoccupation with issues of natural reproduction. In both Patricia Woods's and Neil Diamant's chapters, the story revolves around states' sometimes clumsy efforts to govern who may marry whom, who may have conjugal relations with whom. In Woods's Israel case, the leading founder of the state, David Ben-Gurion, thought he could pull in the support of religious political parties by offering them the sop of control over the "unimportant" issues of marriage and divorce, while he and his party retained sway over the important ministries, such as defense, treasury, and foreign affairs. Control over marriage and divorce proved to be far from "unimportant," as it turned out. It enabled the religious parties to establish the lines of Jewish identity and to help blur any distinction between the categories of Jew and citizen. The new leaders of the People's Republic of China were much more attuned to the importance of domestic issues of intimacy than was Ben-Gurion. One of the first pieces of legislation passed in revolutionary China in 1949 was a law dealing with marriage and divorce. As Diamant indicates, the state sought to establish a class identity for the Chinese citizen that would be achieved by restricting unions between those of the "good" classes with those of the "bad." In practice, the state found it extremely difficult to govern marriages and, therefore, to meld personal identity with class and the state. Dissolving the boundaries of the private in favor of the boundaries of the public has turned out to be much more difficult for most states than many ambitious political leaders ever imagined. Being a part of society, right into the bedroom, is fraught with problems for the state standing apart from society.

Kenneth Lawson demonstrates in his essay in this book that nothing highlights this paradox – the state as a part of society and apart from society, as standing above society and yet as inferior to the people – more than war. "Wartime mobilization is one that accentuates the boundary separating state and society as people are presumed to resent and resist the encroachment of the state on their lives and on their wallets." But, he notes, simultaneously,

[30] Edmund S. Morgan, *Inventing the People: The Rise of Popular Sovereignty in England and America* (New York: W. W. Norton, 1989).

"one of the chief and likely indispensable means by which state officials seek to mobilize large segments of a population for war is through the invention, adoption, and appropriation of imagery to incite nationalist identification and passions.... The synthesis between society and the state is exactly what national ideologies and movements purport to bring about and accomplish." Lawson calls this the nation-state fusion.

The Image and Practices of the State

This image of the state and its two sets of boundaries, territorial and state-society divide, has gained wide currency in the last couple of hundred years, becoming the universal picture of what political regimes everywhere are or should be. The power of this image should certainly not be lightly dismissed. Even in Africa, where state boundaries are weaker than elsewhere, the creation of new states in the image of European states was momentous; "the imposition of citizenship on each and every African was a revolutionary event."[31]

But states are more than this common image. They are characterized, too, by an actual set of practices.[32] Some practices validate and reinforce the common image. Rituals and ceremonies, for example, can elevate the state as a special social organization in society and set it apart from more prosaic other social groups, such as families, churches, and businesses. Practices at checkpoints, such as checking passports, can reinforce the image of the state and its boundaries. Border crossings may effectively keep out products and people banned by law; a judge may sentence someone to jail for flouting those laws, and the bureaucracy may carry out the judge's sentence. For all the talk of globalization, labor migration may actually have decreased in the second half of the twentieth century compared with the century before that, especially where new states imposed boundaries that effectively stemmed the movement of peoples in various regions of the world. Validation of the image also comes through the actions of international organizations and other states, which accept the theoretical right of the state to be preeminent rule maker in its claimed territory.

Actual practices, however, may not reproduce this common image of the state at all. They may not imply its coherence, the sanctity of its boundaries, or the unity of its citizenry. Border crossings, to return to that example, may serve as sites of practices undermining the state image and neutralizing its boundaries. A border guard may be party to a smuggling ring; a judge may use criteria other than those found in the law, such as kinship, racial prejudice, or desire for personal wealth to dictate the court's ruling; a state

[31] Herbst, *States and Power in Africa*.

[32] Migdal, *State in Society*; Joel S. Migdal and Klaus Schlichte, "Rethinking the State," ed. Klaus Schlichte (forthcoming).

official may choose not to carry out the court's order. In Watt's chapter, the Turkish state's legal and military practices resulted in just the opposite effect from the creation of a single Turkish nation that state officials sought. Their measures actually "produced a sense of exclusion and difference among many Kurdish citizens of the Republic."

Callahan's chapter on Burma demonstrates dramatically the sharp disjuncture between image and practice. Until 1988, postcolonial regimes in that country differentiated between two territories, the center and the margins. In the center, the state adopted practices subjecting the population to its day-to-day rules and moving various ethnic groups toward a Burmese sense of nationhood. But far from the capital city, the state did little more than rhetorically assert its control over the dispersed, mysterious peoples with their distinct languages and cultures. Even after the opposition began courting support in the margins and the military regime countered by adopting supposedly inclusive policies in the 1990s, state practices acted simultaneously to homogenize the population and to differentiate it, setting off those in the margins from the core population in the center.

In Lawson's essay on Canada during World War I, the disjunction between image and practices takes an ironic turn. In the case of his town of Rossland, the effect of pulling together as Canadians during this critical time had a paradoxical effect. The daily practices of civic leaders, community associations, and ordinary citizens did not reinforce the image of the state and its political-social boundaries. Instead, they created a different set of boundaries, which distrusted, ostracized, and repressed particular segments of the population. Identity did not include all citizens but redrew national boundaries to exclude certain groups of citizens. World War I "helped forge an emotional link between the people of Rossland and the Canadian state in a qualitatively new and deeper way." But at the same time, this link "involved drawing new social boundaries that defined who did and did not count as a 'true' Canadian."

The contradiction between image and practices, between intent and outcomes, between rhetoric and action, is not, of course, limited to states. It can exist in any social formation, from a small family to a global religion. In all sorts of cases, one's sense of belonging and communities of belonging are constructed in the swirl of often seemingly contradictory forces. The relationship between membership and identity even when the state is not directly involved can also be quite complex and take unexpected turns. In the late Ottoman Empire, as Sarah Abrevaya Stein demonstrates in her contribution, important institutions, notably a key Jewish newspaper, were fashioning a new category of Jew through the creation of a modern secular culture in the Ladino language. At the same time, the newspaper editorially discouraged Jews from actually belonging to or even accepting the legitimacy of precisely that secular Ladino culture it was constructing.

The Ottoman Empire, because of its ambivalence and uncertainty regarding some of the characteristics of states coming out of Europe in the period leading up to the twentieth century, presents a much clearer lens to view the gap between actual practices and the idealized image of the state. Reşat Kasaba writes in his chapter of the Ottoman Empire as dubious in maintaining both a firm territorial boundary separating it from other political entities and the state-society divide. For long periods, the imperial borders had an indeterminate status. And constructing the state-society boundary demanded that the Empire have some sort of vision for what Ottoman society was, what actually might integrate it. But it lacked such a vision, and as territorial boundaries were redrawn in the Empire's long retreat, it became even more difficult to achieve, as groups ended up within several different states.

For most people at the beginning of the twenty-first century, in the swirl of contradictory forces, of conflicting images and practices, the state remains at the center of the vortex. It is a state in which daily practices portray a picture quite different from its common image, a picture whose spatial logic varies from that of the state nestled inside hard borders and above its society. These practices depict a state that is composed of diverse fragments, whose parts often operate in divergent ways. Such practices conflicting with the image of the state, then, are not just quirky exceptions to the rule, corruption or criminality that can simply be eliminated by better policing techniques. No, the diverse fragments represent spatial logics different from that implied in the state's image. The struggles representing the most important social dynamics in today's world are found at the crux of these contending mental maps.

The two boundaries of the state, the territorial and the state-society divide, are not inviolable, no matter how much state officials claim to the contrary. Other practices, many of which are incorporated into the state by its own agents and officials, blur, erase, or diminish these two boundaries, boundaries that the state image portrays as sacrosanct. Through manifold alliances, state officials and other social actors engage in practices that reduce the importance of the line separating the state from other social groupings – collectively, society – as well as that separating it from other states. The border guard in cahoots with the smuggling ring neutralizes the boundary between state and society by giving primacy to the alliance with other smugglers over his or her role as a cog in the state machinery. And he or she diminishes the importance of the state's territorial boundary by making it porous to goods banned by law. That smuggling ring establishes a very different mental map and succeeds in having its checkpoints take precedence over those represented by the state map.

The debate in the social sciences between those claiming that the state's boundaries are no longer relevant in a globalized world and those who continue to see the state as the ultimate purveyor of people's status and identity[33] – citizenship and nationhood – may be creating a false dichotomy. It may be more accurate to think of a world of multiple types of boundaries overlapping one another. These boundaries produce numerous mental maps, and they generate many different forms of belonging. Sometimes different bounded social and political formations sit comfortably with one another, but many times they do not.

Individuals are thus often caught in a swirl of contradictory forces – or vectors, as Stein calls them – each maintaining powerful sanctions and rewards. To some extent, people can accommodate multiple boundaries and multiple senses of belonging, even ones with radically different principles underlying their practices.[34] They make such accommodations by activating different mental maps, varying principles and practices, in different sorts of situations. All of these groups apportion respect and privilege and use their checkpoints as an important means of determining and assigning privilege.

But this sort of accommodation has its limits. Contradictory mental maps and checkpoints can tear people in different directions. Varying systems of status hit up against one another, forcing people to create a hierarchy inducing them to choose which boundaries, principles, and practices to submit to and which to violate (with all the attendant consequences). It is in such situations that one finds the sites of social struggle and social change.

[33] Stephen D. Krasner, *Sovereignty: Organized Hypocrisy* (Princeton, N.J.: Princeton University Press, 1999).

[34] Migdal, *State in Society*.

PART II

ON THE EVE OF THE NATION-STATE

The Ottoman Empire

2

Do States Always Favor Stasis?

The Changing Status of Tribes in the Ottoman Empire

Reşat Kasaba

From the very early years of their struggle to carve out a space for themselves in medieval Anatolia right to the final days of their existence as an independent polity, the Ottomans were caught between two conflicting tendencies. One of these was the tendency toward continuing flux and mobility that characterized the lives of both the nomadic tribes that were indigenous to this part of the world and the early Ottomans. The other tendency was the drive to form an effective imperial bureaucracy to govern what became the largest empire of the early modern era. When I first started working on this project, I had assumed that these two tendencies represented two irreconcilable forces; that the formation of the Ottoman Empire and the Ottoman and Turkish states involved a protracted contest between, on the one hand, an officialdom that had always been for "stasis" and, on the other, the masses of real and potential subjects who wanted to continue their peripatetic lives at all costs. Along with many historians, I thought that it would be inconceivable for an early modern polity such as the Ottoman Empire to survive and expand as the Ottomans did without developing an effective way of settling and controlling the nomads and without abandoning their own nomadic past.[1]

As I examined the policies that were designed to impose stasis as the norm of the realm at various points in Ottoman history, however, I found that these were much more than simple directives designed to bring about a settled and sedentarized society. For one thing, many of these measures included elaborate safeguards for protecting the structure, organization, and leadership of some of the very tribes whose nomadism they were trying to alter and control. I also discovered many examples of migrants and nomads who

[1] Rudi Lindner says that by the end of the fourteenth century, tribal form had ceased to be relevant for the Ottoman Empire. "What Was the Nomadic Tribe?," *Comparative Studies in Society and History* (1982): 709. See also his *Nomads in Medieval Ottoman Anatolia* (Bloomington: Indiana University Press, 1983).

incorporated sedentary forms of farming and/or urban occupations into their nomadic and migratory cycles and managed to comply with the new laws without abandoning completely their nomadic and pastoral lives. I could see that neither stasis nor mobility ever became the exclusive characteristic of the state or the itinerant communities. Instead, simultaneously and in contention with each other, they had permeated all segments of the Ottoman state *and* Ottoman society. Consequently, the emergence of the modern state in the Ottoman Empire was accompanied, on the societal level, by the creation of a framework that guaranteed the continuing movement across spatial and social divides. The porosity and permeability of these internal boundaries were partly responsible for the very high degree of uncertainty and flux that shaped the questions of belonging in the Ottoman Empire well into the nineteenth century.

This situation changed radically within the context of what Rogers Brubaker calls the "unmixing of people" during the last quarter of the nineteenth century.[2] Then, a more rigid insistence on stasis, management, and legibility became the norm not only for the Ottoman but also for all the other states of that era and that region. Under these specific conditions, many nomadic communities became the specific targets for relocation and sedentarization by the late Ottoman and its successor states. This change of policy and crystallization of priorities were dictated in part by the global environment that put a very high premium on stable borders and manageable society, which came to imply homogeneous and mostly settled populations in the course of the late nineteenth and early twentieth centuries.

This chapter contextualizes the relationship between stasis and mobility without assuming that their simultaneous existence necessarily conflicts with the imperatives of state formation. In most of the chapter, I examine the relationship between stasis and mobility by looking at the imperial officials and tribes. I start by describing the imprecise nature of the boundaries that defined the contours of the Ottoman Empire, especially in the early parts of its history. I see this impreciseness as resulting partly from the pragmatism of the Ottomans in their dealings with the tribes but also from the ability of the local nomadic groups to negotiate with and make their priorities part of the priorities of the Ottoman officials. In the following two sections, I give examples from the Ottoman sedentarization policies in the eighteenth and nineteenth centuries and show that the intermeshing of the goals of the central bureaucracy and the nomadic elements of this region make it impossible to posit either stasis or mobility as the prevailing objective of these policies. These three sections show that the question of belonging was highly contested and contingent for most people who lived in the Ottoman Empire during most of its history. The chapter ends with a brief discussion

[2] Rogers Brubaker, "Aftermath of the Empire and the Unmixing of People," in K. Barkey and M. von Hagen eds., *After Empire* (Boulder, Colo.: Westview, 1997).

of the shift toward separation and rigidity that came to the forefront as ethnicity became a central concern of the Ottoman state during the latter decades of the nineteenth century. Needless to say, this shift would have profound implications for questions of identity and belonging both in the late empire and in its succeeding states.

Early Years

Historical atlases of the late medieval and early modern Europe pretend to tell us the exact limits of the territories of the Ottoman Empire. It is as if the makers of these maps could hover over Europe and see which river bend belonged to what state, where a border line made an angle to divide a specific valley, and how far west or east a traveler could go and still be in the Ottoman Empire. Given the difficulty of answering these questions with any degree of certainty, the map makers use only recognizable, natural barriers such as rivers, mountains, or sea basins as their benchmarks. Even these are far from being unambiguous since, in the absence of reliable methods of harnessing waters, the rivers changed their size, direction, and volume and the mountains were inhabited by nomads who defied the barriers in their paths.[3] Despite these problems, we use these maps not only to get a series of static snapshots of the empire but also to deduce from them the shrinking or expansion of its borders. The latter is important because implicitly or explicitly we have come to accept the changing size of the border as the single most important indicator of the empire's and fortune.

These historical maps have become such an integral part of our thinking and writing about the Ottoman Empire that we hardly ever question the nature of the boundaries they depict and the relevance of these divisions for people who lived in these regions of the empire that abutted the neighboring polities. Ottoman expansion involved the conquest of a series of castles, major towns, and crucial waterways and passes. Beyond these, one would be hard-pressed to find any indication of where the Ottoman lands ended. There were no border posts or barbed wires that separated the Ottoman Empire from its neighbors, and one certainly did not need a passport to travel to and from the territories of the surrounding states.[4]

If the absence of clear markers was one of the factors that made it particularly difficult to tell where the territory of the empire ended and where that of another state started, the other, and in some ways the more important

[3] Jeremy Black, *Maps in History* (New Haven: Yale University Press, 1997), p. 25.

[4] At least not until 1869, when the law of nationality was adopted. It must be added, however, that the Ottoman officials did not look favorably on travel abroad, especially in large numbers, because this was interpreted as a failure of the state to keep its subjects content (Engin Akarlı, *The Long Peace, Ottoman Lebanon, 1861–1920* (Berkeley, Calif., University of California Press, 1993), p. 61).

factor, was the intense movement of goods and people in and across the border regions. In addition to nomads, about whom I will say more later, hundreds of itinerant merchants constantly crisscrossed the border areas and kept the Ottoman Empire always linked to its neighbors and to the world at large. There is some merit to the observation that the Ottomans directed their expansion deliberately in order to capture all the important passages between Europe and Asia. Indeed, by taking a large part of the Balkans in the fourteenth and fifteenth centuries, the Black Sea basin in 1475, and Mesopotamia and Egypt in 1516–17, they had placed themselves in control of all the important trade routes that linked Europe with Asia in the Middle Ages.[5] Furthermore, their trade policies suggest that the Ottomans were intent on not subverting but facilitating this trade and profiting from it.[6]

Within the context of Ottoman expansion, it became quite typical for the nomadic tribes who populated the border regions of the empire to form a human link between the Ottoman heartlands and other places that were under the control of the neighboring states. Their vast arcs of migration extended to hundreds if not thousands of miles and frequently went right through the frontier regions. Even deserts and large bodies of water and seas were traversed by pirates, corsairs, Bedouins, and Berbers, who had no permanent village or a port where they lived permanently. As such, nomadism not only was a prominent feature of the border regions of the empire but was present in large parts of the rest of the Ottoman lands as well. To give but one estimate, İnalcık thinks that as much as 27 percent of the population of Anatolia might have been full or semi-nomadic in the 1520s; according to another historian, in a province such as Baghdad, this percentage could be as high as 60 percent.[7] Historical atlases sometime represent these groups and their movements but only with distinct arrows that have a beginning and an end point. Hence, as constructs that are conditioned by our modern sensibilities of sovereignty, sedentary life, and control, historical maps are ill equipped to reflect the real conditions on the ground, especially in the territories that straddled the area between the Ottoman Empire and its neighbors.[8] In an alternative portrayal that did not privilege stasis but focused on groups such as nomads, itinerant traders, and migrant workers who routinely transgressed these lines of demarcation, the border zones would appear more as areas that connected the Ottoman Empire with other parts of Asia,

[5] Janet Abu-Lughod, *Before European Hegemony* (New York: Oxford, 1989).

[6] Halil İnalcık, "Bursa and the Commerce of the Levant," *Journal of the Economic and Social History of the Orient* 3 (1960): 131–40.

[7] Halil İnalcık and Donald Quataert, eds., *Social and Economic History of the Ottoman Empire* (Cambridge: Cambridge University Press, 1994), p. 35; Rhoads Murphey, "Some Features of Nomadism in Ottoman Empire," *Journal of Turkish Studies* 8 (1984): 192.

[8] In his excellent study, Black shows that historical atlases reflect more the concerns of the time in which they are produced than the historical situation which they depict. Black, *Maps in History*.

Europe, and Africa and not as barriers that separated these lands from each other.

The origins of nomadic pastoralism in the Ottoman Empire should be sought in the synergy between the indigenous nomads who had inhabited this part of the world for many centuries and the Türkmen tribes who arrived there in the eleventh century.[9] The high degree of mobility that prevailed in these parts of the world served the Ottoman officialdom well in its early drive in Europe and Asia between the thirteenth and seventeenth centuries.[10] By relying on the nomadic resources of the society, Ottomans were able to mobilize large numbers of fighters quickly, and with their agility and speed, these troops repeatedly and easily overwhelmed the smaller and land-bound troops of the weak feudal states of eastern Europe. Similarly, the Ottoman government took advantage of the relative rootlessness of these tribes in ordering them to move over long distances and resettle in the newly conquered territories as part of its effort to populate these regions.[11] Far from trying to turn all nomads into settled peasants, in the early part of its history, the Ottoman officials would pass specific laws and regulations designed to protect pastoral nomads, regulate their migratory routes, and guarantee their livelihood and safety.[12] On some occasions, the central government would even appoint a traveling judge to accommodate the tribes.[13] So pervasive was the nomadic influence in the social organization, institutions, practices, and culture of the early Ottoman period that İnalcik describes them as "the backbone of the entire imperial organization."[14]

Given this context, the question of who the Ottomans were or who "belonged" to the Ottoman Empire was not relevant for the organization and functioning of the Ottoman Empire, especially in the early part of its history. Even after they started to build their bureaucracy, the Ottomans did not consistently use a rigid classification to divide their tax-paying subjects into hermetically sealed categories. The divisions that were introduced

9 For example, in the Balkans, the nomadic groups were collectively referred to as the Vlachs. When the Ottomans arrived, these and other Türkmen tribes, such as Cumans, Pechenegs, and Tatars, had already been involved in many years of conflict, contention, and cooperation. Fikret Adanır, "The Ottoman Peasantries," in T. Scott, ed., *The Peasantries of Europe* (London: Longman, 1998), p. 275.

10 In Cemal Kafadar's words, "The Ottoman success was due to the fact that they harnessed that mobility to their own ends while shaping and taming it to conform to their stability-seeking centralizing vision" (*Between Two Worlds* (Berkeley: University of California Press, 1995), p. 141).

11 Ömer Lütfi Barkan, "Osmanlı İmparatorluğunda bir iskân ve kolonizasyon metodu olarak sürgünler," in three parts: *İstanbul Üniversitesi İktisat Fakültesi Mecmuası* 11 (1949–50): 254–69; 13 (1952): 56–79; 14 (1953–4): 209–36.

12 İnalcık and Quataert, eds., *Social and Economic History of the Ottoman Empire*, p. 37.

13 Cengiz Orhonlu, *Osmanlı İmparatorluğunda Aşiretlerin İskâni* (Istanbul: Eren, 1987), p. 20.

14 Halil İnalcık, "The Yürüks," in R. Pinner and H. İnalcık, eds., *Oriental Carpet and Textile Studies* (London, 1986), p. 56.

to facilitate overrule were fluid, imprecise, and prone to change over time. Religion was the main and the only substantial exception to this; hence, generally, the Christians were referred to as "*zimmi*" or "*nasrani*" and Jews as *Yahud*, *Yehud*, or *çıfıt*, but occasionally *zimmi* covered all non-Muslims, not just the Christians. Some groupings within the Muslim community were differentiated, as well. For example, the names of the individual gypsies were always qualified with "*kıpti*," and after the sixteenth century, those who belonged to the Twelver branch of the Shi'i Islam, known as *Alevi* (or Alawite), were identified as *Kızılbaş* (red-head) in reference to their defection to and service under the Shah of Iran in specially designated troops that were distinguished with their red caps. If a person or a group of people belonged to a religious order or ethnic group, such as the *Kızılbaş*, Yezidis, or the Kurds, which had the potential of undermining Ottoman authority, the official documents took care to specify this fact when they mentioned that person or the group, or even their village.[15]

As the largest and the most formidable group, the status of the Kurds was always a sensitive issue. The Ottomans applied a policy of currying favor (*istimalet*) and used Sunni Kurds as a buffer against Iran and as an ally in their lengthy battles with the Kızılbaş communities. Some of the Kurdish chiefs used their ties with the Ottoman government to amass fortunes and extensive power in eastern Anatolia, enabling them to influence the Ottoman policy and campaigns in this area.[16] In 1632 and 1633, Sultan Murad IV issued a series of imperial orders reinforcing the hereditary nature of Kurdish tribal chiefdom and prohibiting the local military commanders and governors from harassing and abusing the Kurdish tribes. In one of them he said, "Just as God, be He praised and exalted, vouchsafed to Alexander 'the two horned' to build the wall of Gog, so God made Kurdistan act in the protection of my imperial kingdom like a strong barrier and an iron fortress against the sedition of the demon Gog of Persia."[17] In another he stated, "The Kurdish commanders are loyal and faithful well-wishers of the Ottoman state and have from the noble time of our great ancestors until the present time performed a variety of praiseworthy services on behalf of the crown and expanded incalculable laudable efforts thus making it incumbent on the imperial zeal that they be treated with respect and care."[18]

As for the non-Kurdish Muslim tribes who did not have a clear affiliation with a distinct religious order, these are mentioned in the government documents with names that referred either to their line of work, such as *Keçili*

[15] See Ahmet Yaşar Ocak, *Osmanlı Toplumunda Zındıklar ve Mülhidler* (Istanbul: Tarih Vakfi 1998).

[16] Robert Dankoff, *Evliya Çelebi in Bitlis* (Leiden: E. J. Brill, 1990), pp. 12–18, 273–90.

[17] Rhoads Murphey, ed., *Kanun-name-i Sultâni Li Aziz Efendi, Sources of Oriental Languages and Literatures*, vol. 9 (Cambridge: Harvard University Near Eastern Languages and Civilization, 1985), p. 14.

[18] Ibid., p. 16.

(sheepy), *Koyuncu* (sheep seller), *Saraç* (tanner), *Kaşıkçı* (spoon maker), *Yarı-Çoban* (half-shepherd), *Kürkçü* (fur maker), *Yağcı* (oil maker), *Yaycı* (bow maker), *Çeng* (musician), *Atçeken* (horse puller), *Koyuneri* (sheep master), or some aspect of the history of the group in question, such as *Öksüzler* (orphans), *Sakallı* (bearded), or *Şehitler* (martyrs).[19] After the sixteenth century, the tribes were subjected to a broad, empire-wide classification on the basis of where their movements concentrated. Those who had moved (or, more typically, who were made to move) to the west of the river Kızılırmak during the previous centuries were designated as Yürüks and registered as such; whereas those who stayed on the east continued to be referred to as Türkmens.[20]

While it is true that in the fifteenth and sixteenth centuries, as a reflection of their status as a world empire, the Ottomans undertook a vast effort to classify and register their subject people, the categories they used in this endeavor were far from being unambiguous. They did not provide a clear demarcation or indicator of where people belonged or what their ethnic or other identity might be. Even the religious categories were blurred on the margins. There were plenty of people in Anatolia, the Balkans, and North Africa who practiced religions that borrowed not only from Christianity, Judaism, and Islam, but also from the pre-Christian shamanistic belief systems of the earlier periods.

It is thus not surprising that when it came to describing who they were and what they ruled, the Ottomans hardly ever referred to the identity of the people under their suzerainty. Geography and space were the far more typical referents, as we can see in this passage from Suleiman I's proclamation to the Venetian ambassador in 1527, referring to himself as "I, emperor of emperors, crowned king of men over the whole face of earth, shadow of god on the two continents, emperor of the White Sea and the Black Sea, of Romania and Anatolia, of the countries of Greece and of Caramania, of Dulkadir, Diyarbekir, Dirinâzim, Damascus, Aleppo, Cairo, Holy Jerusalem, and sublime Mecca and revered Medina, of Zide, of Yemen, and of many other countries."[21]

Settling Nomads

By the end of the seventeenth century it had become clear to the Ottomans that in the newly emerging circumstances of early modern Europe, flexible borders and imprecise identities no longer served them well. They had spent

[19] See Ahmet Refik, *Anadolu'da Türk Aşiretleri* (Istanbul: Devlet Matbaası, 1930).

[20] İnalcık, "The Yürüks," pp. 42–3; Faruk Sümer, "Anadolu, Suriye ve Irak'ta Yaşayan Türk Aşiretlerine Umumi Bakış," *İstanbul Üniversitesi İktisat Fakültesi Mecmuası* 11 (1949–50): 515–16; Salahaddin Çetintürk, "Osmanlı İmparatorluğunda Yürük Sınıfı," *Ankara Üniversitesi Dil ve Tarih Coğrafya Fakültesi Dergisi* (1943), p. 109.

[21] Lucette Valensi, *The Birth of the Despot* (Ithaca, N.Y.: Cornell University Press, 1993), p. 53.

most of the seventeenth century in war with several of their neighbors while trying to deal with internal unrest, rural rebellions, and military uprisings. They had little to show for the extraordinary effort and resources they expanded for ventures such as the disastrous second siege of Vienna in 1683. The seventeenth century ended with the Treaty of Karlowitz in 1699, where the Ottomans experienced their first major loss of territory in Europe and left Hungary, Transylvania, Croatia, Slovenia, Dalmatia, the Morea, some Aegean Islands, Podolia, and southern Ukraine.

It was in this environment of seemingly uncontrollable downward slide in external fortunes and continuing internal chaos that the priorities of the Ottoman officialdom started to clash more visibly and consistently with the interests of the nomadic tribes. Not surprisingly, agriculture was of particular concern to the state. Rural insecurity of the preceding decades had pushed large numbers of people into the cities. This and the lengthy periods for which the peasants were drafted to fight in wars, away from their farms and families, had undermined the agriculture of the empire. For example, a survey that was conducted in Karasi in western Anatolia in early eighteenth century found that of the 170 households that had been previously registered there, only 56 were still there, and 12 of the 54 villages that were part of the district were in ruins.[22] By restricting and controlling the migratory routes of the nomads, the Ottoman government was trying to improve rural security and protect the peasants and their properties. Also, it was expected that the nomadic tribes and the peasants who had escaped from their lands in the chaotic conditions of the seventeenth century would take advantage of the land grants, free seeds, free oxen, free irrigation, and tax exemptions that were offered by the Ottoman government and would agree to return to farming.[23] All of this, it was hoped, would contribute to the reversal of the trends that had pulled the empire into a long period of crisis and shore up the agricultural basis of the Ottoman economy.

With such concerns in mind, the Ottoman officials started to register the affiliation, size, and wealth of the Yürük tribes in the Balkans and the Beduin, Kurdish, and Türkmen tribes in the Arab provinces between 1689 and 1691. Similar steps were taken in earlier centuries, especially at the end of the sixteenth century when the empire went through a lengthy period of rural depredations. But the seventeenth-century measures were more comprehensive. They were formulated when the empire was in the midst of a war against the combined forces of the Russian, Polish, and Habsburg armies, and they were supposed to address several of the most pressing problems the Ottomans were facing at the time. In addition to revitalizing the agriculture, they would reinforce the borders of the empire and develop new pools of

[22] Yusuf Hallaçoğlu, *XVIII. Yüzyılda Osmanlı İmparatorluğu'nun İskân Siyaseti ve Aşiretlerin Yerleştirilmesi* (Ankara: Türk Tarih Kurumu, 1988), p. 79.

[23] Orhonlu, *Osmanlı İmparatorluğunda Aşiretlerin İskânı*, pp. 33, 49, 55.

manpower for the armed forces and for repairing and rebuilding the citadels, castles, fortresses, roads, and bridges. Hence, the suitable members of tribal communities were drafted into the Ottoman army and trained in special companies of infantry troops with these tasks in mind. In an effort to evoke a previous era when the nomads had played a key role in expanding the Ottoman presence in the Balkans, the newly constituted Yürük companies were given the name of Evlâd-ı Fatihan (Children of the Conquerors).[24]

Given the territorial losses of the late seventeenth and early eighteenth century, it was not surprising that the indeterminate status of the imperial borders was of particular concern to the Ottomans as they implemented these first measures of sedentarization. Hence, in addition to repairing the existing citadels and building new ones on the Austrian and Russian borders, the central government continued to settle the Yürüks in the Balkans and took steps, such as banning the use of forced labor, in order to prevent the flight of especially the Christian peasants to the other side of the newly drawn borders.[25]

Similar policies were implemented in other borders areas, such as Mesopotamia, where large numbers of nomads were given land and settled in.[26] Those ethnic and religious groups that were likely to undermine the state's efforts or those that were inclined to form cross-border alliances were broken up and dispersed in other parts of the empire, or other groups were settled amongst them in order to weaken their capacity to resist. For example, in 1691, the Badıllı clan of Turkmen origins, which normally spent its winters around Ankara in central Anatolia, was settled in Harran, in northern Syria,[27] and some among the Kurdish Mihmadlu tribe were moved from eastern Anatolia to the area around Izmir in 1713.[28] Generally, the island of Cyprus and the desert region of Rakka in Syria became two of the most frequently mentioned penal destinations in the seventeenth and eighteenth centuries. These places were used for punishing tribes in groups, in retaliation of specific criminal behavior, as well as for mass relocations and resettlements. Here are two examples: A group within the Danişmendli clan was moved from around Sandıklı in the west-central Anatolia to Rakka in 1719 because it was inflicting damage on villages and farmers.[29] The example for how Cyprus was used comes from even earlier: In 1572 some among the Akçekili tribe in Kütahya tried to force their way into a bathhouse and kidnap several of the bathing women "even though a towel was hung on the

[24] Tayyib Gökbilgin, *Rumeli'de Yürükler, Tatarlar, ve Evlad-ı Fatihan* (Istanbul: Osman Yalçın Matbaası, 1957), pp. 255–6; Ismail Hakkı Uzunçarşılı, *Osmanlı Tarihi*, vol. IV, part 1 (Ankara: Türk Tarih Kurumu, 1956), p. 31.

[25] Uzunçarşılı, *Osmanlı Tarihi*, vol. IV, part 1, p. 4.

[26] Orhonlu, *Osmanlı İmparatorluğunda Aşiretlerin İskânı*, pp. 57–70.

[27] Ibid., p. 59.

[28] Ibid., p. 71.

[29] Refik, *Anadolu'da Türk Aşiretleri*, pp. 164–5.

door to indicate the presence of women inside." More than fifty men who were involved in this incident were banished to Cyprus.[30]

The Ottomans also tried to better define and defend the maritime borders of the empire in the eighteenth century. Among other steps they issued a decree in 1701 that prohibited the Algerian seafarers from raiding the Aegean coastal regions and forcing men to join them as fighters.[31] Incidentally, this had been a commonly used method of draft for centuries.

For a short time during the first half of the eighteenth century, these reform attempts seemed to bear fruit. The Ottoman Empire went through a period of relative peace in 1718–30. These were also years of openness to western ideas and some economic growth that even included the start of new manufacturing and industrial establishments.[32] But this proved to be a period of limited and short-lived enlightenment. By the second half of the eighteenth century, the Ottoman Empire had once again been drawn into a series of lengthy and destructive wars and was faced with rural uprisings, especially in the mountainous regions.[33] Also, local leaders, who had benefited from their positions as intermediaries in the implementation of the reform measures of the eighteenth century, had now become de facto independent, wielding extensive power in their localities and seriously undermining the power and authority of the central government. With their small armies, loyal peasants, and nomads whose protection they assumed as their responsibility, these provincial notables became so well entrenched and powerful that the last decades of the eighteenth century have come to be designated as the "Age of the Notables (*ayan*)" in Ottoman historiography.[34]

Despite the century-long policies that aimed at creating a more stable, sedentary, and internationally secure empire, the circumstances did not look much better at the turn of the nineteenth century than they did a hundred years earlier. The borders maintained their imprecise character, and a vast portion of the empire's population was still not settled or established in terms of geography, ways of living, or identities. In the beginning of the nineteenth century, the Ottoman administration tried to deal with this situation by attacking it from several directions. One of these was by curbing the growing independence of the local notables; the other was to conduct periodic surveys as well as an empire-wide first census in 1831 to keep track of the size, nature, and changes in the population of especially the border regions in the

30 Ibid., pp. 15–16.

31 Uzunçarşılı, *Osmanlı Tarihi*, vol. IV, part 1, p. 4.

32 Mehmet Genc, "Ottoman Industry in the 18th Century: General Framework, Characteristics and Main Trends," in Donald Quataert, ed., *Manufacturing in the Ottoman Empire and Turkey, 1500–1950* (Albany: SUNY Press, 1994), pp. 59–86; "Osmanlı Ekonomisi ve Savaş," *Yapıt* 49, no. 4 (April–May 1984): 52–6; 50, no. 5 (June–July 1984): 86–93.

33 Yücel Özkaya, *Osmanlı İmparatorluğu'nda Dağlı İsyanları* (Ankara: Ankara Üniversitesi DTCF, 1983).

34 İnalcık and Quataert, eds., *Social and Economic History of the Ottoman Empire*, pp. 637–758.

Balkans and in the southeast.[35] Collecting accurate information on the empire's demography and assessing the availability of land became particularly pressing after the Crimean War of 1854–6, when waves of refugees retreated with the shrinking borders of the empire. It is estimated that between the Crimean War and 1866, at least 500,000 Muslim subjects of Russia's tsar took refuge in the Ottoman Empire.[36] The Ottoman government drafted a Regulation (Talimatname) in 1856 that specified how the refugees would be moved within the empire, who would be responsible for their well being, and where they would be settled.[37] In 1860, these tasks were put under the purview of a Commission of Refugee Affairs (Muhacirin Komisyonu).[38] The 1877–8 war with Russia created the largest wave of immigrants until that point. To absorb and settle the 1.5 million people who were brought to various ports within the empire's borders, the commission was expanded and renamed the Commisssion for the General Administration of Refugee Affairs (İdare-i Umumiye-i Muhacirin Komisyonu) in 1878.[39]

It was inevitable that the problems associated with finding land for the growing number of refugees and immigrants and settling them in the Ottoman Empire would eventually and inevitably become linked with the continuing process of sedentarizing and integrating the nomadic tribes into the imperial society. The vast network of officials, commissions, and initiatives that dealt with tribes and immigrants and refugees was finally centralized on the eve of World War I, through the creation of the General Directorate of Tribes and Immigrants (Aşair ve Muhacirin Müdüriyet-i Umumiyesi) in 1914.[40]

By the nineteenth century, the Ottoman government was registering tribes with as much information as possible, including not only their names and reputations, but also the areas of their circulation and the names of the governors who were responsible for them. Here are some examples from government documents that involved tribes: Selanik Yürükleri (Yürüks of Salonica), Naldöken Yürükleri (Yürüks of Naldöken), Kütahya'ya tabi Ak Keçili Yürükleri (White Goat Yürüks who belonged to Kütahya), Halep Yeni İl Türkmenine bağlı Emir cemaati (Emir community that was part of the Yeni İl Türkmen Confederation that was based in Aleppo), Karahisar-ı Sahib

35 Enver Ziya Karal, *Osmanlı İmparatorluğu'nda İlk Nüfus Sayımı* (Ankara: Başvekalet Istatistik Umum Müdürlüğü, 1943).

36 Alan Fisher, "Emigration of the Muslims from the Russian Empire in the Years after the Crimean War," in *A Precarious Balance: Conflict, Trade, and Diplomacy on the Russian-Ottoman Frontier* (Istanbul: Isis, 1999), pp. 170–91; Kemal Karpat, *Ottoman Population, 1830–1914* (Madison: University of Wisconsin Press, 1985), p. 66.

37 Orhonlu, *Osmanlı İmparatorluğunda Aşiretlerin İskânı*, p. 119.

38 Ibid.

39 Nedim Ipek, *Rumeli'den Anadolu'ya Türk Göçleri* (Ankara: Türk Tarih Kurumu, 1994), pp. 41, 69.

40 Orhonlu, *Osmanlı İmparatorluğunda Aşiretlerin İskânı*, p. 120.

Piyadeleri (infantry from the district of Karahisar-ı Sahib), İç İl'den çıkıp Alaiye'ye gelen yürük taifeleri (Yürüks who moved from İç İl to Alaiyye), and Mihmadlu Kürdü (Kurds of Mihmadlu).[41]

In addition to registering and counting the peoples of these tribes and creating specific administrative units, the Ottoman state tried to strengthen the ties between nomads and the central government also by creating a School for Tribes (Aşiret Mektebi) in 1892. This school was set up with the explicit purpose of training the sons of the leaders of the Arab tribes with the hope that they would learn to behave properly as members of the larger Islamic community and be loyal followers of the Sultan Caliph.[42] Later, the sons of the Kurdish and Albanian chiefs were also admitted to this school, and it remained in operation until 1902.

Compared with the previous centuries, in the nineteenth century, the Ottoman government became much more direct in targeting specific tribes and in enforcing its orders of settlement. Frequently, tribes and clans were broken up and settled in different villages. Sometimes, the places of settlement were chosen with the requirements of the imperial economy and the conditions in local markets in mind. It was with such concerns that the government moved and settled many tribes into the wheat- and cotton-farming regions of central and southern Anatolia.[43] To be sure, banning all kinds of nomadism and pastoralism was unthinkable since the empire relied on these communities for its supply of animal products and also beasts of burden. Accordingly, tribes were permitted to continue animal husbandry, but instead of a whole community moving with its animals, some of the tribes were now required to send a limited number of shepherds with their flocks.[44] The government also made the customary routes of tribal migration impassable by setting up roadblocks and, occasionally, even staging robberies along these paths.[45]

In the second half of the nineteenth century, the Ottoman government resorted to military force with more regularity in order to make it very difficult, if not impossible, for the tribes to continue their uncontrolled peripatetic lives. In 1863–6, a new mobile military force was constituted under the name of Fırka-i Islahiye with the specific task of controlling and sedentarizing the nomads in Southeastern Anatolia. Partly as a result of the activities of Fırka-i Islahiye, this region was pacified and attracted a sizable number of new

41 See Refik, *Anadolu'da Türk Aşiretleri.*

42 Alişan Akpınar, *Osmanlı Devletinde Aşiret Mektebi* (Istanbul: Göçebe, 1997); Eugene Rogan, "Aşiret Mektebi: Abdülhamid II's School for Tribes (1892–1907)," *International Journal of Middle East Studies* 28 (1996): 83–107; Selim Deringil, *The Well Protected Domains* (London: I. B. Tauris, 1998), pp. 101–4.

43 Orhonlu, *Osmanlı İmparatorluğunda Aşiretlerin İskânı*, p. 117.

44 Orhonlu, *Osmanlı İmparatorluğunda Aşiretlerin İskânı*, p. 49.

45 Norman Lewis, *Nomads in Syria and Jordan* (Cambridge: Cambridge University Press, 1987), p. 30.

immigrants such as Türkmens and Circassians, who sought refuge there from other parts of Anatolia and the Caucasus.[46] The newcomers were broken up into small groups and interspersed among the Armenian, Kurdish, and Alevi concentrations in the southeast, which led to the emergence of a much more diverse and sedentary society. The towns of Hassa, Islahiye, Osmaniye, Reyhanlı, Kadirli, and Kozan all emerged in the nineteenth century as a result of the policies of settlement that were enforced by Fırka-i Islahiye.[47] Tribal divisions among the Kurds made it easy for the central government to use some of the Kurds as allies while continuing to inflict heavy punishments on others. The clearest example of the latter policy can be observed in the operation of the Hamidiye Regiments that were formed in 1891 and were staffed by Kurds. In the closing decades of the nineteenth and the early years of the twentieth century, the Sunni Kurds, who made up the overwhelming majority of the recruits in the Hamidiye, were given a free hand and strong government backing in Eastern Anatolia to go after and pacify the Alevi (Kızılbaş) Kurds, to push out other ethnic groups (particularly the Armenians), to seize their land, and to settle on them.[48] Frequently, the central government took direct action and ejected Kurdish tribes from their regions. For example, after becoming infamous for its fierce banditry in the region between, Mosul, and the Iranian border, the Kurdish Hemvend tribe was broken up and settled in groups in Scutari and Ankara (1886), Binghazi (1887), Tripoli (1889), and Istanbul (1890).[49]

Mobility-in-Stasis

It is undeniable that the state's policies of sedentarization eventually bore fruit, and in the course of the nineteenth century, large parts of the Ottoman Empire became more settled. As a macro-indicator of this trend we can point to the noticeable increase in the rate of growth of urban population, which was higher than the rate of growth of the population of the empire. For example, the population of Izmir increased by about 25 percent (from 160,000 to 200,000) between 1870s and 1890s, whereas the population of empire grew by about 11 percent between 1880s and 1890s.[50]

[46] On *Fırka-i İslahiye*, see Cevdet Paşa, *Tezâkir*, 21–39, C. Baysun, ed. (Ankara: Türk Tarih Kurumu, 1986), pp. 107–91.

[47] Eberhard traces the origins of many of the leading families in Southern Turkey, some of whom are large landlords today, to their nomadic past as Türkmen tribes. Wolfram Eberhard, "Nomads and Farmers in Southeastern Turkey," *Oriens* 6 (1963): 42–6.

[48] On Hamidiye, see Martin van Bruinessen, *Agha, Shaikh and State* (Utrecht, 1978), pp. 233–9; David McDowall, *A Modern History of the Kurds* (London: I. B. Taurus, 1997), 59–63.

[49] Prime Ministry's Archives, Council of Ministers Records (henceforth BBA, MV) 20/6, 20/28, 22/50, 27/53, 47/54, 55/12.

[50] Rauf Beyru, *19. Yüzyilda Izmir'de Yaşam* (Istanbul: Literatür, 2000), p. 53; Cem Behar, *Osmanlı İmparatorluğu'nun ve Türkiye'nin Nüfusu* (Ankara: Devlet Istatistik Enstitüsü, 1996), p. 49.

Yet despite the efforts that stretched for more than 300 years that aimed to create a sedentary basis for the empire and for the states that succeeded it, the nomadic basis of the large parts of the Balkan, Anatolian, and the Middle Eastern societies survived much of Ottoman history. While touring Anatolia on behalf of the British Museum in 1838, Charles Fellows wrote: "I have not seen a village or even a mosque . . . the people all living in tents and from this circumstance they are less capable of paying the prompt attention to the rites of hospitality."[51] In another source we read that as late as in 1840 there were only twenty-two villages between Aleppo and the Euphrates.[52] German geographer W. Hütteroth finds that as much as nine-tenths of the cultivated parts of inner Anatolia were settled only in the last fifty years of the empire.[53] As he was recounting the preparations for the establishment of the Firka-i İslahiye in 1863, Cevdet Paşa writes that the entire southeast had remained under the control of local tribes, even though nominally this region had become part of the Ottoman Empire in 1517.[54] And in 1914, approximately fifty years after Fellows, André Gide echoed him: "The earth is cultivated but where are the cultivators? As far as one can see, and for some time now, not a single creature, not a single village, not even an isolated tent."[55] A survey that was conducted with the Ministry of Interior in the 1940s found that as much as 63 percent of the land in Turkey was used, at least in part, for raising animals.[56] The map that is included with this study plots the paths of migration of those tribes that had remained within the borders of the new Turkish Republic. This map shows that the relative distance over which people moved had become considerably shorter by the early decades of the twentieth century. The new patterns of circulation appear to be much more closely knit, indicating a clear point of origin and giving some substance to the claim that these tribes had to have some kind of spatial identity. Nevertheless, since each one of the arrows in this map shows a different flow of migrants, based on the number of arrows in this representation, there must have been at least a hundred distinct flows. What is particularly striking is the almost symmetrical placement of some of the settlements across the Syrian and Iraqi borders in the south and the two-way movements that continued to cross these lines.

The persistence of nomadism and nomads can be observed also in the cultural artifacts and life styles of even the most "settled" groups in both the

[51] Charles Fellows, *Travels and Researches in Asia Minor* (London: John Murray, 1852), 1852, p. 155.

[52] Lewis, *Nomads in Syria and Jordan*, p. 51.

[53] Wolf-Dieter Hütteroth, "The Influence of Social Structure on Land Division and Settlement in Inner Anatolia," in P. Benedict, E. Tümerlekin, and F. Mansur, eds., *Turkey: Geographic and Social Perspectives* (Leiden: E. J. Brill, 1974), p. 21.

[54] Paşa *Tezâkir*, 21–39, p. 108.

[55] *The Journals of André Gide*, translated and annotated by Justin O'Brien, vol. 2 (New York: Alfred A. Knopf, 1948), p. 13.

[56] Marcel Clerget, *La Turquie passé et présent* (Paris: Armand Colin, 1947), p. 89.

Ottoman and post-Ottoman periods.[57] On a lighter note, Turkish author Demirtaş Ceyhun observes that well into the twentieth century, with extra beds that were stored in their closets and sparse furnishings, even the highly urbanized middle-class homes in Ankara and Istanbul conveyed a sense of portability, a readiness to move at a moment's notice.[58]

Hence, if we were to observe the empire from the point of view of the central officials who had declared nomads to be living in a state of "heresy, savagery, and ignorance"[59] or the cities whose urbane ways were flourishing, we would agree that the Ottoman Empire was determined to become and indeed becoming more sedentary. If, on the other hand, we were to focus on the population movements that continued to underlie most forms of social organization across these lands, we would have to conclude that much remained in a state of flux despite the intentions and the determination of the imperial government.

One way of making sense of the simultaneous existence of movement and stasis would be to posit the Ottoman state and Ottoman society as exclusive and inherently antagonistic entities. In such a perspective, we would see migration as another means of resistance used by the nomads against the centralizing precepts of the state, purely as acts of resistance or rebellion. Recently, by asking "why states are the enemy of people who move around" and "why civilizations can't climb hills," Scott has assumed such an antagonistic relationship and focused on the fate of specifically migratory communities as they become the targets of modern states that are bent on enhancing their power.[60] Indeed, one could come up endless examples of Sufi groups, as well as the Kurds, Circassians, Türkmens, and Yürüks who were successful in preserving their communities, networks, and migratory lives in defiance of an increasingly powerful and centralizing state. It is not very clear, however, when and under what conditions we can see such efforts as stemming directly and exclusively from sources that were completely independent of the Ottoman state.

Through all the modalities of sedentarization policies, the Ottoman officials were dealing with a society that was many-layered, with complex lines of authority and power tying different units within and across one another. The Ottoman Empire had been successful in the first two centuries of its history and established one of the largest empires of the early modern era by leaving many of these local units intact, providing security to the people and most importantly recognizing and securing the privileged position of

57 Walter Denny, "Türkmen Rugs and Early Rug Weaving in Western Islamic World," *Halı* 4, no. 4 (1982): 329–38.

58 Demirtaş Ceyhun, *Ah Şu Biz Kara Bıyıklı Türkler* (Istanbul: E Yayinlari, 1993) p. 218.

59 Deringil, *Well Protected Domains*, pp. 19, 41.

60 James C. Scott, "La montagne et la liberté, ou Pourqui les civilisations ne savent pas grimper," *Critique Internationale* 3 (2001): 85–104. See also his *Seeing Like State* (New Haven, Conn.: Yale University Press, 1998).

the leaders of these communities. Tribes were no exception to this. Now in the eighteenth and nineteenth centuries, the central government had little choice but to enlist the support and services of these leaders in the cause of reform. In a frequently utilized approach, tribal chiefs were required to provide financial and personal guarantee that their tribes would stay at their designated places of settlement.[61] In return, they were given better quality of land and privileged access to higher echelons of the bureaucracy. In the early 1850s, during his travels in eastern Anatolia, Robert Curzon spoke with some Kurdish chiefs and discovered that some of the tribes had kept the post of chieftainship within one family for as many as seven generations.[62] Naturally, the implementation, if not the conception, of these policies involved negotiations between the central government and the leaders of the tribes who were supposed to be the main targets of these very policies but who, in many cases, were empowered by these policies. Hamidiye regiments provide the best example for such an outcome. Not only were these designed to strengthen and reward certain "loyal" tribes, they also contributed to the long-term survival of the tribal structure, since tribesmen were kept together in one unit in order to take advantage of their cohesion and solidarity. Consequently, in many instances nomads' interest in mobility was preserved as one of the tenets of these policies even though the overwhelming concern of the central government was with sedentarization. Hence in the 1880s, a high-ranking government official stated that "it would be against reason to construct a mechanism of government which would be totally in contradiction to the customs and beliefs of the nomadic population."[63]

We should also note that, even though state's interests and the society's preferences did not always conflict with each other, this did not mean that nomads and other itinerant groups never resisted the pressures of the Ottoman officials. Nomadic tribes, in particular, had numerous ways of avoiding the demands of the government and continuing the established ways of circulating in and out of their regions despite the state's interest in confining their movements. They could easily hide among the villagers or flee, abandoning their designated plots and villages and resuming their nomadic lives or becoming bandits or mercenaries. They could, in other words, take advantage of the space created by the policies of the central government. Needless to say, such defiance made their relationship with the state even more antagonistic.

Reading the primary and secondary sources, one comes across many instances where the state officials were forced to give up or modify their original plans because of the actions of peasants or nomads. For example, in the

61 Orhonlu, *Osmanlı İmparatorluğunda Aşiretlerin İskânı*, p. 50 n.87.

62 Robert Curzon, *Armenia, A Year at Erzurum and on the Russian Frontiers of Russia, Turkey, and Persia* (New York: Harper and Brothers, 1854), p. 84.

63 Cited in Deringil, *Well Protected Domains*, p. 110.

early eighteenth century, the villagers around Buca near Izmir protested the government plans to settle more tribes in their midst, explaining that their lands were already congested and not rich enough to sustain the newcomers. In this case their complaints were heeded and the plans were scrapped.[64] At the same time, the tribes that had been settled in western and west-central Anatolia complained about the size of their designated holdings and expressed a desire to expand these. It is likely that they were seeking to gain official recognition for the expansion they had already undertaken on their own. The Ottoman government referred these petitions to one of the highest-ranking officials, Anadolu Beylerbeyi, who recommended the addition of more than twenty villages to the previously designated area on the condition that the settlers would have to pay the taxes that were due on these properties.[65] In 1692, a group of Türkmens was moved from Tokat in central Anatolia to Raka. On protesting their living conditions, they were relocated to the region around Sivas, in central Anatolia. In 1695, the same group was moved once again because it had refused to pay its taxes and was inflicting damage on the villagers.[66]

Some of the negotiation between the local tribes and the central government involved the use and interpretation of old and new legal categories that, depending on the specific conditions, could serve either as a means of enforcement by the state or as a shield of protection by the tribes. Yürüks, who were the first and constant targets of settlement policies, routinely tried to avoid the obligations of their new status by claiming that they were not tax-paying subjects (*reaya*) or that they were performing crucial services to the government as guards, horse trainers, and trainers of falcons (for hunting), which should accord them special exemptions.[67]

In many instances, instead of complaining or petitioning, the tribes complied with the demands of the officials by simply expanding the settled portion of their activities, which had always been a part of their lives anyway. Hence, travelers such as Fellows noted how the newly settled villages emptied out in the summer when the inhabitants moved into higher grounds. Also, until the very last years of the empire, the Ottoman government encouraged such integration of nomadism and sedentary farming by allowing and even encouraging the tribes to settle in places of their seasonal migration, mostly in already existing villages.[68] Looking at such examples, it is hard not to conclude that it was not their resistance to but accommodation with the state power that made nomads a fixture of Ottoman society throughout its history

64 Orhonlu, *Osmanlı İmparatorluğunda Aşiretlerin İskânı*, p. 76.

65 Ibid., p. 77.

66 Refik, *Anadolu'da Türk Aşiretleri*, pp. 111–12 (Document 163).

67 Ibid., pp. 36, 37 (Documents 67, 70).

68 Orhonlu, *Osmanlı İmparatorluğunda Aşiretlerin İskânı*, p. 109 (Orhonlu gives the example of how the Reyhanli clan was settled in Amık valley.)

and helped this form of social organization survive in the social networks of the successor states of the empire.

In addition to the empowerment of the chiefs and tribal flexibility, there were other factors that contributed to this situation, which I describe as "mobility in stasis." Some of the state policies of supporting sedentarization induced, inadvertently or otherwise, other groups to move, creating a domino effect of sorts. For example, as the Türkmens moved west and south, their place in the east was taken over by Kurds, who "reintroduced the long range north-south migrations between the Anatolian high plateau and the southern foothills of Taurus";[69] they eventually were instrumental in pushing the Armenians out of these regions. Consequently, some parts of Anatolia witnessed even more migration in the nineteenth century than in the earlier centuries. Even though the Ottomans were trying to create a more sedentary society, some of their policies initiated new movement where there had been none or expanded the scale and direction of existing paths of migration. Kurdish tribes that were sent across long distances as punishment or the uprooting of existing communities in order to open up space in the fertile western and southern lands for the growing number of refugees constitute examples of such state policies. In the late 1890s, many Kurdish tribes decorated themselves with false insignia and pretended to be a part of the Hamidiye troops, fighting their rivals and pushing them out of their lands.[70] Hence for all these reasons, in the midst of massive settlement policies that were carried out after the 1860s, parts of the Ottoman lands appeared to be experiencing even more flux than they had in previous centuries.[71]

Boundaries and Belonging

The borders that were redrawn repeatedly in the course of the eighteenth and nineteenth centuries cut across and split the networks in the Balkans and in the Arab provinces of the Ottoman Empire. Consequently, Kurdish, Arab, Türkmen, Yürük, and other Christian and Muslim communities were divided and their parts were left within the borders of several different states. Much more than the sedentarization policies of the central government, it was the drawing of these borders that ultimately constrained the movement of tribes by confining them within these national spaces. As the policies of drawing borders and settling communities matured, the frontier areas ceased to be areas through which people moved to connect two territories; they were

[69] Xavier de Planhol, "Geography, Politics and Nomadism in Anatolia," *International Social Science Journal* 11, no. 4 (1959): 529.

[70] McDowall, *A Modern History of the Kurds*, p. 60.

[71] Bruinessen interprets the establishment of the Hamidiye troops as a reversal of the state's previous policy of sedentarization, since these regiments clearly strengthened at least some of the tribes. *Agha, Shaikh and State*, p. 238.

now becoming true borders that differentiated from each other the territories that belonged to two different political entities. When the communities and, in some cases, even the villages were sliced in this fashion, those who were left within the Ottoman Empire either followed their relations and kinsmen and took refuge in the neighboring states or, bereft of their means of livelihood, were seriously impoverished.

In one of the many surreal outcomes of the new restrictions, the tribes that lived in these zones were now forced to apply for permission to import and export livestock each time they took their herds for grazing in the places they had used for this purpose for generations.[72] When the borders were drawn, the identity of not only the people but also the animals, especially those that were separated from their owners, became subjects of intense debate among the people involved.[73]

Especially in the southeast and eventually across all the commercially active regions of the empire, the interruption of these networks had an adverse effect not only on these communities, but also on the supply networks of the major Ottoman cities whose trade was supported through these channels. Toward the end of the nineteenth century, the Ottoman state tried to reconstitute these networks in truncated form in order to reinforce the authority of the central government. Growing pressure of the state made these groups even more vulnerable and hence prone to agitation to carve out their own space for survival. Serbia, Montenegro, Albania in the Balkans, Crimea in the north on the Russian border, Kurdish areas on the Iranian border, Basra and Korna in the South, and Tripoli and Algeria on the Mediterranean – in short, all the territories that used to define the frontier regions of the empire – all became sites of such unrest and agitation in the eighteenth and nineteenth centuries.

To add another layer of complexity, the already difficult circumstances of settling nomads became even more complicated during the last quarter of the nineteenth century when the waves of refugees retreated into the shrinking borders of the empire. Not only did the urgency of finding land for these people complicate the policies of sedentarization, but the growing number of refugees also brought to the forefront the question of the ethnic and religious composition of the population in various parts of the empire, especially in the border areas. Taking care of these refugees and settling the large numbers of nomads and other circulating groups in an ethnically charged environment required a new approach to rule on the part of the Ottoman state and a new social compact between the Ottoman state and the society.

Initially, the Ottomans limited their attention to specific places and conditions rather than thinking in universal terms of identity, citizenship, or nationality of everybody living in the empire. Accordingly, in settling nomadic

[72] MV 40/20.
[73] MV 62/6.

communities as well as refugees, the government tried not so much to separate and disengage different ethnic and religious groups from each other as to create symbioses among them. It is in this spirit that the Ottoman authorities gave the nomad Kurds in eastern Anatolia the right to shelter with their flocks in the villages of the Armenian peasants.[74] Incidentally, this had precisely been the policy of early imperial settlement in the Balkans.

It would not be accurate to state that the Ottomans never embraced a general framework in trying to bring some stability to the quickly changing circumstances of the empire. In fact, several models, such as supranational Ottomanism, Islamism, and Romantic and ethnic nationalism, were used in succession and combination with each other, but none of these gained the power or inspired the imagination that some Ottoman officials and intellectuals hoped to cultivate. For example, the curriculum of the Tribal School that was set up in Istanbul in 1892 was heavily biased toward the teaching of religion, creating the impression that these schools were trying to teach how to become not good Ottomans but good Muslims. Ironically enough, the Kurds and Arabs fought frequently in these schools, most of the time over the correct rendering of the Koran.[75] Occasionally, the Ottoman officials tried to meld some of these frameworks, combining, for example, a narrowly defined official Islam with more secular symbols of nation building. Across the frontier regions in the Balkans, especially in places such as the semi-autonomous Eastern Rumelia, Ottomans insisted that their postage stamps be used.[76] They made teaching of Ottoman Turkish mandatory in Greek and Bulgarian schools[77] and prohibited Muslim students from attending foreign-owned schools.[78] In Beirut, when an Italian school attempted to raise the Italian flag, the government immediately and forcefully protested, forcing the school to retreat.[79] The Congress of Berlin in 1878 (where, incidentally, the Ottoman government was represented by an Ottoman Greek) created a Bulgaria that was autonomous but tributary and an Eastern Rumelia that was semi-autonomous, with a Christian governor who was to be appointed by the Ottoman government. Given the complexity and contradictory nature of some of these arrangements, it was no surprise that everything from the appointment of governors to the use of currency became points of serious contention involving the Ottoman state, local groups, and the European powers.[80]

74 Planhol, "Geography, Politics and Nomadism in Anatolia," p. 530.

75 Akpınar, *Osmanlı Devletinde Aşiret Mektebi*, p. 40.

76 MV 33/36.

77 MV 34/24.

78 MV 16/23.

79 MV 43/71.

80 In *The Well Protected Domains*, Selim Deringil shows how sensitive the Ottomans were in sustaining not only the substance, but also the symbols of their power and sovereignty during the reign of Abdülhamid.

We know that ultimately, the reforming bureaucrats and intellectuals fell short of creating a vision for a well-integrated Ottoman society, with its immense ethnic and religious diversity. Instead of building such an integrated but diverse totality that would have required the genuine participation of these groups, they chose to coopt the leaders of some of these communities and enlist their services in the top-down construction of a centralized identity. Failing in this project, they came to regard the ethnic and religious separation of their subjects as a prerequisite for creating the stable and predictable society for which they hoped.

Conclusion

The historical trajectory I have reviewed here involves the interplay of three sets of boundaries. The first of these is the external boundaries of the empire. Until the end of the sixteenth century, it was the natural barriers such as the Arabian and North African deserts, Caucasus mountain ranges, the Mediterranean Sea, and the northern steppes that set limits to the expansion of the Ottoman Empire. These expanses were uncertain by definition; they stretched over a large territory and contained hybrid communities with overlapping cultures and histories. Between the fourteenth and the sixteenth centuries, it would be impossible to run a clear line across any of these places and divide them into zones that "belonged" to the Ottoman Empire and those that were of another state. As sovereignty became the governing principle of international relations in the early modern era, the European states, including those that bordered the Ottoman Empire, tried to be more specific about the territory over which they could exercise legitimate power. Some of the European states succeeded in coming up with a vision that gave some meaning (in terms of a common experience, manufactured ideology, or collectively imagined identity) to the collectivity over which they claimed a right to rule and managed the transition to the modern era more or less intact. As for the Ottomans, there was no historical, cultural, or ideological ground on which they could lay unequivocal claim to any of their changing borders. Consequently, starting with their first major territorial loss in 1699, Ottomans repeatedly revised their "inviolable" boundaries as they continued to cede region after region to neighboring states or indigenous nationalist movements. It was only after World War I and under the nationalist leadership that a precise territory was defined in advance with a clear stipulation that the nationalist army would fight to defend it.[81]

The other border that is relevant for our discussion is the line that separated the Ottoman state from the Ottoman society. In the early part of

[81] As it turned out, even the exact extent of these territories was uncertain. The status of Mosul province was not finalized until well after the peace settlements that ended World War I. Andrew Mango, *Atatürk* (New York: Overlook Press, 1999), p. 378.

the history of the empire, this line was also highly porous. High-ranking bureaucrats who staffed the Ottoman government were routinely recruited from all segments of the society, especially from among Christian boys, and were trained specially for government service. Partly because of the relatively open access that the societal elements had to the domain of the state, the nomadic character of vast sections of the Ottoman society influenced the laws and institutions of the imperial bureaucracy and left a deep imprint in the practice and ideology of the Ottoman state. Each one of the sedentarization policies that the Ottoman officials implemented between the seventeenth and eighteenth centuries was designed as part of a broader policy of institutionalizing and codifying the practices. To put it another way, each can be seen as a deliberate attempt at instituting a separation and a conceptual and practical distinction between the Ottoman state and society.

By the time the Tanzimat reforms were instituted in the nineteenth century, many of the channels that provided opportunities for social mobility were blocked. With its multiplying offices, laws, and formal procedures, the Ottoman state had acquired the characteristics of a functionally differentiated, "modern" polity. But effective rule under such circumstances required that this separation be followed by a reintegration that would give the newly institutionalized state the right to rule legitimately over the society. The ideologies of Ottomanism, Islamism, and ethnic nationalism all fell short of providing the comprehensive vision that would, in fact, pull the subjects of the Empire into a collectivity that was larger than their tribes or religious or professional communities.

The third set of boundaries defined and contained the hundreds of ethnic and religious communities that came under the Ottoman rule over the long history of the empire. In some ways, this is the most misunderstood part of Ottoman history and society. Often, this picture is one of neatly drawn boundaries separating different ethnic and religious groups from each other in their respective millet communities. In fact, every constitution of these separate millets was the product of the state's attempts at distinguishing and institutionalizing its own rule. If we move beyond the formal categories that were created by the state or by the communal leaders and examine the interactions that prevailed in the society, we see that the boundaries of these groups remained amorphous and as such they defied easy categorization. Not only among the Sufi groups, but also between the different religions, there were many gray areas that permitted cultural cross-fertilization. Ultimately, fitting the national borders around these communities proved to be an impossible task – so much so that in the early twentieth century, creating a nationally viable state proved to be possible only with the massive displacement of millions of people and exchange of populations across national boundaries.

3

The Permeable Boundaries of Ottoman Jewry

Sarah Abrevaya Stein

At the turn of the twentieth century, over a quarter of a million Jews lived in the European regions of the Ottoman Empire.[1] Most were Sephardim, Jews who came to the region after being expelled from Spain and Portugal in the late fifteenth century and who retained a Judeo-Spanish language known as Ladino or Judezmo. For the next five centuries, Ottoman Jews would constitute a critical role in the Ottoman economy and political system, developing, in the meanwhile, a rich and unique culture that differentiated this population from Jews elsewhere in Europe.

In the middle of the nineteenth century, a modern, secular culture in Ladino (still the mother tongue of the vast majority of the empire's Jews) began to emerge in the Ottoman Balkans and European Turkey.[2] By the late nineteenth century, Ladino was being used to produce new genres of Jewish culture: original works of poetry, drama, fiction, scholarly essays,

[1] Two useful studies of the empire's multiethnic demography are: Kemal H. Karpat, *Ottoman Population, 1830–1914: Demographic and Social Characteristics* (Madison: University of Wisconsin Press, 1985), and Justin McCarthy, *Muslims and Minorities: The Population of Ottoman Anatolia and the End of the Empire* (New York: New York University Press, 1983).

[2] As late as the Second World War, 85 percent of Turkish Jewry identified Ladino as their native language. In 1895, some 80.35 percent of Serbian Jews spoke Ladino, and in 1926, some 89.43 percent of Bulgarian Jews labeled themselves Ladino speakers. Finally, in 1928, some 62,000 of Greece's 73,000 Jews (most of them from Macedonia and Thrace) identified Ladino as their mother tongue. Information about Jewish literacy in Ladino in the era of the Turkish Republic may be found in Walter F. Weiker, *Ottomans, Turks, and the Jewish Polity* (New York/London: University Press of America, 1992). For more on Jewish literacy in Ladino in the Ottoman Balkans, see Harriet Pass Freidenreich, *The Jews of Yugoslavia: A Quest for Community* (Philadelphia: Jewish Publication Society, 1979); Eyal Ginio, "'Learning the Beautiful Language of Homer': Judeo-Spanish Speaking Jews and the Greek Language and Culture between the Wars," *Jewish History* (2002); Astuc Kalev, "Data Concerning the Demographic Situation of the Bulgarian Jews, 1887–1949," *Annual* 16 (1981); Saul Mézan, *Les Juifs espagnols en Bulgarie* (Sofia: "Hamishpat" Publishers, 1925); Bracha Rivlin, ed., *Pinkas Hakehilot – Greece*, vol. 17 (Jerusalem: Yad Vashem, 1998).

dictionaries and encyclopedias, translations of world literature, and a dazzling array of daily, weekly, and monthly periodicals. In these media, readers and writers of Ladino debated and displayed what it meant to be modern and Jewish. Without a doubt, the single most prolific genre of Ladino print culture was the popular press. The first Ladino periodical, *La buena esperansa*, was published in 1842, and, over the course of the next century, Jewish periodicals blossomed in the Ottoman Empire and its successor states; by 1913, there were no fewer than 389 Jewish periodicals published in Turkey and the Balkans.[3] This, of course, was at roughly the same time that secular print cultures emerged in the many other languages of this extraordinarily multilingual empire.[4]

This chapter considers the complex ways in which the contributors to the Ladino press envisioned Ottoman Jews and the Ottoman Empire in an era in which the structure of empire was giving way to newly created successor states organized around ethnic and national affinities from which Jews would (by and large) be excluded.[5] The ensuing pages explore the multiple

[3] Gia Aivazian, "The Role of the Armenian Press in Istanbul, 1908–1915 in the Shaping of the Armenian National Identity," paper presented at the Middle East Studies Association, San Francisco, 1997; Ami Ayalon, *The Press in the Arab Middle East, a History* (Oxford: Oxford University Press, 1995); Abraham Galanté, *La presse judeo-espagnole mondiale* (Istanbul: Societé Anonyme de Papeterie et d'Imprimerie (Fratelli Haim, 1935); Moshe David Gaon, *Ha-itonut be-ladino: Bibliografia* (Jerusalem: Ben Zvi, 1965); Iacob Hassan, "El estudio del periodismo sefard," *Sefarad* 26 (1988): 229–236; Gad Nassi, ed., *Jewish Journalism and Printing Houses in the Ottoman Empire and Modern Turkey* (Istanbul: ISIS Press, 2001).

[4] English language studies on the Ottoman press include Palmira Brummett, *Image and Imperialism in the Ottoman Revolutionary Press, 1908–1911* (Albany: State University of New York, 2000); Elizabeth Brown Frierson, "Unimagined Communities: State, Press, and Gender in the Hamidian Era," Ph.D. dissertation, Princeton University, 1996. Turkish language sources on the Ottoman press include M. Orhan Bayrak, *Türkiye'de Gazeteler ve Dergiler Sözlüğü, 1831–1993* (Istanbul: KÜLL Yayinlari, 1994); Nesim Benbaneste, *Örneklerle Türk Musevi Basininin Tarihçesi*, (Istanbul: N. Benbaneste, 1988); A. Alâaddin Çetin, *Basbakanlik Arsivi Kilavuzu* (Istanbul: Enderun Kitabevi, 1979); Hasan Duman, *Istanbul Kütüphaneleri Arap Harfli Süreli Yayinlari Toplu Kataloğu, 1828–1928, Bibliographical Series/Research Centre for Islamic History, Art, and Culture*, vol. 3 (Besiktas, Istanbul: Islâm Tarih, Sanat, ve Kültür Arastirma Merkezi, Islâm Konferansi Teskilâti, 1986); Selim Nüzet Gerçek, *Türk Matbaaciliği*, vol. 1: *Müteferrika matbaasi* (Istanbul: Istanbul Devlet Basimevi, 1939); Server R. Iskit, *Türkiyede Matbuat Rejimleri* (Istanbul: Ülkü Matbaasi, 1939); Server R. Iskit, *Türkiyede Nesriyat Hareketleri Tarihine bir Bakis* (Istanbul: Devlet Basimevi, 1939); Server R. Iskit, *Türkiyede Matbuat Idareleri ve Politikalari* (Istanbul, Turkey: Tan Basimevi, 1943); Server Iskit, *Turkiye'de Matbuat Hareketleri ve Politikalari* (Istanbul, 1943); Alpay Kabacali, *Baslangiçtan Günümüze Türkiye'de Basin Sansürü* (Istanbul: Gazeteciler Cemiyeti Yayinlari, 1990); Zafer Toprak, "Fikir Dergiciliginin Yuzyili," in *Türkiye'de dergiler, ansiklopediler (1849–1984)* (Istanbul: Gelisim Yayinlari, 1984); A. D. Zheltiakov, *Türkiye'nin Sosyo-politik ve Kültürel Hayatinda Basin (Pechat v obshchestvenno-politicheskoi i kulturnoi zhizni Turtsii)* (Ankara, Leningrad: Basin Yayin Genel Müdürlügü, 1979); Zafer Toprak, "Fikir Dergiciliginin Yuzyili," in *Türkiye'de dergiler, ansiklopediler (1849–1984)* (Istanbul: Gelisim Yayinlari, 1984), 273.

[5] *El tiempo* ran continuously from 1872 until 1930, appearing first as a daily, soon after biweekly, and, from July 1882 to 1930, three times a week. The newspaper was created by

communities and identities to which popular Ladino sources envisioned Ottoman Jewish readers cohering: vectors of belonging that unsettle our assumptions about the relationship between minority communities and the multiethnic empires in which they lived. Studying these intertwining identities not only enriches our understanding of Sephardic history and culture but offers a profound lesson about the complexity of "belonging."

This chapter also explores the porousness of ethnic and regional boundaries. As we see below, even in the earliest days of the Ladino press, readers were encouraged to think of themselves as Jewish, Ottoman, Sephardic, participants in a Western European cultural economy, Francophilic, and antinationalist. In this way, Ottoman Jewish readers of Ladino were encouraged to harbor a sense of self that was multivectored but nonetheless free of paradox or conflict. This may appear contradictory to the contemporary eye, accustomed, as it is, to perceiving identity as a single, reducible phenomena, but late nineteenth- and early-twentieth century Ottoman Jewish culture and identity was far from single in inspiration or nature. Which is not to say it was "hybrid" or irreducible, at least not in the sense implied by many contemporary theorists of identity.[6] At its core, Ottoman Jewish identity

Merkado Fresco, David Fresco, Sami Alkabez, and Isaac Carmona, and was at first patronized by Hayim Carmona, scion of a prominent family of Constantinople. After Carmona's death in 1883, patronage of the paper was assumed by Hayim's son Isaac, who had been *El tiempo*'s editor since 1872. For the next few years, the paper was edited by Sami Alkabez and Merkado Fresco until 1878, when the position was assumed by David Fresco, who would edit it for some fifty years. These and other technical details of the newspaper's publication are described in the following sources: Moshe David Gaon, *Ha-itonut be-ladino: Bibliografia* (Jerusalem: Ben Zvi, 1965); Avner Levi, "The Ladino "El Tiempo" of Istanbul During 1882–83," *Qesher*, no. 13 (May 1993): 22e–24e.

6 I refer here, in particular, to Homi Bhabha's notion of hybrid identity as a site of colonial resistance. To quote Bhabha:

> Hybridity is the sign of the productivity of colonial power, its shifting forces and fixities; it is the name for the strategic reversal of the process of domination through disavowal. . . . [Hybridity] unsettles the mimetic or narcissistic demands of colonial power but reimplicates its identifications in strategic subversion that turn the gaze of the discriminated back upon the eye of power.

Though Bhabha's theories of hybridity have helped to shape my understanding of Ottoman Jewish culture identity, I depart from him in several significant regards. First, I stop short of equating Ottoman Jews' ability to marvel at French culture with a political process of "resistance." This term, I would suggest, fails to describe the many nuances in the relationship between Ottoman Jewry and French Jewry and between France and the Ottoman Empire. In particular, Bhabha's theory elides the eagerness with which many Ottoman Jews embraced the influence of Franco-Jewry and the various cultural and material reasons that lay behind this choice. For Bhabha, the absorption of Western influence by colonial (or semi-colonial, in this case) subjects is always born of inauthenticity or cultural or material corruption. For Jews of the turn-of-the-century Ottoman Empire, however, Westernization represented not the demise of modern Ladino culture but its reformulation. Such a reformulation was necessary in part because the changing political landscape of the Ottoman Empire was turning Jews into

was not plural but self-consciously "Jewish," an essentialist category that held tremendous meaning, particularly insofar as it differentiated Ottoman Jews from their Christian and Muslim neighbors.[7] But this Jewishness was articulated through and alongside the articulation of other allegiances: with the Ottoman Empire, with Europe, with other Ottoman millets, and with the modern.

This chapter takes as its case study the first Ladino newspaper published in the Ottoman capital and among the most long-lived of them all: *El tiempo* (Constantinople, 1872–1930). There is evidence that by the First World War, one of every two Jewish adults in the Ottoman capital subscribed to *El tiempo*: Its reach was extended further still by the practice of sharing papers.[8] The influence of *El tiempo* stretched beyond the imperial capital. The newspaper published letters to the editor penned in cities far from Constantinople, and at least some readers outside the city subscribed to the publication on a regular basis.[9] Perhaps more striking still, Ladino newspapers based in Salonika, Izmir, and as far away as Jerusalem and Cairo not only reprinted articles from *El tiempo* but engaged in active debate with it: responding to the paper's polemical articles, challenging its editor, querying whether or not this influential newspaper could be allowed to speak (which it often assumed it did) for all of Ottoman Jewry.[10]

a minority (and nonindigenous) culture. In this sense, by the turn of the century, Ottoman Jews were becoming doubly imperial subjects, quite unlike Bhabha's much-simplified imperial subject.

The above quotation is selected from Homi Bhabha, "Signs Taken for Wonders: Questions of Ambivalence and Authority under a Tree outside Delhi, May 1817," in *The Location of Culture* (New York: Routledge, 1994), 102–123, 113.

7 Bruce Masters has recently developed a similar argument about Jewish identity in the Arab regions of the Ottoman Empire. Bruce Masters, *Christians and Jews in the Ottoman Arab World: The Roots of Sectarianism* (Cambridge: Cambridge University Press, 2001).

8 This estimate is derived from a circulation identified by Avner Levy (who identifies *El tiempo*'s circulation as 10,000) and on Justin McCarthy's age pyramids, which are based on the Ottoman census of 1912. Justin McCarthy, *Muslims and Minorities*, Appendix 4, 193–226; Levy, "The Jewish Press." For more on the Jewish population of Constantinople, see Riva Kastoryano, ed., *Ottoman and Turkish Jewry, Community and Leadership*, vol. 12, *Indiana University Turkish Studies Series* (Bloomington: Indiana University Turkish Studies, 1992); Stanford Shaw, "The Population of Istanbul in the Nineteenth Century," *Turk Tarih Dergisis* 32 (1979): 412.

9 Elias Canetti, for example, has recalled in his memoir that his grandfather read *El tiempo* in Ruschuk (Rus), a town situated on the Danube, some 250 miles from Constantinople. Elias Canetti, *The Tongue Set Free: Remembrance of a European Childhood*, trans. Joachim Neugroschel (New York: Seabury Press, 1979).

10 Arguably, such interlocution was the norm rather than the exception. Ladino newspapers of the late nineteenth and early twentieth centuries tended to be in conversation with one another: Their editors, be they friends or foe, often knew one another well, collaborated on projects, or, indeed, were related. Consider, for example, the close relationship between Abraham Galante (editor of the Cairo-based *La Vara*) and David Fresco, or the relationship between Fresco and Elia Carmona, editor of the humorist *El Gugeton* (the longest-lived

As the interlocution between *El tiempo* and other Ladino newspapers suggests, *El tiempo* was – despite its visibility and popularity – in many ways an anomalous source, shaped by the city in which it was produced, the editors and journalists who dictated its content, and the readers who consumed it. Indeed, *El tiempo* is a useful historical source in part because its relevance was continually being challenged. The paper's pages were rent by rifts that divided Jewish readers from one another and from the ideological project – which can loosely be described as Westernization – by which it was inspired. In the pages of this newspaper, one can discern not a unified voice of Ottoman Jewry, but vociferous public debate, particularly over the question of what it meant to be Ottoman and Jewish. To understand these rifts and situate them in the turn-of-the-century Ottoman landscape, this paper focuses on *El tiempo*'s discussion of the question of language choice, an increasingly politicized issue not only for Jewish subjects of the Ottoman Empire but for Jews in Central and Eastern Europe as well.[11] As we see below, the newspaper's stance on the relative merits of French, Ladino, Hebrew, and Turkish can be used as a barometer of the constraints and opportunities facing Jews in the Ottoman heartland.

Debates over language choice in the turn-of-the-century Ottoman Jewish press also invite fascinating and often surprising historiographic conclusions. The following pages suggest that we should resist the assumption that there is an intimate and inviolable connection between the emergence of print cultures in ethnic vernaculars and the emergence of a sense of nationalism or community among their readers.[12] An exploration of the Ladino press of

Ladino journal after *El tiempo*). In both instances, these writers and editors exhibited a profound influence on one another. Albert E. Kalderon, *Abraham Galante, a Biography* (New York: Sepher-Hermon Press, 1983); Robyn Lowenthal, "Elia Carmona's Autobiography Judeo-Spanish Popular Press and Novel Publishing Milieu in Constantinople, Ottoman Empire, circa 1860–1932," Ph.D. dissertation, University of Nebraska, 1984).

Mention of *El tiempo*'s influence on the Ladino press of Jerusalem has been made by Michelle Campos in her unpublished Ph.D. dissertation, where she notes that the Jerusalem-based Ladino newspaper *ha-Herut* ran numerous articles responding to *El tiempo*'s coverage of Zionism. See *ha-Herut* 2 nos. 49 and 50, January 19 and 21, 1910. Michelle Campos, "A 'Shared Homeland' and Its Boundaries: Late Ottoman Palestine between Imperial Commitment and Communal Identification, 1908–1914," Ph.D. dissertation, Stanford University, 2002.

11 I elaborate on this comparison in greater detail in a book that compares the emergence of the Ladino press in the Ottoman Empire with that of the Yiddish press of the Russian Empire. See Stein, *Making Jews Modern: Yiddish and Ladino Press of the Russian and Ottoman Empires* (Bloomington: Indiana University Press, 2003) For a survey of the language debates that occupied Ottoman Jewries, see David M. Bunis, "Modernization and the Language Question among Judezmo-Speaking Sephardim of the Ottoman Empire," in *Sephardi and Middle Eastern Jewries, History and Culture in the Modern Era*, ed. Harvey E. Goldberg (Bloomington: Indiana University Press, 1996), 226–239.

12 I respond here to a growing body of scholarship that studies the relationship between ethnic and national identity formation and print culture. Among the most influential works on this

the Ottoman Empire exposes a far more complicated reality. It is true that newspapers in Ladino were available to an exclusively Jewish reading public (some non-Jews were literate in these languages, but they were rare exceptions). But ironically, this did not mean that these newspapers sanctioned readers' use of this language or encouraged them to imagine themselves as a national entity. The Ladino press, as we see below, hoped its readers would adopt European or Turkish languages and even went so far as to denounce Ladino as a corrupt tongue, a patois, an embarrassment, and a jargon.[13] This antagonism toward Ladino reflected the mood of Ottoman Jewish politics on the eve of the twentieth century, which tended to be antinational, Francophilic, and committed to the maintenance of the Ottoman Empire as a whole. To put this another way, readers of the turn-of-the-century Ottoman Ladino press were discouraged from belonging to (or, indeed, from believing in) the very culture the press itself was helping to create: a distinct and distinctly modern secular culture in Ladino.

Ottoman Jews and the Hazards of Modernity

The Ottoman Empire underwent many changes in its 600 years of history. To simplify this history dramatically, one could say that throughout, the empire was headed by a patrimonial state that sought legitimation in Islam: Muslim law, the *shari'a*, was implemented by the Sultan Caliph (though the Sultans did not use the title "Caliph" from the mid-sixteenth century to the rule of Abdulhamid II).[14] This being said, much government business was conducted according to secular regulations: For example, social and economic groups, such as merchants, often served as intermediaries between the central government and the majority of Ottoman subjects.[15] Though

subject are Benedict Anderson, *Imagined Communities* (New York: Verso Press, 1983); Eric J. Hobsbawm, *Nations and Nationalism since 1870* (Cambridge: Cambridge University Press, 1992); Miroslav Hroch, *Social Preconditions of National Revival in Europe: A Comparative Analysis of the Social Composition of Patriotic Groups among the Smaller European Nations* (Cambridge and New York: Cambridge University Press, 1985); Anthony Smith, *The Ethnic Origins of Nations* (Oxford: Blackwell Press, 1986).

[13] For more on the Ladino term "*zhargon*," see Winfried Busse, "Le judeo-espagnol – un jargon?," in *Hommage a Haim Vidal Sephiha*, ed. Marie-Christine Varol-Bornes Winfried Busse (Berne: Peter Lang, 1996), 239–246.

[14] According to traditionalist and textualist views of Islam, the *shari'a* divided Ottoman society into two: the bureaucracy, the military, and janissary corps (slave army), and the clergy composed the elite, a group accessible only to Muslims that was exempt from the payment of taxes. Everyone else was known as the *reaya* (the flock), and subject to heavy tributary taxes. See, e.g., Metin Heper, *The State Tradition in Turkey* (North Humberside, Eng., 1985); Serif Mardin, "Power, Civil Society and Culture in the Ottoman Empire," *Comparative Studies in Society and History*, no. 11 (1969): 258–281.

[15] The study of the Ottoman merchant class and of local elites has inspired a rich array of scholarship. See, e.g., the contributions to Benjamin Braude and Bernard Lewis, eds., *Christians and Jews in the Ottoman Empire, the Functioning of a Plural Society* (New York: Holmes &

Ottoman society was technically ordered by Islamic texts and practices, in fact an entirely different reality – one that might be thought of as functional coexistence – existed on the ground.

Similarly, relations between Muslims and certain non-Muslims (those who were thought to possess a divinely inspired Holy Book, which included Christians and Jews, but often excluded Zoroastrians) were technically regulated by a pact called *dhimma (zimmet* in Turkish) but in fact were conditioned by a complex web of social, religious, and economic practices that undermined – or at least provided alternatives to the strict observance of – Islamic law. According to the traditional pact regulating relations between the *ahl al-dhimma* (people of the dhimmi) or *dhimmis* (*zimmi* in Turkish) and Muslims, "rights" of non-Muslims were not guaranteed. Indeed, the notion of rights did not exist until it was introduced by Westernizing reformers in the late nineteenth century.[16] Prior to liberalizing reforms of the nineteenth century, *dhimmis* were reminded that they were inferior to Muslims by legislation that circumscribed their dress, use of animals, weapons, and places of worship and by the threat of *sürgün* (forced migrations, which certain Muslims were subject to, as well).[17] Simultaneously, however, the *dhimmi* in general – and Ottoman Jewry in particular – were protected in ways that minorities under Christian rule were not. Non-Muslims were allowed to maintain their own courts and institutions, and as a result, they evolved into corporate structures. In this way, ethnic and religious difference was respected and juridically sustained. The success of this system – insofar as the empire's Jews were concerned – was reflected in the virtual absence of anti-Semitism from the Ottoman landscape.

For Ottoman Jews, this social map translated into economic success in the early modern period. While the majority of the Sephardim were involved

Meier, 1982), 171–184, and Edhem Edhem, Daniel Goffman, and Bruce Masters, eds., *The Ottoman City between East and West, Aleppo, Izmir, and Istanbul* (Cambridge: Cambridge University Press, 1999). See also Beshara Doumani, *Rediscovering Palestine* (Berkeley: University of California Press, 1995); Daniel Goffman, *Izmir and the Levantine World* (Seattle: University of Washington Press, 1990); Reşat Kasaba, *The Ottoman Empire and the World Economy in the Nineteenth Century* (New York: University of New York Press, 1988); Caglar Keyder, *State and Class in Turkey: A Study in Capitalist Development* (London and New York: Verso, 1987); Sevket Pamuk, *The Ottoman Empire and European Capitalism, 1820–1913: Trade, Investment, and Production* (Cambridge: Cambridge University Press, 1987); Ehud Toledano, "The Emergence of Ottoman-Local Elites (1700–1900): A Framework for Research," in *Middle East Politics and Ideas: A History from Within*, ed. Ilan Pappe and Mose Ma'oz (Tauris, 1997), 145–162.

16 Aron Rodrigue, "From *Millet* to Minority: Turkish Jewry," in *Paths of Emancipation: Jews, States, and Citizenship*, ed. Pierre Birnbaum and Ira Katznelson (Princeton, N.J.: Princeton University Press, 1995).

17 For a comparative look at the treatment of *dhimmis* under Ottoman control, see Benjamin Braude and Bernard Lewis, eds., *Christians and Jews in the Ottoman Empire: The Functioning of a Plural Society*, vol. 1 (New York: Holmes & Meier, 1982).

in small-scale trade and artisanal occupations, a small Jewish elite became influential in finance and international commerce, tax collecting, and the fabulously successful production of woolen textiles based in Salonika and Safed. Sales of textiles linked the Jewish economy to the Ottoman regime, a "vertical relationship" that the empire strove to cultivate. Salonikan cloth was designed to be consumed by the Janissary Corps (a segment of the Ottoman army dependent on the forced conscription on conquered subjects); from the sixteenth century onward, the cities' poll tax was even paid in cloth. This profitable relationship began to decay in the seventeenth century. By then, England had introduced a competitive cloth that undermined the Salonikan market, while fires and epidemics further weakened the industry. In contrast to England, the Ottoman regime did not encourage exports, rendering the textile trade even less competitive (England's mercantilist policies aided the growth of joint-stock companies, such as the English Levant Company, a frequent advertiser in the pages of the Ladino press).[18] The weakening of the Salonikan economy had reverberations throughout the Ottoman Jewish world.

The growing strength of the Atlantic economy did not prevent Ottoman industrial centers from remaining vibrant, local merchants from prospering, or the Ottoman textile industry from surviving: in the early nineteenth century, even the Ottoman monetary system remained strong.[19] And yet in many ways, Salonika's decline reflected an economic crisis that Ottoman Jewry faced as a whole.[20] While Greeks and Armenians responded to regional

[18] For more on the decline of the Ottoman Jewish textile industry, see Benjamin Braude, "The Cloth Industry of Salonika in the Mediterranean Economy," *Pe'amim* 15 (1983): 82–95; Benjamin Braude, "The Rise and Fall of Salonika Woollens, 1500–1650: Technology Transfer and Western Competition," *Mediterranean Historical Review* 6, no. 2 (1991): 519–542; Daniel Goffman, *Izmir and the Levantine World* (Seattle: University of Washington Press, 1990); Snezhka Panova, "The Development of the Textile Industry in the Balkan Countris and the Role of the Jewish Population in the XVIth–XVIIth Centuries," *Annual*, no. 11 (1976): 123–140; Minna Rozen, "Contest and Rivalry in Mediterranean Maritime Commerce in the First Half of the Eighteenth Century: The Jews of Salonika and the European Presence," *Revue des etudes juives*, no. 147 (1988): 309–352; Azriel Shohat, "The King's Cloth in Salonika," *Sefunot*, no. 12 (1971–8): 169–188.

[19] Doumani, *Rediscovering Palestine*; Pamuk, *The Ottoman Empire and European Capitalism*; Donald Quataert, *Ottoman Manufacturing in the Age of the Industrial Revolution* (Cambridge: Cambridge University Press, 1993).

[20] More general studies of the shifting regional economy of this period include Daniel Goffman, *Izmir and the Levantine World* (Seattle: University of Washington Press, 1990); Huri Islamoglu-Inan, ed., *The Ottoman Empire and the World Economy* (Cambridge and Paris: Cambridge University Press/Editions de la Maison des Sciences de l'Homme, 1987); Kasaba, *The Ottoman Empire*; Quataert, *Ottoman Manufacturing*; Keyder, *State and Class in Turkey*. Critiques of the world systems model have been proposed by Janet Lippman Abu-Lughod, "The World System in the Thirteenth Century: Dead-End of Precursor?," in *Islamic and European Expansion: The Forging of a Global Order*, ed. Michael Adas (Philadelphia: Temple University Press, 1993), 75–102; Michael Adas, "Bringing Ideas and Agency Back

economic shifts by diversifying their economies, Jews were unable to do the same: When the Janissary Corps was abolished in 1826, it was a final blow to an already weak Ottoman Jewish economy.[21] For many Jewish subjects of the empire, success in the Ottoman economy would increasingly depend on ties with Western Europe rather than ties with the Ottoman authorities. These economic shifts had implications for the shaping of culture: Increasingly, embourgeoisement became inseparable from westernization in the Ottoman setting, not only for Jews but for budding bourgeoisie of other ethnic and religious groups as well.

To develop ties with Western Europe, Ottoman Jewry turned to the Western European Jewish elite for cultural and economic inspiration. French Jewry soon offered itself forth as a model; in 1860, the Alliance Israélite Universelle (AIU) was founded by the Franco-Jewish elite to educate Levantine Jewry in the French language and culture, "civilizing" them and readying them for success in what scholars have called the capitalist world economy. The AIU would educate over three generations of Levantine Jews, dominating secular Jewish culture in the Ottoman Empire until the Young Turk Revolt in 1908.[22]

In: Representation and the Comparative Approach to World History," in *World History: Ideologies, Structures, and Identities*, ed. Richard H. Elphick, Philip Pomper, and Richard T. Vann (Oxford: Blackwell, 1998), 81–104.

[21] For studies of the shifting economic roles of Ottoman millets, see Charles Issawi, "The Transformation of the Economic Position of the *Millets* in the Nineteenth Century," in Braude and Lewis, eds., *Christians and Jews in the Ottoman Empire*, 261–286; Hagop Barsoumian, "The Dual Role of the Armenian *Amira* Class within the Ottoman Government and the Armenian *Millet* (1750–1850)," in ibid., 171–184; Richard Clogg, "The Greek *Millet* in the Ottoman Empire," in ibid., 185–208; Paul Dumont, "Jewish Communities in Turkey during the Last Decades of the Nineteenth Century in Light of the Archives of the Alliance Israélite Universelle," in ibid., 209–242; A. Uner Turgay, "Trade and Merchants in Nineteenth-Cebtury Trabzon: Elements of Ethnic Conflict," in ibid., 287–318.

[22] For more on the Alliance's activities in the Ottoman lands, see Esther Benbassa, "L'Education feminine en Orient: L'ecole de Filles de l'Alliance Israélite Universelle a Galata, Istanbul (1879–1912)," *Histoire, Economie, et Société* 4 (1991): 529–559; Dumont, "Jewish Communities"; Aron Rodrigue, *Images of Sephardi and Eastern Jewries in Transition, the Teachers of the Alliance Israélite Universelle, 1860–1939* (Seattle: University of Washington Press, 1993); Aron Rodrigue, *French Jews, Turkish Jews: The Alliance Israélite Universelle and the Politics of Jewish Schooling in Turkey, 1860–1925* (Bloomington Indiana University Press, 1990). For studies of the AIU's influence elsewhere in the Middle East and North Africa, see Avraham Cohen, "Iranian Jewry and the Educational Endeavors of the Alliance Israelite Universelle," *Jewish Social Studies* 48, no. 2 (1986): 15–44; Harvey Goldberg, "The *Maskil* and the *Mequbbal*, Mordecai Ha-Cohen and the Grave of Rabbi Shim'on Lavi in Tripoli," in *Sephardi and Middle Eastern Jewries, History and Culture in the Modern Era*, ed. Harvey E. Goldberg (Bloomington: Indiana University Press, 1996), 168–189; Michael M. Laskier, *The Alliance Israelite Universelle and the Jewish Communities of Morocco: 1862–1962* (Albany: State University of New York Press, 1983); Amnon Netzer, *The Jews of Persia and the Alliance in the Late Nineteenth Century: Some Aspects* (Jerusalem: Hebrew University of Jerusalem/Ben-Zvi Institute, 1974); Yaron Tsur, "Haskalah in a Sectional Colonial Society Mahdia (Tunisia) 1884," in Goldberg, ed., *Sephardi and Middle Eastern Jewries*, 146–167; Zvi Yehuda, "Iraqi

While a centuries-old economic relationship between Ottoman Jews and the Ottoman central authorities was in decay by the nineteenth century, the political status of Jews, too, faced demotion. The cause was a century-long process of centralization based on European models that began in 1774 and culminated in a series of rationalizing measures known collectively as the Tanzimat reforms, the first of which was issued in 1839.[23] In 1856, equality was granted to non-Muslims. In 1869, a law detailed the notion of Ottoman citizenship, which was extended to all subjects of the Sultan regardless of religion. Simultaneously, legislation was introduced that eroded the autonomy of non-Muslim groups, now retroactively labeled millets. While these reforms emulated Western European laws that had integrated Jews into the surrounding society, in the Ottoman context, they represented a diminishment of Jewish (and of non-Muslim and Muslim Arab) autonomy and freedom, one reason why there was little popular support for the reforms.[24] (Arguably, there is good reason to question the government's sincerity in implementing them, or its ability to do so: In certain regions, it was nearly two decades before the Tanzimat reforms were even implemented.)[25] At least so far as the empire's Jews were concerned, when implemented, the Tanzimat reforms often proved disadvantageous; as others have suggested before me, the Tanzimat reforms started a process that would eventually transform Turkish Jews from a millet to a minority – from a corporate body integrated into the Ottoman imperial system to a disassociated ethnic body.[26]

The Language of Change

This story of Ottoman Jewish economic and political disenfranchisement at the turn of the twentieth century is critical to the history of modern Ladino

Jewry and Cultural Change in the Educational Activity of the Alliance Israelite Universelle," in ibid., 134–145.

23 For more on the Tanzimat reforms, see Feroz Ahmad, *The Making of Modern Turkey* (London and New York: Routledge, 1993); Roderic Davison, *Reform in the Ottoman Empire 1856–1876* (Princeton, N.J.: Princeton University Press, 1963); Sukru M. Hanioglu, *The Young Turks in Opposition* (New York: Oxford University Press, 1995); Aykut Kansu, *The Revolution of 1908 in Turkeys* (Leiden and New York: Brill, 1997); Hasan Kayali, *Arabs and Young Turks, Ottomanism, Arabism and Islamism in the Ottoman Empire, 1908–1918* (Berkeley: University of California Press, 1997).

24 For a comparative study of the effects of emancipatory and liberalizing decrees on Europe's Jews, see Pierre Birnbaum and Ira Katznelson, eds., *Paths of Emancipation: Jews, States, and Citizenship* (Princeton, N.J.: Princeton University Press, 1995).

25 Beshara Doumani, for example, has argued that the Tanzimat reforms were not immediately felt in Palestine. There, he suggests, the Tanzimat reforms gave local merchants access to official political posts and institutions (such as the Advisory Councils), which in turn allowed them to manipulate and resist the central government's economic policies. Doumani, *Rediscovering Palestine*, 107.

26 Kemal Karpat, "*Millets* and Nationality: The Roots of the Incongruity of Nation and State in the Post-Ottoman Era," in Braude and Lewis, eds., *Christians and Jews in the Ottoman Empire*, 141–169; Aron Rodrigue, "From *Millet* to Minority," 260.

letters. Published less than twenty years after the initiation of the Tanzimat reforms, the creation of the first Ladino daily newspaper in the empire was quite consciously considered an act of economic and political desperation. In its first issue, editors intimated that a daily newspaper in Ladino might resuscitate Ottoman Jewry's drowning economy and culture, rendering Ottoman Jewry competitive with the increasingly successful Armenian and Greek millets. "Readers, we know well," *El tiempo*'s first editorial stated, that knowledge of "*la lengua de su patria* [the language of your country]" is necessary for survival, self-defense, and advancement. In this, it continued, "we are deficient in comparison to other *millets* that have already published journals in Turkish transliterated into the script of their *nasyon* [millet]."[27]

As this suggests, the earliest editors of the Ladino press understood legible news in print to be critical to the vivacity of any Ottoman millet. Thus *El tiempo*'s first editorial outlined that every second or third day, the journal would include a section written in Turkish transliterated in Hebrew letters: a practice employed by four papers published in the empire between 1867 and 1889.[28] A fluency in Turkish, *El tiempo* editors explained, was important "because we find ourselves under the Ottoman government."[29] This was hardly an expression of patriotism. On the contrary, it reflected a classic diasporic view of government, illustrating the extent to which the paper's producers conceived of a commitment to the Turkish language (and, by extension, Turkish culture) to be produced by physical rather than ideological conditions. In any case, the paper's promise to offer readers instruction in Turkish was formulaic, perhaps designed to assuage censors or critics, and would not be honored. Indeed, it would take some thirty years for the paper to reassert or even outline its commitment to facilitating readers' acquisition of Turkish, by which time, as we see below, the paper's professed devotion to Ottoman Turkish reflected the gradual erosion of its own influence and, not coincidentally, the cohesion of the empire as a whole.

Before *El tiempo* renewed its promise of instruction in Turkish, however, the paper was firmly set on facilitating readers' knowledge of French. This was, in large part, because *El tiempo*, like so many Ottoman Ladino newspapers and cultural institutions, was supported by the AIU. The producers of *El tiempo*, like the leaders of the AIU, saw fluency in Western European languages and cultural trends as necessary tools for readers wishing to succeed in an Ottoman economy that was understood to revolve around Western economic interests. To this end, *El tiempo* republished telegrams announcing the day's news that reported on events in Paris, London, Vienna, Berlin, and Budapest, a focus that was reiterated in the paper's advertisements, which

[27] *El tiempo*, no. 1, September 19, 1872.

[28] Abraham Elmaleh, "HaSifrut v'haitonut Ha'Espanoliot," *HaShiloach* 26, no. 1 (1912): 67–73, 253–260, 255–256. See also Moshe David Gaon, *Ha-itonut be-ladino: bibliografia* (Jerusalem: Ben Zvi, 1965).

[29] *El tiempo*, no. 1, September 19, 1872.

promoted goods and stores based in these European cities. In the process, *El tiempo* by and large neglected news of Ottoman urban centers, though it occasionally reported on events in "the provinces." Izmir, Salonika, and Edirne – major Jewish centers in the empire – began to receive regular attention only in the mid-1880s, and even news of Constantinople was hard to come by in the paper's earliest years.

By the 1890s, however, the paper's adulation of French culture would assume a secondary position. Or, better put, it was simply taken for granted. One can find nearly no explicit support of the use of the French language in the pages of *El tiempo* after about 1892. Still, though *El tiempo*'s support for French culture faded, it did not disappear. The fiction serialized in the paper was all European, and mostly French, in origin.[30] Orations on the importance of learning Turkish, like all articles in *El tiempo*, were often composed in Frenchified Ladino, a practice that did not go uncriticized.[31] To put this another way, by the 1890s the paper's adulation of French culture had not disappeared, but was thereafter advanced only tacitly. This reflected the influence of the AIU: By this decade, a generation of students (and a generation of *El tiempo* readers) had graduated from AIU schools, and their fluency in French language and culture was simply assumed. But it was also a response to changes in the Ottoman political landscape. By now, the paper was intent on fashioning itself as an Ottomanist journal; that is, it had begun to support the maintenance of the imperial system and the Turkicization of all Ottoman subjects. Accordingly, it became an ardent opponent of nationalism of all forms, particularly Zionism, which was gaining a foundation in the Ladino cultural area.[32] To respond to Zionist (and, by extension, all separatist nationalist) claims, the contributors to *El tiempo* subdued their lionization of Western Europe and began to argue that Jews were guaranteed a secure home in the Ottoman Empire. By 1899, an article in the paper

[30] In recent scholarship, Olga Borovaia has demonstrated that the genre of the Ladino translation was not derivative or literal but an original and creative mode of cultural production, a conclusion that significantly expands our sense of the scope and significance of the modern Ladino literary canon. Olga V. Borovaia, "Translation and Westernization: *Gulliver's Travels* in Ladino," *Jewish Social Studies* 7, no. 2 (2001): 149–168.

[31] In 1893 Nissim Yehuda Pardo, journalist for the Izmir-based *Novelista*, accused *El tiempo* of corrupting Ladino by its inclusion of too many French words. Perhaps, Pardo suggested, *El tiempo*'s writers could offer parenthetical translations into Ladino after each imported word. To some extent this bit of advice was heeded, though with an unintended result: Parenthetical translations did begin to follow *El tiempo*'s "French" words (these words were not so much French as French-inspired), with the result that journalists could include more, rather than less, foreign-sounding words and had even more freedom to jettison select words in Ladino, particularly those with Hebrew roots. Nissim Yehuda Pardo "El judeo espanyol," *El tiempo*, no. 72, June 22, 1893.

[32] Aron Rodrigue and Esther Benbassa, *The Jews of the Balkans: The Ladino Community, 15th to 20th Centuries* (Oxford: Blackwell, 1995), 116–143.

spoke of the importance of Jews' "Ottoman nationality," a notion that was unthinkable two decades earlier.[33]

To appreciate the radicalism of the phrase "Ottoman nationality," it must be understood that prior to the early 1890s, *El tiempo* had self-consciously stressed the Jewishness of its readers. The paper referred to its readers in terms that would remind them of their affiliation to one another: the *puevlo judeo* (Jewish people), *keila de mosotros* (our community), *muestra komunidad* (our community), *komunidad judia de oriente* (Jewish community of the Orient), *komunidad izraelita* (Israelite community), *komunidad relijoza* (religious community), *judaizmo de turkia* (Jews of Turkey), *muestra nasyon* (our millet). These were terms that stressed Jewish particularism, the cohesion of the Jewish community, and a strong sense of group identification. Though they relied on phrases that would reappear in Zionist discourse, these terms did not have nationalist implications. References to Jewishness, instead, were incredibly flexible and not self-consciously ideological. One week, the paper might reproduce an article from a Western European newspaper on the eternal nature of the "*rasa judea*" (the Jewish race) and the Jewish "national spirit," and the very next week publish a piece decrying the politics of ethnic particularism. The fact that these positions were not seen as contradictory is not so much a sign of *El tiempo*'s disorganization as it is a hint to how fluid was the notion of identity in the Ottoman Empire in the late nineteenth century. For the producers of *El tiempo*, "the Jewish community" was an entity that was delineated by language and culture but could be subdivided by city, religious practice, political belief, language, or dialect (which is to say nothing of the many ways in which readers must have interpreted these phrases). Thus the paper acknowledged that their readers constituted multiple Jewish worlds even as they allotted space for news of what a column called "*del mundo izraelita*" (the Jewish world). To put this another way, for Ottoman Jews of the nineteenth and early twentieth centuries, community was simultaneously a singular and a plural phenomenon.

To a great extent, this multichromatic notion of community was fostered by a tradition of state policy. Prior to the Tanzimat reforms of the late nineteenth century, the Ottoman political system did not demand or encourage its subjects to be homogenous: There was no assumption that one could, or should, be Ottoman. The category (at least in its secular sense) essentially did not exist prior to the late nineteenth century: For both Jews and non-Jews there existed no sense that the borders of empire provided cohesion or an identity for residents. This is not to say that Ottoman rulers promoted equality, but that they tolerated, and provided for, a multicultural society based on the acceptance of difference.[34] This began to change in the late nineteenth

33 "Las israelitas i la Turkiya," *El tiempo*, no. 46, March 9, 1899.

34 Consider, for example, that the study of the Turkish language was not required by non-Muslim subjects of the empire until 1894. Thus as late as the turn of the century, even Jewish

century, when the state designed the juridical category of the millet, which was meant to uphold difference by providing non-Muslims (at least in theory) with a certain degree of religious, legal, and cultural autonomy.

It is to this newly invented marker of difference, the millet, that *El tiempo*'s many references to Jewish group cohesion refer. The notion that readers were not only Jews but Ottomans, then, was an anathema in the paper's early years: This idea would emerge only at the turn of the century, when the paper began an active campaign to encourage readers to engage in a process of "*Turkifikasion*" (Turkicization), a verb first used in the pages of *El tiempo* in 1901.[35] This semantic choice is telling: Rather than emphasizing Ottomanization, this term, "*Turkifikasion*," actually indicated that the salience of Ottomanness was being subdued by nationalist rhetoric almost as quickly as it was being introduced. Even as *El tiempo* began to actively support the notion of Ottomanism – which the paper defined as the construction of one country made up of different religious elements – the integrity of this platform, it would seem, was being eroded.[36]

Despite this ironic turn of events, beginning in the 1890s *El tiempo* renewed its rigorous campaign to defend the promotion of Turkish among Ottoman Jewry. *El tiempo*'s pro-Turkish stance is neatly captured in the writing of Isaac Ferrara, a frequent contributor to the paper in the first years of the twentieth century. In a series of articles published in 1902, he offered readers a cultural itinerary for the process of Turkicization. Ferrara urged readers to study Ottoman history; he proposed that Jewish knowledge of Turkish literature and poetry should be raised.[37] Ferrara argued that Ladino, "*muestro espanyol*" (our Spanish), contained over 2,000 words of Turkish, which would make the learning of Turkish easier.[38] Elsewhere, he suggested that Turkish was difficult to learn only because of the strong linguistic influence of Arabic, influences that, he argued, should be purged from the language.[39] Still, though Ferrara's many contributions to *El tiempo* provided readers with the most thorough cultural itinerary to the process of Turkicization that could be found in the paper, his articles did not provide readers with the reliable information or practical suggestions that they needed to embark

authorities vested with a certain degree of authority by the state were neither required nor expected to speak the language. Abraham Galante has, for example, described an official meeting between Sultan Abdülhamid II and Constantinople's Chief Rabbi Moshe Levy in 1900 for which the rabbi's grandson was obliged to serve as translator. Avram Galante, *Histoire des Juifs de Turquie*, 9 vols. (Istanbul: Isis, 1985) vol. 11, p. 183. For more on the theme of "difference" in Ottoman society, see Aron Rodrigue and Nancy Reynolds, "'Difference' and Tolerance in the Ottoman Empire," *Stanford Humanities Review* 5, no. 1 (1996).

35 "La lengua turka i los judios di turkia," *El tiempo*, no. 31, January 17, 1901.

36 "Otomanismo i otomanizasyon," *El tiempo*, no. 116, July 6, 1910.

37 Isaac Ferrara, "De la literatura otomana," *El tiempo*, no. 36, February 27, 1902.

38 Isaac Ferrara, "Los verbos turkos en el judeo espanyol," *El tiempo*, no. 95, September 1, 1902.

39 Isaac Ferrara, "De la literatura otomana," *El tiempo*, no. 48, March 20, 1902.

on this journey. Ferrara discussed the importance of Ottoman history but did not write historical essays. He described the importance of poetry but did not reproduce selections of poetry or offer reading suggestions. Again and again, he reiterated the importance of studying Turkish, but did not include transliterated Turkish, as the paper had once promised it would, did not publish articles in simple Turkish, did not even present the alphabet for readers who wished to memorize it. His articles, like so many in *El tiempo*, outlined a political vision but failed to facilitate its enactment.

El tiempo's promotion of Turkish was intimately connected to its assault on Ladino, which began in earnest in the last decade of the nineteenth century. Prior to the mid-1890s, *El tiempo* gave little attention to the relative worth of Ladino. Contributors referred to the language as "*muestra idioma*" (our idiom) or "*el idioma espanyol*" (the Spanish idiom). These were not terribly insulting terms but not highly complimentary ones, either; a reflection that the language question, such as it existed at this time, was not as politicized as it would soon become.[40] This, too, began to change in the 1890s. In 1893, *El tiempo* ran a series of articles entitled "El judeo espanyol," written by David Fresco, editor of the paper for most of its run. The first of these responded to criticisms of *El tiempo*'s excessive use of French phrases. The reason *El tiempo* draws on French phrases, Fresco argued, is that Ladino has no available synonyms: The language is a "*jirgonza*," and journalists writing in Judeo-Espanyol are simply too dignified to draw on the available terms.[41] Other articles in the series suggested that the reason journalists have turned to French for inspiration is that Ladino lacks words for the sentimental and the philosophical. "Spanish [*espanyol*]," one concludes, "has no moral advantages for the Jewish People [*puevlo judeo*]."[42] Elsewhere, Ladino was labeled shameful (*una virguensa*) and a dying language.[43] These articles all reached the same conclusion: Ladino should be abandoned in favor of Turkish, which should be adopted not only as a mother tongue (*lengua maternala*) but as the language of the country (*lengua de su patria*).

Over the course of 1901, Fresco consolidated his attack on Ladino in a series of articles entitled "*la kuestyon de la lengua*" (the question of language). The Jews of Turkey, he declared, view Ladino as a nonlanguage: They are "a people without a language."[44] When Turkey's Jews left Spain, Fresco explained, they spoke cultivated Spanish ("once," he wrote, "we spoke Spanish like Cervantes"). But over time, their language became corrupted, disfigured,

40 For an outline of the many positions taken on the language question by Ottoman Jews, see David M. Bunis, "Modernization and the Language Question among Judezmo-Speaking Sephardim of the Ottoman Empire," in Goldberg, ed., *Sephardi and Middle Eastern Jewries*, 226–239.

41 "El judeo espanyol," *El tiempo*, no. 72, June 22, 1893.

42 "El judeo espanyol," *El tiempo*, no. 24, December 14, 1893.

43 "El judeo espanyol," *El tiempo*, no. 26, December 26, 1893.

44 David Fresco, "La kestyon de la lengua," *El tiempo*, no. 62, June 13, 1901.

bastardized. Today, the "idiom judeo-espanyol" is not a language in the modern sense of the word. It has no logic to suit the thoughts of man. It follows no grammatical rules. It lacks terms for geography, astronomy, modern science; it cannot be used in diplomacy or for intellectual or commercial purposes. It is relied on only by the illiterate and uncultured, who are unable to prosper because of their lack of a language. Ladino, Fresco concluded, lacks utility, and since the nature of the human body is to refuse a foreign entity, it, too, should be refused, abandoned.[45]

Fresco's attacks on Ladino would be subdued only after *El tiempo* gained ideological and economic competitors, competitors that forced the paper to reorient its focus. The catalyst to these parallel reorientations was the Young Turk Revolution of 1908, a revolution that the paper celebrated, proclaiming that Turkey had, at last, entered the "civilized world" in a moment that "feels like a dream."[46] Indeed, Ottoman Jewish intellectuals seemed to have many reasons to welcome the Young Turk regime on the morrow of the Revolt, though by and large the regime lacked a mass following among Jews.[47] The renewed Constitution of 1876 promised Jews equality under the law. The new parliamentary representatives included five Jewish deputies whose pictures and biographies were reproduced reverentially in *El tiempo*. For the first time in over two decades, a Chief Rabbi was elected to represent Ottoman Jewry, albeit not without controversy.[48] In the same year, the World Zionist Organization (WZO) established its first office in Istanbul. Simultaneously, the lifting of censorship allowed the creation of numerous Jewish newspapers; the new era of political laxity also enabled the creation of Hebrew language associations and youth groups.[49]

The conditions for Jewish publishing in Ladino, French, and Hebrew would change dramatically after the Young Turk Revolt. With the lifting of censorship, dozens of periodicals were introduced in Constantinople and other cities of the empire.[50] Many of these were founded by the WZO,

45 David Fresco, "La kuestion de la lengua," *El tiempo*, no. 63, June 12, 1901.

46 "El imperio otomano salvado por la justisya," *El tiempo*, no. 88, July 27, 1908.

47 Ahmad Feroz, "Unionist Relations with the Greek, Armenian, and Jewish Communities of the Ottoman Empire, 1908–1914," in Braude and Lewis, eds., *Christians and Jews in the Ottoman Empire*, 425–428; Rodrigue, "From *Millet* to Minority," 255.

48 For a detailed study of the controversy surrounding Nahum's appointment, see Esther Benbassa, *Une diaspora sépharade en transition* (Paris: Les Editions du Cerf, 1993); Esther Benbassa, *Haim Nahum: A Sephardic Chief Rabbi in Politics, 1892–1923* (Tuscaloosa: University of Alabama Press, 1995).

49 See, e.g., Esther Benbassa, "Presse d'Istanbul et de Salonique au service du sionisme (1908–1914)," *Revue Historique* 560 (1986): 337–367.

50 For a detailed discussion of the Young Turk Revolt's impact on censorship and the press, see Palmira Brummett, *Image and Imperialism in the Ottoman Revolutionary Press, 1908–1911* (Albany: State University of New York, 2000).

which aggressively sought to woo preexisting presses as well.[51] The WZO tried to woo *El tiempo*, too, and at first the journal seemed interested in a cooperative effort. Quickly, however, Fresco proved an unreliable ally of Zionism and, instead, an unwavering supporter of the anti-Zionist Chief Rabbi Haim Nahum. By 1910, any hope of cooperation between *El tiempo* and the Zionist establishment was dashed. In this year, Fresco published several articles that his critics considered anti-Semitic: one a translation of an anti-Zionist article from a contemporary Turkish paper, the other an inflammatory series, "Is Zionism Compatible with Ottomanism?"

Fresco's answer to the latter question was resoundingly negative. Zionism, he wrote, contradicts Judaism, the mission of Israel, and the aspirations of humanity. He called it primitive, exclusivist, utopian.[52] He saw it as an exploitation of the poor, a ruse that would woo Jews away from the synagogue, a philosophy crudely imported from Russia and Galicia.[53] The Zionists, Fresco argued, call anti-Zionists assimiliationists, as if this were an insult. In fact, assimilation is part of nature, a signal of progress.[54] Imagine, he continued elsewhere, if Jews, Greeks, and Armenians all retreated into isolation, speaking only the language of their *puevlo* (people)?[55] In fact, both Greeks and Armenians have chosen to adopt the language of their country; do we, he demanded of his readers, wish to diverge from our peers?[56] Jews, he consistently argued, are not a race, but a religion: Jewish in origin and Ottoman "in spirit."[57] "I am an Ottoman," Fresco declared, "genuinely patriotic."[58]

As it defended Jews' Ottomanness, *El tiempo* continued to lobby for Jews' use of Turkish, encouraging readers to study the language and parents to speak to their children only in Turkish, insisting all the while that a people could not be bilingual.[59] In fact, the process of adopting Turkish was not succeeding among Ottoman Jewry. Even among Jews who lived alongside Turkish speakers, Ladino would remain a mother tongue late into the interwar period: As late as 1927, for example, some 85 percent of Turkish Jews would identify Ladino thusly (though the number of Jews claiming Turkish as

[51] Benbassa, *Une diaspora sépharade*, see esp. chap. 4.

[52] "Las israelitas i la lengua turka," *El tiempo*, no. 20, November 20, 1908; David Fresco "El tsionismo," *El tiempo*, no. 13, October 25, 1909.

[53] Response to a letter to the editor by David Fresco, *El tiempo*, no. 34, December 15, 1909; "El eksplotasyon tsionista, el muev kongreso," *El tiempo*, no. 132, August 12, 1910.

[54] David Fresco, "El tsionizmo," *El tiempo*, no. 14, October 27, 1909.

[55] Ibid.

[56] David Fresco, "El tsionizmo," *El tiempo*, no. 16, November 1, 1909.

[57] Jed Franko, "El tsionizmo," *El tiempo*, no. 8, September 13, 1909.

[58] David Fresco, "La monstrozo impostura, a Sr. Sokolow," *El tiempo*, no. 20, November 12, 1909.

[59] "Korsos gratuitas de lengua turka en los kuartieras israelitas de konstantinopla," *El tiempo*, no. 19, November 25, 1910; David Fresco, "La kuestyon de la lengua evraika," *El tiempo*, no. 25, December 12, 1910.

their mother tongue rose steadily thereafter).[60] According to Moïse Fresco, an Alliance teacher, few students were interested in a career in the civil service, and this represented the only context in which fluency in Turkish was truly necessary.[61] Nonetheless, *El tiempo* would never recognize the unpopularity (or ineffectual nature) of its position.

If *El tiempo* was overestimating the appeal of its pro-Turkish stance, it was underestimating the popularity of its critics. To a great extent, this was because Fresco's anti-Zionist tracts were blind to the originality and flexibility of Ottoman Zionism. Jewish nationalism in Turkey did not, in fact, advocate the fragmentation of the empire, and there was little outright support among Sephardi Zionists for the creation of a Jewish state in Palestine. Ottoman Jewry feared nationalist claims to Palestine because they represented a threat to their own government. This fear shaped Zionism in the Ottoman setting into a form of nationalism with virtually no territorial dimension. *El tiempo*'s mistake, perhaps, was that it understood Zionism as a rigid institution rather than an inspiration for Ottoman Jewry, failing to anticipate that Zionism might successfully recast Ottoman Jews' nostalgia for the millet system into support for the politics of ethnic particularism. The paper failed to see that while Ottoman Zionism was nationalist in cultural orientation, many of its supporters (like many Arab nationalists of the empire) remained Ottomanists at least until the First World War.[62]

There were concrete reasons that *El tiempo*'s vision of Ottomanism lacked the popularity that Zionism was gaining. "Ottomanism" itself was proving utopian: an adjective that contributors to the paper repeatedly hurled as an epithet at Zionist interlocutors. In the years after the Young Turk Revolt, Ottoman Jews watched as the Committee for Union and Progress (CUP)'s vision of a multiethnic politic of Ottomanism was morphed into a nationalist and increasingly racist philosophy of Turkism. Only months before David

60 Walter F. Weiker, *Ottomans, Turks, and the Jewish Polity* (New York and London: University Press of America, 1992), 303.

61 Rodrigue, *French Jews, Turkish Jews*, 86.

62 Hasan Kayali and Engin Akarli have argued that in the wake of the 1908 Revolt, the empire witnessed a rise in cultural (but not political or territorial) nationalisms, forms of nationalist expression that accommodated Ottomanist thought. These scholars both conclude that the empire's ethnic groups by and large remained loyal to the multiethnic structure of empire until the close of World War I. In this, Kayali and Akarli depart from canonical studies of Arab nationalisms such as that of George Antonius and Zeine Zeine, and recent scholarship by C. Ernest Dawn. Kayali, *Arabs and Young Turks*; Engin Deniz Akarli, *The Long Peace* (Berkeley: University of California Press, 1993); George Antonius, *The Arab Awakening: The Story of the Arab National Movement* (1938; New York, 1979); Zeine N. Zeine, *The Emergence of Arab Nationalism* (Beirut: Khayats, 1966); C. Ernest Dawn, *From Ottomanism to Arabism: Essays on the Origins of Arab Nationalism* (Urbana and Chicago: University of Illinois Press, 1973); C. Ernest Dawn, "The Origins of Arab Nationalism," in *The Origins of Arab Nationalism*, ed. Lisa Anderson, Rashid Khalidi, Muhammad Muslih, and Reeva S. Simon (New York: Columbia University Press, 1991), 3–30.

Fresco looked to the Armenians as an example of successful assimilationists, the CUP had begun its massacres of thousands of Armenians seen as political foes.[63] These were events that *El tiempo* reported on at some length, but with no explicit sympathy. On the contrary, the paper insisted that both ethnic nationalism and irredentism were dangerous threats. In July 1909, the paper published an article that assured readers that the empire had an army strong enough to deter hostile forces from without or within.[64] After the issuing of the conscription law of 1909, which required all Ottoman citizens to serve in the army, *El tiempo* reiterated its faith in the Ottoman military by publishing an article calling for the voluntary conscription of Jewish men, reminding readers that Jews had always been among the empire's most loyal subjects (in fact, far from supporting the conscription law, the rate of Jewish emigration increased dramatically after 1909).[65] This imagined loyalty, in any case, could hardly prevent the disintegration of the empire. By this date, the empire had lost most of its European provinces and could look forward to far more conflict with increasingly nationalistic minorities.

Throughout this massive change of territory, *El tiempo* remained adamantly, even naively, opposed to separatism, but its priorities, by necessity, shifted. Tangles with Zionism all but disappeared from the paper by the autumn of 1911, overshadowed by wars and internal unrest. Clearly, Fresco had misjudged the power of Zionism and nationalist irredentism. Still, his trust of Ottomanism betrayed a kind of insight. Jews had indeed benefited from the Ottoman imperial system: Their cooperation with the imperial regime had allowed them to thrive economically, culturally, and politically. Fresco was not alone in understanding this. As Fresco could not have known in 1911, Jews and other non-Muslim groups would suffer at the hands of nation-states born of nationalist irredentism in the Balkans. In Turkey and the Balkans, the construction of ethnicity and often its wholesale creation (through population transfers or the random drawing of boundaries) was proving essential to the construction of nation-states. Among Jews, dwindling prosperity, anti-Semitism, and the racism of many new nation-states caused a tremendous rise in emigration beginning in 1909. *El tiempo* instituted a new column in 1913 entitled "Across the World," which provided

[63] Fikret Adanir, "Armenian Deportations and Massacres in 1915," in *Ethnopolitical Warfare: Causes, Consequences, and Possible Solutions*, ed. D. Chirot and M. Seligman (2000); Roderic Davison, "The Armenian Crisis, 1912–1914," in *Reform in the Ottoman Empire 1856–1876* (Princeton: Princeton University Press, 1963), 180–205.

[64] "Por la defensa del imperio otomano," *El tiempo*, no. 120, July 19, 1909.

[65] "Por la defensa de muestra kerida patria," *El tiempo*, no. 54, February 2, 1910. The way in which Jews "voted with their feet" in the 1909 may tarnish Çaglar Keyder's suggestion that the period between the fall of 1909 and elections in March 1912 hinted at the potential success of a multiethnic political sensibility. Çaglar Keyder, "The Ottoman Empire," in *After Empire, Multiethnic Societies and Nation-Building*, ed. Karen Barkley and Mark Von Hagen (Boulder, Colo.: Westview Press, 1997), 38.

readers with the financial information they needed to negotiate these changes: the average cost of homes, for example, in Paris, Berlin, and London.[66]

El tiempo would continue publishing until the 1930s, but even by the outbreak of the First World War, it seemed to be in a sort of decay. Arguably, it had been the paper's optimism that made it both a success and a curiosity. Its distrust in Ladino, its empty promises to support Jews' fluency in Turkish, its faith in the already disintegrating imperial system, its attempt to resuscitate the flagging Ottoman Jewish economy, and its persistent attack on the politics of nationalism all could be considered challenges to the onslaught of modernity. And yet, within the context of modern Ottoman Jewish culture, these were distinctly modern impulses: The expressions of a newspaper determined to help readers navigate their way through a changed world. That debates over language should become a barometer to this struggle is hardly surprising, given that language would prove a critical factor in differentiating (and, arguably, inventing) national populations in Turkey and the Balkans, as in Central and Eastern Europe and the Middle East. These debates illustrate the sometimes discordant and always graceful interweaving of Ottoman, Western, and Jewish senses of self that defined Ottoman Jewish secular cultural production – and differentiated it from Jewish culture as it was shaped elsewhere in Europe.

The complex ways in which *El tiempo* spoke to and of readers of Ladino also offers a lesson about the slipperiness of the notion of "belonging" – and, perhaps, even of the notion of "borders" – in the context of the multiethnic empire. In the Ottoman setting, the idea of "belonging" arguably was introduced only with the Tanzimat reforms, reforms that introduced the notion of citizenship. Considered from the vantage of the empire's Jews, these reforms, and, indeed, the meaning of "belonging," simply failed to accommodate the nuances of Ottoman Jewish identity and, as a result, were virtually assured to fail. These reforms were, after all, inspired by Western (and primarily French) assumptions about the meaning of culture and politics – and the necessity of distinguishing between the two. To the extent to which Ottoman Jews had prospered under the rule of empire, however, they did so when culture and politics were intertwined: when Jewish millets were granted the autonomy to exist as political units that were inherently cultural and as cultural units that were inherently political. This is not to say that the rule of the Ottoman Empire was not flawed nor that the experience of every Ottoman millet reflected that of Ottoman Jewry. But it is to suggest that the strengths of the traditional Ottoman system were not appreciated by reformers of the late nineteenth century: The political, economic, and intellectual climate of the day forbade it.

In some sense, historians of empires and nation-states have remained under the spell of liberalism to such an extent that we are only now beginning to create the vocabularies needed to understand empires as functional and

[66] See, e.g., "A traverso el mundo," *El tiempo*, no. 64, February 14, 1913.

often quite successful political units. Contemporary historical vocabularies are still by and large shaped around Western European models. According to these models, ethnic groups are either emancipated or unemancipated; they are either minorities or have been absorbed into majority cultures; they are colonial subjects or enfranchised citizens. Empires or nation-states, accordingly, are either multicultural or exclusivist, democratic or undemocratic. None of these terms, I would argue, truly applies to the Ottoman setting or to the experience of Jews living under Ottoman rule. While it is true that Ottoman Jews were not emancipated, given that no group under Ottoman rule was, the term "unemancipated" has little application. And though Ottoman Jewry numerically made up a minority, this population could not – at least before the liberalizing reforms of the nineteenth century – be said to have minority status. Further, while the Ottoman Empire was ruled according to the laws of Islam, in many senses these empires were far more tolerant of difference than were their contemporaries to the West or East. And finally, while Ottoman Jews were undoubtedly subjects of imperial rule, they cannot be collapsed neatly into the category of the colonial subject, nor, indeed, can they be said to have been passive importers of Western European culture or commodities, as the term "comprador" (which can be roughly translated as "intermediary") – often applied to the Empire's Jews and other non-Muslim groups – implies. Though the producers of *El tiempo* looked to Western Europe for cultural inspiration and economic support, from the perspective of the producers of this paper, French customs were not "foreign." Because they were assumed to be familiar to French Jews, the latest French trends were considered part of the corpus of modern Jewish knowledge (though, in fact, they were more often than not novel to Ottoman readers of Ladino). By the same token, Ottoman Jewish importers who promoted their wares in the pages of *El tiempo* were by no means foreign, certainly no more foreign than the Muslim importers who worked alongside them.[67]

Certainly, it is not only Ottoman Jewry that these terms and concepts can fail to accommodate; as I have argued in other contexts, the Jews of the Russian Empire have been similarly disserviced by the scholarly adherence to liberal vocabularies. Fortunately, our understanding of the many subjects of Russian, Austro-Hungarian, and Ottoman rule is being deepened by exciting scholarship that approaches the study of empires and ethnicity in new ways.[68] To a great extent, this diverse body of work shares one fundamental

[67] Indeed, as Reşat Kasaba has argued, Ottoman Jewish sellers of Western products were deeply embedded in local economies and Ottoman cultural norms. Kaşaba, *The Ottoman Empire*, see esp. chap. 4, "Growth in the Periphery: Western Anatolia (1840–1876)," 87–106, and his conclusion, 113–116.

[68] To mention only a few works among many, consider Masters, *Christians and Jews*; Barkey and Von Hagen, eds., *After Empire*; Istvan Deak, *Beyond Nationalism* (New York: Oxford University Press, 1990); Daniel R. Lazzerini and Edward J. Brower, eds., *Russia's Orient, Imperial Borderlands and Peoples, 1700–1917* (Bloomington: Indiana University Press, 1997); Ronald Suny, *The Revenge of the Past* (Stanford, Calif.: Stanford University Press, 1993).

assumption: that boundaries and belonging are not rigid categories or material realities but more often than not have multiple and contradictory meanings. It is a somewhat delicious irony that to explore this phenomena, we may turn to Ottoman Jewry: not as the quintessential diasporic unit but as a population deeply invested in manifold political and cultural alliances that were the unique products of late imperial Ottoman society.

PART III

THE STATE AND "DANGEROUS POPULATIONS"

4

"Dangerous Populations"

State Territoriality and the Constitution of National Minorities

Adriana Kemp

> They are also our fallen. They were also Israeli citizens. Like us they participated in the national ballots and when they felt hurt, they went out onto the streets. None of them was armed. Yet most of them died from gunfire, or from rubber bullets or from a sniper shot.[1]

Thus reads the beginning of an article published on the eve of the creation of the Or Committee, appointed by the Israeli prime minister Ehud Barak and chaired by former Supreme Court judge Theodore Or, to investigate the circumstances that led to the killing of thirteen Palestinians, twelve of them Israeli citizens, by the Israeli police during the clearing of demonstrations in October 2000. The article, published in Israel's most widely circulated daily newspaper, and the dozens or more that have been published since in Israeli media, are trying to make sense of the tragic events. Although too soon to be lent to academic analysis, as of today, few would dispute that the course of events that led to October 2000 mark a watershed in the history of the Palestinian minority/Jewish majority relations in Israel. Whether interpreted as a legitimate expression of Palestinian protest against five decades of institutional discrimination and nefarious neglect or as a confirmation of the Jewish majority's latent distrust on the "inner enemy," most Israeli observers would agree that things would never be the same.

Known since as the "Bloody Events," the violent behavior of the Israeli police toward the Palestinian demonstrators and the refusal of state authorities to condemn it unequivocally seem to encapsulate most tragically the "double bind" that underwrites the relations of the Jewish state toward the Palestinian citizens. At once included via the mechanisms of formal citizenship and excluded from the community of fate, regarded as right-bearing citizens and serialized state subjects and simultaneously criminalized as "usual

[1] S. Ginosar, "Be'esh haia, metvaj karov, lifamim baayin, lifamim bagav," *Yiediot Achronot Supplement 7 Yamim* (November 17, 2001), pp. 25–34.

suspects" of disloyalty and unfaithfulness, Palestinians stand at the center of the state desire for control, discipline, and regulation of the most minute levels of conduct of those who are members of the society and polity yet do not belong to them.

How were the conditions created so that Palestinians could be excluded, segregated, and discriminated via their incorporation as state citizens? This chapter deals with the intricate relations between state borders, statecraft, and the making of a Palestinian national minority in Israel's first decades. Similar to the vast majority of nation-states, there is no precise fit between the Israeli state and nation, and the state's borders sit uneasily on the model outlined so neatly by socio-political theory that endows borders and belonging with an essential nature of their own.[2] The establishment of the State of Israel and the war that ensued radically altered the country's physical and demographic map. The Palestinians who remained in the territory under Israel's control became "a minority that was created overnight." Severed from their national fellows – the vast majority of whom in 1949 were driven outside the newly established geopolitical lines – and overtaken by a recent alien state that granted them formal citizenship but perceived them as "enemies," Palestinians in Israel share the predicament of "trapped" minorities,[3] that is, minorities who are entrapped in between the incongruent demarcation lines of state control and ethnocultural belonging. Trapped minorities call into question the dual normative role attributed to borders by western statecraft as tools aimed at distinguishing between "internal" and "external" spheres of action, creating external distinction and at the same time internal homogeneity, not of space and territory as such but mainly of what becomes a *territorialized* population.[4]

I explore the modes by which the Israeli border – as a discursive construct of state law and administration – became instrumental in the constitution of the Palestinian minority as a "dangerous population," at once incorporated by the political body (as formal citizens and as subjects of state power) and excluded from it (as "alien" to the community of belonging). I suggest that the constitution of the Palestinian minority as a dangerous population has been the result of a coupling between the national goals of the dominant ethnic group and the constant preoccupation of the disciplinary state with population management and surveillance.

2 R. L. Doty, "Racism, Desire, and the Politics of Immigration," *Millennium: Journal of International Studies* 28. no. 3 (1999): 585–606.

3 See O. Yiftachel, *Planning a Mixed Region in Israel: The Political Geography of Arab-Jewish Relations in Galilee* (Aldershot: Averbury, 1992); D. Rabinowitz, "The Palestininan Citizens of Israel, the Concept of Trapped Minority and the Discourse of Transnationalism in Anthropology," *Ethnic and Racial Studies* 24, 1 (2001): 64–85.

4 A. Giddens, *The Nation State and Violence* (Berkeley: University of California Press, 1987); G. Poggi, *The State: Its Nature, Development and Prospects* (Stanford, Calif.: Stanford University Press, 1990).

While there is an extensive literature dealing with the disparity between the Palestinians' formal definition as citizens, and the exclusionary practices of the ethnic state in Israel, the tendency in critical studies has been until recently to explain the position of Palestinian citizens as directly determined by Zionist ideology.[5] Premised on a unitary image of the state-as-entity,[6] critical studies have underplayed the analytically distinct logics that inform statecraft practices and the modes in which their interaction pattern the position of Palestinian citizens in the Jewish state as ethnicized "dangerous populations" and yet at the same time as modernist subjects of state administration.[7]

Drawing mainly on Knesset records, I offer an analysis of the debates held year after year all through the 1950s over the extension of two pieces of legislation that bore directly on the border question. The first legislation refers to the Emergency Defense Regulations (Security Areas) from 1949 (also known as the Security Areas Law); the second refers to the Mandatory Defense (Emergency) Regulations from 1945, adopted later as state law. Both legal constructs, and the regime of disciplinary practices they enacted, were instrumental for the ethnonational project of "judaization" of the state territory through its concomitant "de-Palestinianisation." At the same time they were part and parcel of the state rationale of surveillance and state administration, of the disciplinary undertaking to connect the vigilance of the state to the minute regulation and supervision of both individual and group conduct. The Knesset debates over the extension of these laws and over the laws' implications for the state's democratic image offer a unique platform for the display of a whole range of attitudes and positions on the status of Palestinian as "citizens" that rarely found their way out to the public sphere during the first decade of the state. As such, Knesset records offer an opportunity to capture a strategic moment in history in which neither

5 See, e.g., E. Zureik, *The Palestinians in Israel: A Study in Internal Colonialism* (London: Routledge and Kegan Paul, 1979); Yiftachel, *Planning a Mixed Region*; O. Yiftachel, "Debate: The Concept of 'Ethnic Democracy,'" *Ethnic and Racial Studies* 15, no. 1 (1992): 125–135; O. Yiftachel, "'Ethnocracy': The Politics of Judaizing Israel/Palestine," *Constellations* 6, no. 3 (1999); A. Ghanem, "State and Minority in Israel: The Case of the Ethnic State and the Predicament of Its Minority," *Ethnic and Racial Studies*, special issue, "Aspects of Ethnic Division in Contemporary Israel," (1998): 428–447.

6 J. Migdal, "Some Framing Thoughts for the Boundaries and Identities Workshop," Seattle, 2000.

7 In that sense, this article is part of a burgeoning body of research that seeks to capture the "doubling" of state-minority relation as one that is premised on the interplay between the homogenizing logic of the state as a "power container" and the differentiating logic of the ethnonational state (e.g., Y. Peled, "Ethnic Democracy and the Legal Construction of Citizenship: Palestinian Citizens of the Jewish State," *American Political Science Review* 86, no. 2 (1992): 432–443; D. Rabinowitz, *Overlooking Nazareth: The Ethnography of Exclusion in Galilee* (Cambridge: Cambridge University Press, 1997); B. Kimmerling and J. Migdal, *Palestinians: The Making of a People* (Jerusalem: Keter, 1999), pp. 145–167.

the institutional framework of the Jewish state nor the particulars of the citizenry were clearly defined. A moment when decisions had to be taken as to who belongs to the political body of the new state and how arrangements had to be made explicit, and thought regarding the institutional practices of the state had to be formulated and implemented. The debates show that the status of Palestinian citizens in the new state was not an open-ended question but rather one subjected to debate and motivated by different, at times irreducible, logics that patterned the limits and the substance of Palestinian citizenship in the state of Israel.

The chapter is divided into three sections. The first section portrays the general background for the creation of the Palestinian minority in Israel. In the second section, I offer an analysis of the Security Areas Law from 1949 that was instrumental in the creation of the borderlands as "security areas" and "protected territory." In this section, I show how the border became a heteronomous[8] space, inverting the meaning of "outside" and "inside" and creating thereby a conflation between Palestinian citizens and a general category of "enemies" of the state. The third section deals with the question of governmentality[9] regarding the Palestinian population as it was embodied in the Military Administration from 1948 to 1966. I describe the array of disciplinary practices that transformed the borderlands of the state into a "total institution" for the Palestinian population. These afforded for the incorporation of Palestinian subjects into the "house of power" of the state as objects of state administration and surveillance, while at the same time setting them aside from the national body as dangerous population. I conclude by making some general remarks on the intricate relations among space, power, and culture in a world of nation-states.

The Border and the Creation of a Palestinian National Minority in Israel

Israel has been portrayed as belonging to the broad category of ethnonational states that are rent by deep national cleavages.[10] The ethnonational character of the state structures its basic institutions within the premises and world view of the dominant ethnic group. Although upon its proclamation as a state, Israel declared its commitment to civil-democratic principles, its self-defined character as a Jewish state poses a serious qualification to the state's democratic nature. Indeed, the tension between the ethnonational and the democratic commitments of the regime in Israel with regard to the

[8] On heteronomous spaces, see J. Ruggie, "Territoriality and Beyond: Problematizing Modernity in International Relations," *International Organization* 47, no. 1 (1993): 150–151.

[9] By governmentality I mean the interlocking between population management and security needs that informs the logic of the modern bureaucratic and territorial state (G. Burchell, C. Gordon, and P. Miller, eds., *The Foucault Effect: Studies in Governmentality* (Chicago: University of Chicago Press, 1991), p. 25.

[10] S. Smooha, *Israel: Pluralism and Conflict* (Berkeley: University of California Press, 1978).

Palestinian citizens has been the matter of serious scholarly debate.[11] Smooha conceptualizes the Israeli case as an "ethnic democracy," a form of regime in which the conferral of political and civil rights to individuals and of collective rights to minorities is combined with the consolidation of control by one ethnic group as the dominant group.[12] Peled later contributed to the debate by developing a model of "stratified citizenship" within which Israel's Palestinian citizens are inserted.[13] According to his model, two types of citizenship exist in the Israeli regime of incorporation: republican citizenship for Jews and liberal citizenship for Palestinians. Within this regime, equal civil and political rights are conferred to the Palestinians as "individuals"; however, the ethnonational structure of the state's institutions creates a highly stratified regime of incorporation that excludes them from the republican community of belonging. Thus, "Although Jews and Palestinians officially enjoy equal civil rights, only the Jews can realize their citizenship in practice, by taking part in defining the common social good."[14]

Despite differences, this vast literature shares an overall interest in two main issues: first, the nature of minority-majority relations in Israel and their incumbency on the regime type; second, the democratic deficit of Israeli regime when compared with the yardstick of western liberal democracy. This is a regime where the commitment to ethnonationalism outweighs the commitment to democracy. My stake in this chapter is neither with majority-minority relations nor with regime types as such. While the former draws on a unitary and essentializing perception of the state, the latter tends to obviate too easily the question of the state, on behalf of regimes. I focus rather on the contradictory and tension-ridden logics that inform statecraft practices (in this case, border-producing practices) in the making of minorities, and how these impinge on our understanding of the borders-identities-state trinity.

The disparity between the Palestinians' formal inclusion as citizens, and the exclusionary practices of the state, was perhaps starkest in the period from the establishment of the Military Administration during Israel's War of Independence until its abolition in 1966. The Palestinians who remained in the territory under Israel's control perceived Israel's establishment as a "catastrophe," and such was the name, "al-Naqba" ("the Catastrophe"),

[11] See, e.g., Zureik, *The Palestinians in Israel*, who sees the Palestinians as subjects of "internal colonialism"; I. Lustick, *Palestinians in the Jewish State: Israel's Control of a National Minority* (Tel-Aviv: Mifras, 1985), who developed the model of "control system"; and Yiftachel, "Ethnocracy," who defies the notion of the Israeli regime being a democracy and conceptualizes it as "ethnocracy." See also N. Rouhana, *Palestinian Citizens in an Ethnic Jewish State: Identities in Conflict* (New Haven: Yale University Press, 1997).

[12] S. Smooha, "Minority Status in an Ethnic Democracy: The Status of the Palestinian Minority in Israel," *Ethnic and Racial Studies* 13 (1990): 389–413.

[13] Peled, "Ethnic Democracy," pp. 432–443.

[14] Y. Peled, "Strangers in Utopia: The Civic Status of Israel's Palestinian Citizens," *Theory and Criticism* 3 (1993): 22.

they gave to the war, which for the Jews was a symbol of independence and revival. This is not surprising, since the war radically altered the country's physical and demographic map. Of the 550 Palestinian villages that existed during the British Mandate period, only 121 remained after the war.[15] According to the first population census conducted in Israel, in 1948, the country's Palestinians numbered 69,000, as compared with 860,000 who resided in the same areas before the war; in other words, the vast majority of the Palestinian inhabitants became refugees, either because they fled or were driven out by the Israeli army. In any event, already in the midst of the war the Jewish leadership decided to prevent the return of the tens of thousands of war refugees.

The decision affirmed the ethnonational status of the nascent state as one seeking to preserve a Jewish majority even at the price of opposition to the international community and the neighboring Palestinian states. This tendency was given expression, for example, in July 1948, when the Central Committee of Mapai discussed the question of the hundreds of thousands of Palestinian refugees who wanted to return. "If we bring those into the country," explained Shlomo Lavi, a well-known party activist, "they will exploit every opportunity to stick a knife in our back." He added, "It is clear that we do not have enough strength to take Palestinians residing in the country and remove them. But we do have enough strength not to let those who have already left return."[16]

In 1949, the number of Palestinians within the bounds of the state increased to 160,000 and constituted 12.5 percent of Israel's population (though less than 20 percent of the prewar Palestinian population in the territory). This growth was accounted for by a "statistical reason": The first census did not count the Palestinians who had not actually left the state's territory but were not present in their homes when the census takers arrived. The state perpetuated this "statistical error," and thus nearly half the country's Palestinian population at the time, about 75,000 of the 160,000, were categorized as "internal refugees" or "present absentees." That is, they were Israeli citizens but their property was declared "abandoned," and they could not claim ownership of it.[17]

Initially, the decision to establish a military administration to deal with the Palestinian population within the state's boundaries was based on solid security reasons, namely, the war situation. However, the decision to leave it in place even after the war was nourished by an emergent perception of Palestinian citizens as a dangerous population, requiring the constant

[15] B. Kimmerling, *Zionism and Territory: The Socio-Territorial Dimensions of Zionist Politics* (Berkeley: University of California Press, 1983), p. 122; B. Morris, *The Birth of the Palestinian Refugee Problem, 1947–1949* (Cambridge: Cambridge University Press, 1989), p. 157.

[16] Mapai Archives, Mapai Central Committee, July 24, 1948.

[17] Kimmerling, *Zionism and Territory*, pp. 134–146.

surveillance and supervision of mechanisms of the state administration. During a meeting of Mapai's political committee to consider ways to establish ties between the party and the Palestinian potential electorate, David Ben-Gurion explained: "We see the Palestinians as a minority – but the Palestinians [also] consider us a minority. Not only are we a minority, we are a minority that dispossessed them of their land, and they are not so quick to forgive.... The State of Israel is a small island in a vast sea of Palestinians."[18] The depiction of Palestinian citizens as an unforgiving "Fifth Column" was made by politicians and public figures time and again.[19] Soon it became an intrinsic part of the state policy toward its Palestinian subjects.

Ironically, the mechanisms that nourished the notion of Palestinians as dangerous population and objectified it as policy during the 1950s and 1960s were enacted through the homogenizing idiom of state administration and law. Their lexicon included terms such as "security areas" and "movement restriction," and their concern revolved around the exact "width" and "length" of protected areas. No allusion was ever made by state legislation and bureaucracy to categories such as ethnicity or nationality. Provided the outward and explicit ethnonational project in which the state of Israel was framed, there are some interesting questions that arise when delving into the administrative and legal constructions of the state, particularly those regarding problematic areas such as the border. Why did the state, from its earlier stages of state building, adopt the language of territorial homogenization and universalized citizenship to enact its laws? And why did it ground its endeavor to "internal pacification" on bureaucratic and administrative mechanisms that spoke about population, territory, and efficiency of management, while it was so clear that ethnicity, nationalism, and segregation were at stake?

Neither the liberal democratic nor the ethnonational paradigms applied to the Israeli case are sensitive to the tension-ridden logics of the state. While the liberal emphasis on formal processes (formal rights) minimizes the definition of democracy close to triviality,[20] the ethnonationals' strict emphasis on ethnic-grounded discrimination and domination overlooks altogether the generative and inclusive power of state's desire for control of populations targeted as dangerous. The interplay between the ethnonational logic of the state and state's desire to render populations "legible"[21] may yield to "unintended

[18] Mapai Archives, Mapai Political Committee, Jan. 24, 1952; Mapai Archives, Mapai Political Committee, Aug. 3, 1952.

[19] U. Benziman, and A. Mansour, *Subtenants: Israel's Palestinians, Their Status and the Policy Toward Them* (Jerusalem: Keter, 1992).

[20] On Israel as a "liberal democracy," see B. Neuberger, "Is Israel a Liberal Democracy?," in N. Gertz, ed., *Viewpoint: Culture and Society in Israel* (The Open University, 1988), pp. 105–126.

[21] J. C. Scott, *Seeing like a State: How Certain Schemes to Improve the Human Condition Have Failed* (New Haven and London: Yale University Press, 1998).

and unexpected consequences" that make of the state a paradoxical, at times oxymoronic, set of practices, at once exclusive and inclusive.

My argument is that in order to understand the constitution of the Palestinians as a national minority in its full complexity, we have to recognize the rationale of governmentality through which the Israeli state operated during its formative years and the ways in which the logic of state governmentality incorporated the Palestinian as state's subjects. As Ian Lustick notes, the attitude of the state of Israel, as a dominant-nation state, toward the national minority in its midst was determined according to one central goal: to supervise that minority,[22] neither to liquidate it nor to integrate it into the fabric of the new society and polity, but to control it and render it manageable and transparent to state power. In that sense, while the ethnonational drive is to exclude and segregate the "Other," the governmentality logic strives toward an ever more total incorporation of the minorities as subjects of the bureaucratic, disciplinary, and administrative mechanisms of the state.

In the following sections, I discuss two pieces of legislation that bore directly on the border question: the Emergency Defense Regulations (Security Areas) of 1949 and the Mandatory Defense (Emergency) Regulations of 1945. While the first set of regulations was given a territorial formulation and dealt with the regulation of "areas" and "space," the second was framed in purely administrative terms as it was concerned with population movement at its most minute and capillary aspects. Furthermore, while the former enacted the totalizing power of homogeneous law, the latter relied on the individualizing power of administration when it deals with the body (literally and metaphorically) of the people.

The Border as "Protected Area": Creating a Heteronomous Space

Under the Emergency Defense Regulations (Security Areas), which were enacted in 1949, all the country's borders were defined, administratively and judicially, as "security areas." On July 5, 1949, the Knesset held its first debate on extending the validity of the regulations, which were enacted in April of that year. Ben-Gurion opened his statement by explaining the regulations' rationale: to ensure the security of the state and the safety of the residents, Jews and Palestinians.[23] This was to be effected by creating a strip of territory bearing a special status along the borders. A "special regime" would be introduced in these "security areas," Ben-Gurion said, to protect Israelis in areas that were the "front line" of the entire state territory.

The Security Areas Law constituted a cardinal legal instrument by which the new state intended to order the lives of its residents in the border areas. The regulations stipulated the creation of "protected areas" in the form

[22] Lustick, *Palestinians in the Jewish State*, p. 76.

[23] *Knesset Records*, July 5, 1949, p. 907.

of ten-kilometer-wide strips along the borders in the north of the country and twenty-five kilometers wide in the south. The Minister of Defense was empowered to issue an order declaring a protected area or part of such an area a "security area." Anyone who was not a permanent resident of a security area was prohibited to enter or to leave it without authorization from an army officer with the rank of lieutenant colonel or higher. Under the regulations, the authorities could also remove permanent residents from a security area and resettle them, and prevent nonpermanent residents of security areas from entering these zones.

The 1949 regulations perpetuated the sweeping powers that had been conferred on the Defense Minister during the 1948 war, which had enabled him to impose a military regime throughout the border areas. The regulations themselves extended the security areas via a series of orders that brought about a tortuous geographical reality. They lined the state with a kind of imaginary "security strip" that no one could enter or leave other than on the basis of the state's security considerations. In this strip, the three principal objects of the modern raison d'etat converged blatantly and openly: population, territory, and security.[24]

The language of the regulations was territorial: They divided the country according to "areas" and "territories" and not according to categories of people. In the discussions concerning the regulations' extension Ben-Gurion constantly reiterated his contention that the law's purpose was to protect both Jewish and Palestinian residents against the Palestinian "gangs" that prowled the border areas and were liable to make the settlements there the prime target of their attacks. The territorialization of the law was important in order to show that at least where security was concerned, the state had no intention of introducing institutional discrimination among the population.

In fact, the law did not distinguish among different population groups, but it did clearly create two different ecological systems within the state: one that was managed according to democratic steering principles that sought the normalization of the citizens' lives, and one that was managed according to emergency principles that were based on the assumption that the war had not yet ended. Already in May 1948, the Provisional State Council declared the existence of an emergency in the new state. That decision, which was made as fierce battles raged within the country, was a kind of governmental declaration of an extraordinary situation that called for the introduction of extraordinary measures. The use of emergency legislation during or immediately after a war was not unique to Israel.[25] What was striking about the emergency legislation in Israel was its transformation into

[24] Burchell et al., *The Foucault Effect*, p. 1.

[25] On other cases of emergency regimes, see M. Hofnung, *State Security vs. the Rule of Law* (Jerusalem: Nevo, 1991), pp. 37–49.

a regular, permanent condition.[26] The state of emergency was not annulled at the conclusion of the war. In the 1950s considerable use was made of emergency legislation, particularly in the border zones, in which their special status as "security areas" that were constantly in an emergency situation was perpetuated by extension laws. The validity of the regulations was thus extended year after year, for twenty-three years, until they finally expired, in the absence of further extension, in 1972.[27]

At the conclusion of the war the use of emergency legislation was justified by what was usually described from the Knesset podium and in various public forums as the "situation along the borders." This referred to the fear of a "second round" – a second invasion by Palestinian states, which incessantly proclaimed their aggressive intentions – and to the presence across the armistice lines of tens of thousands of war refugees who hoped to return to their homes and who, with the demarcation of the borders, became potential "infiltrators." However, the expression "the situation along the borders," which was cited to justify the emergency legislation, derived also from the state's desire to consolidate Jewish rule and presence in the territories that were conquered in the war. This was most pronounced in the border areas, which were the state's front lines in the event of an invasion but were also areas inhabited primarily by Palestinians. As is seen below, the Security Areas Law became the main instrument to "judaize" the borders. Raison d'etat was overlaid by raison de la nation, which sought to consolidate the Jewish majority throughout the state territory.

The extensive use of the Security Areas Law entailed the imposition of severe restrictions on individual liberties and the granting of broad powers to the Minister of Defense, a fact that was not lost on the public in Israel or on the international community. The enactment of emergency legislation meant that the nascent state applied undemocratic principles in broad areas under its control. The extension laws, which were temporary and as such ostensibly indicated the transient nature of these infringements of democracy, served as a convenient political response to domestic and foreign opposition. However, the repeated use of the extension laws with regard to the security areas made the "situation along the borders" – the complex conditions that had prompted the decision to declare the border a security area in the first place – the justification for perpetuating a permanent state of emergency along the borders. A paradoxical situation that assumed the "constant existence of extraordinary conditions" was created, and it implied the use of "extraordinary" methods and instruments.[28] And no less important, the Security Areas Law became a tool with which it was possible to create two spaces in the state territory. Each space operated according to heteronomous principles of

[26] Ibid., p. 51.
[27] Ibid., p. 71.
[28] Ibid.

jurisdiction and implementation, so much so that it could be said to have engendered a kind of *state within a state.*[29]

From the outset, the Knesset was not enthusiastic about the idea of the state maintaining heteronomous spaces by means of emergency legislation. Knesset members from various opposition parties were outraged over the very notion that the government was invoking emergency laws without obtaining parliament's consent. As Zerah Warhaftig, from the United Religious Front, put it, "I have the impression that this [the use of the Security Areas Law] has come to us from a bad habit, to which we became accustomed during the Mandate period, [of thinking] that it is impossible to get along without such laws."[30] Mapam (left-wing opposition party) members warned of an "anomalous" situation in which quite extensive areas of the state and large spheres of its citizens' lives would be subject to the powers of one official and under the authority of military law. They demanded that these powers revert to the Knesset so that it could enact laws on a normative democratic basis.[31]

In an effort to moderate the tension between the emergency legislation applying to the border zones and Israel's image as a democratic state, Knesset members urged that a number of amendments be introduced in the law, including the establishment of an appeals committee, which would be independent of the Defense Minister and vigilant in preserving civil rights.[32] None of these demands and suggestions, which recurred sporadically in the yearly debate on the extension laws, was accepted, but this did not prevent government spokesmen from claiming that the law was liberal. As proof of that "liberality," the chairman of the Knesset's Foreign Affairs and Defense Committee, Knesset member Meir Argov, explained that several articles in the law stipulated the supervision of the legislative branch, in the form of his committee, over the very declaration of an area as a security area.[33] However, the law's true liberal character, he argued, lay in the narrow width of the security strip along the borders relative to the length of the borders and the size of the country's Palestinian population.[34]

29 S. Jiryis, *Palestinians in Israel* (Haifa: Al Itihad Press, 1966), p. 10.

30 *Knesset Records*, July 7, 1949, p. 979.

31 I. Ben Aharon, *Knesset Records*, April 6, 1949, p. 321.

32 M. Rubin, *Knesset Records*, July 12, 1950, p. 2183.

33 *Knesset Records*, Dec. 12, 1951, p. 74; Dec. 13, 1955, p. 530.

34 *Knesset Records*, Dec. 13, 1955, p. 530. The width of the security strip was frequently addressed in the debates over the law's extension. As mentioned, the Security Areas Law drew a distinction between the country's northern and southern sections. North of latitude 31, the law stated, the security area would extend ten kilometers from the border, and to the south, twenty-five kilometers. The difference was due to the fact that the southern borderlands were sparsely populated by Jews, and therefore it was difficult to guard every point along the border. However, the government's representatives continually emphasized that when it came to "kilometrage," as they put it, only the army possessed the authority and the knowledge to decide the meaning of security. Year in and year out, Knesset member Meir

An attempt to repeal the Security Areas Law and to turn it into a permanent, regular parliamentary law in 1953 failed. The acting Defense Minister, Pinhas Lavon, was adamant: "The annulment or weakening of the security strip is inconceivable... in the face of the conspiracies being woven around us."[35] Notwithstanding the debates over the law's implications for the state's democratic image, it was extended year after year for more than two decades, even after the Six Days' War of 1967 had erased the 1948 borders. From the government's perspective, the law was not only a rapid and effective instrument to enforce policy, it was also a means to build the nation-state. As Foreign Minister Moshe Sharett explained, during the Mandate period the emergency regulations "served to suppress the National Home, now they serve to fortify the State of Israel."[36] The logical question is: Against whom did the application of the regulations in the security areas fortify the country's borders?

Protected Against Whom?

Generally speaking, a perusal of the Knesset's debates on the extension laws pertaining to the Security Areas Law shows that in the first years, the majority of the Knesset members did not question the actual necessity of the security zones. The borders were perceived as highly vulnerable given the repeated infiltration by Palestinian refugees who wanted to return to their homes and the fact that Israel's retention of the newly conquered territories was a controversial matter within the international community. The Knesset, for the most part, considered the law a just and effective ruling even if it was not fully consistent with the standards of democratic procedure.[37] At the same time, certain reservations were raised during the extension debates. Some opposition members were incensed at Article 4 of the regulations, which empowered the authorities to remove "types of people" from security areas. The law did not specify which "types of people" were meant, but it was obvious that the reference was to Israel's Palestinian citizens.

In fact, Article 4 was a reminder that behind the law's territorial language, the main object of supervision was the permanent Palestinian population, most of whom resided in places that were defined as security areas and who were perceived by both civilian and military authorities as a potential Fifth Column. A case in point is Bechor Shitrit, who headed the Minority Affairs Ministry in the year of its establishment and was known for his "humanitarian" approach toward the Palestinian population. Shitrit summed up the

Argov reiterated that the size of the security areas was minimal taking into account that "the state's wretched borders effectively make the whole of Israel one border" (*Knesset Records*, Dec. 16, 1953, p. 390; Dec. 24, 1956, p. 547).

35 *Knesset Records*, Dec. 16, 1953, p. 385.

36 *Knesset Records*, May 21, 1951, p. 1804.

37 See, e.g., MK Y. Gil, from the General Zionists, *Knesset Records*, July 5, 1949, p. 918.

government's attitude toward the country's Palestinian citizens as follows: "Security considerations and self-preservation unavoidably dominated Israel's approach to the Palestinian problem. It is clear that the lifting of the security restrictions that were placed on the movement of Palestinians in the frontier areas, or facilitating the return of Palestinians who had migrated from the country, would have been unsafe in a period when the danger of the war's resumption was concrete and constant."[38]

Why, nevertheless, was the law framed in territorial terms? The territorialization of the law's language was more necessary than might have been expected, because of Israel's need for legitimation by the community of nations with their democratic, liberal image.[39] However, the territorial language supplied an added value. Shifting the emphasis from people to territory enabled the reification of the control and supervision that the authorities implemented in the name of the law over Palestinian citizens. Effectively, the law in its territorial formulation served as a convenient and useful means of social supervision that did not have to define or to characterize the individuals and groups to which it applied. Being defined according to a geographical principle, the law did not require the precise identification of the objects of supervision, not even when it invoked the abstract reservation "types of people." Instead, it turned territory into an abstract means of shaping social relations. At the same time, the law enabled the "filling" and "voiding" of the spaces proximate to the border, both conceptually and concretely, by means of an impersonal territorial definition of security relations and needs.[40]

These were the conditions that enabled the advocates of the Security Areas Law to insist that it applied not to people but to territories, and as such was nondiscriminatory and, conversely, that precluded the detractors' objections at the level of principle. For example, the law's territorialization enabled Knesset member Peretz Bernstein (General Zionists) to accuse its opponents of a defective grasp of geography, since according to his calculation Jews were the majority in most of the security areas – proof that the law did not discriminate and that such criticism was unwarranted.

There was a good deal of feigned innocence in the emphasis that was placed on the law's territoriality, since the same law determined the bounds of activity of the Military Government, and together with Regulation 125 of the 1945 Defense (Emergency) Regulations, constituted the principal foundation on which the Military Government's powers rested. Government spokesmen

[38] Quoted in Lustick, *Palestinians in the Jewish State*, p. 67.

[39] Peled, "*Strangers in Utopia*," pp. 26–27.

[40] The territorial definition that underlay the Security Areas Law allowed for the realization of three striking aspects of territoriality in the modern state: (1) conceptual and concrete emptying of space, (2) creation of impersonal relations in a complex bureaucratic state structure, and (3) camouflaging the social (in this case, ethnic) source of rule over people by its reification and transformation into "territory" (R. D. Sack, *Human Territoriality: Its Theory and History* (Cambridge: Cambridge University Press, 1986), pp. 28–51.

took care to assert in every discussion that there was no logical connection between the Security Areas Law and the Military Government. Thus, Lavon: "There could be a security areas law without the existence of a military government; there could be a security areas law and a law concerning a military government; there could be a military government in a certain area without a security areas law."[41] However, although the security areas' map was not entirely congruent with the map of the areas in which the Military Government functioned, there was a clear operative connection between the two. It was manifested, for example, in the case of the Military Governor in the Central District, who was also appointed the responsible authority in the border areas under the Security Areas Law. "The two tasks," critics noted, "were so intertwined that it seemed they appeared virtually inseparable."[42]

The Military Government was officially established on October 10, 1948, and operated in three sectors: northern, central, and southern. The most prominent feature of its map was the inclusion of as many Palestinian localities as possible and the exclusion of as many Jewish localities as possible.[43] The justification for the Military Government was the state of emergency that prevailed during the period of the hostilities and immediately afterward. When the fighting ceased and a central civil administration was installed, the Military Government was not abolished, but neither was it formalized judicially. The result was that for more than a year the Military Government operated without any legal basis.[44] The promulgation of the Security Areas Law in April 1949 afforded legal backing to the existence of the Military Government and its activity in the border areas.

It was the security areas' regulations that effectively defined the geographical contours of the Military Government, even though its operation was in practice directed exclusively toward the Palestinian population. Thus, in reply to a request by the municipal council of Nahariya and Shevei Zion, in Western Galilee, to abolish the Military Government there because it was an obstacle to the region's development, Emanuel Mor, the commander of the Military Government in the Administered Territories, replied: "There is no foundation whatsoever for that contention, because the Military Government in the Jewish settlements in Western Galilee exists only in theory, and in practice there are no restrictions on movement or in any other sphere." Interestingly, the justification Mor cited for leaving the Military Government intact was the need to preserve the continuity of territory and its administrative unity.[45] Thus "territorial continuity" and "administrative unity"

41 *Knesset Records*, Dec. 16, 1953.

42 Quoted in Hofnung, *State Security*, p. 150, n. 79.

43 Jiryis, *Palestinians*, pp. 16–17.

44 Lustick, *Palestinians in the Jewish State*, pp. 65–66.

45 Israel State Archives 11-5434-C, Nahariya Local Council to Minister of Defense, Sept. 28, 1949; E. Mor Commander, Military Government, to Maj. Nehemiah Argov, Defense Minister's Adjutant, Oct. 13, 1949.

became, in the geographical language of the Military Government and the emergency regulations, a convenient substitute for concepts such as "rule" and "supervision," which apply to people.

The 1949 Security Areas Law conferred wide-ranging powers on the Military Governors. The most important of these was the power to impose entry and departure restrictions to and from areas that were defined as security areas. In fact, the border areas were placed strictly off-limits to people who in the population census of 1948 were not registered as permanent residents of these areas. These powers sealed the border areas against the possible return of Palestinian refugees to their prewar places of residence.[46] Refugees in this context included not only those who were on the other side of the border, but also the mass of "internal refugees," or "internal DPs," who had never left the bounds of the state but were placed in this category because they were not present in their homes on the day of the census. These became an oxymoron, "present absentees," as labeled by the administrative nomenclature. The result was that the powers accruing in the Security Areas Law helped to bring about a large-scale if not total "de-Palestinianization" of the border areas.

The most important power that the representatives of the Military Government were likely to invoke appeared in Article 8 of the law, which stipulated that a responsible authority appointed by the Minister of Defense was entitled to order a permanent resident of a security area to leave the area. The law did not stipulate the length of time during which a citizen could be barred from a security area nor, apart from providing for relocation, did it say anything about the fate of these "expelees."

The law also failed to specify which type of population the Defense Minister could distance from the border. Under the territorial formulation, Jews and Arabs alike could theoretically find themselves removed from security areas. As evidence, the chairman of the Security Committee maintained that when the legislators enacted Article 14 of the law, which assured a removed resident of a security area permanent housing, they had not been thinking of Arabs but mainly of thousands of Jews who had suffered during the war of Independence.[47] However, the law's sting lay precisely in the territorial framing of the power to remove residents, since it accorded blatantly nondiscriminatory legal backing to the evacuation of an Arab population from a particular area – which had been declared a "security area" – and transfer elsewhere in the country or across the border.

Under the provisions of the Security Areas Law, Palestinian residents were removed from their villages, their homes were demolished, and thousands of dunams of land were seized from their owners and transferred to others. Even when the evacuees were given housing elsewhere, the action was done

[46] See remarks by M. Begin, *Knesset Records*, Dec. 24, 1956, p. 541.
[47] M. Argov, *Knesset Recourds*, Dec. 11, 1951, p. 619.

against their will. An infamous example is the fate of the inhabitants of the village of Ikrit, in the north. The village was razed to the ground after the residents were granted a show-cause order from the Supreme Court, and the Defense Minister nevertheless invoked his authority under the Security Areas Law to block their return.[48]

The Ikrit case was debated over and over in the Knesset and was cited from public platforms to illustrate the kind of arbitrary actions that could be executed in the name of the Security Areas Law.[49] Nor was Ikrit the only such case.[50] The "language games" that replaced "Palestinian citizens" with "protected areas" and sheer discrimination with "security needs" collapsed in the face of the arbitrary actions that were undertaken in the name of the law in the "protected territories" and which the Knesset learned about yearly, usually from Maki and Mapam (the Communist Party and a left-wing party, respectively). Such actions were committed, according to them, in periods of stability when there was no security justification for them, and even when the Military Government strictly followed the letter of the law. As the abuses of the Security Areas Law by the Military Government became more flagrant with the passage of time, vociferous opposition was heard from across the political spectrum. The realization that the law, which was supposedly meant as protection against outside enemies, had nothing to do with them and was in fact directed against the "inside" Palestinians, began to trickle down not only into the left-wing factions but also into parties such as the General Zionists, the Progressives, and parties from the religious bloc.[51] By 1954, it was possible to sum up six years of the law's application and to indicate clearly the implications of legislation that was ostensibly purely territorial. It was Knesset member Ya'akov Riftin (Mapam) who lashed out at the law: "This law is one of the laws that deceive the population, and it is one of the arms of the same government which also symbolizes the rule

48 For the course of events surrounding the Ikrit affair, see Knesset member Rustum Bastouni (Mapam)'s motion to Defense Minister in the Knesset (*Knesset Records*, Jan. 16, 1952, p. 1011). On the way in which the invocation of the security rationale blocked the possibility of holding a debate on Bastouni's motion, see also Defense Minister Ben-Gurion's answer (*Knesset Records*, Jan. 16, 1952, p. 1012).

49 See, e.g., Knesset member Mass'ad Kasis, *Knesset Records*, Dec. 11, 1951, pp. 616–617; parliamentary query submitted on July 30, 1952, by Knesset member Bastouni to the Agriculture Minister on the housing and rehabilitation of the residents of Ikrit, *Knesset Records*, Nov. 25, 1952; Dec. 16, 1953, p. 394.

50 The evacuation of the Maronite village of Bir'em in the summer of 1948 and its destruction five years later (*Knesset Records*, Dec. 16, 1953, p. 386; Dec. 23, 1953, p. 462), the evacuation of the Palestinian villages of Khisas, Qe'itiya, and Ja'una on June 5, 1949 (Hofnung, *State Security*, p. 151), and the removal of Bedouin tribes in the Negev from their land and their transfer to other areas are additional examples of the dynamic that was generated by the Security Areas Law.

51 *Knesset Records*, Dec. 16, 1953, p. 386.

of the glorious Military Government."[52] A year later, Moshe Sneh (Maki) explained the meaning of the law in these words: "Past experience proves that the use of this law was not for the state's external security needs, but for the suppression of the Palestinian population internally."[53]

Cabinet ministers did not, of course, agree with the law's description as a "fraud," but they, too, could not entirely deny that it was intended less to demarcate the border vis-à-vis the outside than to demarcate it internally and protect it against the Palestinians "inside." That this was the law's purpose was in fact made perfectly clear in 1951 when Acting Prime Minister Moshe Sharett asked rhetorically: "Why does such a law exist? In the first place because peace does not yet exist. Second, because the state has not yet been consolidated internally. In other words, because the state faces dangers from both outside and inside."[54] Two years later, and five years after the war had ended, Acting Defense Minister Pinhas Lavon reiterated the true purpose of the security areas: "A territorial security strip of ten kilometers, in which we can operate militarily without fear of an attack from inside, is a basic position of cardinal importance for our security in the event we will have to face the test [of war]."[55] To Lavon it made sense to distance the Palestinian population from the border areas on the basis of their declaration as "security areas" because Israel was a state of dynamic land settlement and mass immigration. A year later, he added: "I find in this no conflict with my democratic outlook."[56]

The actions carried out by the Military Government based on the Security Areas Law were justified by the concern that Israel's Palestinians were giving shelter to or were liable to assist refugees who were infiltrating into Israeli territory.[57] Another argument was that the Palestinians in Israel were liable to act as a bridge in an attempted invasion of Israel by Palestinian armies. This basic assumption prevailed throughout the 1950s and was effectively the justification for the maintenance of the Military Government until 1966 and of the Security Areas Law until 1972. Yet as early as 1951 the assessment of the internal security service (Shabak) was that no concrete danger was posed by the Palestinians in Israel, primarily because of their fear of how the government would react. The same report added that in the light of the constant breaching of the borders by infiltrators, it was remarkable that few Israeli Palestinians had been tempted to try to undermine the state's security.[58]

[52] *Knesset Records*, Dec. 13, 1954, p. 295.
[53] *Knesset Records*, Dec. 13, 1955, p. 527.
[54] *Knesset Records*, May 21, 1951, p. 1804.
[55] *Knesset Records*, Dec. 16, 1953, p. 394.
[56] *Knesset Records*, Dec. 13, 1954, p. 299.
[57] Lustick, *Palestinians in the Jewish State*, p. 68.
[58] Benziman and Mansour, *Subtenants*, p. 104.

The recommendations made by a panel known as the Ratner Committee, which was established by the government on December 6, 1955, under the chairmanship of Professor Yohanan Ratner, a former senior army officer, to examine the possibility of abolishing the Military Government, clearly reveal the suspiciousness that was still rampant toward Israel's Palestinian citizens. The committee's report, issued in February 1956, recommended that the Military Government not be dismantled for two main reasons: (1) the fact that the Military Government applies in border areas and weak security points – areas in which the distance between a population of Palestinian citizens of Israel and Palestinians across the border is small, and in some places negligible, and (2) the fact that four states that are threatening Israel and declaring their belligerence lie along the state's long and twisting borders, and the fear that these states may draw on the assistance of the Palestinians in Israel in the event of a military confrontation. In the light of these facts, the report concluded, it was necessary to understand the role and importance of the Military Government in four spheres: (1) preventing hostile activity by the Palestinians in Israel, (2) bolstering security in the border zone, (3) preventing infiltration and preventing the return of Palestinian refugees to their homes and their land, together with the development and settlement of new immigrants in frontier locations that are of cardinal military importance, and (4) maintaining the regime of entry and exit permits that enable the authorities "to keep an eye," as the report put it, on a "problematic" population.[59]

The committee's findings affirmed the government's policy toward the country's Palestinian citizens, and as an independent panel they bore even greater weight. Government policy rested throughout on a conception that conflated – whether implicitly or, in some cases, explicitly – Palestinian citizens from "within" the bounds of the state and Palestinians from "enemy territories." The blurring of the difference between the "Palestinians inside" and the "Palestinians outside" was not confined solely to the discursive level; it pervaded the day-to-day operations of the military administration and the Israeli army in the security areas, where Palestinian citizens were subjected to treatment resembling the measures taken against those classified as "infiltrators."[60]

[59] Israel State Archives, *Supplement/Military Government in Israel*, 11-5434-C.

[60] A striking example of the way in which the differences between "inside" and "outside" Palestinians were blurred in the border areas occurred in the village of Ara. On June 25, 1952, an IDF reconnaissance patrol that was training along the Jordanian border opened fire at a large group of villagers from Wadi Ara who were walking toward the border – in broad daylight – to meet with relatives from across the border at the conclusion of the holy month of Ramadan. Two men were killed and five wounded as a result of the shooting. The soldiers alleged they mistook them for infiltrators (*Knesset Records*, Aug. 28, 1952, pp. 3203–3207). Another infamous incident was the Kfar Qassem massacre. In October 1956, a Border Police unit shot to death in cold blood forty-nine residents of the Palestinian village of Kafr Qassem

The classification of the Palestinians citizens in Israel as a dangerous population exposed the dialectical nature of state borders when they refer to a national minority: Instead of creating distinctiveness outwardly and integration inwardly, they did the opposite, creating a buffer internally and blurring the difference between "inside" and "outside." In other words, the discussion of the security areas along the borders disclosed the existence of an interesting politics of meanings under the aegis of which the notions of "inside" and "outside" were reversed.

The Border as a Total Institution

The force of the security areas map lay in the way it set apart the border zones from the rest of the state's territory and thereby enabled the introduction of a permanent emergency regime, mandated by "security considerations," in an administrative strip that circled the country. However, that map did not demarcate the border areas themselves internally. The powers of expulsion and restriction of entry to the border areas, as set forth in the Security Areas Law, did not regulate the movement of people who held the status of permanent residents in the security areas themselves, nor the entry and exit of permanent residents to and from those zones. In theory, a permanent resident was entitled under the regulations to move freely throughout all parts of the country that were not declared security areas.

In this sense, the Security Areas Law left the Military Administration without the legal and administrative tools with which to execute its mission: management and supervision of the Palestinian population within the bounds of the state. Although the Military Administration restricted the Palestinians' freedom of movement and obliged them to obtain various means of identification and permits, that demand had no legal basis. The situation was obviously untenable, but the authorities were also reluctant to initiate special legislation, which would be certain to generate unrest domestically and protests in the international community. The solution to the judicial trap was not found until January 1950, when the Military Governors in the security areas were appointed military commanders under the Defense (Emergency) Regulations of 1945 from the mandatory period. Henceforth the 1945 regulations became the second and, indeed, the main, legal pillar upholding the operation of the Military Administration.

The use of the British-promulgated regulations enabled the government to state for overseas consumption that it was resorting not to discriminatory

who were on their way home at the end of the workday in the fields and who did not know that the village had been placed under curfew. See Y. Elam, *The Executors* (Jerusalem: Keter, 1990), pp. 53–70; *Ma'ariv*, Oct. 27, 1996, "*Forty Years since the Kfar Qassem Massacre*"; B. Morris, *Israel's Border Wars, 1949–1956: Palestinian Infiltration, Israeli Retaliation and the Countdown to the Suez War* (Tel-Aviv: Am Oved, 1996), pp. 645–646.

legislation of the Israeli parliament but to emergency ordinances decreed by the British, which were being applied only in areas that were geographically close to the border, as these areas were the scene of severe security problems, including infiltration, espionage, and sabotage – claims that were fundamentally correct. From the moment the 1945 regulations became the cornerstone of the Military Government's activity, there was virtually no hope that the regulations would be repealed before the abolition of the Military Administration itself.[61] Overall, then, the Security Areas Law can be said to have drawn in practice the geographical contour lines of the areas of operation of the Military Government, while the Defense (Emergency) Regulations of 1945 filled those areas with content.

The defense regulations were framed in administrative language and dealt with problems arising from the "management" of the lives of the residents within the state's boundaries and ensuring their security. Originally, the 1945 regulations were intended to prevent unrest and were directed against both the Palestinian resistance forces and against Jewish underground organizations. Following Israel's establishment, they were absorbed, with certain reservations, into Israeli law. The Defense (Emergency) Regulations of 1945 consist of 170 articles, which vested the authorities with sweeping, almost unlimited powers to administer and to supervise the population.[62]

Ben-Gurion liked to emphasize the "governmental"-administrative character of the Military Administration rather than its military essence. As he explained it, the Military Administration was actually a tool by means of which the state could not only ensure security needs in problematic areas but also provide efficient services based on the needs of the residents in those areas.[63] The concentration of the powers relating to every sphere of life of the Palestinian residents in the hands of the Military Government was justified in terms of administrative efficiency in handling the problems of the population. Indeed, it was presented as being "for the good of the Palestinians": As long as they had not become fluent in Hebrew, it would be best if their contacts with the Israeli governmental system were conducted through a military agency, which the Palestinians, "by their nature," tended to hold in awe.[64] Nor were claims that the Military Government was an apparatus of progress and development absent from the discourse. Thus, for example, Knesset member Ezra Ichilov (General Zionists) said that anyone passing through the security areas and through the territory of the Military Government could not help but marvel at the tremendous development in the economic conditions and in the civil life of the Palestinian population: "Not only is there no example of similar conditions in the Palestinian states, but

61 Hofnung, *State Security*, pp. 82–83.
62 See Jiryis, *Palestinians*, p. 7.
63 Israel State Archive, *Supplement-Military Government in Israel*, 11-5436-C, no date.
64 Benziman and Mansour, *Subtenants*, p. 36.

even in comparison and in relation to the situation and standard of living of the majority of the Hebrew [*sic*] population."[65] In other words, the Military Government was portrayed as a "problem solving" body able to streamline the modes of state management of the Palestinian population while at the same time bringing them progress and modernization.

The interlocking of "security needs" and "population management," which the mechanism of the Military Administration was supposed to embody, according to Ben-Gurion, is central to understanding the distinctiveness of rule in the modern state. Once the borders had been demarcated, the cardinal effort of the European territorial state was directed toward ensuring internal security by consolidating and stabilizing its domestic affairs. The tendency toward centralism, standardization, regulation, and homogenization that characterized state praxis stemmed from a preoccupation with questions such as the optimal method to collect taxes and recruit soldiers; how to apply the state's laws and regulations while preventing people from evading them and setting appropriate punitive measures; how to regulate and plan the commerce, education, health, housing, and birth rate of the state's subjects; and how to supervise their movements and activities.[66] In this sense, "population management" involves being preoccupied with the question of the suitable technique of governmental activity that will enable the sovereign to reach each of its subjects and thus ensure political and social security. Population management is thus the very heart of the "art of government" in the territorial state.[67]

The territorialization of state rule portended the birth of what is sometimes called the "police state," the Polizeistaat – a term more closely related to policy and governing, and in this sense not necessarily associated with its popular use nowadays. It refers to a system of disciplinary practices that connect the supervision that is wielded from the sovereign's "overview" of the population – which he achieves by means of the law – and the thorough, almost microscopic, methods of control and regulation that are applied to each subject's individual behavior.[68] "The things of each moment," including "the little things," are the police's object of action, which become particularly important in connection with groups designated as "dangerous populations," those liable to challenge the authority of the central government.[69]

65 *Knesset Records*, Dec. 24, 1956, p. 543.

66 C. Tilly, "Reflections on the History of European State Making," in C. Tilly, ed., *The Formation of National States in Western Europe* (Princeton. N.J.: Princeton University Press, 1975), pp. 601–638; A. D. Smith, "State-Making and Nation-Building," in J. A. Hall, ed., *States in History* (Basil Blackwell, 1986); Giddens, *The Nation State*.

67 Burchell et al., *The Foucault Effect*, p. 19.

68 Ibid., p. 25.

69 J. Simons, "Rationalities of Government and Peace: Israeli Thought on the Palestinian-Israeli Conflict," *Millennium* 20, no. 2 (1991): 143–153.

The concern for "the little things of each moment," which took place within the Palestinian population residing in proximity to the border, was part of the underlying rationale of the Military Government apparatus. Like the attitude of the modern state toward the "lunatic," the "criminal," and the "deviant," the Military Administration's attitude toward the national minority as a dangerous population was based on a regime of disciplinary practices consisting primarily of the "taking of freedom" and regulation of movements. The situation in the field was succinctly defined by the Military Governor of the "Little Triangle" in 1958: "My role is not to protect. That task devolves on the Border Police and on the Jewish settlements along the border. My task is to supervise the Palestinian population in the region as long as there is no peace. Thus the need exists for checks, surveillance, and supervision."[70] It is important to emphasize that the Military Administration did not neglect the use of military methods in order to achieve internal pacification. But its administrative actions were no less important and exercised a far-reaching influence on the lives of the Palestinian residents in the areas of the Military Administration.

Not surprisingly, given the police logic that guided the Military Administration, the Palestinian residents felt the full power of the restrictions on their movement precisely after the state's boundary lines were demarcated in the armistice accords.[71] Once the contours of the geopolitical body were demarcated, the state then concentrated on developing disciplinary practices for supervising the members of the minority. A Palestinian from Nazareth who wanted to visit a relative in Jaffa, for example, had to apply one or two days ahead of the trip to the Military Governor for an exit permit. He or she had to fill out an application, bring it to the local Military Administration headquarters, and wait in line for a reply, which might be negative. An unemployed Palestinian from Shfar'am who wanted to look for work in Haifa had to go through the same procedure,[72] as did any Palestinian who had to get to another area for medical treatment.[73] The travel permit contained an expiration date, the bearer's destination, the route he or she was permitted to take, and the date of return. Movement could also be restricted outside the area of the Military Administration if deemed necessary by the military commander.[74]

The emergency regulations turned the areas of the Military Government, which were defined as "security areas" or as "closed areas," or as both together, into a "total institution" in which the Palestinians' day-to-day lives

70 Quoted in Lustick, *Palestinians in the Jewish State*, pp. 78–79.

71 D. Peretz, *Israel and the Palestine Palestinians* (Washington D.C.: Middle East Institute, 1958), pp. 97–98.

72 *Knesset Records*, Jan. 18, 1956, p. 826; July 15, 1953, p. 1951.

73 See, e.g., *Knesset Records*, June 8, 1953, p. 1523, regarding an Acre man who was denied an entry permit to Nazareth in order to obtain medical care there.

74 *Knesset Records*, May 23, 1956, p. 1853.

were conducted. During the 1950s the Defense Minister declared fifty-four areas of the Military Administration, some of which also had subdivisions.[75] Galilee, for example, was divided into more than fifty areas, enabling the authorities to upgrade population supervision.[76] The regulations prohibited the residents in Military Administration areas not only from moving freely inside or outside them, but also from choosing their place of residence freely and from changing their place of residence from one area to another.[77]

These areas became a kind of "inspection house," to use Jeremy Bentham's metaphor, containing transparent walls through which the ever-vigilant eye of the Military Administration could follow the residents' movements and actions and watch their property. As explicitly expressed by the Ratner Committee in 1955, the Military Government was essential for the authorities in order "to know better the Palestinian population and to keep an eye on it."[78] The craving to know everything about the actions, opinions, and behavior of the Palestinian population in Israel and to "keep an eye on it" was realized primarily through the introduction of a rigid and comprehensive regime of permits that involved the surveillance and disciplining of every single sphere of life: distribution of transit permits, work permits, entry and exit permits, marriage permits, food and clothing coupons, and supervision of delivery of mail, organized transportation, and the like. So all-embracing was the regime of permits introduced by the Military Administration that some claimed it had turned every Palestinian resident in Israel, no matter where he resided, into a "closed area" in himself.[79] Indeed, the regime of permits enabled the border to be shaped as an area protected against the Palestinians in Israel by imposing restrictions not on the territory itself but on the people residing in it.

It was not by chance that the opponents of the Military Administration often spoke of it in terms of the "ghettoization" of the country's Palestinians. As Knesset member Emil Habibi (Maki) explained: "Two weeks ago the General Prosecutor declared to a military court in Acre, in an unequivocal manner, that these security areas are ghettos for the Palestinian citizens, and that only the Palestinian citizens are required to obtain permits to enter or leave these areas."[80] And Knesset member Avraham Berman, from the Left Faction, issued an impassioned statement from the Knesset rostrum: "We,

75 Hofnung, *State Security*, pp. 151–152.

76 Lustick, *Palestinians in the Jewish State*, p. 131.

77 See, e.g., a parliamentary query of May 12, 1953, submitted by Knesset member Tawfiq Toubi to the Interior Minister, asking why the Musa family, which moved from Galilee, a closed area, to Acre, which lay outside the area of the Military Government, had to obtain authorization from the Military Governor in order to register the change of address. *Knesset Records*, June 8, 1953, p. 1525.

78 Peretz, *Israel and the Palestine*, p. 101.

79 MK Meir Vilner, from Maki, *Knesset Records*, 1951, pp. 241–242.

80 *Knesset Records*, Dec. 16, 1953, p. 391.

the ghetto fighters, will never reconcile ourselves to this disgrace, to [the establishment] of ghettos for Palestinian citizens in Israel."[81]

Like the Security Areas Law, the Military Administration, too, applied – according to the language of the law – to a defined geographic area rather than to a specific population. In theory, then, Jews, too, were subject to the same restrictions – but not in practice. The shortcomings of the arrangement were addressed in a report issued by the State Comptroller: "Anyone who enters or leaves a closed area without a written permit from the military commander in theory commits a criminal act. In practice, we do not demand such a certificate from Jews and do not generally draw a criminal conclusion [*sic*] against these residents when they violate the provisions of this regulation. There is a defect in the arrangement, which was laid down in a general form so that it includes all the country's residents but is effectively implemented with regard to only some of them."[82] The arrangement was flagrantly discriminatory and was the cause of one of the principal violations for which Palestinians in Israel were detained or fined: "A Jew can violate such a law and never be brought to trial, but an Palestinian who goes one kilometer from his house is sentenced to two months in jail, he is taken from his wife and children and imprisoned for the most minor nonsense."[83] In 1951, for example, according to a report drawn up by the Defense Minister, 2,028 individuals throughout the areas of the Military Government were accused of illegal exit without permits and were fined a total of 13,606,440 Israeli pounds.[84]

Only residents who held an ID card could obtain a travel permit. Whether residents were granted permits bore directly on the quality of their lives, since a permit could mean the difference between obtaining work or being condemned to unemployment, or between receiving food coupons and getting medical treatment or not. The various permits and licenses thus constituted both the "stick" and the "carrot" in the relationship between the Military Administration and the Palestinian citizens. A perusal of the parliamentary queries that were submitted to Cabinet ministers exposes clearly the mechanics of favoritism and bribery fostered by the permits system.[85]

81 *Knesset Records*, Dec. 21, 1953.

82 State Comptroller's Report on the Defense Establishment for Fiscal 1957–8, Jerusalem, February 15, 1959, p. 78, from Hofnung, *State Security*, pp. 151–152.

83 MK Meir Vilner, *Knesset Records*, Dec. 11, 1951, p. 616.

84 *Knesset Records*, Aug. 19, 1953, p. 2397. On the criminalization of Israel's Palestinian population by the Military Government, see A. Korn, "Crime and Law Enforcement in the Israeli Arab Population under the Military Government, 1948–1966," in I. Troen and N. Lucas, eds., *Israel: The First Year of Independence* (Albany: SUNY Press, 1995), pp. 659–682.

85 In a query to the Interior Minister, MK Tawfiq Toubi related the story of Fadila Salah Fahmawi, who moved from Umm el Fahm to Tamra. The Military Governor delayed the registration of her son in the birth registry, as a result of which the two did not receive their food rations nor were the authorities willing to provide their other needs (*Knesset Records*, Feb. 23, 1953, p. 780). A similar and representative case was the refusal of the governor to

It was only in 1959 that the government, at the recommendation of a new cabinet committee headed by Justice Minister Rosen, introduced a series of measures enabling Palestinian citizens to move freely outside Military Administration areas. These included a free day of travel to Be'er Sheva without the need for permits; freedom of movement during daylight hours for residents of the Triangle and of the north to the major cities (Afula, Nahariya, Haifa, Hadera, Netanya, Petah Tikvah, Tel Aviv-Jaffa, Ramle, and Lod) apart from security areas, and organizing school outings by means of a collective permit rather than individual permits for each child.[86] But it took another seven years before the restrictions on movement and the permits regime were fully abolished: This occurred in 1966, when the Military Administration was finally dismantled.

Concluding Remarks

The relations of power and identity at borders and between the borders and their respective states are manifold and defy simple generalizations. According to an old but still vital historical paradigm, modern nation-states, especially in Western Europe, are built from political centers outward and imposed on marginal groups and peripheral regions in a process of institutional integration and cultural assimilation.[87] But the "border" can also be a contradictory site whose meaning and form shift in subtle and sometimes not so subtle ways according to setting.

As my analysis of the Israeli nation-state making shows, the "border" has not been one and the same for state citizens; it bore dramatically different significance for Jews and Palestinians. Indeed, the "border" – both as a spatial stage of power relations and as discursive object – has been the site of a twin process. On the one hand, the "borderlands" and "border people" were subjected to the intensification of state power through centralization, territorialization, and surveillance. In this sense, state rationalization and disciplinary statecraft, regarded by western socio-political theory as the "essence" of *stateness*, have been enhanced precisely at the margins. On the other, the "border" functioned as a heteronomous space in which the Palestinian citizens could be constituted as dangerous populations, simultaneously

extend the travel permit of a Taibeh resident who worked as a driver unless he agreed to work in the service of the Military Government (*Knesset Records*, Jan. 18, 1956, p. 826). See also *Knesset Records*, Jan. 18, 1956.

86 *Knesset Records*, Aug. 5, 1959, p. 2923.

87 K. Deutsch, *Nationalism and Social Communication: An Inquiry into the Foundations of Nationality* (1953); E. Weber, *Peasants into Frenchmen: The Modernization of Rural France, 1879–1914* (Stanford, Calif: Stanford University Press, 1976); for a critique, see P. Sahlins, *Boundaries: The Making of France and Spain in the Pyrenees* (Berkeley: University of California Press, 1989).

included in the house of power of governmentality and excluded from the ethnonational project of the nation.

The constitution of the "border" as heterotopy, a particular space that inverts regularized and standardized relations of power in a mirror fashion, sheds light on our understanding of the predicament of Palestinian citizens in Israel as a "trapped minority." As such, Palestinians are doomed to prove their loyalty to a state that cannot be loyal to them by its very definition as a Jewish state. The perception of Palestinian citizens as a "Fifth Column" is still widely prevalent among the Jewish population. The results of a poll taken a year before the October 2000 events show that most Israeli Jews believe that Israeli Palestinians support terrorist attacks. Findings showed no significant variance between left-wing and right-wing political camps.[88] No less important, as recent events indicate, this perception is still widely prevalent among state officials that repeatedly "denounce" Palestinian citizens' involvement in activities and pronouncements that presumably jeopardize the state's well-being.

At the same time, the exclusion of Palestinians as minority via their inclusion as citizens yielded to the creation of a democratic Palestinian "civil society" within the state bounds. This is evinced by Palestinians' increasing participation in parliamentary politics, the growing autonomy of their local politics, and the launching of autonomous political parties, interest groups, and new social movements that make use of state institutions (such as the High Court of Justice) as a means of claim making in their struggle over redistributive justice.[89]

The incompleteness of exclusionary and inclusionary practices of statecraft affords for a more nuanced understanding of domination structures. In the last account, these are never complete, as they are never that perfect.

88 "The Peace Meter – September 1999," *Haaretz*, Oct. 5, 1999, sec. B, p. 3. It refers to the periodical poll led by the Steinmetz Centre on Peace Research at the Tel-Aviv University.

89 A striking example of these developments is the appeal to the High Court of Justice known as the Katzir case, lodged by an Arab citizen who was prevented from leasing state land in the village of Katzir on grounds of not being a Jew. The court unprecedented decision was that land policy discrimination is against the state's law. See N. Ziv and R. Shamir, "'Politics' and 'Sub-Politics' in the Struggle against Land Discrimination," *Theory and Critique* 16 (Spring 2000): 45–66.

5

Making Myanmars

Language, Territory, and Belonging in Post-Socialist Burma

Mary P. Callahan

In the 1990s, an elite-level struggle over political power in Burma remapped the politics of belonging and language in the country for the first time in over a century. National borders did not change, but an internal divider that marked off the unquestioned political center from its attendant margins suddenly became permeable and contentious. First established as a colonial administrative simplification in the late nineteenth century, this boundary between the central areas and what became known as the "Frontier" or "Excluded" areas demarcated where politics happened, who could be what kind of citizen or subject, and which language would animate struggles for power throughout the twentieth century. After political independence in 1948, the colonial-established distinction between center and margins persisted until just after the 1988 pro-democracy uprising, which sprang up mostly in the central region. The uprising toppled the weak Burma Socialist Program Party regime, but the struggle for control over the successor state took several years to play out. Along the way, the seemingly solid barrier between the center and frontier became porous, destabilizing the spatial logic that had characterized and pacified political conflict in the modern era. After 1988, ethnic minority populations long held in ambivalent categories of lesser citizenship and territory that rarely crossed the central state's radar screen became potentially formidable threats to those in power in the center. As a result, populations in these formerly more marginal areas began to find their behavior and language under the optic of the central state, and the century of the latter's disinterestedness was replaced by the demands and commands of citizenship in an authoritarian political system. This process has produced a range of new kinds of contacts, negotiations, enterprises,

The author appreciates the insights of Elizabeth Angell, Vincent Boudreau, Kyaw Yin Hlaing, Patrick McCormick, Joel Migdal, and the participants in the September 2000 Workshop on Boundaries and Belonging. They read an earlier draft of this paper and offered helpful advice. Any remaining weaknesses are solely the responsibility of the author.

trespasses, and struggles, all of which challenge the spatial logic of power that mapped politics in Burma in the colonial and postcolonial eras.

Among these new interactions and struggles is an unprecedented state-engineered redefinition of the terms of belonging in Burma. This redefinition entails the most concerted government effort at minority assimilation and disempowerment in the twentieth century and has at times endangered those who conduct their affairs outside the home in an indigenous language other than Burmese (the language the regime now calls "Myanmar"), the language of the centrally based ethnic-majority group that comprises about 65 percent of the national population. This state's language requirement has become especially clear in the realm of education. For example, in the 1990s, the teaching of the ethnic minority, Mon language in southern Burma, an area where a former rebel group (the New Mon State Party (NMSP)) concluded a cease-fire agreement with the military junta in 1995, became a dangerous enterprise. Thein Lwin writes that "the teachers of the Mon language and literature run the risk to be punished by the [Rangoon] government authorities. Some teachers have been arrested." In 1998, the government shut down 120 Mon schools, stranding 6,000 students. Subsequent negotiations between the New Mon State Party's education committee and the junta led to the reopening of the schools, but "the teaching of the Mon language and literature was not officially allowed."[1] In most regions beyond the center where the government has established any kind of authority, non-Burmese languages may be studied only in the first few years of education, but not after fourth grade or outside of school hours. Religion, too, has been a target of this linguistic intolerance by the regime. For example, in 1991, two Mon Buddhist monks and a Rangoon University lecturer were arrested for trying to promote usage of Mon, a historic language by which Buddhism was introduced to Burma.

Until the 1990s, the central state may have proclaimed the intention of making Burmese the only public language across the territory that spanned to the British-drawn borders, but it never committed any significant resources, political will, or criminal sanctions to back up such a proclamation in geographical areas beyond the colonially designated central region. This chapter attempts to explain why all this changed after the pro-democracy uprising in 1988. The chapter begins by explaining how the elite-level political struggle

[1] Thein Lwin, "The Teaching of Ethnic Language and the Role of Education in the Context of Mon Ethnic Nationality in Burma: Initial Report of the First Phase of the Study on the Thai-Burma Border, November 1999–February 2000," available online at http://www.students.ncl.ac.uk/thein.lwin (accessed May 29, 2000). The Mon case is the most documented of minority-language persecution, in part because of the ongoing research of one graduate student. There are also reports of the military regime eliminating other minority languages from school curricula. See coverage of the issue in Chin schools in *Burmanet News*, issue 405, May 12, 1996; the issue of language repression is highlighted more generally in Amnesty International, *Myanmar Ethnic Minorities: Targets of Repression*, ASA 16/014/2001, June 2001.

in Rangoon after 1988 destabilized the predictable, century-old, territorially bound mode of power politics, leaving the military exposed and vulnerable in the absence of a clearly defined set of rules as to how to consolidate and to maintain its power. I argue that in its effort to impose form and order over the political chaos in the center, the military elevated language affairs to a national agenda, newly mapped all the way out to the borders drawn around the country by British surveyors. Language became one tool in the regime's broader efforts to rebuild the post-1988 state and pacify the population.

The chapter then steps back and considers why language in these remote regions never appeared on a Rangoon regime's agenda before 1988 and considers the way the evolution of language policy was conditioned by territorially defined ideas about and practices of politics. The following section analyzes the military's response to the 1988 political crisis, which was to deploy a series of counterinsurgency-type tactics to try to reorder the practices of politics and to create new boundaries to define and enforce the terms under which the population throughout the country could belong, be left alone, or be heard. At the heart of the regime's reconstruction process was its attempt to create, to deploy, and to animate a new racialized definition of citizenship. This new Myanmar citizen was to be born out of programs of homogenization and differentiation, both of which aimed at rebuilding the state and pacifying the population. In this process, the regime's activities established new markers for how language could (and could not) be used by native Burmese speakers and new demands for linguistic homogeneity among those whose first languages were different. Drawing new boundaries around who belongs, what one can belong to, and how one can express belonging, however, inevitably produces unintended consequences, which are covered in the conclusion of the chapter.

Before proceeding, it is important to note the limitations of the argument here. The chapter does not attempt to impute subjective feelings of belonging to any populations – elite or otherwise – in Burmese territory. Given that very little systematic anthropological research has been conducted among any populations inside or outside the center in more than fifty years, the essay cannot even assume any integrity to the categories of ethnicity and linguistic identity long assumed to be "real" or "natural" by scholars and practitioners of Burmese ethnic politics. Instead, this chapter analyzes the quite serious and equally unprecedented attempt by a Rangoon regime to fabricate a monolingual body politic mapped across spaces long considered beyond the realm of politics in pre-1988 Burma.

Why Non-Burmese Languages Became Dangerous

The political struggle between the military regime established in 1988 and the opposition leader and Nobel Peace Prize laureate Aung San Suu Kyi brought ethnic minority cultural and language politics into dangerous new terrain for the first time in modern history. Prior to 1988, postcolonial politics, belonging, and citizenship mapped to the central plains, Irrawaddy Delta, and southeastern archipelagic areas – all constituent parts of the region originally targeted for direct rule by British colonial officials, who called this territory "Burma Proper" or "Ministerial Burma." In the colonial and early postcolonial eras, struggles over who would rule and who would be disenfranchised pitted various groups of ethnic Burmans against Chinese, Indian, and other lowland indigenous groups all living in these central regions. There was never much more than lip service paid to populations living in the territory beyond, which the British called by a number of evocative names, including the "frontier fringe" or the "Excluded Areas."[2] By the 1960s, ethnic minorities living in the central region had been eliminated from political contention, but various ethnic Burman elites continued to compete among themselves for the power, resources, and prestige associated with the independent state. These intra-elite struggles remained remarkably fixed in their central territorial domain. Centrally based contenders rarely recruited ethnic minorities who lived beyond the colonial-designated center in any notable fashion. On the rare occasions that Burman politicians sought support from non-Burman leaders outside the center, they built neither durable nor successful coalitional forces.[3] From the viewpoint of elites in the center, there were neither potential political allies nor equal citizens in the regions beyond. This perception was reinforced in the 1950s and 1960s, when separatist insurgencies broke out in the remote, former frontier regions, capturing the attention and sacrificing the young of the *tatmadaw* (Burmese for "armed forces" of the national state) without ever really threatening the spatial logic of national-level politics. Since none of these "rebel" groups considered Rangoon a target or a prize to be won, remote territory and its inhabitants rarely stirred the imaginations of political rivals and contenders in Rangoon and environs.

All this changed in 1989, when opposition leader Aung San Suu Kyi began touring the country and crossing the seemingly impermeable boundary between center and margin that only the *tatmadaw* had crossed before. In trips and speeches to ethnic minority communities far from Rangoon, beyond the center, she canvassed this "new" terrain for political allies, along the way inspiring the creation of local incarnations of her political party, the National League for Democracy (NLD). Appearing at times in ethnic

[2] This territorial hierarchy of administration persisted in postcolonial constitutions. For example, under the 1974 constitution, the former frontier areas (mapped almost identically to the colonial "frontier") was divided into "states" comprised mostly of ethnic minority populations. Under that constitution, central Burma – which was populated mostly by ethnic Burmans – was divided into administrative units called "divisions."

[3] The only significant attempts at legal multiethnic political coalitions came in 1958 and 1960, when Prime Minister U Nu promised concessions to Arakanese and Mon politicians in return for support for his flailing government and subsequent electoral campaign, respectively.

minority costumes – a Karen *htamein* (sarong) or a Shan *khamauk* (conical peasant hat) – she captured the attention and affections of long-ignored populations. Perhaps most evocative was her party's decision to use a drawing of that Shan *khamauk* as the ballot pictogram indicating a candidate's membership in the NLD; the symbolism of the *khamauk* connecting Aung San Suu Kyi to populations beyond the center was lost on no one.[4] Of course, on these tours, Aung San Suu Kyi spoke in Burmese, and just like the army in its past counterinsurgency campaigns in these regions, she also employed translators to convey at least parts of her message to non-Burmese-speaking populations. It worked, and in the 1990 election, the NLD won 392 out of the 425 seats it contested for the new parliament. Nineteen ethnic minority parties also won parliamentary seats, with most of the victors sympathetic to the goals of the NLD.

This parliament was never permitted to meet, as the military regime quickly began disqualifying, arresting, or chasing out of the country many of the victorious opposition candidates. Ultimately, the junta – called the State Law and Order Restoration Council (SLORC; in 1997 renamed the State Peace and Development Council, or the SPDC) – squashed the opposition's attempts to build a multiethnic political coalition that crossed the boundary between center and margins. SLORC came to view that experiment in coalition building as the single greatest threat to the military's power and to Burma's continued existence as a unitary state spreading to the British-drawn borders. The military's response does not suggest that Aung San Suu Kyi and the opposition had in fact built an integrated multiethnic coalition of forces that successfully rendered irrelevant the old interior divide between center and frontier. But it does highlight the panic that the mere possibility of such an alliance inspired in the military. In the aftermath of the bloody, divisive 1988 uprising, military leaders calculated correctly that the army did not have the capability to fight battles in border regions and in Rangoon should an alliance develop between the NLD in central Burma and armed, ethnic minority rebels beyond the center. In the new order of post-Socialist politics, the SLORC/SPDC[5] no longer could afford to concede border regions as irrelevant to struggles for power in Rangoon but could less afford to move troops away from the rebellious central region to deal with tensions beyond.

As a result, the junta tried to drive a wedge between potential allies in the center and frontiers by launching a somewhat coordinated political campaign to march peripheral populations into national formation according to

[4] Pictograms of every party appeared on the ballot, in recognition of the population's multilingual nature as well as of the quite serious problem of illiteracy nationwide.

[5] The conflation of the two names of the regimes from 1988–97 and post-1997 into "SLORC/SPDC" is deliberate. While the SPDC reorganization of November 1997 did represent some realignment of power among particular generals in Burma, on the surface, the post-1997 SPDC has not shown any serious deviation from previous policies of SLORC.

the military's security-focused terms. For the SLORC/SPDC, the populations of the border areas had to be embraced and remade into "Myanmars," and it accordingly launched a singular cultural heritage industry along with development and educational initiatives in both the center and the former frontier areas. While this attempt to fabricate "Myanmar" and "Myanmar" speakers is analyzed more carefully below, here it is important to note that this component of the regime's response to the transethnic oppositional threat sent a warning to minorities living beyond the center: They will belong to the nation-state on the terms set in Rangoon, at regional military headquarters, and by local military garrisons. The warning instructed minorities that they are, always have been, and always will be "Myanmars," the new putatively biological, racial category constructed by the regime. As a regime spokesperson noted on the educational components of these identity-producing campaigns in the border regions, "National races [i.e., ethnic minorities] residing in the border areas will then be able to think correctly and work together resolutely for reconsideration of national races through common awareness and objective and correct belief and conviction."[6]

This emphasis on teaching citizens to "think correctly" is not new in the history of Burmese politics, but what is new is the fervor with which this campaign has been carried out over more than a decade. Over the last fifty years, Rangoon regimes always have framed their formal policies toward ethnic minorities living beyond the central region as programs aimed at teaching "backward" peoples how to think correctly – that is, to think with a Union mentality (1950s), as Socialists (1962–88), and now (since 1988) as authentic and pure "Myanmars." During the first two time periods, however, one could think, speak, read, and write correctly in any indigenous language, as long as the content of one's utterances were pro-Union and later pro-Socialist. Since 1988, however, the regime's cultural homogenization programs suggest that thinking correctly must be done in "Myanmar" language; any diversity threatens all "Myanmars." Thinking incorrectly is dangerous, as is teaching and preaching in non-Burmese indigenous languages.

Language, Boundaries, and Belonging before 1988

Burma is quite unusual by Southeast Asian standards in that until 1995, its postcolonial governments had never directly promulgated any *coordinated* or *systematic* set of regulations regarding language policy.[7] By "language policy" or "language administration," I mean actions by state officials at all

[6] Lt. Col. Thein Han, "Human Resource Development and Nation Building in Myanmar: Unity in Diversity," in *Human Resource Development* (Yangon: Ministry of Defence, 1998), p. 218.

[7] For comparisons with Indonesia, the Philippines, Malaysia, Thailand, and Vietnam, see the case studies in Michael Brown and Sumit Ganguly, *Fighting Words: Language Policies and Ethnic Conflict in Asia* (Cambridge, Mass.: MIT Press, 2003).

levels of the state administrative hierarchy that explicitly compel social and political actors to communicate in the public sphere in a specific language. Nonetheless, language has always been an integral component of the formal government regulations, popular and elite prejudices, and force-backed commands that have constituted and enforced citizenship and belonging in this country. Hence, it is necessary to trace the often uncoordinated and not terribly calculated actions of government and social forces toward administration of language and "correct" thinking.

Before the 1990s, the politics of language were limited to the central arena in which struggles for national power transpired. Throughout the entire territory of Burma's nation-state, more than a hundred languages are spoken, although precise numbers of speakers, dialects, and language families are unknown. In fact, the last attempt to collect statistics on numbers of home speakers or mother-tongue speakers of each language was in 1931, when the British Census of India attempted to group populations into categories according to language. One census official noted with great consternation that "some of the races or tribes in Burma change their language almost as often as they change their clothes."[8] Census takers confronting this bewildering and fluid ethnolinguistic pastiche in 1931 created dozens of new racial categories, finally settling on a figure of 135 races. Until recently, postindependence governments downplayed difference and from 1948 to 1988 recognized only seven major "nationalities" (minorities) in the country. The fact that no subsequent government has seen fit to collect information on languages and their speakers presumably arises from this postindependence political project aimed at discounting the diversity of the population while promoting instead its unity-building programs.[9] Somewhat surprisingly, this data avoidance was continued by the post-1988 military junta, even while it reinvigorated the 135-race framework of the 1931 census in its attempt to divide ethnic minority groups from each other and block political alliances among them and other regime opponents.

This variance in the numbers of ethnolinguistic categories created and embraced by colonial and postcolonial governments before 1988 did not affect the mapping or substance of language politics in Burma throughout the first ninety years of the twentieth century. Throughout this period, the politics of language centered on the territory mapped to "Burma Proper" and focused on a singular and contentious programmatic ambition: to establish one language as the language of administration in the colonial period and of the nation-state after independence in 1948. During British rule,

[8] Census Commissioner, Government of India, *Census of India, 1931*, vol. 11, part 1, p. 245.

[9] Anna Allott, "Language Policy and Language Planning in Burma," in David Bradley, ed., *Language Policy: Language Planning and Sociolinguistics in South-East Asia* (Canberra: Department of Linguistics, Research School of Pacific Studies, Australian National University, 1985), p. 131.

anticolonial, nationalist organizations pressed for the recognition and elevation of Burmese to official status, along with the associated demotion of the languages of colonial collaborators, the Indians and Chinese. Conflict over language in the central region was less between speakers of English and Burmese than it was between Burmese speakers and other non-English-speaking populations. At stake was who would hold postcolonial political power. After independence in 1948, Burmese-speaking elites launched in the central regions a new industry of language "modernization" – that is, unification, standardization, and translation – aimed at elevating Burmese to the status of "national language." Under parliamentary rule in the 1950s, the newly independent, ethnic Burman–dominated government supported the founding of the Burma Translation Society (BTS) in 1948. Later the University of Rangoon opened a Translation and Publications Department. The BTS formed committees on history, science, and the creation of a dictionary and an encyclopedia and by 1965 had produced more than 5 million copies of books in fields such as science, arts, history, Burmese culture, and education. The Vocabulary Committee's forty terminology subcommittees boasted of translating 65,000 technical terms from sixteen specialized subjects and assigning them standardizable Burmese equivalents for a "vocabulary bank."[10] Commissioned in 1949, the Burmese Encyclopedia began appearing volume by volume in the early 1960s. The Socialist government (1962–88) continued and expanded on these language-enhancement programs. During the Socialist period, the aim of policies that affected language usage was to turn everyone – especially Burmans but also non-Burmans – into Socialists first and foremost, or at least to provide everyone with linguistic tools that would allow them to express Socialist ideology in public. Notably, other identity or community linkages were politically irrelevant as long as Socialism came first.

Inside central Burma, language policies did not provoke much resistance.[11] In fact, a Burmese dictionary, vocabulary bank, and translated texts constituted the logical elements of an official language, which for all elite-level political contenders was one uncontested requirement for a modern nation-state. Given that no significant elites in the central region were excluded from access to this language, this "modernization" of Burmese was

[10] Howard Hayden, *Higher Education and Development in South-East Asia: Country Profiles*, vol. 2 (Paris: UNESCO, 1967), p. 56.

[11] There was remarkably little debate about which regional dialect should be designated the "official" language, which is probably a reflection of how few major differences exist among the dozen or so dialects of Burmese. Moreover, no one seriously questioned the idea that one dialect should be crowned "official." On regional dialects, see John Okell, *A Reference Grammar of Colloquial Burmese*, part I (London: Oxford University Press, 1969), and his "Three Regional Dialects," in David Bradley, ed., *Studies in Burmese Languages*, Papers in Southeast Asian Languages No. 13 (Canberra: Department of Linguistics, Australian National University, 1995), pp. 1–138; and Minn Latt Yekhaun, *Modernization of Burmese* (Prague: Oriental Institute in Academia, 1966), pp. 62–3.

seen as a "natural" and unproblematic step in the decolonization process.[12] Prior to 1988, this modernization project spurred conflict only once, when in the 1960s, the Upper Burma Writers' Association in Mandalay which argued in favor of simplifying the quite formal writing style.[13] These writers called for abandoning this inaccessible literary style entirely and replacing it with the colloquial style of Burmese. The writers argued that this reform would accelerate the social revolution under way in Burma, by making literacy more achievable for uneducated peasants and workers. The Burma Socialist Program Party government, backed by the Rangoon-based literati, rejected this proposal, claiming that serious matters of state simply cannot be expressed in a lowly colloquial language. The latter was said to have lacked the prestige, dignity, and authority required of an official language of a modern nation-state.[14]

It is important to note that throughout the postcolonial era leading up to 1988, national leaders' concerns about the politics, cultures, and languages of the frontier regions remained of secondary significance, while the major struggles that dominated national-level politics were still over control of the state based in Rangoon. Because the map of political contention was limited to the center, language policy and administration rarely spilled very far over the internal boundary between center and margin. By drawing borders that became internationally recognized, the colonial state had assigned ethnic minorities in remote locations to the territory that became the Burmese nation-state after 1948. That these populations were equally mapped out of the political struggles and imaginations of the center by the colonial state's internal territorial/administrative grid made it unlikely that Rangoon-based elites would ever care about delivering on the goods of citizenship to these territorially and linguistically distinct populations.

From the frontier areas, however, the view of central proclamations about officializing Burmese and forging national unity was one of threat, intrusion,

[12] During the first decade after independence, non-Burman political and economic elites in the central regions did not consider the elevation of Burmese to be terribly onerous. Most Chinese and Indians spoke Burmese as a second language, and they were still able to send their children to private schools where their mother tongues were used in instruction. Moreover, Martin Smith notes that minority presses "thrived" during this era, and at least eleven newspapers were published in minority languages in central Burma. See his "Unending War," *Index on Censorship* 23, no. 3 (July/August 1994): 113–18.

[13] Burmese language is communicated in two very different styles – one is formal, literary, written Burmese and the other is spoken, colloquial Burmese. In general, literary style is used in formal writing, nonfiction books, newspapers, school readers, comic books, and the narrative portions of serious novels, while colloquial style is used in everyday conversation, classroom lectures, informal letters, and in the dialogue sections of novels. There is "a considerable degree of variation between usages, grammatical forms, and constructions" appropriate to each style. See Okell, *A Reference Grammar of Colloquial Burmese*, p. xii.

[14] Allott, "Language Policy"; Julian Wheatley, "Burmese," in Bernard Comrie, ed., *The World's Major Languages* (New York: Oxford University Press, 1987), pp. 834–55.

and belonging-by-command. This outlook contributed to the emergence in the late 1950s of armed separatist movements seeking political concessions that ranged from increased cultural, economic, and political autonomy from Rangoon to outright political independence. There also emerged a legal united front of representatives of several frontier populations, which many called the "Federal Movement." This group formulated demands to replace the Burman-dominated "Union" constitutional framework with a more explicitly and substantively federal one and forced the issue on to the agenda of the government in Rangoon. When the Federal Movement held a series of high-profile meetings in the capital in 1962, the military accused the civilian-led government of preparing to give away territory to Federal Movement leaders. This became the justification for the military's coup d'etat in 1962. In fact, movement leaders, who negotiated and argued in English and Burmese, demanded not that they separate their territory and administration from Burma but that minority populations simply obtain greater access to the decisions that affected the definitions and methods of belonging to the postcolonial national society. They wanted to be heard in Rangoon. When this movement was crushed by the army in its 1962 coup, many of its backers went into armed rebellion against the government. The military's Revolutionary Council (which initiated the transition to the Socialist government) immediately embarked on a propaganda campaign to broadcast the Socialists' unity theme in the border regions where separatist violence was escalating. As F. K. Lehman argued, many in these regions interpreted the propaganda as a warning that "adherence to a minority cultural tradition is treated as tantamount to subversion of the nation and is branded as a mark of group inferiority within the nation."[15]

Even more directly confrontational was the Socialist government's revision of citizenship laws in 1982, which created three categories of citizens: full, associate, and naturalized. The new requirements made it very difficult for many indigenous minorities throughout the former frontier areas to qualify for anything better than "associate" citizenship.[16] Full citizenship required presentation of government identification cards, which in many cases had never been issued in large parts of rebel-held or even government-held territory where minority populations could not communicate in the language required for the application. Josef Silverstein notes that in a large number of cases, these minorities "lost their equal standing with other indigenous peoples of Burma and were treated as stateless."[17] Such people were

[15] F. K. Lehman, "Ethnic Categories in Burma and the Theory of Social Systems," in Peter Kunstadter, ed., *Southeast Asian Tribes, Minorities, and Nations* (Princeton, N.J.: Princeton University Press, 1967), p. 104.

[16] Josef Silverstein, "Fifty Years of Failure in Burma," in Michael E. Brown and Sumit Ganguly, eds., *Government Policies and Ethnic Relations in Asia and the Pacific* (Cambridge, Mass.: MIT Press, 1997), pp. 167–96.

[17] Ibid., p. 182.

required to hold a Foreigners' Registration Card, which effectively barred them from many occupations and disqualified their children from entrance to the university. Hence, while the Socialist regime preached the necessity for unity throughout the nation-state's territory, its practices and policies neither questioned nor allowed any public reflection over the boundary between the center and its margins. The center was where politics happened, full citizens lived, and Burmese was the currency of public life; in the margins, social affairs were considered "local," lesser citizens lived out "primitive" existences, and language was by definition not a public activity, since the public had been territorially limited to the center.

To summarize, until the 1990s, all postcolonial regimes in Burma expressed formal concerns and issued proclamations about the populations inhabiting the former frontier areas, but these matters were always of secondary importance to intra-elite struggles over who controlled state power in the central region. Even the literacy campaign of the 1960s, which could have been the perfect tool for assimilating a wide swath of citizens across the British-drawn territorial divide between center and periphery, took more than fifteen years to stumble into minority terrain and ultimately had little impact. Despite the center's apparent neglect of these frontier regions, the activities of ethnic Burman elites regarding language and identity were viewed by populations beyond the center as anything but benign or neutral. Many in these regions saw themselves under political, cultural, and linguistic siege from Rangoon. The monolingual bent to all colonial and postcolonial language policy universalized standards and requirements for public language without universalizing access to channels through which large numbers of citizen speakers and writers could have some say over the new requirements. As Bourdieu writes, this involved "the imposition of the dominant language and culture as legitimate and . . . the rejection of all other languages into indignity (thus demoted as patois or local dialects). By rising to universality, a particular culture or language causes all others to fall into particularity."[18] Until the 1990s, no postcolonial regime deliberately forced Burmese on the frontier peoples, but the official functionality of Burmese certainly endowed it with a kind of prestige and potentially a financial payoff that non-Burmese mother tongues would not be able to match in the era of monolingual nation-states.

Language and Belonging in the "Myanmar" Era

As noted above, of all the criticism and resistance that the junta has faced since 1988, it clearly found most threatening Aung San Suu Kyi's 1989–90 popularity with minority populations, in both rebel-held and

[18] Pierre Bourdieu, *Practical Reason: On the Theory of Action* (Stanford, Calif.: Stanford University Press, 1998), p. 46.

government-held territory. The threat of an alliance between opposition groups in the center and in the border regions pushed the military into quite dramatic responses. First, not surprisingly, it carried out a massive expansion of the army and an unprecedented arms modernization plan, so that the *tatmadaw* would never be vulnerable to an onslaught from armed rebels allied across the old center-margins divide. More surprising was SLORC's creative engineering of nonmilitary ways to come between the urban-based NLD and its potential allies in the frontier regions. Toward this end, Lt. Gen. Khin Nyunt initiated cease-fire negotiations with ethnic rebel groups in 1989. Over the next several years, seventeen of the twenty-one major antigovernment forces with as many as 50,000 troops concluded cease-fire agreements with SLORC. These arrangements should not be taken to indicate a shift toward center-frontier reconciliation. Instead, these are nothing more than temporary, ad hoc solutions to the political conflict between Rangoon and the minority populations scattered throughout the border regions. The cease-fires merely bought the junta the opportunity to redirect troops to the center, where the 1988 crisis was felt more deeply. Notably, the cease-fires already have broken down in a number of regions.

As these cease-fire agreements began to fall into place, the shape of the government's strategy for imposing order over what appeared to be the breakdown of the long-manageable, territorialized order of national politics began to emerge. For the first time since the British established the two administrative zones in this colony, a Rangoon regime launched a somewhat coordinated campaign to deal with the centrifugal impulses created by the century-old spatial logic of politics. This campaign entailed the most concerted government effort at minority assimilation and disempowerment in the twentieth century. It started with a number of makeshift, not terribly well-thought-out solutions to what the military defined as the national crisis of 1988. Over the last decade and a half, these practices and proclamations have evolved into an unparalleled obsession with producing cultural homogeneity and purity, while at the same time exoticizing and infantilizing the ethnic minority populations. It might seem contradictory to be pressing for homogeneity and unity among the citizenry of Burma, while also differentiating groups within the population as primitive, tourist-attracting, exotic creatures. But for this military, homogenization and differentiation were integral parts of the same offensive against the disintegration of political order. The 1988 crisis, in the view of the *tatmadaw*, was caused by national disunity. The junta's offensive against disunity had two spatially demarcated objectives: to purify the polluted oppositional politics in the center that brought on the 1988 crisis and to render legible (and hence controllable) the formerly excluded populations in the remote regions.[19] Homogenization

[19] On the concept of legibility, see James C. Scott, *Seeing like a State: How Certain Schemes to Improve the Human Condition Have Failed* (New Haven, Conn.: Yale University Press, 1998).

and differentiation strategies carried slightly different messages to populations in the center and the margins, but these activities all aimed at producing manageable citizens across both these spaces.

Differentiation

The emphasis on exoticizing minorities and differentiating identity-producing association is not entirely new in Burma, nor at all unusual among Burma's neighbors. During the Socialist era, the Burma Socialist Program Party routinely dragged representatives of the major nationality (i.e., minority) groups into Rangoon on Union Day every February to perform folk dances at the National Theatre, while also supporting the translation of some minority folklore into English or Burmese for publication. And next door in Thailand, the government's emphasis on promoting tourism beyond simply its sex resorts resulted in windfall profits for those who tapped into the most "authentic" hill tribes to whom western tourists pay to be introduced. What was unusual about the differentiation programs carried out by SLORC/SPDC in the 1990s was that their scale and complexity was so much grander than the annual theatrical productions of previous postcolonial regimes. Moreover, their target appeared to be domestic audiences (in both the center and beyond), not dollar-laden foreign tourists as in Thailand.

The first expansion on this scale of differentiation came during the negotiations over cease-fires with former ethnic minority insurgents, when the then-SLORC Chairman Sr. Gen. Saw Maung reinvigorated the colonial categorization of indigenous peoples into 135 races. The latter probably appealed to Saw Maung as a classic counterinsurgency (and colonial) divide-and-conquer strategy to limit the size of the groups that might make common claims on the government, so as to weaken their bargaining positions. Over the next decade, the regime brought thousands of actors, musicians, artists, dancers, and writers not just for Union Day but for celebrations of any national holiday, as well as a whole range of new state productions, competitions, and spectacles. Government-authorized textbooks for schools and universities inserted images of ethnic minority figures alongside *tatmadaw* soldiers into drawings representing significant events in Burmese history. In the 1990s, the high-circulation, pop-culture magazine, *Myet-khin-thet* (published by the military intelligence directorate), routinely carried what must have been costly full-color photos of the most exotic of Burma's minority populations, such as the Pao or Palaung. The first nightclubs authorized to open in Rangoon in 1992 all included stage shows in which dancers and musicians (often ethnic Burmans wearing minority costumes) performed "traditional" minority dances, songs, or acts; many foreigners and Burmese in the audiences were not sure which minority was being depicted, and there were often discussions about what the "real" name of the group was that was on display onstage.

Traffic in this differentiation has been two-way across the century-old internal boundary between center and periphery, but the traffickers in each direction are quite different groups of people and are carrying out quite different parts of the regime's program to rebuild the state and pacify the post-1988 society. The regime has tightly controlled the route from the border areas to the center, allowing a trickle of ethnic minority representatives (artists, musicians, former-insurgents-turned-drug-warlords) hand-picked by the regime. The endpoint for them has been some kind of regime spectacle, wherein they played roles ranging from the primitive, childish tribesperson displayed in a festival or competition to the expensively attired, well-armed druglords who proclaim their allegiance to SLORC/SPDC at opening ceremonies for their new banks, toll roads, and office buildings. The audience for these spectacles has been strictly limited to the territory of the center and, more specifically, the performances target those who marched in the streets in 1988 (or were sympathetic to the marchers) but have gone back to quiet lives since the crackdown. The message has been a warning: "These people from beyond the center are not like you; we (the military) will keep the uncivilized primitives and dangerous druglords under control on your behalf." In a sense, then, this warning tries to shore up the old colonial internal boundary, in an effort to keep potential allies territorially separate and, more importantly, incapable of thinking of each other as equal political partners.

By contrast, the traffic from the center out to the margins has been more crowded, mainly with military officers and foot soldiers, as well as a handful of Chinese, Burman, and other entrepreneurs looking for economic opportunities. As in the case of a hearts-and-minds counterinsurgency operation, the military typically has arrived in the remote areas championing the cause of a particular kind of differentiation. What it has wanted the local populations to hear and process was this: "We respect you, and encourage you to escape whatever oppression you may have encountered at the hands of your distant ethnic cousins; you deserve separate recognition." The fact that the message has been conveyed in Burmese, the language of the ethnic majority population long suspected of expansionism by many in the border regions, undoubtedly has reinforced suspicions and inspired intransigence to the *tatmadaw*'s new mapping and identity production in national politics. But there have been signs that some groups embraced the parts of this message that suited their purposes and along the way thwarted the regime's overall aim of consolidating the power of the military over the polity. For example, the new emphasis on the existence of 135 nationalities in Burma reportedly derailed the regime's progress toward finalizing a new constitution back in 1996, according to one member of a National Convention committee assigned to deal with political arrangements for ethnic minorities. This army colonel reported, "We have to accept the 135 races theory, but now all 135 want their own states."[20]

[20] Interview, September 22, 1997.

Homogenization

Along the same lines, the regime's homogenization strategy also has aimed at both purifying the center and increasing the regime's control over populations in border regions. For the former to be accomplished, the power of Aung San Suu Kyi and her political party had to be diminished. The regime's cultural homogenization programs have subsequently emphasized the way impure, heterogeneous, foreign influences (ranging from Aung San Suu Kyi's imperialist British husband to western neo-imperialist governments that colonized Burma and that recognized the NLD's victory in the 1990 election) have destroyed stability and prosperity in Burma over the last two centuries. In this attempt to construct a homogeneous "we," the regime has deployed quite extraordinary language in its attempt to recast Aung San Suu Kyi as both contaminated "other" and a contaminant who is dangerous to those around her. For example, in newspapers and public pronouncements, regime spokespersons have called Aung San Suu Kyi an "axehandle" (she was the handle that foreign oppressors wield to chop up and destroy Burma), "puppet girl," "puppet princess," and "Mrs. Race Destructionist" (by mixing her blood with that of her British husband, her mixed race sons destroyed the purity of the Burmese bloodline). Notably, there is little evidence that these clumsy psychological warfare–inspired initiatives have made any dents in Aung San Suu Kyi's popularity in central Burma.

Beyond the center, the regime's concern was with making potential allies of the NLD more legible and hence more controllable. To accomplish this, the populations in the old "excluded" areas had to be regrouped, and assigned new names and categories of belonging. Most importantly, these names – all 135 of them – were generated, defined, and enforced by the *tatmadaw*, which simultaneously laid out a unifying, genealogical theory of how all 135 were connected via a common and glorious ancestry, called "Myanmar." Under this theory, every Shan, Pao, Chin, Karen, and Lushai is fundamentally a "Myanmar."

Hence, the junta's solution to the political chaos that surrounded 1988 combined the entire population – in the center and in the margins – into a single target of this strategy of cultural homogenization, albeit for different reasons and toward different ends in each territorial space. At the core of this homogenization strategy was an optimistic, no-holds-barred assault on the everyday language and conceptual referents to be used throughout the country and beyond. The government renamed the country "Myanmar" and renamed some of the major cities, allegedly to eliminate vestiges of imperialism. English-language books were republished with all references to "Burma" whited out and replaced with "Myanmar." After twenty-six years of rewriting history to explain the teleology of Burmese socialism, SLORC in 1989 launched a new growth industry in writing the sacred and ancient history of the singular national race called the "Myanmar." The junta assigned various government bodies responsibility for conjuring a highly improbable unilineal, unified, and peaceful history of a single, millennia-old nationality divided only by the trickery and brute force of the British imperialists. Perhaps most representative of this campaign was the 1997–8 Pondaung Primate Fossil Exploration archaeological project. With little archaeological expertise, the army-led dig has produced specious claims that fossils found in the Pondaung region prove that "human civilization began in our motherland."[21] The government claims the fossils "prove" that harmony among all ethnic groups existed in Burma all the way back to the Neolithic period:

> This irrefutable conclusion is drawn from the very fact that all over the land which now constitutes the Union of Myanmar, there is a surprising consistency and uniformity or rather similarities observed on the Neolithic pottery, . . . common ideas and similar techniques that were responsible for all inventions and evolution in material cultures during the Neolithic period. . . .
>
> [A]mong the Neolithic peoples then, is a total lack of any evidence as to indicate mass mortality or mass burial that could have arisen out of inter-ethnic conflicts; for this reason, divisive inter-racial disharmony and enmity seemed an anathema to the national groups in those days of yore.[22]

Similarly, SLORC/SPDC sponsored numerous large-scale "Myanmafication"[23] performances that revealed the unity campaign's dual purposes: keeping out foreign influences (thus "purifying" Myanmar culture and purging the "impure" (i.e., Aung San Suu Kyi)) and papering over differences among indigenous populations and cultures. The purification and homogenization purposes are reflected in the regime's founding of new versions of historicized "Myanmar" festivals – including annual regatta, equestrian, and music competitions – aimed at "strengthening the national pride of being a Myanmar citizen as a unifying bond."[24] At annual Exhibitions to Revitalize and Foster the Spirit of Patriotism, junta Secretary 1, Lt. Gen. Khin Nyunt, enjoins attendees to study "the origins of the Myanmar race, the flowering of Myanmar patriotic spirit during the Bagan, Pinn-Ya, Inn-wa, Taungu, Nyaung-Yan and Konbaung dynasties, the 3 Anglo-Myanmar wars."[25] Additionally, over the last decade, science, cultural, and national and local history museums have popped up all over Rangoon and the rest of the country. Built by particular

[21] May May Aung, "National Museum, the Symbol of Myanmar Pride and Honour," *Myanmar Information Sheet*, December 29, 1997, available online at http://homepages.go.com/~myanmarinfosheet/1997/1997.htm (accessed June 11, 1999).

[22] *Myanmar Perspectives* (March 1999).

[23] This is Gustaaf Houtman's evocative terminology. See his *Mental Culture in Burmese Crisis Politics: Aung San Suu Kyi and the National League for Democracy* (Tokyo: Institute for the Study of Languages and Cultures of Asia and Africa, 1999).

[24] Uta Gartner, "Old Festivals Newly Adorned," Conference on Tradition and Modernity in Myanmar, Berlin, Fakultatsinstitut fur Asien- and Afrikawissenschaften, 1993, p. 360; Gavin Douglas, "State Patronage of Burmese Traditional Music," Ph.D. dissertation, University of Washington, 2001.

[25] *New Light of Myanmar*, October 30, 1998.

ministries, regional commands, or armed forces directorates, all of them revere the "Myanmar" race as the sacred core of their narratives of progress and history.

Making Myanmar Speakers

In this cultural heritage industry, language has taken center stage, and it has done so by crashing through the old substantive and territorial boundaries that had limited the reach of the monolingual state since the early twentieth century. SLORC's earliest moves were typical of previous centrally focused initiatives: The junta quickly ordered the Myanmasa Ahpwe (Burmese Language Commission) to rewrite the official monolingual Burmese dictionary in order to strip out Socialist terminology and English loan words. Here, as in the previous ninety years, the audience for this language initiative was the population living in the central regions. However, very quickly, language manipulation activities began to spill across the old boundary between center and margins. As the regime has attempted to reassemble the remnants of the Socialist state into one under more direct military control, it has appointed waves of new committees – all under the direction of military officers – that have been charged with addressing the weaknesses of national unity that caused (in the army's view) the 1988 crisis. One of these committees came straight out of the army's forty years of counterinsurgency combat: the Committee for Writing Slogans for Nationals, established on April 16, 1989. From this committee emerged "Our Three Main National Causes": (1) nondisintegration of the Union, (2) nondisintegration of solidarity, and (3) perpetuation of national sovereignty. These slogans and others – such as "Crush all internal and external destructive elements as the common enemy" – have appeared in Burmese and English in every publication produced in Burma after 1989, and on red-and-white signs in all public places. The slogans all emphasize the urgency of maintaining national unity, at any cost.

This unity crusade has moved language politics into new arenas for a Rangoon regime, starting with the June 18, 1989, Adaptation of Expressions Law. The law and the subsequent renaming campaign that came out of it have attempted to regulate two things: First, the regime has tried to standardize the terms Burmese language speakers would use to discuss their public identities, and, second, SLORC has tried to dictate what non-Burmese speakers – inside and outside the country – would call the country and its public institutions (including the official language). The regime also has decreed a new romanized orthography for these names. For example, the 1989 law renamed the country, "Myanmar," while "Rangoon" was henceforth "Yangon." According to one regime spokesman, "The term 'Myanmar' has been used as the name of the nation and the people for years countable by the thousands."[26] The junta appears to be harkening back at least to twelfth-century

[26] Tekkatho Myat Thu, "Call Us Myanmar," *New Light of Myanmar*, April 23, 2000.

Old Burmese inscriptions, wherein "Myanmar" was the written term for the domain of the kings at Pagan and, later, at Pegu and Mandalay. There is some conceptual slippage here, given that for most of these eras, a king's domain was defined by claims not over territory but over scarce labor and populations. Under SLORC/SPDC, the political unit called "Myanmar" has come to refer only to territory. There is also linguistic inventiveness at play here. In modern Burmese language usage, "Mranma/Myanma/Myanmar"[27] has been the formal, written, literary term for the modern nation-state's territory since independence in 1948, while "Bama/Bamar" (from which "Burma" is derived) has been the spoken or colloquial language equivalent for the sovereign domain of the government, that is, the name of the country. Under SLORC's language reforms, Burmese speakers and non-Burmese speakers have been directed to use "Myanmar" as the name of the country, its citizens and the official language, and to use "Bamar" to refer to the ethnic majority group. Speakers of this diglossic language have been directed to scrap the old formal-versus-colloquial distinction and deploy these new terms regardless of setting.

In a sense, the junta's renaming project represents a continuation of the four-decade-old postcolonial – and centrally focused – project of codifying and officializing the Burmese language to enhance its prestige as a language of a nation-state. However, whether or not it was intended, the renaming project represents one of the more naked assertions of the supremacy of the ethnic-majority Burmans over the minorities in the country. Gustaaf Houtman points out, "Neither *Myanma* nor *Bama*, from which Myanmar and Burma are derived, are neutral terms, as both are strongly associated with the Burmese language, the language of the ethnic majority."[28] For speakers of Burmese as a second or third language, the formal, written style – from which "Myanmar" and almost all the other new names are derived – is even more inaccessible than the colloquial style and perhaps most identified with the ethnicity and associated chauvinism of its mother-tongue speakers. One critic writes of the renaming project:

> [It is] clear proof that the Myanmar [i.e., ethnic majority group] want to dominate over all other ethnic groups, and is practising the policy of a great nation of Myanmar, i.e., in the course of time there would be no Shan, Chin, Kachin, Karen, Mon and Arakanese, all would eventually merge into Myanmar. It will be a monolithic whole with one country, Myanmar, instead of the Union of Burma, one religion, Buddhist, and one race, the Myanmarnese [*sic*].[29]

[27] These are common transcriptions, transliterations, and romanizations of the Burmese language term. No single romanization scheme has gained widespread acceptance, which accounts for this variation.

[28] Houtman, *Mental Culture in Burmese Crisis Politics*, p. 49.

[29] Kanbawza Win, *An Appeal to the UN and US* (Bangkok: CPDSK Publications, 1994), p. 44.

Beyond the renaming campaign, there is further evidence that Rangoon cares about everyday politics, social relations, and language in the former frontier regions a great deal more than did any previous regimes. From a century-old policy of malignant neglect, the postcolonial central government has shifted demonstrably into a more invasive, assimilationist set of policies toward these populations. As noted above in this chapter, schoolteachers and monks in widely dispersed border regions have been arrested for conducting instruction in languages other than Burmese. In the regions where cease-fires have been reached with former insurgent groups, Rangoon has deployed the Ministry for the Development of the Border Areas and the National Races (later renamed the "Ministry for the Progress of Border Areas and National Races and Development Affairs") to build roads, Burmese-language schools, hospitals, power plants, telecommunications relay stations, and other institutions aimed at both modernizing and subjugating former rebel-held territory. These border-areas projects, which are on a scale never seen in Burmese history, are carried out by soldiers, officers and local residents conscripted into labor gangs by the *tatmadaw*. This army likewise exists on a scale unprecedented in modern history. Growing from 170,000 in 1988 to over 400,000 (mostly Burman) soldiers in 2000 and expanding its materiel and technology at a similarly breakneck pace, this *tatmadaw* has a capacity to deploy soldiers, guns, trucks, teachers, doctors, nurses, and other resources in ways the unity-conscious Socialist government never could. The Socialists' clumsy attempts to integrate these ethnic minority groups into a Socialist Union of Burma never succeeded because of the utter incapacity of the central government to offer any compelling incentives to locals to work, cooperate, and negotiate with Rangoon. There is little doubt that some local populations still consider the *tatmadaw* an occupying force representing Rangoon's continued attempts at internal colonialism. Nonetheless, these border areas development activities bring new resources and incentives to bear on negotiations over political and economic power that now routinely transcend the old divide between center and the margins.

Conclusion: The Making (or Unmaking?) of Myanmars and Myanmar Speakers

Language policy in modern Burma has come a long way from its original territorially bounded focus on the creation of a monolingual public sphere in the central regions. Rangoon-based regimes throughout the twentieth century dedicated resources and personnel to the task of creating all the trappings of a modern, standardized language in these regions. At stake was how power was to be articulated in styles that favored one elite group over another and that elevated the status of that elite group within the international community as well. Out of intra-elite power struggles, various postcolonial coalitions of ethnic Burmans grasped the reins of rule and generated an extensive array of programs aimed at codifying, empowering, and modernizing their own mother tongue. These programs have been quite successful in their transformation of the Burmese language. Indeed, the latter now seems inevitably and naturally the language of this nation-state. No one in central Burma with any serious claims on ruling power would ever question the status of Burmese as the official language of the public sphere – a significant change since the colonial era, when English was paramount. For those in the center, belonging is now unquestionably a process that can be practiced and imagined only in Burmese.

During the entire twentieth century, it was only in these spatially limited central regions that any explicit language policy materialized in formal policy pronouncements. However, this does not mean that the impact of the policy to "modernize" Burmese – as well as other outcomes of intra-elite struggles in Rangoon – did not have far-reaching implications for populations living, speaking, struggling, and thinking beyond the central regions. From the colonial era onward, cultural, symbolic, and political capital became centralized in Rangoon's environs. This centralization led to a hierarchical ordering of territory and populations that located sophistication, civilization, and power in the center. Distance from Rangoon was associated with political insignificance and social backwardness. Reinforced by deeply rooted Social Darwinist views about the evolution of civilizations, this systematic and tidy ordering of state and society placed at a distinct disadvantage the territorially distant, linguistically distinct populations that lived in the juridically "excluded" areas. After independence in 1948 and especially after the takeover by the military-Socialist regime in 1962, central politics became increasingly contestable only in Burmese, which turned thinkers, writers, and speakers of other languages into lesser citizens in the roster of the modern nation-state.

From the point of view of populations living in the former "excluded" areas, postcolonial military, political, and cultural power has been displayed in Burmese language and narrated according to putative ethnic Burman traditions. Minority populations have viewed postcolonial, national-level politics as a series of theatrical acts pitting arrogant, intolerant, expansionist, and often incomprehensible Burmans against increasingly self-identifying, oppressed, indigenous minorities. Little has changed since independence in 1948 to inspire revisions of this interpretation. In areas where the SLORC/SPDC concluded cease-fire agreements in the 1990s, local populations have gained little from integration with Rangoon, although some of their leaders – especially those involved in the production of heroin and methamphetamines for the global market – may find easier access to money-laundering services in Rangoon. Few villages and towns view the "border areas development" programs as anything but a new, more invasive round of Rangoon expansionism;[30] the fact that the army carries them out and does so exclusively in Burmese language reinforces this view. As a result of decades of exclusionary state practices, anything Rangoon does is automatically suspect among populations living in many of the more remote regions. Importantly, this may not change when the state is no longer in the hands of the military.

Despite the hostile reception to development and Burmanization programs in remote areas, the use of Burmese language therein nonetheless is probably spreading. In terms of language policy in the border areas, the SLORC/SPDC regime did not promulgate an explicit Burmese- or "Myanmar"– only policy, but local and regional commanders handling day-to-day law and order affairs have consistently made it difficult for educators, monks, and other public figures to operate in anything but Burmese. As a matter of survival interest, many people living in these remote regions – confronting the presence of tens of thousands of recently arrived Burman soldiers – have a range of incentives to speak and to understand Burmese so as to navigate the new power corridors of their localities. Fluency or comfort with Burmese language allows the possibility of negotiating with the soldiers who claim the locals' husbands, sons, rice, land, or bullocks for use in development or counterinsurgency projects. A generation from now, this bilingualism may lead to what SLORC feared most after 1988: the ability of ethnic minorities to communicate fluently enough in Burmese language that they can team up with the monolingual Burman opposition. In other words, the post-1988 regime's state-building and pacification practices pushed language manipulation beyond the old boundaries of Central, Ministerial Burma, where these practices may end up empowering social forces that could destabilize the Rangoon military junta.

Considerations of the regime's differentiation, homogenization, and language practices highlight both the new permeability of the century-old territorialized logic of politics and the remarkable durability of that boundary-generating logic. The regime itself exhibits mixed feelings about this. In the central region, the regime wants ethnic Burmans – who have not thought of the former border regions as political spaces inhabited by equal fellow citizens – to sustain the colonial demarcation between center and periphery. It wants to rehabilitate practices and images of differentiation that ensure a disjuncture between politics and nonpolitics, center and margins, civilized and primitive populations, the NLD and potential allies in border regions.

30 The use of forced labor to carry out the "development" projects has created not only local hardships and hostility among ethnic minority villagers, but also waves of displaced people as rural populations flee the depredations of the military labor recruiters. See, for example, the report of the International Labour Organisation, *Forced Labour in Myanmar (Burma)* (Geneva, July 1998).

The regime also wants to make populations on the periphery legible enough that they cannot slip through the permeable border and politically ally with centrally based opposition. Creating this legibility has entailed an explosion of state building in territory beyond the center, which asserts a bureaucratic impulse toward administrative uniformity across the two spaces. Quite unintentionally, these state-building projects require and in some ways force the internal boundary to become increasingly permeable and irrelevant.

6

Institutionalizing Virtual Kurdistan West

Transnational Networks and Ethnic Contention in International Affairs

Nicole F. Watts

> [T]he Kurdish problem is no longer an exotic affair of a people living at the other end of the world. It is largely perceived as a European problem – to such an extent that the German Foreign Minister, on a visit to Ankara, had to reply to his Turkish interlocutors that, even if, as they claimed, there was no Kurdish problem in Turkey, there was a major Kurdish problem in Germany!
>
> Kendal Nezan, President, *Institut Kurde de Paris*, April 17, 2000

Introduction

On a cold day in mid-February of 1999, staff at the Kurdish Institute in Paris arrived at work to find journalists knocking on their doors and their normally quiet offices flooded with phone calls, urgent faxes, and e-mail. Kurdish guerrilla leader Abdullah Öcalan had been captured by the Turks in faraway Kenya, and the reporters all needed the same thing: the Kurdish Reaction. "They all came here – TV cameramen and reporters from Europe, and around the world," remembered one Institute representative. "They saw us as the voice for the Kurds."

Field research for this article included personal interviews in Turkey, France, and England with human rights and pro-Kurdish activists, all of whom were generous with their time and ideas. My interpretive analysis of their work is strictly my own, and those I interviewed may not necessarily agree with it. Some of the research for this article was supported by a Peace Scholar award from the United States Institute of Peace; likewise, the views expressed herein are mine, and do not necessarily reflect those of the institute. I am grateful to the institute for its support. I wish to thank Professor Joel Migdal and other participants in the first workshop on Boundaries and Belonging, whose enthusiasm for an early draft of this paper encouraged me to further develop many of the ideas herein. Further appreciation goes to Professor Reşat Kaşaba and members of the 2001 Turkish Studies group for their constructive critiques, some of which vastly improved this paper, some of which I chose to ignore at my own peril. Any errors are my own.

Not simply a solitary group, the Kurdish Institute in Paris sits at the heart of a transnational web of organizations and individuals dedicated to the promotion of Kurdish identity and rights. While Kurds struggled to maintain explicitly Kurdish representation in the public sphere within Turkey, by the late 1990s "pro-Kurdish"[1] activists working in Turkey, Europe, and across national borders had produced a new phase of transnational contention that had critically altered the terms of negotiation between Turkish officials and Kurdish activists. Kurdish rights were being pursued not only in the mountains and cities of eastern and western Turkey but in corridors, offices, and assembly rooms in Strasbourg, Paris, Berlin, and London. Linked by ideas, institutions, technology, and travel, Kurdish activists had constructed a transnational advocacy community, a kind of "Virtual Kurdistan West" that could not be located on any political map but had become a persistent presence in international affairs.

The growing political, cultural, and economic relevance of such deterritorialized[2] or transnational communities, of which the Kurds are but one, has encouraged a great deal of new research across a range of disciplines. Commenting on an increasingly crowded international stage, social scientists have described a world populated by "nations unbound," "ethnoscapes," transnationals, transmigrants, cosmopolitans, and network societies.[3] Distinguishing these communities from earlier diaspora or migrant communities has been the extent to which they maintain relations with their "home" communities, their regular use of travel and technology as a unifying mechanism, their accelerating rates of migration, and their often overt challenges to the authority of home states. They have, in the words of Michael Shapiro, created a "different and nonstatic planetary map"[4] that coexists in often uneasy

[1] I apply the term "pro-Kurdish" to any individual or group who publicly and explicitly lobbies for expanded Kurdish cultural or political rights. Not all pro-Kurdish actors are of Kurdish ethnicity, and not all ethnic Kurds are pro-Kurdish.

[2] I use the term loosely, following Arjun Appadurai, who applies the term "deterritorialization" not only to transnational corporations and money markets but to "ethnic groups, sectarian movements, and political formations" that "increasingly operate in ways that transcend specific territorial boundaries and identities." See Arjun Appadurai, "Global Ethnoscapes: Notes and Queries for a Transnational Anthropology," in *Recapturing Anthropology: Working in the Present*, ed. Richard G. Fox (Santa Fe: School of American Research Press, 1991), 192. Many such communities might also be referred to as diasporas, but see Khachig Tölölyan for a careful review of the use of the term. Khachig Tölölyan. "Rethinking Diaspora(s): Stateless Power in the Transnational Moment," *Diaspora* 5, no. 1 (1996): 3–36.

[3] See, variously, Linda Basch, Nina Glick Schiller, and Cristina Szanton Blanc, *Nations Unbound: Transnational Projects, Postcolonial Predicaments, and Deterritorialized Nation-States* (Amsterdam: Overseas Publishers Association, 1994); Pheng Cheah and Bruce Robbins, eds., *Cosmopolitics: Thinking and Feeling Beyond the Nation* (Minneapolis: University of Minnesota Press, 1998); and Appadurai, "Global Ethnoscapes."

[4] Michael J. Shapiro, "Introduction," in *Challenging Boundaries: Global Flows, Territorial Identities*, ed. Michael J. Shapiro and Hayward R. Alker (Minneapolis: University of Minneapolis Press, 1996), 3.

relationship with more traditional maps of state-demarcated sovereignty. It is no secret, then, that boundaries of belonging have increasingly been formed distinct from territorial homelands and overlaying borders and in contradistinction to nation-states.

The formation and evolving identities of transnational communities, as well as their multifaceted relations with both "host" and "home" actors, has been the subject of extensive study, especially in the fields of anthropology, sociology, and migration studies. What has been less well understood is the process by which some transnational communities translate their grievances into concrete political pressure, how they encroach on domains formerly dominated by states, and how and when they become not merely cultural "formations" but collective actors with political agency in domestic and international affairs. Although some of these communities may form governments-in-exile (as did the Palestinians), many fall short of both actually declaring such representation and of seeking the "total claims to power" a government-in-exile demands.[5] Nonetheless, as Fiona Adamson notes, because many of today's transnational communities are produced in part due to political conflict, repression, and economic dislocation, the "relationship of a transnational community to its 'home' is . . . as likely to be defined by a desire for transformation, contestation and political change as it is by nostalgia, continuity and tradition."[6]

Given the internal fragmentation and economic marginalization of most transnational communities, it is far from clear how they actually go about "bypassing, erasing, and neutralizing" the monitoring devices and mental maps of the state, to paraphrase Joel Migdal in his introduction to this volume. This paper, then, analyzes some of the specific mechanisms transnational actors use to exert political agency in international affairs. More specifically, I examine how, despite vehement Turkish state opposition and significant internal divisions,[7] pro-Kurdish activists created a political advocacy

[5] Yossi Shain defines a government-in-exile as "opposition groups that struggle from outside their home territory to overthrow and replace the regime in their independent, occupied, or claimed home country." Although other groups may hold similar goals and use similar strategies, many politics of diaspora differ from those of a government-in-exile because "they do not make such total claims to power." See Yossi Shain, "Introduction: Governments-in-Exile and the Age of Democratic Transitions," in *Governments-in-Exile in Contemporary World Politics*, ed. Yossi Shain (New York: Routledge, 1991), 2.

[6] Fiona B. Adamson, "Mobilizing for the Transformation of Home: Politicized Identities and Transnational Practices," in *New Approaches to Migration? Transnational Communities and the Transformation of Home*, ed. Nadje Al-Ali and Khalid Koser (London: Routledge, 2002), 155–168.

[7] Kurds are divided into several different linguistic groups and by religion. There is some contention among these groups themselves and among outside analysts as to whether all should be defined as "Kurdish." Some Zaza-speaking and some Alevi "Kurds," for instance, do not consider themselves Kurdish, while others do. For a good discussion of Kurdish ethnic identity, see Martin van Bruinessen, "The Ethnic Identity of the Kurds," in *Ethnic Groups in*

community capable of challenging Turkish state authority as it was exercised in the international arena.[8] As indicated above, I term this community "Virtual Kurdistan West" and conceive of it as a dynamic "tendency," composed not of a fixed set of practices or individuals but of a "family of related yet mutually competing stances," in the words of Rogers Brubaker.[9] As a cumulative effect, it has been produced not *by* a nation, Kurdish or otherwise, but by certain segments of various Kurdish communities working in conjunction with non-Kurdish actors. Virtual Kurdistan West is "virtual" because it lacks an "actual" sovereign territory and relies extensively on new technology resources. I modify it as "west" to distinguish it from other possible virtual Kurdistans: because it is geographically rooted in what might loosely be termed "western" Kurdistan (Turkey) and western Europe, because its leadership is primarily from Turkey and is inspired by and embedded within western European political and social institutions, because its institutions primarily target Turkey and Turkey-origin Kurds, and because approximately 85 percent of Kurds in western Europe are from Turkey.[10] It is "western," in other words, to distinguish it from the more "eastern" Kurdish movements of Iraq and Iran, which operate under very different social and political conditions.[11]

I argue here that key to the emergence of Virtual Kurdistan West was the institutionalization of a distinctive set of pro-Kurdish norms and practices within nongovernmental and governmental arenas in Europe. This institutionalization provided Kurdish activists with a concrete array of legal, material, political, and ideational resources with which to sustain their agenda. Perhaps counterintuitively, such institutionalization was facilitated by the linkage of a specifically Kurdish agenda with transnational campaigns

the Republic of Turkey, ed. Peter Alford Andrews with the assistance of Rudiger Benninghaus (Wiesbaden: Reichert, 1989), 613–621. Also see Paul White, *Primitive Rebels or Revolutionary Modernizers? The Kurdish National Movement in Turkey* (London: Zed Press, 2000), chap. 3.

8 I am focusing, then, not on the Kurdish diaspora community in its entirety but on a specific section of this community and its political activities.

9 Rogers Brubaker, *Nationalism Reframed: Nationhood and the National Question in the New Europe* (Cambridge: Cambridge University Press, 1996), 60–61.

10 See, among other sources, Institut Kurde de Paris (IKP), "Kurdish Diaspora," http://www.institutkurde.org; Internet; accessed February 2001.

11 Notwithstanding the Kurdish pseudostate established in northern Iraq after the 1991 Gulf War, there are substantial differences in the international status of Iraq, Iran, and Turkey that significantly alter the dynamics of the pro-Kurdish movements in these countries. As a European Union candidate and signatory to numerous international human rights conventions and treaties, Turkey offers activists the potential to exert substantially more leverage than those targeting Iraq or Iran. On the other hand, Turkey-origin pro-Kurdish activists and institutions do not receive the kind of financial aid the Iraqi pro-Kurdish movement does from the United States. This said, I am not suggesting that there is no mingling of Iraq- and Turkey-origin Kurds in this Virtual Kurdistan West (the Kurdish Institute in Paris provides a clear example to the contrary) but remarking on a tendency for their political activism to follow divergent paths.

promoting a "universal" norm of human rights. While an emerging body of work on human rights networks in international relations has provided valuable insights into the ways nonstate actors and "advocacy networks" may exert influence in international affairs,[12] the use of such networks to promote a particularistic, national agenda has been largely ignored. An examination of the Kurdish case, however, suggests that regular and supportive interactions between Kurds and non-Kurdish actors, often operating through transnational human rights networks, provided a space for the emergence of new expectations about "appropriate" behavior among Kurds and new legal, cultural, and political practices that collectively came to constitute *national* practices.

Such practices have been promoted by a large number of organizations I here classfy into justice, cultural, and foreign affairs "ministries."[13] Thus Virtual Kurdistan West possesses a kind of "Justice Ministry" that offers its Kurdish "citizenry" alternative legal recourse via the European Court of Human Rights, a "Culture Ministry" that reconstituted and promoted notions of Kurdish culture, and a "Ministry of Foreign Affairs" that promotes a pro-Kurdish political agenda in international (and particularly European) affairs. The organizations within these "ministries" have each developed extensive relationships with various European governments, intergovernmental organizations such as the European Parliament, and nongovernmental organizations including charities and human rights groups. They have each poached on a portion of the Turkish state's established rights to rule its "own" citizens: the justice ministry by offering citizens an alternative system of law, the culture ministry by offering an alternative community of belonging, and the foreign affairs ministry by offering alternative political norms to those of Turkey.

Conceptualizing Virtual Kurdistan West as a product of the collective efforts of a wide range of actors is a divergence from usual depictions of the Kurdish movement that locate the Kurdistan Workers Party (PKK) at the center of analysis,[14] where PKK leaders have indeed sought to be. First coming

[12] See, e.g., Margaret Keck and Kathryn Sikkink, *Activists beyond Borders: Advocacy Networks in International Politics* (Ithaca, N.Y.: Cornell University Press, 1998); Thomas Risse, Stephen C. Ropp, and Kathryn Sikkink, eds., *The Power of Human Rights: International Norms and Domestic Change* (Cambridge: Cambridge University Press, 1999); Audie Klotz, *Norms in International Relations: The Struggle against Apartheid* (Ithaca, N.Y.: Cornell University Press, 1995); Thomas Risse-Kappen, ed., *Bringing Transnational Relations Back In* (Cambridge: Cambridge University Press, 1995).

[13] I use the world advisedly, for although it usefully captures these organizations' proto-state-like function and the cumulative effect of their actions, it must be taken figuratively: These "ministries" report to no central hierarchy, are unconstrained by bureaucratic borders, and are made up of a multiplicity of organizations with no necessary relationship to one another. Nonetheless, taken *collectively* they approximate the function of a ministry in a traditional territorial state.

[14] See, e.g., White, *Primitive Rebels*; David McDowall, *A Modern History of the Kurds* (London: I. B. Tauris, 1996), chap. 20; Michael Gunter, *The Kurds in Turkey: A Political Dilemma*

to public attention in 1984 with attacks on Turkish guardposts, the PKK soon expanded its "repertoire of contention" to encompass not only guerrilla activities but lobbying and protest in Europe. By the late 1990s the PKK had wide-ranging support within Europe and controlled many Kurdish cultural and political groups there. Simultaneously, it sought recognition as the sole legitimate representative of the Kurdish people, something it never quite achieved. While recognizing the PKK's enormous political and economic influence, particularly at the level of grass-roots mobilization among Kurdish diaspora communities, my attention here to organizations other than the PKK is meant to highlight the important and multiple roles played by other, less well-known pro-Kurdish actors, especially at the level of "high" politics, where the PKK's status as a guerrilla organization has constrained its access. It is true that the PKK (and its successor, the Kurdistan Freedom and Democracy Congress) is influential, but it is nonetheless one actor in a hotly contested political terrain.

The remainder of the chapter is organized as follows. I first provide a brief overview of the ways nonstate actors are pursuing their goals in the international arena, and how pro-Kurdish activists in Turkey began linking a pro-Kurdish agenda with international norms of human rights. I then examine the ways in which pro-Kurdish activists institutionalized Virtual Kurdistan West via its justice, cultural, and foreign affairs "ministries," facilitating the formation of a national actor in international politics. The organizations selected here for discussion within each category are not the only important or even the largest ones within the realm of Kurdish politics in Europe, but they are among the most significant in the world of international diplomacy.[15]

Transnational and Ethnic Networks in International Affairs

That increasing numbers of people are spilling over the boundaries once imagined to define and contain them is indisputable. In 1972 there were about 2.8 million refugees in the world; in 2002 there were about 19 million, or about one out of every 300 people on earth, according to the United Nations High Commissioner for Refugees.[16] In total, there are about 90 million

(Boulder, Colo.: Westview, 1990). An exception is Robert Olson, ed., *The Kurdish Nationalist Movement in the 1990s* (Lexington: University of Kentucky Press, 1996).

15 Furthermore, although Turkey-based organizations do not receive much attention in this chapter, it is important to remember that they also constituted vital parts of pro-Kurdish advocacy networks.

16 See United Nations High Commissioner for Refugees, "Basic Facts," http://www.unhcr.ch/cgi-bin/texis/vtx/basics; Roger Zegers de Beijl, International Labor Organization, "Combatting Discrimination against Migrant Workers: International Standards, National Legislation and Voluntary Measures – The Need for a Multi-pronged Strategy," http://www.ilo.org/public/english/protection/migrant/papers/disstrat/index.htm; and the International Labor Organization, http://www.ilo.org/public/english/protection/migrant/about/index.htm, accessed October 2002. Also Myron Weiner, *The Global Migration Crisis: Challenge to States and to Human Rights* (New York: HarperCollins, 1995), 1–20.

migrants worldwide; collectively, workers residing abroad send more than $100,000 million per year back home, with more than 60 percent going to developing countries.[17] Driving this "world in motion" is the restructuring and internationalization of postindustrial global capitalism, revolutions in communication and transportation, rapid population growth, the ever-widening gap between poor and rich countries, and armed conflicts.[18] As Arjun Appadurai writes, "tourists, immigrants, refugees, exiles, guest-workers, and other moving groups and persons constitute an essential feature of the world and appear to affect the politics of and between nations to a hitherto unprecedented degree."[19]

Linking these "moving groups" of exiles and activists abroad with actors back home are transnational networks that send money, people, resources, and ideas back and forth across national boundaries. Within political science, analysts of international relations have focused in particular on a type of network that has come to be known as a "transnational advocacy network" and on how networks like these can empower relatively weak actors in their struggle to reform or revolutionize state policy.[20] Bound together through "shared values, a common discourse, and dense exchanges of information and services,"[21] transnational advocacy networks may include nongovernmental organizations, intergovernmental organizations, parts of states, foundations, the media, academics, and segments of diaspora communities.[22] They tend to form when activists seeking to change state behavior find access to their state blocked and turn to actors outside the target country. In what Margaret Keck and Kathryn Sikkink describe as a "boomerang pattern" of transnational activism, these coalitions or networks pressure other states or an intergovernmental organization to apply pressure to the target country.[23] Because transnational advocacy networks are in and of themselves not powerful, they use information, ideas, and strategies "to alter the information or value contexts within which states make policies."[24]

Most political scientists working on transnational advocacy networks have focused on their use by "principled" actors pursuing "universal" goals such as human rights, bans on land mines, and environmental protection. However, transnational advocacy networks are also commonly used by activists promoting ethnic and particularist agendas. Macedonians in Australia,

[17] On remittances, see Susan F. Martin, "Remittances as a Development Tool," http://usinfo.state.gov/journals/ites/0901/ijee/martin.htm, accessed October 2002.

[18] See, e.g., Benedict Anderson, "Nationalism, Identity, and the World-in-Motion," in Cheah and Robins, eds., *Cosmopolitics*; Basch et al., *Nations Unbound*; Appadurai, "Global Ethnoscapes."

[19] Appadurai, "Global Ethnoscapes," 192.

[20] See, e.g., Keck and Sikkink *Activists beyond Borders*; Risse et al., *Power of Human Rights*; Klotz, *Norms in International Relations*.

[21] Keck and Sikkink, *Activists beyond Borders*, 2.

[22] Ibid., 9.

[23] Ibid., 12–14.

[24] Ibid., 16.

Hmong in America, Cypriots in London, Tamils in Canada, and Palestinians in Tunisia have all formed part of ethnic advocacy networks that have contributed to the redefinition of their peoples' sense of national self, provided critical economic and human resources for mobilization, and helped to reconfigure state-society relations in the societies from which they come.[25] In some cases, moreover, advocacy networks may function dually as promoters of both "universal" causes, such as human rights, and more particularistic national or ethnic causes. As Lisa Hajjar writes of the Palestinian case, for example, human rights activism in the occupied territories during the 1990s did not function as a rejection of nationalist politics but was "drawn upon to advance national goals and secure national rights (foremost Palestinian self-determination)."[26] This blurring of human rights and national goals within transnational networks is a topic left largely unproblematized in the international relations literature,[27] but as the Kurdish and Palestinian cases demonstrate, it may have profound implications for the likelihood of the domestic implementation of human rights norms, as well as the ability of ethnic or national activists to access a variety of legal, economic, and political resources.

The Kurdish Challenge

Once described as a "lost people" of the Middle East,[28] by the late 1990s Kurds had not only become an international cause célèbre but had begun to exercise something like national influence over Kurdish populations within Turkey *and* within international affairs. This development was perceived by

[25] See, e.g., Loring M. Danforth, *The Macedonian Conflict: Ethnic Nationalism in a Transnational World* (Princeton, N.J.: Princeton University Press, 1995); Louisa Schein, "Importing Miao Brethren to Hmong America: A Non-So-Stateless Transnationalism," in Cheah and Robbins, eds., *Cosmopolitics*; Yezid Sayigh, *Armed Struggle and the Search for State: The Palestinian National Movement, 1949–1993* (Oxford: Clarendon, 1997); Fiona B. Adamson and Madeleine Demetriou, "ReMapping the Boundaries of 'State' and 'National Identity': Incorporating Diasporas into IR Theorizing," paper prepared for the 42nd Annual Meeting of the International Studies Association, Chicago, February 20–24, 2001.

[26] Lisa Hajjar, "Human Rights in Israel/Palestine: The History and Politics of a Movement," *Journal of Palestine Studies* 30, no. 4 (Summer 2001): 26.

[27] Keck and Sikkink, who delve further than most into this problem, argue that human rights networks may be distinguished from what they term "solidarity networks" on the basis of "whose rights" are being defended: "although both involve relationships between oppressed peoples and those in a position to support them," solidarity networks promote solidarities of community rather than rights of individuals, they argue. But as the authors acknowledge (but do not further explore), these are ideal types, and "between the two positions are many who see the defense of human rights as the best way to protect the lives of the people whose ideas they defend." See Keck and Sikkink, *Activists beyond Borders*, 92.

[28] See, e.g., F. David Andrews, ed., *The Lost Peoples of the Middle East: Documents of the Struggle for Survival and Independence of the Kurds, Assyrians, and Other Minority Races of the Middle East* (Salisbury, N.C.: Documentary Publications, 1982).

Turkish officials as profoundly worrying and as a potentially serious threat to the country's security. In Turkey, where Kurds constitute anywhere from 12 to 20 percent of the population,[29] concern over potential Kurdish claims to self-determination has encouraged generations of the state and state-sponsored representatives to try to make "being Kurdish" irrelevant and to redefine Kurds as ethnically Turkish. Consequently, officials have pursued a succession of legal and military measures that have curtailed Kurdish citizens' freedom to express elements of a Kurdish identity and seriously punished those who tried. Quite counter to state intent, such tactics helped to produce a sense of exclusion and difference among many (although not all) Kurdish citizens of the Republic,[30] encouraged some to reject the legitimacy of the state's cultural ideals and political institutions, and spawned a host of rebellious organizations and movements. While widely differing in methods and political detail, all pursued the shared mission of reinstating or reinventing "Kurdishness" as a socially and politically meaningful category of belonging.

Although earlier phases of Kurdish contention had already begun to erode the state's discursive authority, it was not until the late 1980s and early 1990s that such challenges began seriously to complicate Turkish internal and external affairs. Beginning in 1994 European and U.S. military aid and loans to Turkey were periodically cut or made conditional on better treatment of the Kurds; Turkey's application to the European Union was repeatedly obstructed in part due to problems with its human rights record and its treatment of Kurds; and in what Ivo Duchacek has described as the "perforation of sovereignty" by subnational authorities,[31] European officials began regularly meeting with Kurdish leaders within and outside Turkey for information on events in Kurdish areas of Turkey, sometimes completely bypassing Turkish officials altogether. Domestically, the challenge was twofold, coming both from guerrilla attacks on Turkish soldiers by the Kurdistan Workers Party (PKK) and from more mainstream activism. In the late 1980s some politicians, writers, and activists began cautiously incorporating a

[29] For a number of reasons, including the fact that Turkish officials have not published census information indicating the ethnic background of Turkey's citizens since 1965, it is unclear exactly what percentage of Turkey's population is Kurdish. For a careful analysis, see Servet Mutlu, "Ethnic Kurds in Turkey: A Demographic Study," *International Journal of Middle East Studies* 28 (1996): 517–541.

[30] For more Turkish state policies toward the Kurds, see Kemal Kirişci and Gareth Winrow, *The Kurdish Question and Turkey: An Example of a Trans-state Ethnic Conflict* (London: Frank Cass, 1997); Henri J. Barkey and Graham E. Fuller, *Turkey's Kurdish Question* (Lanham, Md.: Rowman and Littlefield, 1998); White, *Primitive Rebels*; and McDowall, *A Modern History*.

[31] See Ivo D. Duchacek, "Multicommunal and Bicommunal Polities and Their International Relations," in *Perforated Sovereignties and International Relations: Trans-sovereign Contacts of Subnational Governments*, ed. Ivo D. Duchacek, Daniel Latouche, and Garth Stevenson (New York: Greenwood, 1988), 4–7.

pro-Kurdish discourse into social democratic and human rights platforms;[32] in June of 1990 a dozen members of the Turkish Parliament established a new political party that advocated the extension of Kurdish cultural and political rights through the prism of democratization and human rights;[33] and in 1991 the Turkish Human Rights Association (İnsan Hakları Derneği) announced that it viewed the Kurdish Problem as the most important obstacle to democractization in Turkey.[34] This linkage of Kurdish rights and democracy/human rights was reinforced by the 1991 Gulf War and the creation of Operation Provide Comfort, which created a "safe haven" in Iraq north of the 36th parallel for Kurds seeking protection from Saddam Hussein (thus fulfilling the political goals of some Kurds through humanitarian intervention).

Systematic utilization by Kurds of transnational resources began in the early and mid-1990s, which saw a rapid growth in communication and collaboration among pro-Kurdish actors within Turkey and among human rights organizations, intergovernmental organizations, Kurdish associations, diaspora communities, media, and academics based outside the country. The actors in these networks together came to reframe their cause as a cause of fundamental human rights, and Turkish rejection of their demands as a violation of an international human rights norm. This shifting of the Kurdish agenda from the infinitely more troublesome domain of minority rights and its grafting, as Richard Price calls it,[35] onto the internationally codified discourse of universal human rights opened a large number of legal and political avenues through which advocates might pursue their cause. In particular, Turkey's application for full membership in the European Community in 1987 gave activists new opportunities to apply pressure on Turkey to improve its human rights record and its treatment of Kurds.

Justice Ministry: Kurdish Rights in European Courts

The most explicit coupling of pro-Kurdish politics and human rights norms has taken place through the activities of a transnational legal advocacy network that has come to form an alternative "ministry of justice" for many

[32] For more on the history of human rights organizations in Turkey, see Gottfried Plagemann, "Human Rights Organizations: Defending the Particular or the Universal?," in *Civil Society in the Grip of Nationalism: Studies on Political Culture in Contemporary Turkey*, ed. Stefanos Yerasimos, Gunter Seufert, and Karin Vorhoff (Istanbul: Ergon, 2000), 433–473.

[33] *Halkın Emek Partisi Program* 1990, 18–19. For more on the party and its place in Turkish and pro-Kurdish politics, see Nicole F. Watts, "Allies and Enemies: Pro-Kurdish Parties in Turkish Politics, 1990–94," *International Journal of Middle East Studies* 31 (1999): 631–656.

[34] Personal discussion with officials at the Turkish Human Rights Association, Ankara, September 1998.

[35] Richard Price, "Reversing the Gun Sights: Transnational Civil Society Targets Land Mines," *International* Organization 52 (Summer 1998). Also see Martha Finnemore and Kathryn Sikkink, "International Norm Dynamics and Political Change," *International Organization* 52 (Autumn 1998): 807.

Kurds from Turkey. Extending from Diyarbakir in eastern Turkey to London and Strasburg, this legal network is primarily constituted through the Human Rights Association of Turkey (İnsan Hakları Derneği), the Turkey Human Rights Foundation (Türkiye İnsan Hakları Vakfi), a London-based legal advocacy group called the Kurdish Human Rights Project, and the European Court of Human Rights (ECHR). Working together, these organizations have reshaped legal expectations and practices for Kurds in Turkey and Europe by routinizing the pursuit of justice outside Turkey itself and by helping to change assumptions regarding the kinds of cases that may actually be brought against the Turkish state. A pro-Kurdish agenda has thus been institutionalized legally via the enforcement mechanisms of the European Convention on Human Rights, something that has legally legitimated Kurdish grievances in the international arena and allowed the network to place direct pressure on Turkey to align itself more closely with international human rights norms.

Especially throughout the 1990s, the Kurdish Human Rights Project (KHRP) played a particularly important role within this network in transforming European human rights code into an alternative legal recourse for Kurdish plaintiffs unable or unwilling to find or seek justice in Turkish courts.[36] At the end of the decade, training programs organized by KHRP and other legal groups, along with more relaxed political conditions in eastern Turkey, allowed the Diyarbakir branch of the Human Rights Association in Turkey to begin handling increasing numbers of cases itself, although still relying largely on KHRP assistance for the final submission of cases.[37] KHRP was founded in December of 1992 by Kerim Yıldız, a Kurd from eastern Turkey, and a small group of other human rights and pro-Kurdish activists who reasoned that as Turkey and other states with Kurdish populations had ratified a number of international agreements relating to human rights, "thereby giving their consent to be bound by them," they could be called to account for this treatment at an international level.[38] Although its motto is "working to protect and promote human rights of all persons living in the Kurdish regions" and it has aided individuals of non-Kurdish background (including Turks), KHRP's primary focus, as suggested by its name, is Kurds.[39] Working closely with the Turkish Human Rights Association,

[36] KHRP has done little work on Iraq or Iran because of a lack of legal instruments with which to prosecute cases.

[37] Personal interviews with Osman Baydemir and Reyhan Yalçındağ, Diyarbakir branch of the Human Rights Association, Diyarbakir, July 3, 2002.

[38] KHRP Annual Report 1997, "The Role of the Kurdish Human Rights Project," 4. For many KHRP documents, including this one, see the organization's web site at http://www.khrp.org.

[39] In an interview with the author, KHRP executive director Kerim Yıldız said that the founders of KHRP originally called the organization the Kurdistan Human Rights Project (instead of Kurdish Human Rights Project) better to reflect the group's intent to aid all peoples in geographic Kurdistan. But because the word "Kurdistan" is still something of a taboo in Turkey and thus rarely used in public discourse, "We were told with the word 'Kurdistan'

KHRP lobbies a variety of intergovernmental organizations of which Turkey is a member. It has especially focused its efforts on the European Commission and Court of Human Rights, established in the 1950s as enforcement mechanisms of the Convention for the Protection of Human Rights and Fundamental Freedoms, drawn up by the Council of Europe and ratified by Turkey (an original signatory) in 1954.[40] (The commission and the court were merged to create one new court in November of 1998). Turkey first began recognizing the right of individual petition to the court in 1987 and the jurisdiction of the court on such cases in 1991, thus opening up a legal channel that had formerly been available only to states.

KHRP's ability to frame Kurdish grievances as human rights violations and to channel them into concrete juridical processes has allowed it to situate itself within a broader network of international charities and human rights groups that sustain it financially as well as ideologically. It is primarily staffed and supported by non-Kurds and officially accepts no aid from any individuals or organizations in Kurdish regions of the Middle East, relying instead on financial assistance from a variety of charities and intergovernmental organizations. In 1999 the association received financial assistance from twenty-five organizations including the European Union, the John Merck Fund (U.S.), the Norwegian Bar Association and the Norwegian Human Rights Fund, the Bromley Trust (U.K.), and the World Organisation against

we wouldn't be able to promote the organization in Turkey. So we changed it to 'Kurdish,' but this creates problems because it sounds like we only help Kurds. So although Kurdistan was a problem for us, 'Kurdish' is a problem too" (personal interview with Kerim Yıldız, London, November 15, 1999).

40 The European Council was established in 1949, separate from the European Community, which was not established until 1951. The council was seen as a political body charged with promoting European unity, protecting human rights, and facilitating social and economic progress. Among its most important acts was the creation of the European Convention for the Protection of Human Rights and Fundamental Freedoms (known as the convention), based on the Universal Declaration of Human Rights but including only principles the council believed might be enforceable. To ensure observance, the convention required the creation of the European Commission of Human Rights and the European Court of Human Rights. All plaintiffs to the court were required to first submit their cases to the commission, which would investigate complaints if necessary, reject inadmissible complaints, and attempt to facilitate a friendly settlement if possible. The commission would prepare a report and transfer complaints to the court if necessary. Although fewer than 5 percent of all registered complaints result in a court hearing, the court has an enormous backlog and the average case takes at least five years. In large part due to this, the court and commission were reorganized beginning in 1994 and were merged into one full-time court in November 1998. See *Human Rights: An Agenda for the 21st Century*, ed. Angela Hegarty and Siobhan Leonard (London: Cavendish, 1999), chap. 3; also L. J. Clements, *European Human Rights: Taking a Case under the Convention* (London: Sweet and Maxwell, 1994), 3–4, 12. For a good analysis of Turkey and the ECHR, see Leo Zwaak, "Turkey and the European Convention on Human Rights," in *The Role of the Nation-State in the 21st Century: Human Rights, International Organisations and Foreign Policy, Essays in Honour of Peter Baehr*, ed. Monique Castermans-Holleman, Fried Van Hoof, and Jacqueline Smith (The Hague: Kluwer Law International, 1998), 209–228.

Torture (Switzerland).[41] These funds support nine full-time KHRP employees based in an upscale district of London and a number of projects, including fact-finding missions to eastern Turkey, lawyer training programs, public awareness campaigns in Europe, and, perhaps most important, legal counseling and assistance.

The Justice Ministry and Leverage Politics

Such extensive utilization of available legal and financial resources has allowed KHRP and other members of the network to carry out what Margaret Keck and Kathryn Sikkink call "leverage politics," in which a relatively disadvantaged group allies itself with a more powerful group that can further its goals through issue linkage ("material leverage") or international scrutiny leading to the shaming of the target state ("moral leverage").[42] In 1996 the European Commission received more complaints against Turkey than against any other country; by December of 1998 a quarter of the court's pending applications (1,825 cases out of 7,771) were against Turkey.[43] According to one KHRP official, KHRP was at least peripherally involved in approximately 80 percent of these cases, at least 70 percent of which were Kurdish-related.[44] More precisely, KHRP was the lead agency in prosecuting forty-four of the 360 cases against Turkey that the ECHR had ruled on by July 2002, and in 2001 was involved in 90 percent of the ECHR's fact-finding hearings on Turkey.[45]

ECHR rulings have placed tremendous political, moral, and financial pressure on Turkey, which has responded to the judgments in a decidedly mixed fashion. Turkish officials have frequently grumbled that the court is biased and "misunderstood" political conditions within Turkey, but in certain high-profile cases have publicly upheld its legitimacy (if only for instrumental

41 KHRP Annual Report 1999, "KHRP Funders." Mindful of the import of remaining political neutral, KHRP maintains a wary distance from the PKK and other PKK-dominated Kurdish organizations in England. However, some contact does exist between them. In 1994, for instance, KHRP cosponsored an international conference on northwest Kurdistan with Medico International that "welcomed a statement" prepared for the conference on behalf of PKK leader Abdullah Öcalan. See "Final Resolution: International Conference on North West Kurdistan (South East Turkey)," March 12–13, 1994.

42 Keck and Sikkink, *Activists beyond Borders*, 23–24.

43 Information Document issued by the Registrar of the European Court of Human Rights, "Survey of Activities, 1998" (November–December 1998), 21. Also see Donna Gomien, *Judgments of the European Court of Human Rights: Reference Charts* (Strasbourg: Council of Europe Publishing, 1996), 283–284.

44 Personal interview with KHRP executive director Kerim Yıldız, London, November 15, 1999. Also see European Commission on Human Rights general secretary Hans Christian Krueger, cited in Institut Kurde de Paris, "Update on the State of Affairs in Turkey," no. 20, January 24, 1996, p. 5.

45 Personal correspondence with KHRP Public Relations Officer Angela Debnath, October/November 2002.

reasons). This was perhaps most vividly illustrated by the government's announcement that it would postpone proceedings to execute Kurdish guerrilla leader Abdullah Öcalan until after the ECHR had heard the case. More common, however, has been a quiet failure to comply with the court's verdicts. As of July 2002 the state had paid at least $2.4 million in ECHR fines, but it owed around $20 million,[46] having failed to fully execute payment in ninety cases.[47] Although three reform packages were passed in the spring and summer of 2002 that addressed a wide range of human rights violations cited by the ECHR, among other organizations, Turkish officials had (as of this writing) refused to comply with a number of specific court judgments. Such problems prompted the Commission of European Comunities to write that Turkey's failure to execute judgments of the ECHR remained a "serious problem" as of 2002.[48]

KHRP and Alternative Avenues of Justice

Ceding some rule-making authority to the European court system is a process all states that signed the convention must confront. In the Turkish case, however, well-publicized deficiencies in the Turkish legal system have also permitted the European Court to play an important role in the reconceptualization of institutional justice among ordinary citizens, encouraging them to consider prosecuting the state for certain types of behavior and holding it accountable in ways they would not have done in the past. Organizations such as KHRP and the Human Rights Association have facilitated this by not only channeling grievances but helping to *generate* complaints that might well otherwise have gone publicly unvoiced. This is particularly true for cases originating in Turkey's southeast, where participants in the pro-Kurdish legal network have helped investigate, draft, and prosecute cases of possible violations involving plaintiffs who are not well educated or connected. In *Akduvar v. Turkey*, for instance, filed in May 1993 on behalf of five Kurdish villagers whose homes had been allegedly destroyed by Turkish security forces, Human Rights Association staff conducted an investigation and encouraged the villagers to file a complaint. This was then sent to KHRP, which assigned two legal experts to the case in early 1993 and represented the plaintiffs during European Commission fact-finding delegations sent to Ankara and Diyarbakir. The confused, sometimes fearful, and often contradictory testimonies of the applicants and others involved in the case suggests that the

46 KHRP information sheet, citing the Turkish Justice Ministry. The Justice Minister reportedly stated that the government had, as of July 2002, paid 4 trillion Turkish lira in fines, but because of the dramatic devaluation of the lira it is unclear exactly how much this is in dollars. Using October 2002 conversion figures produces a total of about $2.4 million.

47 Commission of the European Communities, "2002 Regular Report on Turkey's Progress Toward Accession," 26.

48 Ibid.

villagers would have been highly unlikely, left to their own devices, to have organized and conveyed such an appeal.[49]

Although the European Convention requires nationals to exhaust domestic remedies before turning to the Court, KHRP and the Human Rights Association's publicization of ECHR rulings against Turkey and their ability to make the ECHR more accessible has arguably helped create a two-level justice system in which Kurdish-origin citizens of Turkey seek to bypass the Turkish judicial system as much as possible. A substantial number of Kurdish plaintiffs have seen their cases dismissed because the court or commission ruled they had not exhausted domestic remedies.[50] But the court has also sidestepped this requirement in a number of prominent cases, especially those concerning Turkey's State Security Courts, arguing that the Turkish court was not capable of delivering impartial verdicts.[51] Emphasizing the futility of working within Turkey itself, KHRP wrote after one case (*Akduvar v. Turkey*) that in "the absence of effective remedies in Turkey, the European Convention is the only mechanism available to victims of village destructions to seek legal redress."[52]

"Culture Ministry": Preserving and Promoting Kurds as Nation

Virtual Kurdistan West as a distinct set of practices and expectations has also taken shape culturally through the determined efforts of thick networks of associations I group together here as a "culture ministry." This "ministry" has included, at any one time, six daily newspapers published

49 The case finally came to court in September 1996, at which time the court ruled against Turkey on several articles of the European Convention. See the Kurdish Human Rights Project, *Akduvar v. Turkey: The Story of Kurdish Villagers Seeking Justice in Europe* (London: KHRP, October 1996).

50 As occurred, for instance, in *Aytekin v. Turkey*, a KHRP-assisted case involving an accusation of murder by gendarmes.

51 For a critical evaluation of the question of "domestic remedy" and the Turkish case, see Oren Gross and Fionnuala Ni Aolain, "To Know Where We Are Going, We Need to Know Where We Are: Revisting States of Emergency," in Hegarty and Leonard, eds., *Human Rights*, 79–114; and Zwaak, "Turkey and the European Convention." One KHRP lawyer interviewed by the author said that by 1999 plaintiffs from Turkey only needed to file a complaint with their local public prosecutor and then they could turn to the ECHR, because ECHR justices had in effect decided that no effective domestic remedy existed in Turkey.

52 KHRP, *Akduvar v. Turkey*, 23–24. This reliance on an external system of law has worried both some activists and Turkish officials. As Bakır Cağlar, a former Turkish state defendant at the European Commission, told a Turkish newsmagazine: "There is a common peculiarity in the Southeast cases, which are the most numerous class of cases being submitted today. Virtually without exception, appeals of this type are made without first exhausting national appeals.... Two English lawyers whom I faced in Southeast cases... That bothers me too. Of course there is a human rights tragedy in Turkey's Southeast, a crisis. But when instead of a Turkish lawyer describing this tragedy in his own words in Strasbourg, two English lawyers cry out – that bothers me too as a Turkish lawyer. Let us deal with it, because this is our problem, the problem of the individuals who live here." Interview with Bakır Çağlar, "Türkiye'nin etrafina duvarlar örülecektir!," *Nokta*, January 1–7, 1995, p. 21.

in Kurdish, Turkish, and other languages; at least twenty-five Kurdish publishing houses based in Istanbul, Sweden, Switzerland and elsewhere; and more than fifty specifically Kurdish organizations that arrange street festivals, public lectures, musical performances, aid programs, and language classes. In the tradition of nation-building states, many of these associations have sought to transform a variety of "diversified, locality-tied," and largely illiterate cultures or traditions, in the words of Ernest Gellner, into a "great or high (literate, training-sustained) culture."[53] More specifically, they have sought to make speaking, reading, and hearing Kurdish (especially the Kurdish dialect of Kurmanji) normative and to reconstruct and to merge various Kurdish identities into one distinct tradition. In so doing, they have directly challenged Turkish state ideology promoting a Turkish national identity for all citizens, Kurdish-origin or otherwise. Although to a lesser extent than pro-Kurdish legal advocacy, Kurdish cultural claims as advanced by these organizations have also sometimes been framed by human rights discourse, expanding their scope of support. I examine the activities and role of this "culture ministry" through the prism of two particularly influential institutions: the Institut Kurde de Paris (the Kurdish Institute of Paris), founded in 1983, and MED-TV, a Kurdish-language satellite station that broadcast from London across Europe and into Turkey between 1995 and early 1999. Both demonstrate how nonstate institutions drawing on international and particularist norms may emulate a state's ability to define and to perpetuate new boundaries of belonging.

The Institut Kurde de Paris

Kurdish cultural and political organizations have been active in Europe at least since the late 1940s, when the Centre d'Études Kurdes was established in Paris after the French withdrawal from Syria. Kurdish organizational efforts expanded gradually throughout the 1960s and 1970s but were given a substantial boost in 1981 when the French socialists came to power, bringing with them a number of French intellectuals who had supported earlier Kurdish activism. In 1983, after two years of discussion and planning, a group of Kurdish and European activists founded the Institut Kurde de Paris in order to maintain "in the Kurdish community a knowledge of its language, its history and its cultural heritage," to better integrate them into their new countries, and to make "the Kurds, their culture, their country and their present situation known to the general public."[54] Highlighting the role non-Kurdish actors played in encouraging him to reconceptualize Kurdish

[53] Ernest Gellner, *Nations and Nationalism* (Ithaca, N.Y.: Cornell University Press, 1983), 37 and 38.

[54] Institut Kurde de Paris (IKP), "What Is the Kurdish Institute?," http://www.institutkurde.org, accessed July 1999. The institute's web site, like that of KHRP, offers an extensive "library" of information concerning the organization's history and activities.

culture as something that actively needed "saving," Kendal Nezan,[55] one of the institute's founders and its current president, stated:

> As you know, intellectuals' involvement in social issues and support for social struggle is an old and powerful tradition in France. Along with my personal history, this tradition and, especially, the example of some great French thinkers that I had the privilege of being personally acquainted with, inspired me to make some modest contribution to the Kurdish people and culture, along with the scientific and professional work I was doing.[56]

By the early 1990s the institute had become a center of Kurdish scholarly, cultural, social, and political life, with regular visitors from around the world. One of the oldest Kurdish cultural associations in Europe and one of its most important, its activities range from organizing aid to Iraqi Kurdish farmers to high-profile art exhibitions attended by French dignitaries. It also hosts regular literary and music evenings, human rights briefings, and lectures by international scholars, authors, and activists. Its library houses one of the best collections of Kurdish-related materials in the world and is utilized by a wide array of researchers.

Like Kurdish-language newspapers and publishing houses, the institute has played an important role in defining and consolidating notions of "Kurdish culture" and "the Kurdish experience." In particular, members of the institute have contributed to the development of formal Kurmanji-Kurdish and the furthering of its transformation from a colloquial and oral medium to a written language employed by intellectuals. In partnership with the French Freedom Foundation, the Norwegian Labour Movement, and UNESCO, the institute published a series of school textbooks in Kurdish for primary and secondary schools that were distributed in Iraqi Kurdistan with the help of the local Kurdish authorities. Its twice-yearly linguistic magazine *Kurmancî* publicizes the work of the institute's linguistic seminars and publishes word lists in Kurdish, English, French, and Turkish. The institute has also worked to transform the elusive geography of Kurdistan into a concrete and codified place, publishing maps of Kurdistan and the world, with Kurdish place names (many of which had been changed by Turkish and Iraqi authorities).[57]

As with KHRP, the Kurdish Institute often frames its broader appeals for support within a human rights framework, and publicizing human rights violations in Kurdish areas is a key part of its mission. It provided the first Kurdish-language translation of the Universal Declaration of Human Rights and in 1992 distributed 50,000 copies in Iraqi Kurdistan with the aid of

[55] Originally from Diyarbakir in eastern Turkey, Nezan moved to Paris in 1968 for his university studies and in 1974 completed a doctorate in nuclear physics at Paris University.

[56] Written interview with Kendal Nezan by Rafet Ballı, November 3, 1989, published in Rafet Ballı, *Kürt Dosyası* (Istanbul: Cem Yayınevi, 1991), 589.

[57] IKP, "Publishing," http://www.institutkurde.org, accessed July 1999.

the Kurdish Organisation for Human Rights, itself created through support from the institute. Beginning in 1989 it organized a series of high-profile conferences on human rights and the Kurds, attended by Nobel Peace Prize winners and prominent human rights campaigners. The first such conference received several days' worth of coverage in major newspapers around the world, highlighting the plight of Kurds everywhere and associating the Kurdish movement with a broader human rights agenda.[58]

The institute itself has been broadly supported not only by members of the Kurdish diaspora community but by a variety of European non- and intergovernmental organizations and individual states. In particular, the institute maintains strong ties to the French government. After ten years as a nonprofit association, the institute became a French "foundation of recognized public benefit" in 1993, and four members of its fifteen-person board of directors are representatives of the French Ministries of Culture and the Interior.[59] A French government program to bring Kurdish students to study in France is also carried out in coordination with the institute.[60] Although the institute now owns its own building in central Paris and possesses a financial endowment that supports some of its activities, it receives grants from the French Social Action Fund and Ministry of Culture, from the French Freedom Foundation, and from a vareity of other European sources, including the European Union, the Norwegian Foreign Ministry, and the Swedish Agency for International Development.[61] It also boasts international sponsorship by a long list of prominent writers, politicians, and human rights activists, including several Nobel Peace Prize winners.

MED-TV

Not until 1995, however, were the kinds of culture-promoting activities carried out by the Kurdish Institute made easily accessible to the general public and, most importantly, to multiple levels of Kurdish society. In May of that year a group of Kurdish and human rights activists founded MED-TV,[62] the world's first international Kurdish-language satellite television channel. Reaching as many as 16 million viewers throughout Europe, the Middle East,

[58] Paris Kurdish Institute, *Uluslararası Paris Kürt Konferansı, 14–15 Ekim 1989: Kürtler, İnsan Hakları ve Kültürel Kimlik* (Istanbul: Doz Yayınları, 1992).

[59] Prior to 1999 two of the board's directors were French government representatives, but the number was increased in 1999 to maintain and strengthen French governmental involvement in the institute (personal interviews with institute founders Joyce Blau, October 30, 1999, and Kendal Nezan, November 1999, Paris).

[60] Personal interview with IKP President Kendal Nezan, Paris, November 1999.

[61] IKP, "Financing," http://www.institutkurde.org, accessed July 1999. The institute also states that it accepts no funding from "states that oppress their Kurdish population" or from "any non-democratic state."

[62] The station took its name from the ancient Medes, from whom many Kurds trace direct lineage.

North Africa, and the Commonwealth of Independent States, analysts and journalists swiftly dubbed it a "nation in the sky," heralding its potential for Kurdish cultural and political development. One Kurdish specialist wrote of MED-TV:

> To many Kurds, MED-TV seems to be the public sphere denied the Kurds in their homeland, on the earth. It is a political space in the heavens. For the first time in history, Kurds from all parts of Kurdistan debate, free of state repression, the fate of their people.[63]

Like the Kurdish Institute, MED-TV was grounded in European spaces, rules, and norms. It was licensed by Britain's Independent Television Commission, broadcast and directed from London, and had main studios in Brussels and additional production facilities in Cologne, Stockholm, and Moscow. It was financed through Kurdish trusts, businesses, and donations from Kurds in Europe.[64] Its founders envisioned it as a kind of Kurdish version of the BBC,[65] and it was defended and sometimes directly aided by European human rights organizations, members of parliament, and the leftist press. The station's directors took care to characterize it as part of marginalized people's efforts to promote individual freedom and human rights, and it was perceived by many leftist and human rights observers as taking a courageous stand against censorship, something that garnered it technical and ideological support.[66] At least one of the station's founding members worked closely with the human rights organization Index on Censorship.[67]

The existence of an explicitly Kurdish station accessible (at least in theory) to Kurds scattered throughout Virtual Kurdistan West dramatically furthered earlier efforts by the institute and other organizations to reconstruct a new and modern vision of what it meant to be Kurdish. This, indeed, was what station founders consciously sought: to "help forge an identity for the Kurdish people," as station director Hikmet Tabak told an interviewer,[68]

63 Amir Hassanpour, "A Stateless Nation's Quest for Sovereignty in the Sky," paper presented at the Freie Universitat Berlin, November 7, 1995, available at a useful Kurdish web site, http://www.kurdweb.humanrights.de, accessed July 1999. Hassanpour's paper provides a good if sympathetic analysis of early MED-TV.

64 MED-TV, "Finances," http://www.ib.be/med, accessed July 1999. The station was accused by authorities in Belgium of extorting money from Kurdish businesses. These charges were not substantiated.

65 See Gill Newsham, "Med TV License Revoked – Station Silenced," One World News Service, May 7, 1999, available at htttp://www.oneworld.org/news/reports99/medtv.html, accessed July 1999.

66 These included *The Guardian* newspaper and the anticensorship organization Article 19, for instance.

67 See, e.g., Newsham, "Med TV License Revoked." Newsham, a filmmaker and journalist, had worked in Kurdish northern Iraq in 1994 and helped found MED-TV after she returned to Britain. She also worked with Index on Censorship and other human rights organizations.

68 Gene Mater, "Satellite Channel Links Dispossessed Kurds," Freedom Forum Online, http://www/freedomforum.org/international/1998/12/lkurds.asp, accessed July 1999.

elsewhere calling MED-TV "cultural sustenance for Kurds everywhere."[69] And despite insistent and repeated efforts by Turkish authorities to prevent its transmissions by legal and physical means, MED-TV swiftly gained a wide audience among Kurdish communities in Europe and eastern Turkey, where satellite dishes now dot the landscape. Even in the Turkish capital of Ankara, the embattled pro-Kurdish party, the Halkın Demokrasi Partisi, tuned in regularly, risking official ire. In part contributing to its success, MED-TV – unlike most Kurdish organizations – openly recognized Kurdish cultural and linguistic diversity, although it prioritized Kurmanji in its programming. Kurdish specialist Amir Hassanpour, who described the station as a "language academy," argues that even by late 1995 it had already "enhanced the status of the [Kurmanji] dialect."[70] At its height in 1997 and 1998 the station broadcast eighteen hours a day, focusing in particular on news programs in Kurmanji, Turkish, Sorani, and, to a lesser extent, Arabic and Zaza. Also unlike many organizations in Virtual Kurdistan West, MED-TV celebrated diverse Kurdish religious traditions, offering programs and festival coverage for Muslim Sunnis as well as Alevis, Yezidis, and Christians. These programs provided concrete normative models for Kurdish communities scattered in diverse environments. As one Kurdish immigrant to London told a reporter:

> Every family has got it or watches it. It's historical. The first time I watched it, the feeling was amazing. It was the first time the Kurds had been together – you could see the news in your own language; listen to Kurdish music; and see your own, beautiful countryside.[71]

"Foreign Affairs Ministry": Kurdish Politics, Parliaments, and Diplomacy

In addition to their promotion of Kurdish culture, both MED-TV and the Kurdish Institute performed a political function that helped to produce a kind of Kurdish "foreign affairs ministry" in which pro-Kurdish advocates acquired the characteristics and a status approximating that of diplomats, parliamentarians, and government officials. Other "members" of this political network have included the self-styled Kurdish Parliament in Exile/Kurdistan National Congress, originally based in The Hague; the Kurdistan Workers Party (PKK), which has been particularly active in Germany;[72] and other

69 Hikmet Tabak, February 1999, http://www.oneworld.org/wacc/action/213/tabak.htm, accessed July 1999. For more on Tabak and MED-TV, see Stephen Kinzer, "Only Kurdish TV Station May Be Shut Down," *New York Times*, April 5, 1999.

70 Hassanpour, "A Stateless Nation's Quest for Sovereignty in the Sky."

71 Quoted in Nick Ryan, "Scattered Nation United By Satellite TV Broadcasting," *Daily Telegraph*, March 4, 1999.

72 At its eighth congress in April 2002 the PKK officially disbanded and was replaced by a new political organization, the Kurdistan Freedom and Democracy Congress (KADEK). The move was perceived as cosmetic by many in Turkey.

pro-Kurdish organizations working in Europe and Turkey. Collectively, they have institutionalized a series of practices – conducting politics in the Kurdish language, convening parliaments, establishing "foreign" relations with governments, for instance – that reinforce Kurdish identity as a politically relevant marker. Such organizations have also provided pro-Kurdish activists, especially those in Europe, with a set of representative political institutions alternative to those of Turkey.

"Enemy State": Ethnic Kurdish Politics in Virtual Kurdistan West

While significant Kurdish political organizations do exist outside the purview of the PKK, especially in Germany,[73] pro-Kurdish political networks have been dominated by the group, especially its propaganda arm, ERNK (the largest group represented in the Parliament in Exile),[74] and its emphasis has tended to gravitate away from reforming Turkish state agencies and toward a normative treatment of Turkey as an "enemy." This position has been adopted by many other pro-Kurdish organizations with high visibility in Europe, contributing to a solidifying of boundaries between "them" (Turks and the Turkish state) and "us" (Kurds). This has made it increasingly complicated for pro-Kurdish activists based in Turkey to work in Europe as well. Despite its claim to adhere to the guidelines on political objectivity and impartiality required by the Independent Television Commission, MED-TV itself was from the outset openly supportive of the PKK, rarely aired other Kurdish political perspectives, and soon became a regular outlet for sympathetic intervies with PKK leader Abdullah Öcalan.[75] Its license was revoked under heavy pressure from the Turkish government in April 1999 after several supporters of Öcalan appeared on the station urging Kurds to attack Turkish targets in retaliation for his capture. Nonetheless, new satellite Kurdish stations soon began broadcasting from England, and then from France, taking care not to repeat what MED-TV directors concede were some genuinely poor broadcasting decisions.[76]

[73] One of the most important (among Turkish-Kurdish groups) is Kemal Burkay's Kurdistan Socialist Party, based in Germany. His party rejects armed struggle and has long criticized the PKK. For more information, see http://members.aol.com/PSKKurd and http://www.komkar.org.

[74] It remains to be seen how influential the reformed PKK, or KADEK, will continue to be.

[75] In 1998 the station was fined £90,000 by ITC for three "serious" breaches of its impartiality agreement; its offenses included a program wholly devoted to covering a PKK political rally with "no balancing material" or context and a news item in which a journalist described members of the Iraqi Kurdistan Democratic Party (longtime foes of the PKK) as "treacherous and murderous." ITC Press Release, "ITC Fines Satellite Channel £90,000," February 2, 1998.

[76] Ian Black, "Turks Want 'Pro-Kurd' TV Censored by Britain," *The Guardian*, June 21, 1999. On recognition of "mistake," also see Kinzer, "Only Kurdish TV Station," and Newsham, "Med TV License." Another Kurdish satellite station, Medya TV, also began broadcasting from Paris free of control of the ITC.

MED-TV's stance both reinforced and reflected popular opinion in some Kurdish diaspora communities within Europe. Approximately 850,000 Kurds live in Western Europe, about 500,000 in Germany alone, with about 85 percent of this latter population coming from Turkey.[77] Some came with the Turkish guestworker community in the 1960s, but their numbers have been supplemented in recent years by political and economic refugees arriving by the boatload in Italy and Greece and then traveling north to Germany, Switzerland, and elsewhere. Disoriented and often bitter, many refugees have become active in pro-Kurdish politics and especially in the PKK,[78] providing it with valuable fiancial and human resources.[79] In particular, the PKK's ability to mobilize community support at critical moments has allowed it to mount mass demonstrations against Turkey and to attract significant media attention.

Foreign Diplomacy

Ground-level Kurdish political activism in Europe has been supplemented by a "high politics" that has permitted some Kurdish activists to gain extensive practice in diplomacy. As the Kurdish Institute's Kendal Nezan remembers, Kurdish activists' first diplomatic achievements came in 1981 when he and an Iranian Kurdish dissident were officially received by the Austrian chancellor, then by Swedish Premier Olaf Palme, and then by the foreign ministers of several other European countries. "Each time," Nezan said many years later, "we exposed the Kurdish question as a whole, and formulated the demand for regional autonomy for the Kurds within the borders of the existing state, as part of the process of their democratization. This demand seemed realistic and modest to those to whom we spoke."[80] Soft-spoken, multilingual, and highly educated, Nezan has in fact become one of the Kurdish movement's

77 Institut Kurde de Paris, "The Kurdish Diaspora," http://www.institutkurde.org/homea.htm, accessed July 1999. For more on the demographics and settlement patterns of Kurds and Turks in Europe, see Jorgen Nielsen, *Muslims in Western Europe*, 2nd ed. (Edinburgh: Edinburgh University Press, 1995), esp. 27–31.

78 For more on the role of the PKK in Kurdish diaspora communities in Europe, see Osten Wahlbeck, "Transnationalism and Diasporas: The Kurdish Example," paper presented at the International Sociological Association XIV World Congress of Sociology, July 26–August 1, 1998, Montreal, 11. Also Osten Wahlbeck, *Kurdish Diasporas: A Comparative Study of Kurdish Refugee Communities* (New York: St. Martin's Press, 1999).

79 It is unclear how much money is given to the PKK voluntarily and how much through coercion. In January 1994 a London police team was established specifically to investigate allegations of extortion in the "Turkish" community of northeast London, where complaints of racketeering, shooting, fire-bombings, and even murder were frequent. Many police and members of the community (including Kurds) blamed the PKK and accused it of extortion. See Duncan Campbell, "War on the Streets of London: Crime in the Community," *The Guardian*, April 29, 1994 (Guardian 2 supplement), 1–3.

80 Conference speech given by Kendal Nezan at "The Kurds: Search for Identity," April 17–18, 2000, American University, Washington, D.C.

preeminent ambassadors in Europe. He and other institute officials are regular visitors to Strasbourg and Brussels, where they are often consulted prior to important European Parliament and Council votes concerning Turkey.[81] Nezan has often served as the Kurdish counterpart in European public interviews with Turkish officials: In July 1993, for instance, he appeared on French TV's Channel 4 to discuss Kurdish rights with Turkish President Süleyman Demirel,[82] suggesting a symbolically similar status.

The Kurdish Parliament in Exile, which reorganized itself as the Kurdistan National Congress (KNC) in May 1999, also played an active role in constructing explicitly Kurdish representation at the international level. Established on April 12, 1995, in an inauguration ceremony in The Hague, the Parliament claimed to represent all Kurds in Turkey, Iraq, Iran, and Syria, but most of its representatives came from Turkey. It consisted of sixty-five members elected or delegated from areas outside Kurdish "home" countries and was dominated by the PKK.[83] PKK chairman Abdullah Öcalan was the Parliament's honorary chairman, and the Parliament's officials openly stated that they viewed the PKK as a Kurdish liberation organization, "what the FLN was for the Algerians and the ANC for South Africans."[84] Much to official Turkish dismay, the Parliament in Exile and its successor the KNC met regularly with parliamentarians around Europe, forging ties with officials in England, Poland, Italy, and Spain.[85] They also directly disrupted Turkish-European relations: After the Parliament first met in the Hague, Turkey suspended diplomatic relations with the Netherlands, and after a Parliament meeting in Rome in September 1998 Turkey recalled its ambassador, straining relations that would be put to the test later in the year when Abdullah Öcalan arrived in Rome asking for political asylum. Such routinization of a Kurdish political presence in European public spaces helps to elevate the status of Kurdish-based cultural and political claims, as well as to allow pro-Kurdish activists to participate in information politics,[86] serving as alternate sources of information to European officials.

[81] A sampling of these meetings includes a hearing on September 1992 with the Council of Europe on the "human rights situation in Kurdistan"; a June 1993 trip to Brussels to speak to the Belgian Parliament on the human rights situation in Kurdistan; a June 1994 visit to Oslo to participate in a conference in the Norwegian Parliament on the Human Rights situation in Turkey, followed by meetings with NGOs and the media; and a December 1995 trip to Strasbourg for a hearing before the European Parliament concerning Kurds in Turkey "on the eve of the vote on ratification of the Customs Union" between the EU and Turkey. See IKP, "Cultural Activities, 1991–1998."

[82] *Cumhuriyet* newspaper, July 14, 1993.

[83] Chris Kutschera, "Parliament or Propaganda Ploy?," *The Middle East*, June 1995, pp. 11–12.

[84] "A Few Facts about the Parliament of Kurdistan in Exile," http://www.ariga.com/peacebiz/peacelnk/kurd.htm, accessed July 1999.

[85] "Kurdish Parliamentary Delegation Visits Poland," Polish Press Agency, April 25, 1999.

[86] On the role of information politics, see Keck and Sikkink, *Activists beyond Borders*, 18–22.

The extent to which a pro-Kurdish political position had become normalized within Europe was exemplified by a campaign in 1994 and 1995 to promote Turkish-Kurdish parliamentarian Leyla Zana as an international peace symbol. Zana, the first openly Kurdish woman ever elected to the Turkish Parliament, was imprisoned for alleged "separatist activity" in 1994 along with half a dozen other Kurdish deputies.[87] In her early thirties at the time, she became a symbol of the Kurdish cause in Turkey, and after rallying by the institute and other pro-Kurdish organizations, she received a Raftos Prize for Human Rights in Bergen, Norway, in late 1994; a Sakharov Prize for Human Rights in January 1996 from the European Parliament; and a Danish Rose Prize for Peace and Human rights in February 1996. In 1995 she was also nominated for a Nobel Peace Prize and was rumored to be among the five finalists.[88] Turkish authorities fought hard to prevent Zana's nomination for the Nobel Peace Prize and chose not to shorten her jail sentence when it came up for appeal in 1998, prompting an outraged response from the European Parliament.[89] But they could not prevent the international community from lauding her.

Apo Goes to Rome: Abdullah Öcalan in Virtual Kurdistan West

The struggle for legitimacy between Turkey and pro-Kurdish political activists crystallized in late 1998 when PKK chairman Abdullah Öcalan (sometimes known as "Apo") arrived in Rome seeking political asylum. Most Turks assumed he would be promptly extradited to Turkey. Instead, Italian authorities took him to a well-protected villa in Rome and debated whether to give him asylum. Both Turkish officials and the Turkish public were outraged, and anti-Italian sentiment swept the country, with huge demonstrations and attacks on Italian embassies and business, boycotts of Italian goods, and diplomatic recriminations. In Europe, thousands of Kurds crossed into Italy to hold widely covered demonstrations in support of Öcalan, staging what observers agreed was an impressive display of organizational coordination that galvanized media coverage around the world. While politicians talked, Öcalan and his supporters turned to the kinds of institutions that

[87] Zana was sentenced to fifteen years in jail in December 1994 for allegedly disseminating separatist propaganda and aiding Kurdish separatists. International observers agreed the trial and its "evidence" were seriously flawed. Zana was one of seven Kurdish members of parliament given sentences ranging from three and a half years to fifteen years. She had demonstrated her commitment to expanding Kurdish rights in Turkey by publicly challenging official Turkish policies within Turkey and in international arenas, but although clearly courageous, she was a fledgling politician with only a brief history of activism, and the European selection of her as a recipient of a number of major peace awards was in no way an obvious choice.

[88] IKP, "Cultural Activities, 1991–1998." Also see Reuters, "Controversy Surrounds Kurdish MP's Sakharov Award," January 17, 1996, and the American Kurdish Information Network press release, "Remembering Leyla Zana," December 5, 1996.

[89] Bulletin of the European Union, "Human Rights," October 1998.

had supported pro-Kurdish politics in the past, and many members of the Council of Europe and the European Parliament proposed that he be "tried" at an international Kurdish conference or tribunal.

But after two months Öcalan was forced to leave Italy to look for asylum elsewhere: Italian authorities chose not to extradite him, but neither did they want to keep him. In February 1999 Öcalan was caught by Turkish commandos while leaving the Greek embassy in Kenya and forcibly returned to Turkey.[90] That Öcalan arrived in Rome at all, that European authorities refused to send him to Turkey, and that they took months to decide whether he should be treated as a "terrorist" or "president" indicated to what degree Kurdish national claims, even those pursued through violence, had been legitimized internationally. Turkish authorities simply were not able to convince Europe that this was a "domestic" matter. However, the fact that pro-Kurdish advocates[91] were ultimately unable to engineer Öcalan's reconstruction as an diplomat and ensure his safety (at least in the short term) indicated the extent to which they were still reliant on their relations with non-Kurdish governments and intergovernmental organizations, which in this case eventually chose not to keep Öcalan in Europe. The "real" state of Turkey, backed by the United States, was still sufficiently persuasive that Italian authorities could not find it in their interests to keep him.

Conclusions

Examining the institutionalization of what I here call "Virtual Kurdistan West" suggests some of the specific means by which relatively disadvantaged ethnic activists may construct a visible socio-political "territory" within which their representatives carry out state-like functions. Often framing their claims in terms of human rights, pro-Kurdish activists working across national borders constructed legal, cultural, and political advocacy networks and institutionalized a new norm of Kurdish national rights within governments, intergovernmental organizations, and nongovernmental organizations in Europe. Cooperation between Kurdish and non-Kurdish actors provided Kurds who perceived of themselves as deprived of a state of their own with concrete resources with which to structure an alternative political configuration. "Kurdishness" was thus reinvented as not merely an ethnic marker but as a politically relevant community, adding a new actor to what Susanne Hoeber Rudolph has called a transnational universe of "transparent

90 Öcalan was tried by a Turkish court in June 1999 and sentenced to death. In October 2002 his sentence was commuted to life imprisonment by the Turkish State Security Court, as part of a package of reforms aimed at meeting criteria for EU entry.

91 While most prominent Kurdish activists took the opportunity to meet with Öcalan while he was in Rome, not all lobbied on his behalf. Among those organizations that chose not to use its influence to seek asylum for Öcalan in Europe was the Paris Kurdish Institute.

plastic overlays, alternative meaning systems superimposed upon the meaning system of political maps."[92]

Such "alternative meaning systems" do more than "overlay" actual places such as Turkey. They may also significantly redefine the terms of interaction between citizens and their states. On the one hand, they may empower groups such as the Kurds by offering them legal and political tools with which to exert leverage on states. On the other hand, they may also create more firmly demarcated lines of exclusion between states and social groups by formalizing and publicizing difference. Because the central logic of Virtual Kurdistan West (Kurdish rights) ran counter to that of the Turkish state (Turkish nationalism) and because many of the political and cultural institutions within each were not mutually recognized as legitimate, the maintenance of dual "citizenship" in both Turkey and Virtual Kurdistan West has become increasingly difficult. Visions of specifically Kurdish language, music, and "countryside" have often been crafted *against* what is perceived as being Turkish; as one Kurdish immigrant in London told a reporter: "I do not mean to say that Turkish advocates are bad or don't want to help. It is just that they are of the very culture that Kurds came here to escape."[93] Alternative political norms established and maintained by pro-Kurdish activists in Europe have posed particular problems for Kurdish and human rights advocates operating within Turkey: Not only are activists in Europe in closer contact with the PKK/KADEK than in Turkey, but their language is crafted for "domestic" political consumption in Virtual Kurdistan West and may constitute legal treason in Turkey.[94] While the construction of Virtual Kurdistan West has thus offered some Kurds new opportunities for social and political belonging, it has thus also contributed to a sense of alienation among many who still seek to make Turkey their home.

Interaction between transnational advocacy communities such as Virtual Kurdistan West and the political map of Europe also affects the way belonging is ascribed to states. By formulating and recognizing social and political conduct that was identified as specifically "Kurdish," nonstate and state actors in Virtual Kurdistan West brought into question the Turkish state's sovereign rights to hold its citizens accountable to its own laws and institutions. In other words, in matters involving ethnic Kurds, Virtual Kurdistan West has sometimes been accorded more legitimacy than the Turkish state

92 Susanne Hoeber Rudolph, "Introduction: Religion, States, and Transnational Civil Society," in Susanne Hoeber Rudolph and James Piscatori, eds., *Transnational Religion and Fading States* (Boulder, Colo.: Westview, 1997), 10–12.

93 Mark Gould, "Red Crescent Comes to Aid of Kurdish Refugees in Britain," *The Independent*, November 1, 1998, p. 8.

94 A 1994 Turkish court indictment accusing seven pro-Kurdish deputies of treason, for instance, cited numerous instances of pro-Kurdish activity in transnational space as "evidence" of PKK sympathies; among these "treasonous" activities were deputies' meetings with alleged PKK representatives at the Kurdish Institute in Paris.

itself. Because Turkish state officials have sought to suppress the development of a Kurdish ethnic movement at the same time as they have sought closer relations with Europe, this recognition of "Kurdish rights" translated into concrete diplomatic problems. For nearly a decade the European Union (EU) used Turkey's human rights record and, more specifically, its treatment of Kurds as one of its primary rationales for preventing Turkey from becoming an official EU candidate. Turkey's treatment of Kurds also cost it loans, aid, and military equipment. When it finally accepted Turkey as an official EU candidate at Helsinki in December 1999, European lawmakers stated they would not begin negotiations until Turkey had improved its human rights record, particularly its treatment of minorities.

Nonetheless, just as the Turkish state found itself vulnerable to alternative communities of belonging, so has the Kurdish "virtual state." Actors within Virtual Kurdistan West, with their emphasis on Kurmanji and "citizen Kurd," have defined themselves against Turkey. But other groups whom its advocates seek to define as Kurdish – Zazas, Alevis, and others – have also begun redefining themselves against *it*. The transformation of such "subgroups" into politically active, collective actors may also be viewed as evidence of the success of Virtual Kurdistan West, for it is when ethnicity appears monolithically defined from above that some groups will most vehemently seek to assert themselves. Although it functions as a "national" entity in the international arena, Virtual Kurdistan West is thus, like the Turkish state, merely one participant in a fray of ideological competitors, and its activists must contend with many other collectivities seeking the right to establish their own internal norms and external boundaries.

PART IV

INSCRIBING MEMBERSHIP AND CONTESTING MEMBERSHIP IN THE NATION

7

Challenging Boundaries and Belongings

"Mixed Blood" Allotment Disputes at the Turn of the Twentieth Century

Lauren Basson

Introduction

In 1890, Jane Waldron, a woman of American Indian and European descent, asserted that as an Indian head of family, she was eligible for a full allotment of land that had previously formed part of the Great Sioux Reservation. Her claim initiated a local, legal dispute that quickly escalated into a national debate about land allotment policies conducted at the highest levels of the U.S. government. Black Tomahawk, a "full blood" Indian, contested Waldron's claim. His lawyer argued that Waldron was not an Indian but a white woman, on the basis of the common law of paternal descent. In the initial decision in the case, the Secretary of the Interior accepted the latter position and ruled that Waldron was not an Indian and, therefore, ineligible for an allotment. This decision met with immediate opposition because it implied that thousands of indigenous people of American Indian and European descent, commonly referred to as "mixed bloods," who had signed Indian treaties with the U.S. government, were not Indians either and, therefore, may not have been eligible signatories. The Secretary's decision thus had the potential to threaten the validity of many treaties concluded with Indian tribes, and it never achieved the status of legal precedent.[1]

In 1905, fifteen years after the dispute began, a district court judge in South Dakota reversed the initial decision and asserted that Waldron was an Indian and, therefore, was eligible for the contested allotment. According to him, the decision about whether someone is Indian should be based not on common law but on "the laws or usages of the tribe."[2]

The lengthy, complex dispute concerning Waldron's allotment claim and other contested "mixed blood" allotment cases at the turn of the twentieth

[1] See U.S. Senate Ex. Doc. No. 59, 1894.

[2] See *Waldron v. United States et al.*, 1905, p. 413.

century shed important light on the ways in which people of so-called mixed descent challenged the boundaries of both the state and the nation. As responses to the first decision in the Waldron case made clear, U.S. government authorities had a clear stake in defining "mixed bloods" as Indians in order to protect the expanded territorial boundaries of the U.S. state that resulted from treaties with Indian tribes. In this sense, the very definition of the U.S. state depended on a system of racial classification that clearly distinguished Indians from whites and applied different policies to members of these groups on the basis of their racial status. To maintain this system, U.S. officials adopted new approaches to defining race in order to respond to challenges such as those posed by the "mixed bloods." The concern with distinguishing people on the basis of race in order to preserve the territorial integrity of an expanded state occurred at the same time that many American Indians were becoming U.S. citizens and, therefore, ostensibly enjoying the same rights and responsibilities as their white counterparts.

In addition to challenging the territorial boundaries of the state, the "mixed bloods" posed a unique and thorny challenge to conventional definitions of the U.S. nation. All citizens of democratic states theoretically enjoy formal equality based on a written set of legal rights and responsibilities grants (what I call "state citizenship"). The differential implementation of those rights and responsibilities in everyday practice, however, distinguishes between those groups of citizens who are deemed "fit" to be members of the nation and those who are not (what I call "national membership"). State citizenship is an overtly inclusive concept, based on the premise that all citizens will be governed equally. The nation is a more exclusive concept, defined by formal and informal, legal and extralegal practices that delineate a select group of people who are eligible and practically able to govern as well as to be governed. Members of the nation have opportunities to become full and active participants in creating and carrying out the laws and policies that affect their lives that other citizens do not share. At the turn of the twentieth century, ascriptive distinctions, such as those based on race, played a central role in defining the boundaries of the U.S. nation despite their apparent contradiction of the democratic principles to which members of the nation purported to adhere.

"Mixed bloods" exposed and highlighted racial distinctions and their role in policy decisions that affected and reflected one's eligibility for membership in the nation through their failure to conform to the standard racial categories of "Indian" or "white." Debates about policy toward "mixed bloods" reveal that despite official proclamations of equality for all citizens, U.S. authorities routinely distinguished between and discriminated against U.S. citizens on the basis of race. In addition to exposing the racialized underpinnings of U.S. definitions of the nation, the "mixed bloods" also challenged the very logic and purported naturalness of those underpinnings. Their presence explicitly demonstrated the constructed character of the racial categories that formed the basis of many U.S. policies and practices.

What role did understandings of race play in defining the boundaries of both the U.S. state and nation at the turn of the nineteenth century? How did "mixed bloods" challenge these boundaries and, thus, the very definitions of the state and nation? How did state authorities respond to these challenges? And finally, why did the construction and maintenance of racial divisions form such a crucial foundation for the policies developed and implemented by officials of a state that claimed to be a democracy in which all citizens were treated equally?

My contention is that through their contestation of laws and policies that ignored their existence, indigenous people of "mixed" descent demonstrated that constructed racial categories played a central role in defining the territorial boundaries of the state and the socio-political boundaries of the nation. They also challenged and destabilized these boundaries by exposing the inconsistencies and contingencies that characterized definitions of standard racial categories. These challenges forced state authorities to respond by reinterpreting conventional racial categories and the state and national boundaries that they helped define.

"Mixed bloods" thus provoked changes in the relationships among race, state, and nation at the turn of the twentieth century. Unfortunately, however, these changes did not necessarily benefit them. In responding to the challenges posed by "mixed bloods" and other new "nonwhite" citizens, state authorities did not deconstruct the racial categories that limited access to full membership in the nation to "whites." Rather, they sought ways to make the definitions of race more internally consistent and systematic despite obvious empirical problems associated with this project. Whereas definitions of race had previously been multiple, fluid, and flexible, they became increasingly focused around a single, rigid standard known as "blood quantum." The little room for "mixed" identities that had once existed vanished quickly as a single drop of "nonwhite" blood became sufficient to render one a member of the relevant "nonwhite" racial category. The legacy of this new, pseudoscientific construction of race and its inability to acknowledge people of "mixed" descent continues to haunt the U.S. political landscape in the twenty-first century.

Through an analysis of debates about two contested "mixed blood" allotments, I trace the changing relationship among definitions of race, state, and nation in the United States at the turn of the twentieth century. These definitions hinged on dynamics of inclusion and exclusion that were sophisticated and multidimensional but also frequently inconsistent and unintentional. The dynamics did not operate on a simple, dichotomous continuum anchored by full inclusion at one end and full exclusion at the other. Rather, inclusionary and exclusionary policies and practices took place simultaneously and interacted to produce complex but often unpredicted methods of dominance as well as infrequent, unexpected challenges to that dominance.[3] Disputes concerning "mixed blood" allotment claims in the late nineteenth century provided one of those challenges.

"Full Blood" versus "Mixed Blood" Challenges to the Nation

In the late nineteenth century, as the territorial boundaries of the United States expanded to the Pacific Ocean and the frontier era drew to a close, the national status of American Indians became increasingly difficult for U.S. policy makers to define. They could no longer designate the Indians as a foreign population that resided beyond and outside U.S. borders. Nevertheless, U.S. policy makers continued to treat the Indians as separate from and inferior to European Americans. They sought ways to control and to manage the Indian population within the boundaries of the U.S. state and the context of U.S. society without compromising the interests or dominance of European Americans.

These efforts led to two simultaneous trends. On one level, U.S. policy makers adopted a more inclusive approach toward American Indians. Beginning with the Dawes Act of 1887, they gradually began to grant formal U.S. citizenship to American Indians provided that the Indians abided by a strict set of assimilationist prerequisites. On another level, however, U.S. policy makers excluded these new American Indian citizens from membership in the U.S. nation by demarcating and solidifying the racial boundary that separated Indians from whites. This newly reinforced racial boundary marked a semi-formal division between those citizens whom policy makers deemed unfit to govern (e.g., "nonwhites") and those whom they deemed eligibile to govern as well as to be governed (e.g., "whites").[4] Thus, rather than indicating an inclusive, universalistic approach to membership in the U.S. nation, granting citizenship to American Indians actually formed part of a larger project to control the Indian population through partial assimilation while simultaneously limiting their membership in the nation through the institution of a strict racial hierarchy.

While "full blood" American Indians at the turn of the twentieth century held an ambiguous national status, people of both Indian and European descent lived in even greater limbo. "Mixed blood" Indians challenged conventional definitions of the U.S. nation on several levels. First, "mixed bloods"

3 See, e.g., Adriana Kemp, "'Dangerous Populations': State Territoriality and the Constitution of National Minorities," paper presented at Boundaries and Belonging Conference, University of Washington, Seattle, October 2000 (Chapter 4).

4 See, e.g., C. B. Macpherson, *The Political Theory of Possessive Individualism: Hobbes to Locke* (Oxford: Clarendon, 1962), for analysis of similar class-based distinctions. While race was not the only criterion used to distinguish between the "fit" and the "unfit," it was one of the most important criteria used. Other ascriptive criteria, such as gender, were also employed to make this distinction.

did not conform to "Indian," "white," or any other standard racial category. This racial liminality provoked consternation among U.S. officials, who based many of their policies on a set of strict racial categories that did not include "mixed bloods," and it led to heated debates and legal battles over whether "mixed bloods" were Indians or whites. More importantly, the racial liminality of the "mixed bloods" within the United States highlighted the centrality of race as a basic criterion for determining who was eligible for membership in the U.S. nation, a nation whose representatives presented it as a democracy in which all citizens were treated equally. The centrality of debates about whether "mixed bloods" were Indians or whites in land allotment and other key policy decisions indicated the importance of racial status in determining whether someone ought to be granted the full rights and responsibilities associated with membership in the U.S. nation.

Second, the "mixed bloods" posed a challenge to the nation different from that posed by members of populations that corresponded to standard "nonwhite" racial categories, such as Indians or blacks. Indians, for example, gradually received U.S. citizenship, but state authorities continued to assign them to a recognized "nonwhite" racial category and, thus, to deem them ineligible for national membership. These "full blood" Indians challenged the definition of the nation and its false promise of inclusion on the basis of their obvious exclusion from it. Indeed, representatives of the U.S. nation had historically defined its members in contrast to characteristics they associated with American Indians: citizens versus foreigners, allies versus enemies, civilized versus primitive, whites versus Indians, and so on. This dichotomous representation of peoplehood suggests that the definition of the U.S. nation and the U.S. conception of American Indians were inextricably intertwined and dependent on each other. At the same time that policy makers excluded "full blood" Indians from membership in the nation, they required their continued, marginalized presence in the polity as the foil against which they defined members of the nation.

In the Jane Waldron case, for example, H. E. Dewey, the lawyer representing Black Tomahawk, stated that Waldron's "status, far from being an Indian, is the reverse."[5] The implication of this assertion is that Indian and white represent not only separate and different racial categories but opposing racial concepts. To be an Indian meant the opposite of what it meant to be a white, U.S. citizen. Policy makers, lawyers, and other European Americans relied on this opposition of racial and national concepts to define the qualities and characteristics that they used to justify both the inclusion and the privilege of white European-American citizens and the exclusion and subordination of Indians and other nonwhites, regardless of their citizenship status.

[5] See U.S. Senate Ex. Doc. No. 59, 1894, pp. 3–4.

The "mixed bloods," on the other hand, challenged the logic and the conceptual foundation on which this racist, dualistic understanding of the nation was based. By their very presence, they exposed the constructed character of the racial assumptions that underlay the definition of the nation and its social boundaries. They revealed the unnatural, artificial quality of the racial categories that were presented by U.S. policy makers and their associates as both "natural" and "scientific." For this reason, among others, the "mixed bloods" posed both a greater challenge and a greater danger to conventional definitions of the nation than their "full blood" counterparts.[6] And in this sense, they were also subject to greater exclusion than "full blood" American Indians.

"Full blood" American Indians did not have access to membership in the nation. "Mixed bloods," according to the prevailing logic of the times, did not have the right to exist. Not only did they not belong to the U.S. nation. They did not belong to any recognized racial or national category whatsoever. Thus, they were ineligible for even the limited resources and benefits that their "full blood" counterparts received from the U.S. government on the basis of their Indian status. There was less and less room within the increasingly racialized world view that permeated the late nineteenth-century United States to accommodate the "mixed bloods" as "mixed bloods," even in a subordinate status. According to the logic that defined the nation, people of "mixed" descent were not only anathema but incomprehensible. Scientists supported this logic by declaring that such "hybrids" were often sterile.[7] Crossing racial boundaries was prohibited by both law and biology, according to the politicians and scientists who erected and maintained those boundaries. Such crossings and their products were simply "unnatural."

"Head of Family" Debate

Official responses to Jane Waldron's claim to be an Indian "head of family" provide one example of the ways in which U.S. policies and practices construed "mixed bloods" and the "mixed" marriages that produced them as "unnatural." Sioux Indians received allotments of land based on their personal status. A head of family received an allotment of 320 acres. Single people, orphans, and children under the age of eighteen received smaller plots. Jane Waldron claimed her allotment as head of her family and garnered support for her claim from many U.S. government officials, including Indian Inspector James H. Cisney, who stated that he could not

[6] Another threat "mixed bloods" posed to conventional, racialized definitions of the nation was their frequent ability to "pass" as whites.

[7] See, e.g., Robert E. Bieder, "Scientific Attitudes toward Indian Mixed-Bloods in Early Nineteenth Century America," *Journal of Ethnic Studies* 8, no. 2 (1980): 20, 23.

"see how the head of a family question can enter into this case":[8]

> Of course, a white man can not acquire any benefits of an Indian in any way from the Government on his own account. And I can't see how or why an Indian woman, because she is married to a white man, can be deprived of any benefits she may be entitled to as an Indian. She must certainly be considered the head of the family so far as her Indian rights are concerned.[9]

In contrast, H. E. Dewey, attorney for Black Tomahawk, and others argued that as a married woman, Waldron could not possibly claim to be a head of family. Women were never heads of family, according to the Civil Code of Dakota or according to Indian custom, Dewey claimed.[10] Despite other reports of tribal practices that favored maternal descent, U.S. officials granted allotment privileges based on the assumption that men represented the "heads of family."

The only exceptions to this practice occurred in the case of widows and, rarely, in cases of intermarriage, such as the Waldron case. Since the law did not officially recognize interracial marriages, an Indian woman married to a white man had to present herself as though she were a widow in order to be recognized as a female head of family. In other words, she had to treat her husband as legally dead. Waldron's attorney did just that, arguing that "[w]e may . . . safely conclude, that the claimant having borne children as the fruit of such marriage, and residing with them, is as much the head of a family under the law and in contemplation of the act of March 2, 1889, as if her husband had deceased before she made her selection of the allotment in controversy."[11]

Thus, to claim her rights as an Indian, an Indian woman married to a European American man had to assume a conventionally male gender role. This unusual requirement for the purposes of claiming her Indian property rights demonstrates one way in which the U.S. legal system treated Waldron, a woman of "mixed" descent married to a European American man, as both unnatural and foreign. Not only did representatives of that system struggle over whether they could define Waldron as fully Indian or fully white based on her American Indian and European heritage, but they exacerbated her liminal status by treating her as neither fully a woman nor fully a man due to her marriage to a European American man.

The legal refusal to recognize intermarriages extended to the descendants of those intermarriages. In some cases, for example, orphans were defined as those without a living Indian parent for the purposes of Indian property rights.[12] In this sense, the law treated white parents as if they were dead.

[8] See U.S. Senate Ex. Doc. No. 59, 1894, p. 38.

[9] Ibid., p. 38.

[10] See ibid., p. 36.

[11] See ibid., p. 31.

[12] Ibid., p. 125.

These examples indicate the extreme lengths to which the law went in order to preserve the racial divisions that underlay U.S. society.

Jane Waldron offered a very different interpretation of her claim to be the head of her family. Rather than referring to the legal complexities that forced her to assume such a status, she challenged conventional norms by basing her claim on the principle and practice of gender equality. At the same time, however, she supported and invited acceptance of her assertion that her husband treated her as an equal partner by acquiescing to socially accepted, racist attitudes toward Indians. Waldron attempted to prove her husband's progressive attitudes toward women by highlighting them through reference to the racist narratives that framed late nineteenth-century U.S. society:

> I claim to be the head of my family as much as my husband. I am as much the head as he, as we manage our business together. We are equal partners in all things. He is one man that does not put women down lower than him, even if she be but an Indian.[13]

The debate about whether Waldron was eligible to assume the status of head of family in order to claim her property rights as an Indian demonstrates the lack of recognition and legitimacy accorded to intermarriages between Indian women and European American men and to the children of "mixed" descent these marriages produced. It demonstrates how high the symbolic and political stakes were for those who "dared" to cross racial boundaries through marriage or descent. Not only was one's racial identity questioned, but also, suddenly, living relatives became legally dead and women turned into legal men. The implications of interracial crossings extended far beyond constructions of race. The debate about Waldron's status as head of family thus highlights the crucial role that construction and maintenance of racial boundaries played in U.S. policies that helped define the state and the nation at the turn of the twentieth century.

Political Competence

Two distinct, but frequently interwoven, approaches to conceptualizing the relationship between race and eligibility for national membership developed

[13] Ibid., p. 87. Waldron also expressed conformity to the dominant racial social system in a note that she sent to the Secretary of the Interior with a series of affidavits that she had collected to protest her treatment by Indian Inspector James H. Cisney at a local hearing he held to review the case. Waldron wrote that "in order that the Secretary may know as fully as possible how this inspector conducted this hearing, I have caused the affidavits of every white person who was present during the hearing to be taken except Dewey and the farmer, who was present only a short time the second day." By explicitly mentioning that she requested affidavits only from whites, Waldron revealed her assumption that the Secretary of the Interior would feel these were the most reliable and perhaps the only worthy witnesses to the hearing. Waldron presented the case in this manner despite the fact that she herself identified as an Indian.

in the United States during the nineteenth century. Both drew on ideas contained in Locke's liberal democratic theory. The concept of political competence emerged as one approach to reconciling the uneasy disjunction between the liberal democratic promise of equality for all citizens and the empirical reality of significant inequalities between groups of citizens. The definition of political competence derived from a constellation of norms, practices, and traits that characterized an ideal member of the nation, someone who was deemed capable of governing as well as of being governed.[14] By emphasizing competence or fitness, the concept suggested that the criteria used to determine eligibility for full and active participation in the nation were based on acquired skills and abilities rather than on ascriptive characteristics. In practice, however, policy makers routinely judged an individual's "fitness" for political participation or "competence" to assume the responsibilities associated with national membership based on his or her racial status and other ascriptive qualities.

For example, a series of proposed congressional bills inspired by the Waldron case attempted to legislate what proportion of "white blood" was necessary to render one competent enough to sell one's land without supervision by the government. Successive versions of the bill decreased the amount of "Indian blood" that legislators proposed to allow in order for one to sell one's allotment without governmental approval. An early iteration of the bill suggested that "[a]ll mixed-blood Indians who are one-half or less than one-half of Indian blood who have heretofore taken allotments of land in severalty ... shall, upon taking said allotment of land, receive from the United States a patent for the same in fee, and they shall thereupon have the right to sell, convey, or encumber said lands, and the same shall be subject to taxation the same as the lands of any other citizen of the United States."[15]

By April 28, 1896, however, the proposal had changed. Now, only "mixed-blood Indians who are one-quarter or less than one-quarter of Indian blood" would automatically receive a patent for their allotments and have the right to sell them. The proposed bill then stipulated that "any mixed-blood Indian of more than one-quarter Indian blood may apply to the judge of the district court of the district in which he resides for permission to sell and convey or encumber his allotment of land; and if the judge of said court shall decide that said mixed-blood Indian is capable of managing his own affairs, said judge shall enter a decree adjudging said mixed-blood Indian capable of managing his own affairs, and thereupon and thereafter said mixed-blood Indian shall have the right to sell and encumber the whole or any part of his allotment and give a fee simple title therefore."[16]

[14] See Macpherson, *Political Theory of Possessive Individualism*, p. 248.

[15] See S. 1628, 1896.

[16] See S. 2966, 1896.

In their recommendation for passage of one of the later versions of this bill, the Committee on Indian Affairs reported that "it is believed by our committee that a mixed-blood Indian having one-quarter or less Indian blood in his veins is quite as competent to perform the duties of citizenship intelligently as many white men, and that the percentage of incompetency among the Indian tribes of one-quarter or less is not greater that that to be found among a like number of white persons."[17]

The Committee on Indian Affairs thus implied that one's racial status was a reliable indicator of one's political competence. Whiteness implied competency, whereas Indianness implied incompetency. References to competency, such as these, served as a thin disguise for excluding people from membership in the nation on the basis of their racial status.

John Stewart Mill, one of the premier Anglo political theorists of the late nineteenth century, devoted considerable attention to defining who was "fit" for full political participation. Although he presented these definitions in the context of a developmental model, they were nevertheless highly racialized. Indeed, Mill overtly suggested that North American Indians, among other racially defined groups, were "unfit for liberty" due to their "indolence," "carelessness," and "cowardice."[18] According to Mill, "nothing but foreign force would induce a tribe of North American Indians to submit to the restraints of a regular and civilized government."[19]

The notion of race that underlay Mill's discussion of political "fitness" shared certain core assumptions with the monogenist understanding of race favored by many scientists in the early nineteenth century. The monogenists viewed all humans as members of one species that originated from a single pair. Inspired by Christian theology as well as by their scientific beliefs, adherents of this school of thought argued that "mixed bloods" had the potential to assimilate and become "civilized" by adopting a European American way of life.[20]

This expansive, semi-fluid understanding of race and its relationship to political fitness or competence underlay many of the discussions about and decisions made in contested allotment cases involving "mixed blood" Indians in the late nineteenth century. Education, fluency in English, proper etiquette (i.e., the ability to comport oneself as a lady or gentleman), social class, and ownership of private property all figured into judgments about political competence and assumptions about racial status. Policy makers and many other European Americans associated possession of these qualities with civilization, moral authority, and whiteness, whereas they associated

[17] See Senate Report No. 969, 1896.

[18] See John Stuart Mill, *Considerations on Representative Government* (New York: Liberal Arts, 1958), p. 149.

[19] See ibid., p. 148.

[20] See, e.g., Bieder, "Scientific Attitudes toward Indian Mixed-Bloods," 17–18.

their lack with primitiveness, immorality, and Indianness or other forms of nonwhiteness.[21]

"Deserving" Indians and Political Competence in the Jane Waldron Case

The lawyers for both Jane Waldron and Black Tomahawk made associations among political competence, moral authority, and race that were challenged by the circumstances of the Waldron case. Robert Christy, Waldron's attorney, had the challenging task of proving that Waldron was an Indian and, therefore, eligible for allotment rights in a society in which most rights and privileges were reserved for European Americans. Dewey, on the other hand, faced the difficulty of proving that Waldron was a white woman and, therefore, ineligible for an allotment, despite her documented Indian ancestry.

The association of allotment rights with Indian status provided an unusual twist to a case that took place in a society where whites enjoyed clear dominance and privilege with very few exceptions. Clearly aware of this context and of the fact that many European Americans might feel uncomfortable extending Indians even the few rights to which they were legally entitled, Christy attempted to demonstrate not only that Waldron was an Indian but that she was a "deserving" Indian. He did not seem to feel that simply proving her racial status as an Indian was sufficient to demonstrate her eligibility for an allotment. Rather, he apparently felt that he also had to prove that she was morally worthy of obtaining an allotment. The assumption underlying Christy's argument was that Indianness was generally associated with moral inferiority, whereas moral worthiness was implicit in whiteness. Christy, therefore, took it upon himself to demonstrate that Waldron was an unusual, "deserving" Indian based on her moral virtues.

Many of the attributes and activities Christy mentioned in order to "prove" that Waldron was morally "deserving," such as education, cultivation, and usefulness, were the same as those included in contemporary definitions of political competence. Christy emphasized Waldron's role in "civilizing" fellow Indians and her own assimilation into a European American-dominated society. According to Christy,

> Every consideration of right and justice supports the claim of Mrs. Waldron. She is an educated and cultivated woman, deservedly possessing the esteem and confidence of the best citizens of the State of South Dakota. Her entire life has been spent usefully amongst the Indians of the Sioux Nation, and she deserves well of the Republic. It is true she is of the "mixed-blood," but this does not, as we have shown, lessen her claims upon the Government, nor render her ineligible to select an allotment under the treaties with her kinsmen and the laws passed to carry them into effect. The "mixed-bloods" have been faithful to the United States in peace and war, and have,

[21] See, e.g., Linda Gordon, *The Great Arizona Orphan Abduction* (Cambridge, Mass., and London, Eng.: Harvard University Press, 1999).

by their example, encouraged the hostile Indians to seek a higher civilization and cultivate the arts of peace.[22]

Christy seemed to contend that Waldron ought to be granted the allotment *not* primarily because of her national and racial status as an Indian. Rather, Christy argued that Waldron was eligible for an allotment because she was culturally assimilated to dominant white norms and behavioral codes and assisted in assimilating other Indians, making her a "deserving" Indian "fit" to receive an allotment. A number of prominent European American men from the Fort Pierre community supported this view in a note that they submitted on Waldron's behalf, attesting to her good character. According to the President of Citizen's Bank, the President of First National Bank, the Postmaster, the Mayor of Fort Pierre, the State's Attorney, and the County Treasurer, "[w]e feel a satisfaction in being able to say that we have known Mrs. Jennie E. Waldron for a number of years: that she is a graduate of one of the best schools in the West; that she paid the expenses of her education by her own industry, and that she is today the peer of any lady in the State."[23]

Ironically, the attributes that Christy mentioned in his assertions that Waldron was a "deserving" Indian were almost identical to those described by Dewey in his assertion of Waldron's whiteness and, therefore, her status as a U.S. citizen:

[Waldron] is a white woman in appearance, condition, education, habits of living, and every other distinguishing characteristic of the white race as compared with the Indians. The wife of a citizen, white, of the United States, married to, living with, and being supported by him – herself a citizen, the daughter of a citizen, who is regularly married to and living with and supporting her mother, while the plaintiff, Black Tomahawk, is a full-blooded Sioux Indian, whose ancestors have possessed this land for generations.[24]

Whereas Christy referred to Waldron's education and life style as indicators of her status as a "deserving" Indian, Dewey offered them as proof of Waldron's racial whiteness. Just as Christy associated whiteness with U.S. citizenship, Dewey also assumed that by proving Waldron's status as a U.S. citizen, he was also proving her whiteness and, therefore, her lack of either national or racial status as an Indian. In contrast, Dewey firmly distinguished Black Tomahawk as a "full-blooded Sioux Indian."

Dewey claimed support for Waldron's status as a white woman on the basis of her residence among and association with whites, her attendance and teaching at white schools, and her high socio-economic status. He asserted "[t]hat Mrs. Waldron, whose maiden name was Jennie Van Metre, lived with the whites, and, like the whites, attended their schools, and afterwards

[22] Senate Ex. Doc. No. 59, 1894, p. 33.
[23] Ibid., p. 78.
[24] Ibid., p. 25.

taught them – gave music lessons, which she is competent to do – and that her status, far from being an Indian, is the reverse, and her station far above thousands of white women."[25]

Dewey explicitly acknowledged the European American assumption that Indians categorically occupied a subordinate status to whites, not only racially and nationally, but also in terms of socio-economic class. Based on this assumption, Dewey further asserted that the relatively high social and economic status Waldron enjoyed in society was an indicator of her whiteness. As further evidence in support of Waldron's whiteness, Dewey contrasted Waldron's appearance, education, and marriage to a white man with Black Tomahawk's poverty and disability:

> Further, she is a white woman and no trace of Indian blood is discernable in her appearance. She is educated and accomplished, is the wife of a white man, if not of wealth at least in circumstances beyond most of his neighbors, while Black Tomahawk, her competitor for this land, is not only a full-blooded Sioux Indian, but poor and a cripple at that.[26]

In a telling metaphor for the broader condition of Indians in the United States, Dewey sought to inspire sympathy for Tomahawk by acknowledging that his paralysis was accidentally inflicted by U.S. officials while he was working in the service of the U.S. government. On another level, however, the source of Tomahawk's injury became irrelevant as Dewey simply continued to stress his status as a cripple. Tomahawk's disability and his Indianness became fused in the same way that Waldron's competence became a proof of her whiteness. One's presumed competence or incompetence as a human being and one's racial status were interpreted as mutually constitutive, an assumption that had direct implications for eligibility for full membership in the nation.

"Blood Quantum"

In addition to the monogenists, a second scientific school of thought gained strength toward the end of the nineteenth century, claiming that members of different races were, in fact, members of different species. According to the polygenists, assimilation from an "uncivilized" to a "civilized" race was impossible. Adherents to this perspective claimed that Indians were innately inferior to whites and argued that "mixed bloods" and other "hybrids" were likely to be infertile.[27] The assumptions underlying this notion that races comprised distinct, inflexible categories to which individuals could be assigned also underlay a second approach to race that emerged in the debates about contested "mixed blood" allotments.

[25] Ibid., pp. 3–4.
[26] Ibid., p. 5.
[27] See Bieder, "Scientific Attitudes toward Indian Mixed-Bloods," 17–30.

While Mill's logic of political fitness suggested that an American Indian might eventually be able to achieve competence through assimilation, the concept of race as a form of individual possession denied this promise. The notion of race as a form of possession can also be traced back to Locke's theory of liberal democracy. C. B. Macpherson referred to the larger implications of Locke's theory of private property as "possessive individualism" and asserted that Locke held a "conception of the individual as essentially the proprietor of his own person or capacities, owing nothing to society for them. The individual was seen neither as a moral whole nor as part of a larger social whole, but as an owner of himself. The relation of ownership ... was read back into the nature of the individual. The individual ... is free inasmuch as he is proprietor of his person and capacities."[28] Thus, just as the value of land was premised on its status as an acquisition, a form of property, the same held true for selfhood. Identity became an individual possession rather than something that emanated from one's relationship to a collective community or culture. In this new, Lockean understanding, identity also became conceptualized as a separate, static entity rather than as a fluid practice or process.

Race constituted a critical part of this new version of identity in the United States, and as a growing body of scholarship has suggested, race itself became conceptualized as a form of property.[29] Whiteness was a particularly valuable form of property in the late nineteenth-century United States.[30] As we have seen through the example of the Waldron case, it guaranteed those individuals who possessed it unquestioned access to a variety of social, economic, and legal rights and privileges that were denied to those who did not "fit" into the "white" category. The notion of race as an individual possession was a cornerstone of the system that existed for the distribution of rights, responsibilities, and resources in U.S. society.

The racialized concept of Indian identity that developed in the context of possessive individualism adhered to an individual regardless of his or her way of life. Indianness was a form of possession that existed independently of the everyday practices one engaged in and the relationships one upheld. This categorical definition of Indianness was critical to European Americans who sought a means to preserve the exclusivity of their whiteness at a time when the demographic landscape of the United States was changing rapidly and the boundaries of citizenship were being expanded. It allowed

28 See Macpherson, *Political Theory of Possessive Individualism*, p. 3.

29 See, e.g., Cheryl Harris, "Whiteness as Property," in Kimberle Crenshaw et al., eds., *Critical Race Theory: The Key Writings That Formed the Movement* (New York: New York University Press, 1995), 276–91, and Peggy Pascoe, "Race, Gender and the Privileges of Property: On the Significance of Miscegenation Law in the U.S. West," in Valerie J. Matsumoto and Blake Allmendinger, eds., *Over the Edge: Remapping the American West* (Berkeley: University of California Press, 1999), 215–30.

30 See, e.g., David R. Roediger, "The Pursuit of Whiteness: Property, Terror, and Expansion, 1790–1860," *Journal of the Early Republic* 19 (1999): 579–600.

policy makers to preserve an essentialized definition of the Indian as exotic, primitive, and traditional even as they encouraged the partial assimilation of American Indians through legislation such as the Dawes Act. U.S. policy makers developed an understanding of a "traditional" Indian way of life that they construed as static and stuck in the past. They clung to this vision despite the fact that Indians were experiencing tremendous flux in their patterns of living, while European Americans dedicated themselves to increasing and reinforcing restrictions on movement and change in the name of modern, rational order.[31]

"Mixed bloods" exposed both the national obsession with controlling movement across socially and territorially defined borders as well as the impossibility of this project. As prior adherents to nomadic or semi-nomadic ways of life, some "mixed bloods" resisted efforts to "settle" and to "civilize" them within the confines of plots designed more according to geometry than geography. Other "mixed bloods," who lived according to more European American norms, resented the political obstacles that they often encountered in trying to settle and to cultivate their own plots of land due to their ambiguous racial status. Meanwhile, modern state officials became increasingly obsessed with trying to organize both territories and socio-political identities into fixed, stable compartments defined by rigid, inflexible boundaries.[32]

In response to the challenges to conventional racial boundaries posed by "mixed bloods" and other people of "mixed" descent, policy makers demanded increasingly precise, biological definitions of race to bolster their racialized policies. Scientists responded by developing quantitative definitions of race that relied on measures such as "blood quantum," that is, the proportions of one's blood attributed to specific racial categories such as Indian or White. The empirical challenges associated with trying to apply those measures in meaningful ways did not easily discourage their efforts. For example, anthropologists went to extreme lengths in attempting to categorize residents of the White Earth Chippewa Reservation according to race, despite their own admission that the techniques they employed, such as measurements of hair type, were incapable of achieving their desired results.[33] The challenges posed by "mixed bloods" to standard racial categories

[31] See, e.g., Linda Alcoff, "Mestizo Identity," in Naomi Zack, ed., *American Mixed Race: The Culture of Microdiversity* (Lanham, Md.: Rowman & Littlefield, 1995).

[32] See, e.g., Zygmunt Bauman, *Modernity and Ambivalence* (Oxford: Polity, 1991); Richard Handler, "Who Owns the Past? History, Cultural Property, and the Logic of Possessive Individualism," in Brett Williams, ed., *The Politics of Culture* (Washington, D.C.: Smithsonian Institution Press, 1991), 63–74; Timothy Mitchell, *Colonising Egypt* (Cambridge and New York: Cambridge University Press, 1991); and James C. Scott, *Seeing like a State: How Certain Schemes to Improve the Human Condition Have Failed* (New Haven, Conn.: Yale University Press, 1998).

[33] See David L. Beaulieu, "Curly Hair and Big Feet: Physical Anthropology and the Implementation of Land Allotment on the White Earth Chippewa Reservation," *American Indian Quarterly* (Fall 1984): 281–314.

thus led not to an abandonment of these categories but rather to renewed efforts to define race scientifically and to strengthen the rigidity of racial boundaries that determined who was eligible for national membership and who was not. By pointing out the inconsistencies and constructed character of conventional understandings of race, "mixed bloods" actually sparked intensified efforts to preserve and strengthen standard racial categories by redefining them in terms of blood quantum.

Blood Quantum Arguments in Waldron Case

The influence of the growing consensus that blood quantum was the appropriate measure to use in defining race was evident in H. E. Dewey's sometimes contorted efforts to prove that Jane Waldron was a white woman. The circumstances of the case required Dewey to argue that Waldron was a white woman despite her documented Indian ancestry. This position contradicted the conventional and increasingly popular assumption that even a small amount of "Indian blood" was sufficient to make one Indian.

While occasionally stressing how little "Indian blood" Waldron had in proportion to "white blood," Dewey did not rely on a blood quantum argument to prove Waldron's whiteness. Instead, Dewey referred to the common law of descent in order to declare that Waldron was a white woman and "not an Indian by race or adoption nor by the customs of the nation":[34]

> Under the well-known rule that the children follow the status of the father and not of their mother, unless they are illegitimate, which is not claimed in this case, not only is Mrs. Waldron a white woman, but so is her mother, and so were her father and her mother. So these people, Mrs. Waldron and her ancestors, for three generations, have been white people and not Indians.[35]

Both the Secretary of the Interior and the Attorney General ultimately accepted the argument that Waldron was white based on the common law of descent and used it as the basis for the original decision in the case. Nevertheless, Dewey himself did not seem completely convinced by his own argument. In fact, he came close to acknowledging contradictions in his claims about Waldron's racial identity at certain points in the case. In some instances, for example, Dewey asserted that "half-breeds" and "mixed-bloods" had always been treated by the U.S. government as a separate racial category from Indians. He contended that they were neither Indians nor whites:

> [D]uring the whole period of Government dealings with the Indians, whenever any half-breed or mixed-blood has received any advantage, benefit or privilege, under any law or treaty, . . . he has not received it under the name or word "Indian," but always

[34] Senate Ex. Doc. No. 59, 1894, pp. 3–4.
[35] Ibid., pp. 3–4.

under the name of half-breed or mixed-blood . . . mixed-bloods are not Indians and are not whites."[36]

This definition of "mixed-bloods" as a separate racial category appears to contradict Dewey's claim that Waldron was a white woman. Furthermore, in his March 1890 deposition to U.S. Indian Inspector Frank Armstrong, Dewey qualified his assertion of Waldron's whiteness by stating that she "is a white woman, although having Indian ancestry on the mother's side."[37] In addition, while Dewey considered Waldron's mother to be *legally* white based on the principle of paternal descent, he felt it important to emphasize that this was a legal construction of the racial status of a woman whom he described immediately afterward as "of the half blood":

Jennie Van Meter Waldron, is a white woman, although having Indian ancestry on the mother's side, she is the daughter of a white man, regularly married to, and living with the mother of Mrs. Waldron, who is herself, in law, a white woman, although of the half blood, her father and mother being of the half blood, but both the offspring of white fathers, married to Indian mothers. The father of Mrs. Waldron being a white man regularly married to and living with a white woman (in law, although in fact of the half blood), Mrs. Waldron can claim nothing under any law or treaty.[38]

Dewey's acknowledgment reveals the popular acceptance of a definition of race based on blood quantum that, in this case, contradicted the legal principles of descent that Dewey relied on in his attempt to refute Waldron's claim to an allotment. It also demonstrates that Dewey was conscious of his definition of Waldron as white based on the common law of descent as a *legal* maneuver that seemed to contradict his personal, commonsense understanding of racial categories. Dewey seemed to accept the unstated assumption that based on blood quantum, Waldron would unquestionably be classified as a "mixed-blood Indian."

"Mixed Bloods" and the Threat of Ambiguity: The Barney Traversee Case

The various arguments presented in the Waldron case demonstrate the lack of legitimacy that state laws and authorities accorded to "mixed bloods" as people of "mixed" descent. They also demonstrate how Jane Waldron challenged conventional racial categories and the boundaries of state and nation that they helped to define by initiating a debate about how these categories were defined, whom they included, and whom they excluded. Throughout the debate, Jane Waldron maintained that she was an Indian, a claim that was ultimately upheld in court. It was also a claim that matched

[36] Ibid., p. 23.
[37] Ibid., p. 49.
[38] Ibid., p. 49.

the new definition of race according to blood quantum, although this was not the basis on which Waldron's particular case was decided.

Barney Traversee, on the other hand, took the debate about racial categories and its implications one step further. Like Waldron, Traversee was of both Indian and European descent. In his initial deposition in a contested allotment case, Traversee, like Waldron, claimed to be an Indian. When this position failed to yield the desired result, however, Traversee tried another approach. In a second deposition, Traversee claimed that he was white. By making this switch and articulating two different perspectives on his identity and its implications through his attorney, Traversee illuminated the threat that "mixed bloods" posed to a political and legal system that depended not only on racial categories but also on firm distinctions between them.

Not only could many indigenous people of "mixed" descent "pass" as whites based on their appearance, but many of them could "pass" based on their cultural and behavioral affinities to whites as well. Their striking similarities to whites and the frequent "invisibility" of their Indianness made them seem a particular threat to European Americans committed to preserving the fragile boundaries of whiteness and restricting access to national membership.

Barney Traversee's father was of French descent and his mother was of partial European and partial Indian descent. After approval of the Sioux treaty, Traversee claimed an allotment of 320 acres as the head of his family. R. B. Stearns, a European American man, filed a competing claim to Traversee's allotment with the assistance of attorney H. E. Dewey, alleging that Traversee was ineligible for the allotment because he was an Indian.[39] Stearns and Traversee agreed to settle their competing claims by engaging in a compromise, whose details were worked out by Dewey. Facing the possibility of bankruptcy, Traversee agreed to relinquish his claim to the original allotment and apply instead for a homestead on half of the land in exchange for $400 that he needed to pay off his debts.[40]

Stearns paid Traversee the $400 and, accompanied by Dewey, went to the local land office to file for the relinquishment. Traversee applied for U.S. citizenship and for a homestead on half of the land at the same time that he filed for relinquishment of his allotment. Mr. Bailey, the land registrar, accepted the citizenship and relinquishment applications but denied the homestead applications filed by both Traversee and Stearns without any explanation.[41]

Traversee and Stearns both filed depositions. In Traversee's initial deposition before U.S. Indian Agent George McKean in September 1892, he stated that he had never been a U.S. citizen. His allotment claim implied that he

39 Ibid.
40 Ibid.
41 Ibid.

identified as an Indian, and state authorities clearly assumed that Traversee was an Indian based on the information he provided.

Q: State what proportion of Indian blood is in you.
A: You can judge, my father was a white man, and my mother was a half-breed Sioux.
Q: Have you at any time or before any official ever stated or swore that you were not an Indian, but a citizen?
A: Not that I know of or so understood. I never was a citizen and I have never given up my tribal relations. I have voted and have said so, but not that I was a citizen.[42]

Later in the deposition, Traversee stated that he "wanted to be a citizen because I did not want to be any longer under an agent and a boss farmer that didn't know as much about farming as I do."[43]

U.S. Special Agent George McKean recommended that Traversee be allowed to relinquish his allotment and file for a homestead on half of the land. In a letter dated October 1, 1892, R. V. Belt, Acting Commissioner of Indian Affairs, advised the Secretary of the Interior that "it appears from the testimony of Travirsie [*sic*] that he has never denied under oath his Indian nativity or character; that he has been carried upon proper 'issue rolls' for many years, and that he has voted two or three times at certain elections because he was furnished a ballot and requested to do so, and not because he claimed such rights on account of citizenship."[44]

Further on, Belt remarked that he felt that Stearns and Dewey had deliberately misled Traversee regarding the need to apply for U.S. citizenship. Belt explained that all Indians who received allotments became automatically eligible for U.S. citizenship based on the Dawes Act and, therefore, had no need to apply and pay a fee for citizenship. According to Belt, "fraud and deception have been practiced upon the Indian in this matter."[45]

On the other hand, Belt felt that despite his status as a U.S. citizen, Traversee, as a racial Indian, should not have the same rights with respect to his allotment that a white U.S. citizen would have with a homestead. Belt strongly objected to allowing Traversee to relinquish his allotment for monetary compensation. His justification for this position, while seemingly inspired by good intentions, nevertheless smacks of paternalism:

> Indians should not be allowed to take allotments for the purpose of speculation. If so, the object of the Indian allotment laws, intended to secure permanent homes for Indians and their families, will be defeated. If the Indian was ignorant of his rights and was misled in relation to his allotment, as appears to be the case, he should be protected, and no doubt that Mr. Stearns will be able to secure himself otherwise in the payment of the amount advanced to the Indian.[46]

[42] Ibid.
[43] Ibid., p. 137.
[44] Ibid., p. 143.
[45] Ibid., p. 144.
[46] Ibid., p. 144.

In contrast to the Waldron case, in which all participants seemed to equate U.S. citizenship with whiteness, Belt acknowledged Traversee's national status as a U.S. citizen but advocated restricting his access to national membership on the basis of his presumed racial status as an Indian. John W. Noble, Secretary of the Interior, concurred with Belt's opinion that Traversee be denied relinquishment. He agreed with Belt's reasoning that Indians with allotments, despite their status as U.S. citizens, should not be allowed to sell their land.[47]

On receiving word of the initial decision in the case, Traversee switched tactics. His lawyer filed an appeal asserting that, in contrast to all of his previous claims, Traversee was actually a white man and should never have received an allotment in the first place. In a second deposition, Traversee provided a new version of his identity and life story. Not only did he now claim to be a white man, but he claimed that both of his parents were white as well. According to Eakin, Traversee stated "that he was not at that time, is not now, never has been, and has never desired to be, a Sioux Indian; that on the contrary he was at the time he signed said Indian allotment application under the circumstances above stated, a white man, a citizen of the United States, and had been since his birth; that he has always been and is now a citizen of the United States."[48]

Traversee continued his deposition by retelling his story about voting. In this version, he referred to his participation in elections as proof of his U.S. citizenship rather than as simply a meaningless action that he performed at the request of European Americans. In addition, Traversee frequently referred to both his family's engagement in farming and their residential integration with white people as support for his own claim of whiteness. Throughout this deposition, Traversee seemed to assume that by proving his status as a white man, he was simultaneously proving his U.S. citizenship and vice versa. In this context, he equated whiteness with U.S. citizenship and implied that they were mutually constitutive.[49]

Traversee explained that he came to be identified as a Sioux Indian when he began residing on the Sioux Reservation in 1881 "with many other white people" while working in the freighting industry nearby.[50] His parents moved to the reservation a few months later. Traversee's mother put his name on the roll of the Cheyenne Indian Agency so that he could receive rations. Traversee claimed that he did not object to receiving these rations because it was his understanding that he was entitled to them through his wife, who was of Sioux Indian descent. In the same deposition, however, Traversee claimed that his wife, like his mother, was a "white woman" despite her

[47] Ibid., p. 144.
[48] Ibid., p. 149.
[49] Ibid., p. 149.
[50] Ibid., p. 150.

Indian ancestry. His aim in making this claim was apparently to support his own assertion that he was a white man and a member of a white family.[51]

Traversee reemphasized the key roles of language and education as components of racial identity later in his deposition. Eakin reported "that affiant has a wife and four children; all speak the English language and use the English in all their conversation; that affiant's children can not talk the Sioux language or dialect; that affiant desires that his children shall continue to attend the public schools and continue to be educated therein."[52]

At the conclusion of his deposition, Traversee strongly objected to being treated as a ward by the U.S. government given his newly proclaimed status as a U.S. citizen. According to the deposition, the "affiant denies the right of the Government to insist on him being and remaining its ward when he has been, and is now, one of its citizens, and by his votes has helped to make laws and elect the officers who execute and interpret its laws."[53] Traversee thus challenged the paternalistic, racist attitude of the Acting Commissioner of Indian Affairs, who insisted on "protecting" Traversee by denying his request to relinquish his allotment on the basis of his racial status as an Indian. He also exposed the dividing line between members of the nation and those excluded from it. Full members participate in making and implementing the laws. Those nominal citizens denied full national membership are simply governed by the laws.

Finally, Traversee asked that his relinquishment be granted "that he may then be a free man, to do and act as other citizens of the United States; that to be a ward of the Government and to be under the directions of the agents and officers is repugnant to him."[54] White citizens had full control over both their territorial and racial "properties." Indian citizens, by contrast, had to defer to government officials in decisions regarding both the sale of their land and the definition of their racial status.

Traversee's lawyer, Owen Rowe, echoed Traversee's demand for independence in his argument for the appeal. Rowe asserted that it was an infringement of Traversee's rights to treat a "free white man" as an Indian:

> The position or condition of a ward may not suggest to the savage or semi-civilized mind any repugnance, for when in that condition he does not feel or understand that his position is an inferior one, but to the person who may have in his veins some tinge of Indian blood, but to all intents and purposes is a free white man, the word "ward" has an entirely different meaning. Such a man naturally enough feels that to be kept in such a condition is to infringe upon his rights.
>
> It would not be strange that Barney Traversee, who, having all his life enjoyed the sacred boon of citizenship and liberty, should now refuse to assume the attitude of

[51] Ibid., p. 149.

[52] Ibid., p. 151.

[53] Ibid., p. 151.

[54] Ibid., p. 151.

an Indian. He stands before you in the dignity of a citizen of the United States and asks to be relieved of all supposition that he is a ward.[55]

According to Rowe's logic, freedom is a natural right of white men (he did not mention women), but need not be granted to nonwhite "savages" who are incapable of even recognizing or understanding their subordinate position, much less challenging it. This assumption dovetails with Mill's notion that members of some racial groups are "unfit for liberty."[56] Rowe also associated U.S. citizenship with whiteness, although other parties in the case had distinguished between the two. Citizenship for Rowe, however, was associated not just with a formal, legal status but with the liberty and dignity that members of the nation enjoy. By presenting his argument in this manner, Rowe demonstrated that although the Secretary of the Interior distinguished between race and citizenship when he asserted that Traversee was both an Indian and a U.S. citizen, he nevertheless continued to judge Traversee's political competence and his eligibility for national membership on the basis of his presumed racial status as an Indian.

Ultimately, the Secretary of the Interior granted Traversee's request for relinquishment on the condition that he dissolve all of his ties to the Sioux Indian tribe. The decision never directly addressed the question of Traversee's racial identity, but the fact that it was premised on Traversee's dissolution of tribal ties suggests that the Secretary of the Interior continued to regard him as an Indian.

The Traversee case shows how one man of "mixed" descent challenged racist U.S. policies and practices by demonstrating how fragile and empirically unsound were the constructions of race that European Americans used to define and restrict access to the U.S. nation. Furthermore, it demonstrates how differently European American lawyers and state authorities interpreted the same individual's political competence and eligibility for national membership, depending on whether they labeled him Indian or white. Finally, the case provides a stark example of how European Americans began to employ race as a means of denying full membership in the nation to those racially defined as Indians despite their status as U.S. citizens.

Redefining "Mixed Bloods"

As illustrated by the Traversee case, U.S. officials responded to the challenges posed by "mixed bloods" by attempting to "eliminate" them in a variety of ways.[57] Most often, they recategorized people of American Indian and European descent as either Indians or whites. In the majority of cases, "mixed

[55] Ibid., pp. 154–5.
[56] See Mill, *Considerations on Representative Government.*
[57] The words "eliminate" and "liminal" share the same etymology. They are derived from "limen," the Latin word for "threshold."

bloods" became Indians based on the widespread practice of designating anyone with non-European ancestry a member of the nonwhite racial category. But U.S. officials did not stop at forcing "mixed bloods" to one side or the other of the conventional racial boundary. They also sought to push them outside the territorial boundaries that defined both Indian reservations within the U.S. and the U.S. state itself. Thus, many "mixed bloods" became homeless wanderers within the U.S., while others were deported to Canada.

The growing focus on racial identity as an individual, biological phenomenon made the notion of "mixed" descent increasingly incomprehensible within U.S. society. Discussions about political competence that may have originated from a perspective closer to that of Mills, who assumed that competence, while not easily achieved, could be attained through assimilation, became entangled in arguments about blood quantum. Competence, in this view, was a function no longer simply of one's behavioral and cultural attributes (understood in racialized terms) but of the proportion of "white" versus "nonwhite" blood that one possessed.

While the notion of "mixed blood" identity became increasingly incomprehensible in U.S. society, being "mixed" was not nearly as much of an issue in collective societies where identity was defined in terms of one's relationship to the larger group rather than as an individual possession. In such contexts, what mattered most was one's recognized affiliation with a collective rather than the details of one's individual ancestry or blood quantum. U.S. officials trying to resolve contested allotment cases implicitly acknowledged the inadequacy of their own conceptual approaches to racial and national identity when, failing to identify a clear rationale for declaring "mixed bloods" either Indian or white, they delegated the decision to Indian tribes. The decision as to who qualified as an Indian, they said, should be made according to the customs of the tribe. This strategy conveniently absolved the officials of the need to answer a question for which they had no adequate conceptual response.

Attorney General Richard Olney, for example, offered the following opinion of how he thought the Waldron case should be resolved:

> The persons entitled to such [allotment] rights are the persons who, at the time of the agreement, constituted the Sioux Nation and were lawful members thereof. The question, therefore, whether any particular person is or is not an Indian, within the meaning of this agreement, is to be determined, in my opinion, not by the common law, but by the laws or usages of the tribe. Presumptively a person apparently of mixed blood residing upon a reservation and claiming to be an Indian is, in fact, an Indian.[58]

By asserting that the decision as to who constitutes an Indian should be left to the tribe, Olney avoided the difficult task of making the decision himself.

[58] Senate Ex. Doc. No. 59, 1894, p. 109.

He conveniently sidestepped the European American controversy about how to define race by assigning responsibility for the decision about who was an Indian to the tribes.

The final decision rendered in an appeal of the Waldron case in 1905 was based on similar arguments. Waldron's team contested the U.S. government's issuance of a trust patent for the disputed allotment to Black Tomahawk and its authorization of Waldron's removal from the allotment before the Circuit Court of South Dakota. District Judge Carland reversed the earlier decision in the case and ruled that Waldron was an Indian, supporting this assertion through reference to Indian laws and customs and his belief that common law was inapplicable to Indian tribes.[59]

Further on in his opinion, however, the district judge provided a different rationale for why "mixed bloods" should be considered Indians. The judge asserted that the treaty granting allotment rights should be regarded not as an ordinary law of Congress but as a contract between the United States and the Sioux Indian Nation.[60] Its terms, therefore, including the definition of "Indian," had to be interpreted as they were understood by both parties to the treaty. According to Judge Carland:

> The Indians were an ignorant and uncivilized race. They knew little or nothing of the terms of the law which they were to accept except what they were told by the commissioners who negotiated its acceptance. A man who can read cannot be heard to say that he understood a contract to mean something different than its terms imply; but a man who cannot read, and signs a contract on the faith of what the other party to the contract tells him, stands in a very different position. The commissioners of the United States stated to the Indians before obtaining their signatures that the law included mixed bloods as well as full bloods. It must be presumed that Congress knew when the law was submitted for acceptance that there were numerous mixed bloods living on the reservation about to be divided and drawing rations at the different agencies, and it cannot be presumed that these mixed bloods were intended to be deprived of their rights to tribal property by a law that, without their signature, would not have become effective for any purpose. These observations are made for the purpose of showing that the law must be looked at as a contract and construed with reference to the understanding the Indians had of the law at the time they accepted its provisions.[61]

Here the Indian definition of who was an Indian had nothing to do with Indian custom or law. Rather, Judge Carland asserted that the Indian understanding referred to that which they had been told by U.S. Indian commissioners seeking to further the strategic interests of the state, although this oral definition of the term "Indian" did not appear in the written treaty. The judge thus attempted to protect the treaty and the benefits it provided

[59] *Waldron v. United States et al.*, 1905, pp. 415–16.
[60] Ibid., p. 418.
[61] Ibid., p. 418.

to the United States, including territorial expansion, under the guise of a paternalistic protection of Indian signatories to the treaty.

Indeed, immediately following this passage, the judge returned to a discussion of the Sioux Indian understanding of the meaning of the term "Indian" based on "the usages and customs" of their tribes. He quoted another case that concluded that "the treaty must therefore be construed, not according to the technical meaning of its words to learned lawyers, but in the sense in which they would naturally be understood by the Indians."[62] Thus, while acknowledging the political and pragmatic context of the treaty and its centrality to the case, the judge continued to try to justify his claim that Waldron was an Indian by casting it as simply a reflection of the *natural* way in which Indians defined themselves. This approach diverted attention from both the strategic interests of the United States at stake in the case and from the problematic construction of race within European American society.

Conclusion

Analysis of the Waldron and Traversee allotment cases demonstrates how "mixed bloods" challenged the conventional racial categories that played such a key role in defining the boundaries of the U.S. state and nation at the turn of the twentieth century. Not only did state authorities explicitly associate U.S. citizenship and national membership with whiteness, they also included race in their definitions of state and nation in somewhat more subtle ways, such as by linking it to ostensibly universalistic concepts such as political competence. Racialized assumptions permeated thinking about the territorial and socio-political character of the United States, on both conscious and subconscious levels. Indeed, the racialization of U.S. law and society was so complete that no one, not even those most disadvantaged by and critical of the system, could speak outside of a racialized discourse. At the most, they could attempt to direct attention to its internal inconsistencies and lack of correspondence to empirical realities, as Traversee did when he switched his identity from Indian to white in an attempt to win a legal victory.

While the difficulty of assigning "mixed bloods" to standard racial categories provoked confusion and, perhaps, aggravation among U.S. officials, lawyers, and others, it did not suggest to them that the task or the classification system should be abandoned. Indeed, if anything, it seemed to have the opposite effect. Definitions of race became even more precise, and efforts to "measure" race increased. As the citizenry of the United States became less white, efforts to preserve and protect whiteness accelerated.

"Mixed bloods" thus challenged the boundaries of state and nation, but the changes these challenges provoked were not necessarily the ones they anticipated or intended. Instead, by exposing internal inconsistencies within

[62] Ibid., p. 419.

definitions of racial categories, "mixed bloods" inspired efforts to develop stricter measures of race. By demonstrating the salient role that race played in defining the boundaries of state and nation, they encouraged state officials to devise more subtle and sophisticated ways to mask reliance on race as a criterion for national membership. Of course, the state officials, lawyers, and others who responded to these challenges were often themselves unaware of the ways in which their particular responses were contributing to changes at a broader socio-political level. In an incremental and inconsistent fashion, however, the challenges posed by "mixed bloods" and the responses to them changed the boundaries of the state and nation. While the boundaries of the state gradually expanded to encompass both more territory and more citizens, the racialized boundaries of the nation became more rigid. Contestations of these boundaries inevitably occurred and led to changes, but the continual redefinition of state and national boundaries often led to more sophisticated methods of limiting access to national membership based on racial distinctions, rather than to greater inclusion of all citizens.

8

Belonging and Not: Rossland, British Columbia, during the Great War

Kenneth G. Lawson

> At the present time often purely emotional means are used . . . to set the masses in motion. One may call the existing state of affairs a "dictatorship resting on the exploitation of mass emotionality."
>
> Max Weber, *Politics as a Vocation*[1]

Weber's statement, made not long after the First World War, reflected the apparent ease with which modern states were able to mobilize society to wage war. According to Weber, the danger, risk, and sacrifice associated with war could easily be accepted by the mass of people through "the fervor of emotional influence."[2] This emotion is directed toward the state not as a bureaucratic apparatus, but rather as an embodiment of the nation, resting on a "sentiment of solidarity in the face of other groups."[3] War, in short, activates a strong consciousness and awareness of the nation and its distinctive institutions that somehow deserve to be defended in the strongest possible way.

Yet inasmuch as officials of the state may "want the state to matter most, enough to die for,"[4] as Migdal suggests, the state's achievement of such a goal should not be regarded as a forgone conclusion. When one stops to think about it, the popular internalization of the state as the embodiment of the nation is actually a rather remarkable achievement, resting both on the

[1] Max Weber, "Politics as a Vocation," in Hans Gerth and C. Wright Mills, trans. and eds., *From Max Weber: Essays in Sociology* (New York: Oxford University Press, 1946 [1977]), p. 107.

[2] Max Weber, *Economy and Society*, vols. 1 and 2 (Berkeley: University of California Press, 1978), p. 921.

[3] Ibid., p. 922.

[4] Joel Migdal, "The State in Society: An Approach to Struggles for Domination," in Joel Migdal, Atul Kohli, and Vivienne Shue, eds., *State Power and Social Forces: Domination and Transformation in the Third World* (Cambridge: Cambridge University Press, 1994), p. 13.

infrastructural power at the disposal of the state and on the opportunity to forge mass emotional bonds with significant segments of society.

Indeed, the realization of the link between the nation and the state probably requires mutual constitution between state and society, and favorable historical circumstances. Stated in more highly conceptual terms, I want to suggest that the state is rooted in a fluid social network: a vast array of social relationships that produce and reinforce a set of mental maps and checkpoints supportive, even constitutive, of the state. The central nodes that comprise the state are not merely the official agents of the state but often ordinary citizens who reproduce and creatively generate the power of the state. This dependence on social networks to buttress the power of the state can be observed in remote communities where there is remarkably little official presence, such as a post office, a local law-enforcement agency, municipal government and the courts, and perhaps an occasional tax collector or military recruiter. Yet the social effects of the state's mobilization for war are widespread and significant, far exceeding the actual capacity of official state agents directly to produce, to manage, and to control these effects.

Chief among the social effects of war are the production and intensification of social boundaries. It is perhaps a truism that war inspires and intensifies civic activity geared toward the definition, promotion, and protection of particular conceptions of national identity. Moreover, civic associations are apt to be transformed into agents of nationalism, armed with a combat task to identify, to target, and to expel "dangerous" or "subversive" elements from civic life. Mobilization for war, in other words, generates social movement that increases national sentiment, which simultaneously *includes* and *excludes* certain groups of people and classes of activity.

The point of this chapter, however, is not about the intensification of the social boundaries of nationalism as such; it is about who produces these boundaries and how. To borrow from William Sewell, Jr., I want to emphasize how, at the grassroots level, war potentially acts to "reconfigure and give new meaning to existing social networks and cleavages, thereby creating new collective identities."[5]

National Belonging, the State, and War

In a recent book that examines the relationship between armed forces and the state, Diane Davis credits scholars for "developing the notion of protection rackets and focusing on predatory states" as a helpful way in which to

[5] William Sewell, Jr., "Three Temporalities: Toward an Eventful Sociology," in Terence McDonald, ed., *The Historic Turn in the Human Sciences* (Ann Arbor: University of Michigan Press, 1997), p. 253.

understand state formation and national politics.[6] The writings of Charles Tilly are among the best-known work in this tradition.[7] Tilly's account of wartime mobilization draws a sharp and antagonistic separation between state and society. To prosecute a war successfully, states are driven toward the "extraction" of people, resources, and revenue from society. And because citizens are assumed to be "reluctant to surrender [essential resources] without strong pressure or compensation,"[8] this extraction generates social resistance to the state's activities. Citizens are presumed always to resent and to resist the encroachment of the state on their lives and on their wallets, and they apparently have little emotional connection to or identification with the state.

Along similar lines, Arthur Stein argues that mobilization for war typically generates higher levels of social fragmentation and discord.[9] Stein rests his argument on a rational choice approach in which individuals are assumed to resent the demands of wartime mobilization, since it is in the individual's interest to freeload on the public contribution of others. According to Stein, the greater the scope of mobilization – in terms of both resources and time – the greater the degree of social unrest:

> Individuals who are called upon to make sacrifices when the nation is threatened are likely to want to minimize their personal contribution.... They are likely to resent the taxes they must pay.... Thus the greater the amount or level of the mobilization effort, the greater the number of individuals who are likely to feel resentment, and... the less the degree of social cohesion.[10]

I do not deny that these approaches serve as a useful corrective to the simplistic but popular view that war unambiguously increases civic spirit and social solidarity. It is true as both Tilly and Stein suggest that war tends to produce social conflict and strife.[11] However, the existence of civic strife does not necessarily prove a decline in civic spirit. The two phenomena – increased civic spirit and increased social strife – may be taking place at the same time, and they may also be logically related. My contention

[6] Diane Davis and Anthony Pereira, eds., *Irregular Armed Forces and Their Role in Politics and State Formation* (Cambridge: Cambridge University Press, 2003), p. 6.

[7] Charles Tilly, "Reflections on the History of European State-making," in Tilly, ed., *The Formation of National States in Western Europe* (Princeton, N.J.: Princeton University Press, 1975), and Tilly, *Capital, Coercion, and States, AD 990–1990* (Cambridge: Basil Blackwell, 1990). See also Robert Bates, *Prosperity and Violence: The Political Economy of Development* (New York: Norton, 2001), and Margaret Levi, *Of Rule and Revenue* (Berkeley: University of California Press, 1988).

[8] Tilly, *Capital, Coercion, and States*, p. 27.

[9] Arthur Stein, *The Nation at War* (Baltimore: John Hopkins University Press, 1981).

[10] Ibid.

[11] See Michael Stohl, *War and Domestic Political Violence: The American Capacity for Repression and Reaction* (Beverly Hills: Sage, 1976). See also Arthur Stein, "Conflict and Cohesion: A Review of the Literature," *Journal of Conflict Resolution* 20, no. 1 (March 1976).

is that the experience of war is likely to generate a heightened sense of civic spirit throughout the centers of civil society to advance the national cause. Yet the emotional character of this civic engagement is often expressed through violence and directed against those who are perceived to fall outside predominant conceptions of who belongs to the nation.

This is clearly not to say that everyone within civil society becomes happy and cheerful to contribute to wartime efforts, especially not those who become targets of exclusion. But neither is mobilization simply a matter of the state coercing and coaxing a resistant and unwilling public. It is difficult to explain the reactions of society to wartime mobilization under the assumption that individuals will conceive and pursue their interests in strictly individualized or instrumental terms, or that they will resent mobilization by the state. This way of formulating the issue poses it too starkly as the state *against* society. The modern state, after all, also claims to speak for the nation, and insofar as it is successful, the state is not perceived so much as acting *against* society but rather *for* or even *as* society. The emotional force of nationalism "sets the masses in motion" as Weber claimed, and allows the state to act *with* society during a time of war.

To be sure, not all approaches that explore the relationship between state and society during wartime treat the boundary between state and society as overtly antagonistic. Margaret Levi's *Consent, Dissent and Patriotism* offers a more sophisticated rational choice approach that embraces the notion that individuals might respond to the call to arms based on an acceptance of normative commitments, but only if citizens trust the state and only if they perceive other citizens doing their bit. Still, in spite of Levi's attempt to take normative commitments seriously as an explanation for behavior, she ultimately portrays the relationship between state and society as a matter of individuals rationally calculating their interests in the frame of social fairness. What is missing from Levi's account (but, strangely, not from her title) is patriotism: an emotional connection to the nation.

Nationalism invites a strong emotional identification between masses of people and the state so that state institutions are themselves popularly perceived as an embodiment or expression of a unique, bounded society. To the extent that officials of the state are successful in this regard, there is a high probability that a significant mass of people will identify with, mobilize for, and creatively constitute the power of the state. Notice that this requires a mental map or way of thinking that fuses state and society together such that *people perceive the* state *as an ontological representation of the will of society and thus a constituent element of their* national *identification*. This conflation of one's own identify with that of the state helps to explain why so many people have shown a remarkable degree of self-mobilization and support for the effort to wage war, producing significant social effects that produce and actualize state power outside official channels.

The ability to produce emotional attachments, in which people feel a strong sense of identification, allegiance, and connection, is perhaps a little appreciated power of most successful human institutions and associations. Modern states are not unique in this regard – people also feel such strong attachments to their schools, churches, universities, sports teams, clubs, and so on. I do not aim to explain the importance of emotional connection generally, but I do aim to examine the way in which the state becomes invested with an emotional quality and meaning at the grassroots level of society. Mass war helps to establish a mass emotional bond to the state by providing a strong sense of a shared political destiny that transcends individual interests and gives substance to the nation. The violent, material, and psychological sacrifices that are experienced in war generate a type of charismatic attachment to the community. As Max Weber observes:

> The individual is expected ultimately to face death in the group interest. This gives to the political community its particular pathos and raises its enduring emotional foundations. The community of political destiny, i.e., above all, of common political struggle of life and death, has given rise to groups with joint memories which often have had a deeper impact than the ties of merely cultural, linguistic, or ethnic community. It is this "community of memories" which . . . constitutes the ultimately decisive development of "national consciousness."[12]

To argue, as I have, that an emotional attachment to the nation can fuel civic movement is not to say, however, that everyone is consistently inspired to action. It is to suggest that enough people are so moved as to create strong social examples, pressures, and institutional forces to draw people continually into the mobilization process. Now, there is perhaps a tendency to presume that the state achieves a seamless response from civil society in which state elites easily manipulate and control social networks and movement through nationalism and emotional appeals. Jürgen Habermas, for example, argues that "the artificiality of national myths, both in their learned origins and their dissemination through propoganda, makes nationalism intrinsically susceptible to misuse by political elites. The fact that domestic conflicts can be neutralized by foreign military successes rests on a sociopychological mechanism that governments have repeatedly exploited."[13] Habermas tends to give the impression that the violence and intolerance associated with nationalism rest on the corrupting influence of political elites to manipulate the masses. While I agree that nationalism can be, and sometimes is, used by political elites as a political tool, it is useful to keep in mind that an appeal to nationalism is not always merely an instrumental attempt to claim power but, to the contrary, is sometimes the political goal to be realized. Nor are

[12] Max Weber, *Economy and Society*, vol. 2 (Berkeley: University of California Press) p. 903. See also Ernest Renan, *Qu'est–ce qu'une nation?* (Paris: Calmann-Levy, 1882), pp. 26–29.

[13] Jürgen Habermas, "The European Nation-State: On the Past and Future of Sovereignty and Citizenship," Ciaran Cronin, trans., *Public Culture* 10, no. 2 (1998): 407.

political elites necessarily able to control the meaning and stir the emotions of nationalism with impunity. State officials probably hope to influence and to exploit national passions, but I argue that their success in large measure depends on the active movement of local community leaders and citizens to support, to interpret, and to produce this emotional identification with the state.

There is another important simplification implicit in Habermas's statement that deserves to be addressed here. His suggestion that nationalism integrates society and produces group cohesion is only partly accurate. It is not altogether clear that nationalism manages ever fully to integrate all citizens within a bounded territory. For while the logic of nationalism certainly helps to establish the external boundaries among nation-states, it also establishes boundaries *within* the nation-state. Nationalism defines who belongs to the political community and the manner of living particular to that community. In doing so, it creates social boundaries; it signifies who is accepted and what kind of activities are acceptable, who is included and who is excluded. These boundaries are, of course, fluid and contested. Precisely because there is rarely a real consensus regarding the particular content of nationalism – that is, the particular way of life that a given nation claims to value – there are often struggles as to who really represents or speaks for the nation and its unique way of life. If we think of the state as a social network with a multiplicity of nodes and competing understandings, it seems plausible that the boundaries are fluid in terms of defining what is a core national value and what is marginal. Moreover, the official agents of the state are themselves likely to be dependent on these networks to generate and reproduce the social boundaries of nationalism.

The empirical focus of this chapter is limited to the small mining town of Rossland, British Columbia, during the Great War. There is no particular reason that Rossland was chosen as a case study over other outlying towns in Canada; nonetheless, a study of the interaction of civic leaders, community associations, and ordinary citizens during wartime allows a careful examination of the ways in which the state's official activities are transmitted to the furthest stretches of society. The remainder of this chapter is organized into three sections that examine Rossland's wartime experience: The first section emphasizes the way in which war awakened nationalist sentiments that intensified the integrative forces within the networks of civil society. I recount how the war drew together civic associations to empower and to facilitate the mobilization of Rossland's people and resources, and how that mobilization was imbued with and partly inspired by nationalist identification. Next, I stress how the boundaries of civil society were both contested and made more explicit along the lines of national identification that shifted the central understandings or mental maps of patriotic sensibility. Finally, I analyze how social boundaries were constructed and enforced to ensure the patriotic conformity and participation of Rossland in support of Canada's involvement in the Great War.

The Golden City Goes to War

It is important to keep in mind that if I were an English-speaking resident of Canada in the year 1900, the mental map of my political allegiances would not stop at or be defined solely in terms of being "Canadian," for I would also probably have a strong identification with the British Empire. Indeed, it could be fairly argued that I would identify as much as a citizen of the Empire rather than merely as a citizen of Canada. Being a "Britisher" was equally if not more central to the way in which many, if not most, English-speaking Canadians conceptualized their political identity at the turn of the twentieth century.

The First World War, however, would help forge a social network that influenced the way people prioritized their sense of group belonging by emotionally linking the people and the Canadian state in a qualitatively new and deeper way. The production of this emotional link between state and society, moreover, involved moving the social boundaries that defined who did and did not count as a "true" Canadian. The war would sharpen the experience and broaden the meaning of Canadian nationalism beyond previous conceptions that had been tightly coupled with Canada's place in the British Empire.[14]

My purpose in this section is to establish the way in which the Great War elicited a patriotic response throughout Rossland's civic sphere. I stress how the mobilization, fund-raising, and celebratory activities associated with the war increased people's sense of belonging to a shared national community that went beyond the reach and control of the government's official efforts to mobilize the people of Rossland. Ordinary citizens witnessed, observed, participated in, and created a shared, expressive national community. Furthermore, a significant number of Rosslanders were drawn into a shared network of mobilization as an additional stratum of civic organization took shape that worked to include residents in the mobilization effort and to raise national identification. Civic networks became more robust partly as a result of the state's encouragement and direction. Yet even so, state officials relied on the active and free participation of community leaders and ordinary citizens. And in many cases, community groups took it upon themselves to organize and to mobilize society for war.

[14] See Carl Berger, *The Sense of Power: Studies in the Ideas of Canadian Imperialism, 1867–1914* (Toronto: University of Toronto Press, 1970). See also Paul Maroney, "'The Great Adventure': The Context and Ideology of Recruiting in Ontario, 1914–1917," *Canadian Historical Review* 77, no. 1 (March 1996).

Rossland was a typical western mining town; it was small, ethnically diverse, and economically dependent on the success of mining operations. In 1910, the population of Rossland was at about 3,000. Many of the residents, perhaps over a third, were immigrants from the United States. Germans and Austrians together accounted for close to 5 percent of the population. There were over 350 Irish and 150 Russians. By 1914, a few dozen Montenegrins had moved to Rossland. Social life was situated in these ethnic communities. Most of the diverse ethnic groups lived in a particular section of town and had a club or organization where cultural traditions were celebrated and native languages were spoken. Some had their own halls, including the Italians, Norwegians, Swedes, Finns, Protestant Irish, and the Chinese. The remembrance and partial enactment of ethnic traditions represented "not only a carry over from the old world, but a point of attachment, a manageable, controllable facet of lives which were unfolding in new, uncertain paths."[15]

With the exception of the Chinese, who were largely excluded from prominent civic spheres,[16] there were significant forces within civil society that acted to integrate the diverse ethnic strands of Rossland's population. Perhaps the most significant integrative force was the development of a common class-consciousness, especially among the 600 or so miners who populated Rossland. Not only did they share a dangerous occupation; they also socialized together in the show houses, gambling halls, and saloons. The Miners' Union Hall was another important site of civic connection. The union operated a small library in the hall, and miners could come together to discuss work, sports, relationships, and other concerns of daily life. Ripmeester argues, "Although there were drunken scuffles which often reflected ethnic tensions, similar occupational and everyday experiences and membership in a common institution [the union] helped to alleviate [ethnic] strain between miners."[17]

Rossland had a variety of civic events and public celebrations that also brought people together into a wider circle of contact and shared experience. Parades and a variety of sporting competitions were a regular part of the calendar. Shared religious affiliation that cut across ethnic lines additionally served to broaden social networks and civic relations. Churches sponsored a good deal of the town's civic activity, spawning numerous other associations such as ladies' aid societies, young people's associations, temperance societies, and men's clubs. Finally, Rossland had a fair share of fraternal associations, the most prominent being the Knights of Columbus, Knights of

[15] Michael Ripmeester, "Everyday Life in the Golden City: A Historical Geography of Rossland, British Columbia," Master's thesis, University of British Columbia, 1990, p. 124.

[16] See Rosa Jordan and Derek Choukalos, *Rossland: The First Hundred Years* (Rossland: Harry Lefevre, 1995) p. 48.

[17] Michael Ripmeester, "Mines, Homes, and Halls: Place and Identity as a Gold Miner in Rossland, British Columbia, 1898–1901," *Canadian Geographer* 38, no. 2 (1994): 107.

Pythias, and the Friends of the Eagles. Women's auxiliaries and social clubs, too, were very active. These groups jointly helped to weld the town together by sponsoring drives, dances, and other social activities that potentially cut across the lines of class and ethnicity.

The Great War activated the social networks that generated a shared public world in Rossland. The war brought people together in both new and expected ways that provided for greater contact, greater civic movement, and greater mobilization of civic energies.[18] The *Rossland Miner* – Rossland's only newspaper at the time – soon noted the apparent unity and civic attitude inspired by the onset of war. "Nothing forces public opinion into its proper channels so effectively as a crisis such as the present one."[19] A small example of this increased awareness of patriotic commitment was demonstrated by "some of the mothers of Rossland" who headed a movement to teach patriotism in the schools. "Realizing the all-importance of patriotism, and the heavy calls that are now being made upon the stock of patriotism possessed by the people of this Dominion and the Empire, they are reflecting upon the negligence shown in teaching and training the young."[20]

Canada offered Britain up to 50,000 men, all British subjects by law.[21] A handful of military authorities assigned to Rossland did their part by sponsoring a public meeting in the Rossland Armory to sign up volunteers. Scores of citizens responded. "Volunteers are numerous who are prepared to go to the front," exclaimed the *Miner*. "The youngest of these so far coming to notice are a pair of nine year old boys.... These two youngsters have been fired by the warlike spirit and their youthful patriotism has been aroused."[22] The boys begged the Chief of Police to enlist them as drummer boys, claiming that their mothers had given full consent. They would have to settle for banging the drums of war at home.

When several dozen of Rossland's volunteers finally departed from the town late in the evening on August 26, an intense, spontaneous celebratory farewell ensued that produced a depth of patriotic meaning and enthusiasm. The *Rossland Miner* reported the night's events in detail, which are worth reproducing at length to gather a sense of the collective national sentiment generated and unleashed in the early phase of the war:

While some were rounding up the volunteers, others mobilized the celebrating machinery. At half-past eleven o'clock, when nine-tenths of the residents were just

[18] In the context of Canadian society taken as a whole, see Robert Rutherdale, "Canada's August Festival: Communitas, Liminality, and Social Memory," *Canadian Historical Review*, 77, no. 2 (June 1996): 235.

[19] *The Rossland Miner*, August 26, 1914, p. 4 (hereafter cited as RM).

[20] *RM*, November 24, 1914, p. 4.

[21] Enlistees from Canada made up the Canadian Expeditionary Force. They were required to be British subjects and they fought under the command of the British Army.

[22] *RM*, November 24, 1914, p. 4.

dropping off to sleep, they were recalled into startled consciousness by the other tenth just getting busy. The cheering soon became organized and more voluminous. Later it became harmony as the city band mobilized and started at work on the good old patriotic airs, with the mob supplying the words in song. The fun was on – not the light, meaningless fun, but patriotic exuberance that had a double motive in existing: there were hearts to cheer, and there was the need of letting the world know that we are Britons. So the thing was done up right. Most of the citizens knew that at the time, for no matter in what part of the city they lived, they could hear the cheers, the music, the beat of the drums. This was not all – there was Bob Stewart and the bagpipes; and there were firecrackers and rockets. And so the soldiers' farewell was given. The pride of the citizens at sending their young men to battle for King and country knew no bounds. The streets were filled with cheering, singing throngs. From end to end of the city marched the men who will fight and the men they leave behind. Over five hundred people formed that procession, keeping time to martial music, swelling the sound with their voices and united in cheers for Rossland's first contingent boys, the land they fight for or the lands whose sons in this war will be made their comrades. Twelve o'clock, one o'clock, two o'clock, three o'clock! Time seemed only to add to the numbers and to the enthusiasm. The city was in the hands of the celebrators and nobody slept. The whole category of patriotic airs was gone through from the front and rear and back again.... They were sung with vim and with a meaning.... So the hours were spent and so Rossland gave its sons a farewell.... Good Luck to every man of them! [23]

Similar patriotic celebrations accompanied all six public farewells for Rossland's recruits, although the send-off of June 15, 1915, appeared to raise patriotic sentiments to a near fever pitch. The *Miner* noted the intensity of the patriotism that moved the crowd:

What Rossland can do, when stirred by a deep and consuming patriotism, is beyond even the hopes of the most ardently patriotic of her citizens. Such vast applause as that which shook the structure of the Ring, last night, will live in the history of the city and the memory of her residents and her residents' children. The grandeur, the glory of such a tribute to national patriotism and sentiment will live for long. Never has such an event of such magnitude been held in Rossland. Some events are too deep for words. Feelings were engendered last night that true patriots do not flaunt. The roots of loyalty were laid bare and an enormous gathering of people found themselves gazing upon their own sacred allegiance to a flag, to a principle, the existence of which have been endangered by the challenge of a powerful foe, as they did not deem possible. In the same way that no loyal Briton can describe the all-possessing, soul-consuming devotion to his King and country, so words fail to describe a meeting, the true significance of which lay in those things which are as deep as love of life.[24]

The war not only supplied a reason to celebrate and express patriotic sentiment; it also provided civic opportunities for groups to demonstrate

[23] Ibid., p. 8.
[24] *RM*, June 5, 1915, p. 1.

their patriotic attributes, to mark themselves as loyalists to the cause. The Rossland Rifle Association, for example, invited citizens to practice shooting and offered the public use of the club's rifle range "in view of the fact that there may be other Canadian Contingents needed at the front." Rifles were lent and ammunition supplied at cost. The *Miner* lauded the practicality and patriotism of the offer. "It is an example of the strong sentiment which is noticeable over Canada today and which every Canadian should firmly grasp in view of the present world-wide situation."[25]

The Rossland Farmers' Institute pointed out that Canada had given a gift of one million barrels of flour and called on its members to contribute either produce or funds to alleviate the "want and suffering" caused by the war. The institute explained:

> In view of the national crisis, which confronts the British Empire... and the consequent necessity of all her subjects standing shoulder to shoulder in her defence and support, the members of the Rossland Farmers' Institute are asked to put themselves on record... in raising funds to be devoted to the amelioration of conditions amongst the poor of Great Britain and elsewhere, which must of necessity arise in consequence of the present war.[26]

Canadian Masons were asked to contribute one dollar to build a military hospital for the "relief of wounded soldiers of the empire who are fighting for Canada and for the principles upon which free masonry is founded."[27]

Note that much of this initial movement and involvement by civic groups were not the product of state directives, but rather were the spontaneous emotional response and expression to protect and to rise to the defense of the political institutions with which one identified. Society was on the move. The immediate outpouring of patriotism and civic activity at the beginning of the war was, moreover, sustained by the growth of an additional layer of civic organization that increased the nodes of civic activity and acted to mobilize Rossland throughout the war. Sometimes the state played a significant role in encouraging and organizing participation – such as efforts to fund the war through the sale of war bonds – at other times it played no role at all. In all cases the state's actual presence was extremely limited; it relied on only a small number of enforcement agents, the active involvement of local officials, and the enthusiasm of civic leaders and followers.

One telling example is the Canadian Patriotic Fund (CPF), a citizen's association that sought to provide care for soldiers' dependents. The Canadian government stood behind and supported the CPF by legally recognizing the fund. The involvement of the government was necessary in part to centralize a dizzying array of citizen-initiated fund-raising activities to aid soldier's

[25] Ibid., p. 1, see also August 29, 1914, p. 4.
[26] *RM*, August 26, 1914, p. 4.
[27] *RM*, September 23, 1914, p. 5.

families – such as benefit concerts, programs, and subscription drives – that had already been organized throughout Canada by early September 1914.[28] The movement and activity of the state was hardly in response, then, to the resistance of society to mobilize for war, pace Tilly, but rather was precipitated by the demand for a more standardized system to cope with the fluidity and multiplicity of social movement.

The fund-raising efforts of Canadian society, moreover, went well beyond those initiatives that had the backing or support of the Canadian government. There were also smaller drives initiated by civic groups at the national and local level to increase soldier's comforts. There were separate collection drives in Rossland for tobacco, razors, and personal "kit bags" for the troops. A local fund was collected for Rossland's military regiments, begun by a $100 donation by a local businessman.

In 1915, community-driven efforts to buy machine guns for local military companies were popular throughout Canada. Two drives were initiated for this purpose in Rossland, one of them begun by none other than the *Rossland Miner*. The *Miner* urged that "machine guns are the best form of aid. No more acceptable gift can be made . . . than one of these."[29] Rossland raised enough in a little over two months to buy at least three machine guns at $1,000 each for the Rossland-Trail Company of the 54th Battalion. Indeed, the response had been so overwhelming throughout the "Dominion"[30] that the government found it necessary to discourage machine gun funds, since the military need was more than met. In Rossland, the subscribers to the various gun funds decided at a public meeting instead to donate the funds to the local Patriotic Fund.[31]

Fraternal lodges also mobilized on behalf of soldiers' comforts. The Knights of Columbus of Canada, for example, orchestrated a campaign to raise $500,000 to establish army huts at military bases in France and elsewhere. Several public meetings were convened to organize a canvass of Rossland. Ads were also published in the *Miner* that made an appeal to – and, indeed, helped to construct the meaning of – patriotic sensibility. An emotional link was drawn from the soldiers of the state to the lives of the citizens in a direct personal way that bridged any gulf between state and society, and thereby established the citizens' patriotic responsibility:

> There is a call reaching Canada NOW. It comes from the bloody fields of France; from the lips of loved ones "Over There." It is to YOU – to every big-hearted, loyal Canadian in every rank of our great Nation. The pick of our man-hood, the pride of our hearts, are NOW, this minute, enduring all the anguish of a man-made hell.

[28] See *RM*, September 2, 1914, p. 1, and October 14, 1914, p. 1.

[29] *RM*, July 15, 1915, p. 1.

[30] Canada did not legally achieve Dominion status until 1926, but the residents commonly referred to Canada as a Dominion. I employ their vocabulary.

[31] *RM*, September 30, 1915, p. 1.

> They are wounded, bleeding, dying that YOU might live. They have fought, suffered, given all, feeling that every heart they left behind would gladly come to their rescue to comfort and relieve the agonies of their illustrious sacrifice.... We know that YOUR response will be fully worthy of the loyal hearts for whom our heroes fight.[32]

The *Miner* reported that residents in Rossland were "responding in generous manner." Rossland's target contribution of $1,000 was met easily and exceeded.

Other fraternal associations contributed to the cause of soldier's welfare in various ways. The Independent Order of Oddfellows, in cooperation with the women's auxiliary, the Daughters of Rebekkah, sponsored several dances to raise money for a Returned Soldiers Home.[33] The Oddfellows of Rossland also purchased over $6,000 in Victory bonds,[34] as did the Knights of Pythias.[35]

Along with the material efforts to support the war effort, fraternal lodges engaged in symbolic boasts of patriotism. Lodges liked to tout how many of their members were at the front, as a sign of their patriotic commitment. The Knights of Pythias as well as the Oddfellows paid the monthly lodge dues of their members who had enlisted. During the war, the Knights of Pythias arranged an annual "Patriotic Week." Members were reminded that "this war has been thrust upon them [by the enemy]. Our order is first of all things patriotic. Loyalty to country and the upholding of the principles of liberty and justice is our first pledge."[36] In the Knights of Pythias lodge, a Roll of Honor was hung that named the eleven members of the lodge who were in the service.

Perhaps more than any other segment of civil society, women's groups stood at the forefront of the effort to increase soldier's comforts. A community clothing drive for soldiers begun in late September 1914 would evolve quickly into Rossland's Red Cross organization. Button sales, bake sales, dances, concerts, work parties, and drives on behalf of the Red Cross were a regular feature of civic life in Rossland throughout the war. A good deal of women's Red Cross work was performed through local churches. Ladies' Aid Societies, for example, would often devote a day of their work to the Red Cross. According to G. T. Moir, "the call for Red Cross work made its inroads very deep in all citizens" and facilitated the union of the Methodist and Presbyterian Churches in 1917.[37] Fund-raising benefits for the Red Cross were sponsored by a diverse set of civic associations and actors, ranging

[32] *RM.*, September 11, 1918, p. 3, emphasis in the original.

[33] *RM*, November 15 and May 17, 1919.

[34] Record books of the Rossland Lodge no. 36, I.O.O.F., November 26, 1919.

[35] *RM*, September 17, 1918, n.p.

[36] *RM*, July 25, 1917, p. 5; see also June 24, 1918, p. 4.

[37] Correspondence from Geo. T. Moir to Rev. Daly of the United Church, dated Oct. 5, 1929, Drawer 3, Folder 8, Rossland Presbyterian, Rossland Historical and Museum Association (hereafter cited as RHMA).

from Gladys Attree's dancing class to the Curling Club to the Sacred Heart Church. In addition to fund raising, of course, there was the mundane work performed by women on a regular basis:

> Here in Rossland the mother, the wife, and the sister of practically every household is interested in the cause [of the Red Cross]. . . . The work of every officer and member of the Rossland branch has been whole-heartedly and unselfishly for the men at the front. There are those who make it a rule to turn out, complete, one garment a day for every working day in the month. Some of them do their sewing or knitting at home, and others at the Red Cross headquarters, while the huge numbers of boxes and bales of bandages, socks, garments and other articles of comfort shipped from Rossland each month are the best evidences of the unceasing and untiring efforts of these women.[38]

The contribution of women to war work did not go unnoticed and arguably shifted popular understandings of the acceptable roles of women in public life. The *Miner* acknowledged that the "patriotic and sacrificing work" of women was helping to break down social barriers and resistance to equal rights. The patriotic response of women established a powerful reason for their inclusion within all spheres of civic participation, including the right to vote, which was partially extended in 1917 (see below). The extension of citizenship rights for women moved from the margins of social acceptability toward the center. The *Miner* wrote:

> Their [war] work has been recognized everywhere, and has been the means of winning for their sex privileges long desired by many which previously have been widely resisted. The recognition of women's right to the suffrage . . . has come easily in the new atmosphere created by women's part in the war work. . . . Women have entered into a great many lines of service for which a few years ago they would have been deemed unfit, and they have proved their ability to render valuable services.[39]

In sum, the war involved Rosslanders in civic life through an intensification of celebratory, fund-raising, and associational activities that emotionally linked residents to a shared national community even in this location far from the centers of state power. Much of the social involvement took place outside official channels even though social movement was overwhelmingly supportive of state activity. Moreover, as national identification and patriotic enthusiasm increased in Rossland as a result of the war, the same might be said for the exclusionary tendencies and points of social control. In the next section, I examine the way in which the war helped to define acceptable forms of civic participation as well as the meaning of Canadian nationalism. A broad range of social markers and checkpoints were established that helped to define those who could be trusted and those who could not.

[38] *RM*, September 8, 1916, p. 2.
[39] *RM*, March 3, 1918, p. 2.

Mobilizing Conformity

I now examine how the boundaries of civil society – who and what were included or excluded from accepted forms of participation – were drawn more explicit, guarded more carefully, and policed with a more serious intensity. I argue that the national identification aroused by the war provided an impetus to exclude all those who were popularly perceived as a threat to the national effort. Enemy aliens, shirkers, slackers, conscientious objectors, and radical labor agitators were chief among these groups.

Yet it is not enough merely to notice that war excluded certain classes of people and activity. The war also more generally redefined and transcended the established boundaries of political allegiance. People were forced to prioritize their sense of belonging, as the elevation of national community tended to trump the demands of other group identities and obligations. Perhaps it is indicative of this process that by the end of the war, Rosslanders were much less apt to think of themselves as a part of and to use the language of Empire. Instead, allegiance to "Canadianism" and the Canadian flag became the primary markers of one's political identity and the proper receptacle of one's patriotic loyalty.

Finally, it is worth pointing out that mobilization for war restructures social relations by thrusting people into new roles and new occupations and by generally upsetting the prevailing, ordinary routines of life. Groups and individuals must struggle to cope with the new relationships and roles fostered by wartime mobilization, and they must do their best to fix some sort of meaning to them. So the issue at hand is not merely that mobilization drives or reshapes civic participation, but that it also transforms the meaning and collective significance attached to this participation. I argue, more specifically, that the widespread sacrifice associated with modern mass warfare tends both to connect people to existing institutions and to generate a perceived need for social discipline and togetherness to maintain the integrity of the national community. And, I argue, unless there is a fairly significant popular consensus on the terms of this collective meaning of war, the demands for national unity are, paradoxically, likely to produce greater division as groups struggle to establish the criteria of national loyalty. This dynamic aspect of war to reshape existing social boundaries along the lines of patriotic loyalty is discussed in light of an extremely divisive election in 1917.

Exclusion and Appropriate Behavior

At the beginning of the war, the Canadian government promised to recognize and to protect the civil rights of immigrants from Germany and Austria-Hungary provided, that is, that these "enemy aliens" did not attempt to leave, to criticize, or in any way to obstruct the war effort. A proclamation was printed in newspapers throughout Canada: "It is provided that all persons in Canada of German or Austro-Hungarian nationality, so long as they quietly pursue their ordinary avocations, be allowed to continue to enjoy the protection of the law and be accorded the respect and consideration due to peaceful law-abiding citizens." The *Miner* noted, "It may thus be seen that the civil and property rights of these foreigners will be safe so long as they go quietly about their own affairs."[40] In short, Germans and Austrians could participate and function within civil society, so long as they did not offend the predominant population or raise suspicions about their loyalties.

The protection of civil rights for Germans and Austrians was inconsistent at best. Enemy aliens were required to surrender their firearms. Searches of homes and persons without a warrant were legal, and enemy aliens were required to report monthly to the local police for the duration of the war.[41] Arrests were made of those failing to report. In 1915, a handful of Austrians were arrested in Rossland after holding "secret meetings." Police were reportedly tipped off that one of the men "celebrated the sinking of the passenger ship *Lusitania*."[42] These men were sent to an internment camp, a common practice also for people accused of loyalty to Germany.

While there were no newspaper reports of violence in Rossland, as there were in some other mining communities in western Canada, people suspected of pro-German sympathies were nonetheless vilified and subjected to increased public scrutiny and surveillance. Several "German sympathizers," for example, who complained of the anti-German bias in the *Miner*, discontinued their subscriptions. The *Miner* responded that "these aliens constitute a class of people whom we do not wish to pollute our mailing list or our delivery system with. We neither desire nor require their support."[43] Several days later, still in the wake of the German sinking of the *Lusitania*, the paper added a more ominous warning:

> To exult over the loss of the *Lusitania*... [exemplifies] as perhaps no other instance of war has done, the depths of repulsive crime to which Germany has degenerated.... Such incidents provide a stimulus to violence, an impulse to take vengeance that is very natural, for the defenseless lives of men and women and weak children, born of Canadians have been taken, and desire for retribution consumes the heart of every Briton with red blood and a sense of duty. The world must be purged of these monsters, of that there is a certainty.... Consequently, the grievously strained toleration of the Canadian people, necessitates the German in our midst to cultivate silence, for henceforth that will constitute the greatest virtue of the race. Rossland is unhappily plagued with one or two of these pro-Germanists, who are alleged to have celebrated the recent *Lusitania* atrocity. It is to these that we address this warning: One or two have, on account of the editorial views expressed by this paper, discontinued their subscriptions, and, as we have before stated in these columns,

[40] *RM*, September 2, 1914, p. 1.
[41] *RM*, November 18, 1914, p. 4.
[42] *RM*, May 22, 1915, p. 1.
[43] *RM*, May 13, 1915, p. 2.

we are glad to have them do so.... So it is that we counsel individuals of German sympathies to pursue that "silent" thinking which naught but a psychotherapeutist can divine, and, we might add: There are few telepathists in our city.[44]

The *Miner* conceded that danger of anti-German violence was low in Rossland largely due to the "men themselves" who have been "careful and doing all possible to avoid friction with fellow workmen. Good feeling therefore exists, even though racial tensions run high and, coupled with extra vigilance on the part of the authorities, all seems done that can be to ensure harmony."[45] This "good feeling" was perhaps more precarious than the paper acknowledged. The local Orangeman Lodge – a fraternal association representing Ulster Protestants – passed a resolution that appeared in the *Miner* the very next day. The resolution encouraged authorities to intern aliens, in part for their own protection:

Whereas there are many alien enemies in the City of Rossland who have voiced their opinions and anti-British sentiments. Therefore be it resolved that the authorities be requested to exercise greater surveillance in the matter of resident aliens, and to intern all Germans and Austrians giving expressions of sympathy with the Empire's enemies. This, we contend, will conduce to the peace of our city and the mutual protection of aliens in our midst.[46]

The surveillance of "aliens," however, was in large measure dependent on and performed through civic pressures and checkpoints that the state did not necessarily control. Accusations of pro-German sympathies, for instance, carried clear social consequences beyond the threat of physical violence. As an example, a Swissman named Hermann Haefliger found it necessary to prove his nationality because a rumor had spread that he was pro-German. The rumor was hurting his watch-making business. In a letter addressed to the editor, Haefliger wrote: "I can understand that at this time there is a very strong feeling against those of German nationality or tendency. This may direct criticism unjustly however, but I wish the people of Rossland to understand that in my case they have been mistaken, and that although I am not naturalized, I am still the holder of warm feeling for Canada and her people."[47] The *Miner* explained to residents:

In order that the dignity and the reputation of the Empire be maintained, it is of most vital necessity that all foreigners may be treated with the consideration, and that before christening anyone with the odious name of Germany, or before charging individuals of other nations with disgraceful birth in that country of horrors, that

44 *RM*, May 17, 1915, p. 2.
45 *RM*, May 25, 1915, p. 4.
46 *RM*, May 26, 1915, p. 1.
47 *RM*, May 21, 1915, p. 2.

the authenticity of such statements should be qualified, in order that no unwarranted harm may result, and justice fail in its mission.[48]

Of course, Bill Elletson, the editor of the *Miner*, had qualified and prefaced his editorial comments by noting that those who *were* sympathetic to Germany had best be quiet about it:

Canada is at war and the sentiment of the nation is very naturally antagonistic to the alien German, Austrian, or Turk. If these people, however, show disposition to conform with the laws of the country, conduct themselves as decent and respectable citizens, and maintain a discreet silence with regard to their sympathies and beliefs, then the people of Canada will be enabled to tolerate them. On the other hand, their deviation from the restricted pathway . . . exposes them to summary and decisive treatment.[49]

The internment of enemy aliens represented perhaps the most obvious and perhaps even expected way in which the boundaries of civil society were redrawn by wartime conditions. In addition, however, to the exclusion and contraction of the sorts of civic participation allowed to enemy aliens, there were other activities that could make one the object of suspicion and the target of public hostility. In particular, anyone who was perceived as failing to carry a fair share of wartime burdens was labeled as a slacker or a shirker and encouraged, sometimes rather harshly, to contribute to the national cause.

There was, for example, an enormous amount of social pressure for eligible men to enlist in the armed forces. "In them days," remembers Martin Colby, "it was rather annoying to go out at all because the men in uniform . . . they'd come up and tap you on the shoulder and say, 'Why ain't you in the army?' . . . Oh Jesus, they used to pressure the life out of you. It was hell."[50] It was not only servicemen but children, too, who applied social pressure. Methodist children, for example, "were taught to badger young men on the street in the hope of shaming them into enlisting."[51] One citizen wrote to the *Miner* to declare publicly that he would recognize no man who claimed exemption from military service.[52] And when the Spanish flu ravaged Rossland in 1918, "slackers who would not to go to war were forced to dig graves."[53]

A series of efforts to define acceptable consumption patterns also emerged to mark those who were loyal to the cause of Canada. After all, the war not

[48] Ibid.

[49] Ibid.

[50] Quoted in Daphne Read, ed., *The Great War and Canadian Society: An Oral History* (Toronto: New Hogtown Press, 1978) p. 103.

[51] J. M. Bliss, "The Methodist Church and World War I," *Canadian Historical Review* 49, no. 3 (September 1968).

[52] *RM*, December 18, 1917, p. 3.

[53] Moir, Rossland Presbyterian, Drawer 3, Folder 8, RHMA.

only demanded that men be willing to sacrifice their bodies; it also demanded thrift and financial sacrifice on a wide scale that in one way or another involved all of Rossland's residents. Food shortages were prevalent and economy was necessarily practiced: Even the consumption of donuts and pastries was prohibited and punishable by imprisonment.[54] Profiteering and lavish spending were equally regarded as unpatriotic. People who failed to contribute to wartime causes or who were perceived to spend too freely were commonly criticized and roundly denounced. "Financial shirkers should be condemned in every community," wrote the *Miner*. "People who indulge in extravagance, who are guilty of wastefulness, who persist in living in luxury are unworthy of the Dominion and deliberately betraying the men who are fighting for them at the front."[55]

Personal thrift was extolled as a national virtue, and spending one's money to support the war was regarded as a patriotic duty that demonstrated one's loyalty. Sacrificing consumption in favor of contributing to war-related causes was cast as a small sacrifice compared with that of the soldier. Citizens were indeed encouraged to contrast their sacrifice with the sacrifice of soldiers, who, after all, were portrayed as making a personal sacrifice on behalf of all those at home. "Won't you give as freely of YOUR MONEY as HE has of HIS BLOOD?"[56] asked one ad sponsored by the Knights of Columbus for the construction of army huts. An editorial in the *Miner* explained:

> Duty for you, Mr. At Home, involves no danger. For the soldier it is full of perils; but for you, who are but asked to sacrifice and save, it has none. Thrift holds no dangers. It is a safeguard. It is a paramount duty. The danger for you and for Canada lies in waste. Canada demands of all her people that they save, and stop at no sacrifice to save. She will need the loan of their savings to shorten the war and to build up peace and prosperity. Do your full duty! Sacrifice to save; save to lend.[57]

The emphasis on thrift linked the private and public spheres together under the banner of national purpose. "In the life of the nation, the home occupies a position of strategic importance. The citizens of tomorrow will be what our homes make them. . . . If Canadians are to be a thrifty people it will be largely because thrift is taught in the homes of Canada."[58] This was all taken seriously enough that an ordinance was passed to make waste a crime, and it became a patriotic duty to notify authorities of food hoarding and waste. "The Canada Food board has put into every woman's hand a weapon to fight against those who have hoarded, say sugar or flour beyond their needs, and have allowed such to go to waste in some cases. Hereafter

[54] *RM*, July 11, 1918, p. 3.
[55] *RM*, June 20, 1917, p. 2.
[56] *RM*, September 19, 1918, p. 3.
[57] *RM*, October 16, 1918, p. 2.
[58] *RM*, February 15, 1919, p. 2.

it will be the privilege for any woman to report any case of hoarding that comes within her knowledge."[59]

I doubt whether anyone in Rossland was actually reported for hoarding. But certainly, if one wanted to maintain one's status and standing as a loyal Canadian, certain patterns of conduct were required and expected, and not simply by the distant powers of the state but by one's neighbors, acquaintances, and friends.

It is perhaps little wonder that groups and individuals who were perceived as not contributing to or not sharing equally in the sacrifice associated were subjected to greater social surveillance and possibly even outcast from the commonly accepted protections and legal rights within the sphere of civil society. The sacrifice associated with war, after all, links people emotionally to the state as a central node of social activity and meaning. And this emotion appears directed toward the state not as a bureaucratic apparatus, but rather as an embodiment of the nation.

Yet by the same token, the construction of boundaries, checkpoints, and social mechanisms of enforcement that delimit behavior are not the outcome of some coherent plan that easily sweeps across society. The acceptance of new rules, behaviors, and conceptions of group loyalty were the product of social and political struggle. This sort of struggle was particularly evident in the "conscription election" of 1917, to which I now turn.

Reconfiguring Allegiances

Sacrifice in war is not just limited to those who give and risk their lives, although that is likely the most dramatic and compelling sort of sacrifice. Yet in wars of mass mobilization, whole populations endure hardship in the form of increased taxes, inflation, shortages, and demands made on time and personal resources. The wide-ranging sacrifices associated with war may on one level be resented, but they also generate a feeling of pride that derives from making contributions and suffering for the national cause. These sacrifices that strain personal relationships and tax family budgets are thus invested with significant meaning and purpose. This is not to say, however, that the construction of the social understandings of the nation and war are absent from the forces of social resistance or struggle. To the contrary, groups and individuals emotionally responded to the war by contentiously seeking to define the "genuine" meaning of Canadian nationalism and patriotic loyalty.

While the war had given rise to a perceived need for acting in social concert and solidarity, the exact terms of this social solidarity – the organizing principles around which people were to rally together – were, ironically, sometimes a matter of great dispute and political struggle. The election of 1917 – commonly referred to as the "conscription election" – can indeed

59 *RM*, April 29, 1918, p. 2.

be presented as a microcosm of the whole effect of the war on civic life, which reconfigured the boundaries of civic participation, drawing some in and others out. The election transcended old political divisions and unified people who passionately believed that Canada had a prominent role to play in the war. Yet the inclusion of people in a common cause was coupled with the active exclusion of all those who, by choice or by ascription, failed to identify with the perceived patriotic purpose of "true blue" Canadians. Although some Canadians clearly felt united by a common patriotic purpose, just exactly what this patriotic purpose entailed was itself a matter of debate, and it left a good number of people out of the discussion altogether.

The election of 1917 was popularly interpreted as a referendum for Prime Minister Borden's policy of conscription enacted in late August 1917. To garner political support and power, Borden managed to form a new Union party made up of his own Conservative party and the proconscription wing of the Liberals. Borden also was able to secure the passage of the Wartime Elections Act, which simultaneously included and excluded whole groups of people from participation in federal elections. On the one hand, the act disenfranchised both conscientious objectors and immigrants from enemy countries naturalized after 1902 and, on the other hand, extended the franchise to women who were directly related to soldiers and servicemen. This weighted the election in favor of voters who would presumably be in favor of conscription.

While the election of 1917 was in one way or another connected to the issue of conscription, it needs to be emphasized that conscription itself signified something broader than simply the means by which Canadian society was going to be mobilized to prosecute the war. For many, the conscription issue involved the very status and meaning of Canada's place in the world. It is significant to notice that the whole language and vocabulary of the war clearly shifted now from loyalty to the Empire to loyalty to Canada – and to those who had already given or risked their lives for the nation. Shortly before the election, the *Miner* described what was at stake:

> When the result of the voting is announced every country in the world will say, either that Canada is still in the circle of countries fighting for liberty, or that Canada is finished and is skulking from further battle shock. Four hundred thousand of our sons have engraved with bayonet points the word "Canada" upon the granite pillar of history. The name cannot be chiseled out, but the voters of the land, if a majority declare against the military service measure, can add the words "faltered and failed" to Canada's record on the monument. Our warriors have done their part; it remains for our voters to be true. In this election the marking of ballots should be looked upon as a sacred ceremony. By ballots is Canada to be consecrated or condemned.[60]

[60] *RM*, December 12, 1917, p. 1.

The Union party was a testament to the ability of the war (and the conscription issue) to induce a change in the way people thought about and ordered their group loyalties and allegiances. When, for example, R. W. Grigor, a staunch and lifelong Liberal, was unanimously chosen as president of the Rossland Union party, he explained in his acceptance speech that while he had become "case-hardened politically... the issue in the present conflict was different." He remarked that he would regret to see social upheaval as a result of conscription, but "rather than see Canada disgraced among the nations by not sending assistance to the Canadians overseas, he would rather see the Dominion disrupted from one end to the other."[61]

Perhaps not surprisingly, those Liberals who remained opposed to conscription also used the rhetoric of loyalty to Canada. Many Liberals decried conscription and the Union party as a political trick that degraded Canadian democracy. For Liberals who did not favor conscription, defections such as Grigor's amounted to political and national hypocrisy. Liberals in fact, labeled Grigor as a "traitor," concerned more with political office than with political principles.[62]

The character and quality of civic discourse were affected by the strong emotions stirred by the Union movement. "Rowdies" often broke up political meetings on both sides of the political divide. The Liberal candidate for the West Kootenays, Winfield Maxwell, struggled to address a political meeting in Vancouver above strenuous heckling and jeering from a group of returned soldiers. The meeting was eventually broken up when the soldiers attempted to lasso one of the speakers.[63] Likewise, an "organized band of hoodlums" broke up a Unionist meeting in Trail by "whistling, the stamping of feet, using insulting language, and otherwise making [the meeting] hideous."[64]

More than even Union government, the Wartime Elections Act was considered by some Canadians as a blatant attempt to play politics with the war effort by redefining the boundaries of political participation. Of course, the disenfranchisement of immigrants and the restriction of the vote to women related to servicemen did appeal to many Canadians as the appropriate and patriotic thing to do under wartime conditions. The president of the National Equal Franchise Union, for example, indicated that "loyal women who have no relatives at the front are willing to forego the ballot in the pending contest in order to ensure the return of a genuine war parliament."[65] For Liberals and Labor party supporters, however, the act looked less patriotic and more like a gerrymander to suit Conservative party purposes. Immigrant groups, after all, traditionally supported the Liberal party. This is not to say that

[61] *RM*, December 5, 1917, p. 1.
[62] *RM*, December 10, 1917, p. 1.
[63] *RM*, December 3, 1917, p. 1.
[64] *RM*, December 11, 1917, p. 1.
[65] *RM*, October 1, 1917, p. 2.

Liberals were above this sort of redefinition of who rightfully deserved the vote. The Liberals indeed engaged in the same kind of inclusionary and exclusionary tendencies that war and nationalism produce, only they desired to draw the lines in a slightly different way, expanding acceptable civic participation for women and contracting it as much, if not more, for certain classes of immigrants.

Maxwell, speaking at the opening of the Liberal campaign in Rossland, agreed that women with relatives at the front were entitled to the ballot, but argued that "the disenfranchisement of those women who were working at home in a patriotic way" also deserved the vote. He favored extending the franchise to all women. Other Liberals in Rossland echoed this view. C. R. Benner "referred to the 'discrimination' in giving the women of men at the front the vote and not those at home engaged in Red Cross and other patriotic work, the Red Cross being the noblest work under the sun."[66]

While the Liberals were prepared to go so far as to support universal suffrage rights for women, they headed in the opposite direction with regard to enemy aliens and nonwhite immigrants. Even if immigrants tended to be strong supporters of the Liberal party, this was no time to seek the immigrant vote (especially given that a good deal of them had been disenfranchised!). And in any case, for many establishment Liberals, the conscription issue was closely tied to the question of immigrants. Benner again expressed what appears to have been a common sentiment: "'We have the best class of people under the sun, and yet we ask the English-speaking classes to leave their families and their homes to go and fight while the Hindoos, Doukhobors, Mennonites, and Chinese are permitted to remain at home and draw the pay of the white man."[67] Applause followed. Another speaker added:

> They are taking the Canadians out of the mines of British Columbia and ordering them to report for service overseas while they send Chinese, Japs and Austrians to take the jobs in the mines. They are conscripting the boys from the farms in the Fraser Valley and from the Kootenays. This in spite of the shortage of food right here in Canada and right here in this city. I predict that is will be a sad day for British Columbia when the yeomanry of the country is composed of slant-eyed Chinese. . . . If we turn the great industry of agriculture over to Chinese, to the Doukhobors and the foreigners generally we will strike at the very basis of Anglo-Saxon civilization.[68]

While the Liberal party by and large was supported by the working classes, the war had given stimulus to the formation of an independent Labor party that tended to be even more outspoken against Union government and went

[66] *RM*, October 25, 1917, p. 3.
[67] Ibid.
[68] Ibid.

so far as to advocate the repeal of conscription.[69] Some supporters of labor now felt forced to choose between national and class allegiances.

Picking sides was not always easy. The war had elevated the issue of national loyalty in political discourse. Even for longtime loyalists of organized labor, a patriotic commitment to win the war – and specifically, support for conscription – had become a litmus test that transcended existing political categories. The anguish involved in making such a decision was reflected in the voice of Rupert Bulmer, an Alderman in Rossland who addressed a local Labor meeting. Bulmer quoted President McKinley, "who had said the Democratic party in the United States 'could always be depended on doing the wrong thing at the right time,' and in his opinion labor had acted very much in the same manner in the West Kootenay." The *Miner* continued:

> He had never in his life opposed labor, but that all present could proclaim his stand from the housetops if they liked, for this time he was going to be against labor; that he would not be placed in the position of supporting autocracy against democracy.... He said he sympathized with the men who were opposing conscription, but that there was a time in every man's life when he had to fight, and that time had arrived.[70]

Bulmer clearly regretted the situation. He had hoped to work for and to support the Labor candidate. Yet while "[h]e felt he should be with the class that works,... he could not accept the plank opposing conscription, and would work and vote against [the Labor candidate]."[71]

When all was said and done, the Unionist candidate, R. F. Green, handily won the election, although the returns revealed that Rosslanders were clearly divided on the conscription issue. Green garnered 354 votes to 193 for the Liberals and 161 for Labor. "It will be seen that the combined poll of [the Liberal and Labor candidates] is exactly the same as the poll in Mr. Green's favor."[72] The latter point deserves to be emphasized as it can reasonably be assumed that the split between the Liberals and Labor was an imperfect reflection of the division within the ranks of the labor movement itself regarding the meaning of the war and the demands of patriotism.

These differences within organized labor that arguably arose from different interpretations of the meaning of conscription and patriotism are significant, for they probably played a role in the decline of the miners' union in postwar civil society. The strong stand taken by some segments of the labor movement against conscription and Canada's full involvement in the war made the movement susceptible to broad-based attacks from both within and without the labor movement. Not only government repression but popular hostility to those groups who bucked Canada's newly intensified

69 See Martin Robin, "Registration, Conscription, and Independent Labour Politics, 1916–1917," in Carl Berger, ed., *Conscription, 1917* (Toronto: University of Toronto Press, n.d.).

70 *RM*, November 12, 1917, p. 1.

71 Ibid.

72 *RM*, December 18, 1917, p. 1.

nationalism spelled an early end to so-called labor radicalism after the war ended.

Conclusion: Loyalty, Labor, and the Networks of the State

"Labor Day, 1919," the *Miner* optimistically asserted, "will dawn on the opening of a new world order. The Great War has made many things new, and given a new impetus to old impulses and movements."[73] The new civic environment created by the war was, however, largely defined and governed by more traditionally oriented "old impulses." Challenges to the existing order did not go very far. The shared social understandings that help to embed the power of the state within a social network had shifted firmly in the direction of maintaining existing institutional relationships. Powerful segments of society conflated mere criticism of *government policy* with an assault on *national identity*. This did not bode well for labor groups that sought a fundamental reordering of economic relations and institutions.

The status and standing of organized labor was on the wane even during (and because of) the war. G. C. Marshall, a union official, pointed out "the very unsatisfactory condition that obtains practically all over the continent":

> Never in history have... labor prosecutions been more prevalent than today, while... not long ago the President of the Canadian Trades and Labor Congress was not permitted to address a public meeting.... In my estimation, there exists only one method that we can successfully utilize to protect ourselves from such lawlessness... and that is through political unity.[74]

For all the talk and presumption of the social unity produced by the war, the truth is that a great struggle had taken place over the exact terms of this unity. To suppose then that labor could protect itself through its own "political unity," as Marshall hoped, was perhaps overly optimistic. Genuine political unity is perhaps never easy to achieve, but it was especially difficult in the Canadian wartime atmosphere, in which some workers and leaders demanded that labor back every effort to win the war, and others saw the war as a continued example of class exploitation and oppression. Workers in the latter category tended to challenge the conservatism of conventional craft-based trade unionism and turned to more radical forms of organization, such as the One Big Union (OBU). Radical labor initiatives and movements, however, had to struggle against "increased cooperation of government with the owners of industry" and suffered a "decline in membership and effectiveness" both during and after the war.[75]

[73] *RM*, August 30, 1919, p. 2.

[74] *Supplement to the President's Report, 1917, District 6 Annual Convention*, Mine Mill Papers, Box 160, Folder 4, University of British Columbia, Special Collections.

[75] Morris Wright, *Takes More Than Guns: A Brief History of the International Union of Mine, Mill and Smelterworkers* (Denver, Colo.: IUMMSW, 1944).

The radical labor movement not only had to contend, however, with the hostility of the government and capital. Other civic actors had their own visions of what Canada was to be like after the war, and these visions generally celebrated and vowed to advance existing institutional patterns. This is perhaps to be expected after a period in which people's connection to and sacrifice on behalf of the nation have increased dramatically and provided an emotional sense of purpose. The United Church, for example, vowed to "make permanent" the "new devotion to eternal principles of right" to which the war had apparently given rise.[76] And the Imperial Order Daughters of the Empire promised to help with "the Canadianizing of the thousands of immigrant families in our Northwest."[77]

Perhaps more than any other single group, the Great War Veterans (GWV) took a lead in postwar civic life and played a prominent role in defining and policing the boundaries of legitimate civic activity – and labor radicalism, with its presumed "foreignness," was one of their chief targets. The radical labor movement, as it was claimed, was dominated by "foreign elements," and the GWV had called for the deportation of all enemy aliens from Canada to help ensure against the spread of radicalism. The *Miner* echoed this view and cautioned all "those who cherish the sanctity of the home" to be aware that propaganda was taking root in Canada by "a foreign element shooting the wads being prepared by our enemies to get a hold on our nation." The *Miner* reasoned:

> It is not Canadianism that is asserting itself through industrial upheavals; it is insidious and vicious foreignisms that find easy material in foreign-born workers.... What the I.W.W. [International Workers of the World] and bolshevists want is to create dissatisfaction among the true blue Canadian workers and soldiers so they will join them and help raise hell. But these workers and soldiers are not going to be fooled. They know that forceful methods cannot change society. Peaceful and sensible methods are what they are looking for. And, Mr. Employer, remember this: Our soldiers and sailors should not be treated as mendicants. They are the ones who gave jobs; marched away to save the country and offered their lives that the rest of us might be saved. Nothing in Canada is too good for them. They should have their old jobs back or be given others. If there are not enough jobs for everyone, the returning veterans should not be the ones to suffer. They should be served first. There are those men who sought work as a safe haven to escape military service. They made good money while the boys were in the trenches. If anyone has to go jobless for a while it should be those slackers.[78]

The GWV generally took a fairly strong stand against labor radicalism, a stand that was partially shaped by the fact that Canadian troops were now serving in Russia against the Bolsheviks. In neighboring Trail, for example,

76 Rossland Presbyterian, Drawer 3, Folder 8, RHMA.

77 *RM*, February 15, 1919, p. 6.

78 *RM*, May 17, 1919, p. 2.

the GWV prevented a meeting of the OBU and demanded that J. Naylor, a member of the central committee of the OBU, leave town. Naylor appealed to the police for protection but was denied. The *Miner* noted approvingly that the Trail GWV "have done their bit at the front and are ready to aid their brothers fighting Bolshevists, not permitting the 'one big union' advocate to speak."[79] In Rossland, the GWV did not break up or prevent any meetings, but it did send a committee to attend an OBU meeting and managed to "convince" those present to pass a resolution renouncing any sympathy "to the Bolsheviki of Russia."[80]

The patriotism of the OBU was on occasion questioned by the *Miner* but without the ringing rhetoric or call to arms that had prevailed in some other Canadian and U.S. communities. There was, in fact, little popular violence against labor radicalism in Rossland. This is not to say that civil relations were always calm and subdued. Tensions indeed sometimes erupted that raised the issue of patriotism and loyalty. In 1920, for example, two "foreigners" were given stiff jail sentences after provoking a "rough house" in the City Cafe. Apparently, the two men belonged to the IWW and had too much to drink. They were "speaking at times most insultingly of the Canadian flag," and customers took exception to the "vile language." Several "well-known townsmen" asked them to leave, which they did only after the police chief arrived and directed them to go home. They returned, however, and a fight ensued in which "much blood was said to have flowed." The police captured one of the men as he tried to flee the scene, while the patrons held the other until he was taken into custody. They were sentenced to eighteen and twelve months, respectively, of hard labor in the Nelson jail.[81]

Compared with some communities where vigilantism and violence had erupted against so-called labor radicals, the situation in Rossland appeared relatively tame. But even if the reaction against labor radicalism was not as violent or intense, it might still be noticed that radical challenges to existing institutions were not easily tolerated. Radical forms of labor organization were attacked as unpatriotic, dangerous, and foreign. The immediate postwar environment, in other words, perpetuated the trend of civic reconfiguration along the lines of patriotic loyalty, that is, an emotional identification with the Canadian state as the embodiment of established national institutions and practices.

The war had significantly structured the character of civic life in Rossland by broadening people's involvement in civic life – from increased public celebrations and events to fund-raising campaigns and political activities – that connected them to a common national project in publicly shared ways.

[79] *RM*, April 5, 1919, p. 1.
[80] *RM*, April 15, 1919, p. 5.
[81] *RM*, May 15, 1920, p. 1.

Another side of this restructuring of civil society, however, was the active exclusion of those who were generally perceived as a threat to the national cause. Shirkers, slackers, conscientious objectors, pro-Germans, and finally radical labor agitators were all identified in this category. The mobilization of civil society for war created a strong emotionally driven impulse to define, to identify, and to police residents who fell into these categories.

None of this is meant to suggest that everyone within society sustains or harbors the same sort of emotion day in and day out. Mass war no doubt upsets many prevailing routines and practices, but it does not change everything. People still need to earn a living, still need to raise their children, and still must carry on as best they can with the tasks of daily living. Few people can or would want to devote themselves entirely to patriotic callings. To say that war fuels an emotional attachment to the state is not to say that everyone is consistently inspired to action. But enough people are so moved, even in a small remote town like Rossland, to produce a robust network of social boundaries that reinforced allegiance to the war effort and disciplined those who might challenge, threaten, or simply neglect that effort. The experience of the Great War in Rossland thus brought some people closer together and pulled others further apart. It did so in novel ways that transformed the character of civic interaction and redefined the boundaries of civil society along the lines of patriotic identification.

9

Boundaries and Belonging in Conditions of Extreme Politicization

The Chinese State in Public and Private Places, 1949–1968

Neil J. Diamant

Introduction

The modern state, we have come to learn, is an extremely ambitious organization, prone to deep societal penetration, territorial expansion, and boundary creations. But among modern states, or at least those that aspire to this status, few are as ambitious as those whose leaders rose to power claiming the birth of a new, revolutionary order. In revolutions, very little is sacrosanct; everything is open to debate and change. The perquisites of class, status, and privilege are rethought and sometimes radically altered, as are criteria for membership in favored and out-of-favor groups when revolutionaries go about rewarding those who supported them and punishing those who did not. In addition, the sources of authority, legitimacy, and methods of governance are reexamined in light of new understandings of what is "fair," "right," and "just." Domestic and private matters, such as love, marriage, divorce, and the appropriate sexual division of labor in the family, are also reexamined. Tellingly, some of the very first pieces of legislation passed by French, Chinese, and Soviet revolutionaries dealt with marriage and the family.[1] Methods of chronicling time itself also change. In China, for instance, the Republican revolution of 1911 renumbered all subsequent years as if 1911 was year "0"; in Taiwan the year 2004 is "92."[2] Conceptions

[1] On the impact of China's Marriage Law (1949), see my *Revolutionizing the Family: Politics, Love, and Divorce in Urban and Rural China, 1949–1968* (Berkeley: University of California Press, 2000); for France (1792), see Roderick Philips, *Family Breakdown in Late 18th Century France: Divorces in Rouen, 1792–1803* (Oxford: Clarendon, 1980); for the Soviet Law (1919), see Kent H. Geiger, *The Family in Soviet Russia* (Cambridge: Harvard University Press, 1968).

[2] Several excellent studies have been published about time and its relationship to politics, revolution, and society (and vice versa). See, e.g., David S. Landes, *Revolution in Time: Clocks and the Making of the Modern World* (Cambridge: Belknap Press of Harvard University Press, 1983); Eviatar Zerubavel, *Hidden Rhythms: Schedules and Calendars in Social Life* (Chicago: University of Chicago Press, 1981); Wen-hsin Yeh, "Corporate Space, Communal Time: Everyday Life in Shanghai's Bank of China," *American Historical Review* 100, no. 1 (1995): 97–122;

and use of the state's internal space are not exempt from reevaluation, either. Formally closed-off spaces (such as the Forbidden City in China and the Bastille in France) are partially opened to the public to demonstrate the regime's democratic or populist impulses, as well as its power; other spaces, such as Beijing's Tiananmen Square, are artificially constructed to become symbolic centers of the state, from which point power and authority radiate to the rest of the polity.[3] In a volume devoted to questions related to the processes and contestations surrounding the establishment and fortification of different types of boundaries and belonging, the analysis of revolution allows us to look at these processes in conditions of extreme politicization, as revolutionaries, far more than officials in relatively stable regimes, place numerous political and social arrangements under the microscope and on the operating table. In revolution, we can observe the impact of the "soft rules" determining boundaries and belonging – those norms and practices implicitly encouraged or overtly, but gently, nudged by cultural elites – as well as the "harder" ones, whose enforcement is backed by sanctions and the state's coercive apparatus.

This chapter takes a close look at one of the most ambitious efforts by a state to redraw political boundaries and people's sense of belonging: the People's Republic of China (PRC) during the 1950s and 1960s. During this period in China, local political institutions were staffed by those either who actively supported the Chinese Communist Party in its rise to power or who were designated as "revolutionary" according to Marxist class analysis (the proletariat and poor peasants), while groups that were deemed politically suspicious owing to their personal or family history or Marxist analysis (such as capitalists, landlords, or the urban middle classes) were systematically purged and frequently vilified in the official press. The new state also made unprecedented intrusions into the private sphere. For instance, the Maoist state, for the very first time in Chinese history, required that people undergo physicals prior to getting married, as well as register their marriages with the state. This sort of intervention was driven both by ideology – arranged and coerced marriages, the norm in China, were said to have no place in socialist China where personal and class "liberation" were key motifs – and by eugenic concerns: The state wanted to create a "healthy" and "strong" citizenry, and this could be accomplished only by making sure that people who

Stephen E. Hanson, *Time and Revolution: Marxism and the Design of Soviet Institutions* (Chapel Hill: University of North Carolina Press, 1977).

3 For a brilliant study of revolutionary uses of space, see Mona Ozouf, *Festivals and the French Revolution*, trans. Alan Sheridan (Cambridge: Harvard University Press, 1988). For a useful review of architectural changes in urban China, see Piper Rae Gaubatz, "Urban Transformation in Post-Mao China: Impacts of the Reform Era on China's Urban Form," in Deborah Davis et al., eds., *Urban Spaces in Contemporary China: The Potential for Autonomy and Community in post-Mao China* (Washington, D.C.: Woodrow Wilson Center Press, 1995), pp. 28–60.

were physically unfit not reproduce.[4] Other forms of intervention in the family were intended to differentiate between classes that were deemed friendly or supportive of the revolution from those whose support was questionable or whose stance vis-à-vis the regime was downright antagonistic. The PRC sought to create a status hierarchy that was the polar opposite of what had existed prior to the revolution. Poor peasants, who had been discriminated against because of their poverty and lack of education, were now deemed one of the most revolutionary classes, while bankers, capitalists, and the like were politically suspicious. To prevent excessive "fraternizing" between citizens who belonged to the new "revolutionary community" (poor peasants, workers, cadres, etc.) and those who were clearly outside it, the PRC's propaganda apparatus and its registrars were under orders to convince the former that political identity really mattered and that friendship with and marriage to someone of the "bad" classes were unrevolutionary acts, subject to state disapproval and possible sanctions. These efforts are considered in the first part of this chapter, which deals with state-society interactions in "private" or "domestic" spaces such as marriage, divorce, and sexuality. In this section I ask, To what extent was the regime successful in generating *politicized boundaries* between people whose identity up until that point was intimately bound up *not* with politics, but rather with cultural attainments, class, and wealth – those qualities the regime hoped to subvert as markers of high status in society?

The Communist regime, however, did not stop at trying to create new and unprecedented political boundaries between people in social space that had hitherto been considered "domestic" or "private" (even as it simultaneously trumpeted its success in leading and "liberating" a unified "Chinese people" from feudal and capitalist oppression). The state also encouraged certain types of behavior in officially designated and supervised *public* spaces. This is not surprising, as most states seek to impose some sort of order on their societies. In post-1949 China, this task acquired particular urgency given nearly two decades of warfare and chaos that preceded the Communist victory. "Order," however, was surely not the only motive. The Communists, much like their Republican predecessors, wanted China to be a "modern" country, and modernity implied the imposition of certain rules and ideas about the way people should interact in public spaces.[5] Paradoxically, at the same time that the party-state sometimes demanded that people "rise up" against various injustices, it simultaneously encouraged them to act in a more "civilized" (*wenming*) fashion in state-monitored public spaces, such

[4] For an elaboration of how officials and citizens reacted to these rules, see Neil J. Diamant, "Making Love 'Legible' in China: Politics and Society during the Enforcement of Civil Marriage Registration, 1949–1966," *Politics and Society* 29, no. 2 (2001): 447–80.

[5] Henrietta Harrison, *The Making of the Republican Citizen: Political Ceremonies and Symbols in China* (Oxford: Oxford University Press, 2000).

as streets ("modern" citizens do not spit in public[6]), mediation sessions, and courts. For instance, the state designated public spaces for organized social interactions between the sexes, such as intramural sports and ballroom dancing. In such spaces, people were expected to comport themselves according to "socialist" decorum, which often meant that the sexes should not engage in public displays of affection. In an even bolder attempt to impose rules governing the use of public space, in the 1950s the state attempted to cordon off rural from urban areas through the imposition of the household registration system (*hukou*), which limited residence in cities to those with a coveted "urban identity card."[7] Given that in China (and worldwide, with the possible exception of the kibbutz in Israel from 1930 to 1985 or so), it was far better to "belong" to a city and acquire urban identity than to remain a peasant bound to rural land, the *hukou* system is said to have created a static, place-bound population and caste-like, rigid boundaries between urbanites and peasants. Living in urban space, therefore, became a source of a highly valued sense of belonging and identity, whereas rural space was a source of inferior identity. To be sure, the Communists did not create these identity markers de novo, but their spatial policies reinforced tendencies that had been in place for a long time. The second part of this chapter looks at behavior in public spaces in terms of the degree of "fit" between actual behavior and what the regime aimed to achieve: Did organized dancing, for instance, have the desired effect of creating a bounded space for young men and women to meet and to court? Were courts and mediation sessions the civilized and orderly public spaces for couples to settle their disputes? Did the *hukou* system actually prevent the acquisition of urban status, or did people find ways around its restrictions? My argument, stated in its most terse form, is that even in a state that is generally considered to be "strong," such as China, we should not confuse intentions with outcomes or deduce the latter from the former without examining all of the messy processes in between. As many officials in China found, state-mandated boundaries in

6 The Communists' concern about spitting and other forms of hygiene was not particularly novel. Municipal officials in some of China's most important cities (Beijing, Shanghai, Tianjin, Canton) were concerned about public hygiene and health from the early part of the century, largely under the influence of Japanese and Western urban reformers. Public hygiene was directly linked to modernity and to nationalism, as improvements in public health would lead to a stronger nation. These concerns carried over to the post-1949 period. For one example of this effort, see Ruth Rogaski, "Hygienic Modernity in Tianjin," in Joseph W. Esherick, ed., *Remaking the Chinese City* (Honolulu: University of Hawai'i Press, 2000), pp. 30–46.

7 On the success of the household registration system in the 1950s and 1960s and its role in the reform period, see Hein Mallee, "Migration, Hukou, and Resistance in Reform China," in Elizabeth J. Perry and Mark Selden, eds., *Chinese Society: Change, Conflict and Resistance* (London: Routledge, 2000), pp. 83–8; Cheng and Selden, "The Origins and Consequences of China's *Hukou* System," *The China Quarterly*, no. 139 (1994): 644–68; Kam Wing Chan and Li Zhang, "The *Hukou* System and Rural-Urban Migration in China: Processes and Changes," *The China Quarterly*, no. 160 (December 1999): 818–55.

public space were as difficult to maintain as the more "private" boundaries among lovers, friends, and married couples.

The State in Intimate Spaces: Politics, Marriage, Divorce, and Sex

"Real love," according to one article in the official press in the early 1950s, "cannot exist between a feudalistic and progressive person."[8] While many of us recognize and smirk at the way politics makes strange bedfellows (e.g., James Carville and Mary Matalin; Maria Shriver and Arnold Schwarzenegger) and bedfellows embrace different politics, the Chinese Communists went out of their way to prevent bedroom alliances between people from opposing political classes. Having divvied up society into two classes of good/"red" (poor and middle peasants, workers, soldiers, cadres, and families of revolutionary martyrs) and bad/"black" (capitalists, landlords, rich peasants, local bullies), the Communists sought to dissuade "reds" from befriending or marrying "blacks": It simply would not do for a high-level party or military official to marry the daughter of a capitalist, a wealthy landlord, or former GMD (Nationalist Party) official. Not only were they exhorted to marry within their class category in the press, they might be interrogated about such an alliance when registering their marriage. On marriage registration forms prospective couples had to tick off their political class, and registrars were expected to investigate suspicious relationships to weed out the most dangerous ones. Since everyone had a personal dossier whose contents shaped his or her future job prospects, a relationship with someone from the bad classes or with a particularly problematic political history could jeopardize one's career. While poor peasants might care less about such matters (since they already occupied the lowest rung in the hierarchy), party officials and privileged urban residents should have paid this matter due attention. The incentive structure would have certainly made it reasonable, even rational, to marry within their class status. Indeed, scholars and former PRC residents who have written about personal and intergroup relations in China during this period have noted that the state was generally successful in creating senses of belonging based on class labels. That is, politically progressive people tended to avoid relationships that transgressed officially designated status boundaries, formed strong "in-group" identities (similar to a Weberian "status group"), and, partially as a result of this, developed hostile feelings toward those of the subservient political classes. On the other hand, those of the "bad" classes came to see themselves as belonging to an inferior group. Among many, "friendship" was replaced by "comradeship" owing to the penetration of politically divisive methods

[8] *Nanfang Ribao*, February 12, 1952.

of identification.[9] Liu Binyan, a well-known writer and critic now at Princeton University, writes, for instance, "In the days of Mao Zedong, politics permeated every aspect of life in China, and was considered more important than happiness, love, and even life itself."[10]

Fortunately, recently opened archives in China allow us to add much more nuance to this perspective.[11] In matters of love and marriage, new documents show a great deal of boundary transgression and that class polarization was not nearly as acute as others have suggested. State pressure on relationships did not result in a "civilizing process" à la Norbert Elias nor in what might be called a "politicized process," à la Liu Binyan. Instead, Judith Kranz and Danielle Steele, whose novels focus on the vicissitudes of romantic love and the role of beauty and wealth, seem to have been closer to the mark in capturing social relations in China, even in a city as political as Beijing during the most politicized period in PRC history.

Probably the best examples of this come from the capital, whose archives chronicled the inner lives of the young and restless political elite. The political elite, as noted earlier, had ample incentives to avoid relationships that would get them into political trouble. In fact, one feminist scholar has argued that Communist officials tended to avoid sexual relationships altogether, except within the (hard) boundaries of marriage: "The Chinese Communists of the revolutionary period were not Victorians, but they consistently demanded that sexuality be confined to marriage and never allowed to interfere with a person's broader social responsibilities," Judith Stacey argues.[12] Archival evidence, on the other hand, suggests that the appropriate metaphor to account for the marital practices of high-ranking officials in Beijing is not "patriarchs" but "conquerors": This elite was the (rural) knights who captured the castle and took for themselves its "spoil" – power and, equally important, beautiful (urban) maidens. State officials in China acted not as the tool or "representatives" of an overarching ideology, such as "socialism,"

[9] Lynn T. White III, *Policies of Chaos: The Organizational Causes of Violence in China's Cultural Revolution* (Princeton; N.J.: Princeton University Press, 1989); Ezra F. Vogel, "From Friendship to Comradeship: The Change in Personal Relations in Communist China," *The China Quarterly*, no. 21 (January–March 1965): 46–60. Susan Shirk, *Competitive Comrades: Student Incentives and Career Strategies in China* (Berkeley: University of California Press, 1984), emphasizes growing class divisions in schools, and Andrew Walder, *Communist Neotraditionalism: Work and Authority in Chinese Industry* (Berkeley: University of California Press, 1986), stresses the role of having good political class in shaping authority relations in factories. Richard Kraus, in *Class Conflict in Chinese Socialism* (New York: Columbia University Press, 1981), argues that, by the Cultural Revolution, class turned to caste.

[10] Liu Binyan, "Jiang Zemin's 'Stressing Politics,'" *China Focus* 4, no. 4 (April 1996): 1.

[11] Archives included two cities (Shanghai and Beijing), suburbs (Tong and Qingpu Counties in northern and eastern China, respectively), and rural areas (mostly western Jiangsu province and Chuxiong Prefecture in southwestern China).

[12] Judith Stacey, *Patriarchy and Socialist Revolution in China* (Berkeley: University of California Press, 1983), p. 186.

"communism," or "patriarchy," but rather as flesh-and-blood human beings, whose desires and interests cannot be easily deduced from abstract ideas. Many high-ranking officials in the capital were, after all, young peasant men when they joined the Communist revolution in the 1930s and 1940s and, like most men of their age, had had their marriages arranged by their parents. Rising through the ranks during the war in the hinterland, many came to see cities as a welcome destination, and the cities' women as the "spoil" to which they were now entitled by virtue of their new status. As such, these officials ignored calls to erect politicized boundaries between classes and took the lead in divorcing "politically correct" rural wives to marry younger, and to them more beautiful, urban ones, even if these women had problematic political histories. As one report from Beijing put it:

> Cadres who come into the city want to divorce their village wives, even though they have feelings for one another. They see them as clumsy and awkward, and without culture. They see young, beautiful, cultured, and brightly colored city women and want to marry them. They then request divorces from their wives.[13]

Witnessing such divorces among high-status males, Women's Federation officials offered conflicting views about their motives. One noted that veteran cadres are "politically progressive" and, as a result, "look down upon their wives in the village, and because of this seek divorce." But others complained that such cadres are "Marxist-Leninist in their work, but feudal in their own relationships."[14] In an internally circulated report, however, the chief judge of the Dongcheng District Court, Shi Lei, offered few paeans to their revolutionary credentials. Cadres who abandoned their rural wives and had affairs with urban women were criticized for "capitalist and corrupt thinking."[15]

An important dimension of high-ranking cadres' avoidance of political prescriptions for "appropriate" relationships was their quest to use marriage to attain better "symmetry" between their high political identity and status and their low cultural capital. Having come from rural areas, which were usually considered to be "backward," "civilization" (as might be expected given that word's Latin root, "civil") was decidedly urban. Now that they lived in urban areas, they hoped to present themselves publicly as "urbane" as possible. And because Beijing had many public squares and parks for twilight and evening strolls, cadres needed appropriate "accessories," such as beautiful women, hanging on their arms. According to some reports, these new urban cadres divorced their peasant wives to marry urban ones because they did not want to be seen in public places with women who were uncultured or unattractive. Shi Lei, the district court judge, complained that

[13] Beijing Municipal Archives (BMA hereafter) 84-3-21, p. 29.

[14] BMA 84-3-21, p. 29.

[15] Dongcheng District Archives (DCA hereafter) 1-1-194, p. 11.

not a few high-ranking cadres petitioned for divorce because their wives "do not know how to have fun or speak well.... When strolling through the park they want someone who is young and beautiful. They think this is 'glorious,' and 'gives them face.' They do not ask about their political status." This quest for an urban face and identity led to not a few boundary-trespassing affairs and marriages. Court and Women's Federation reports complained that the newly arrived cadres married dancing girls, female "hoodlums," secretaries, staff, typists, women just out of labor reform, students, nurses, and even people with serious political problems.[16]

Usually, these marriages (and divorces) were approved within party units. On occasion, however, higher-up party officials tried to prevent these boundary crossings. When they did, however, they encountered significant resistance. In Beijing, the Women's Federation complained that if party branches disapproved of a divorce claim, male cadres would then "threaten their unit by saying they'll leave the Party, send someone else to do their job, or commit suicide."[17] Other cadres said, "I'd rather have a wife than party discipline," and "Marxism-Leninism cannot control people's private lives; the party cannot interfere with marriage freedom."[18]

Such problems continued to vex the Communist Party (CCP) throughout the mid-1950s and 1960s in both urban and rural areas. Urban space marked civilization and culture, and rural space ignorance and colorlessness. In 1954, for instance, the Women's Federation in Beijing continued to complain that male officials sought to divorce their peasant wives because they "lacked culture" and were "backward," and because "they did not want to be seen with them in public." According to statistics from the first six months of 1954, one-third of all divorce cases at the Beijing Municipal Court were those of new urban cadres seeking to divorce their peasant spouses.[19] Such was also the case among workers in both Shanghai and Beijing. Many workers hailed from suburban and rural areas, coming to the city to escape rural poverty. Many left behind husbands and wives in the countryside. After living in the city for some time, these former peasants sought to quickly "upgrade" their status by divorcing their (good-class) spouses and taking up with new lovers. Some men even attempted to kill their wives and children, because courts were reluctant to grant divorces to men, believing that their divorce claims stemmed solely from adultery.[20] Rural women, too, were eager to divorce peasant men, whether for better jobs, pay, or identity as an urbanite. Even rural men with good political status could not prevent women's mobility to urban areas in search of what they hoped would be a better life. In the

16 DCA 1-1-194, pp. 11–13.
17 BMA 84-3-21, p. 29.
18 DCA 1-1-194, p. 13.
19 BMA 84-3-28 (Oct. 1954), p. 34.
20 Shanghai Municipal Archives (SMA hereafter) C31-2-417 (1955), pp. 10–11.

mid-1950s in Hunan province, as the records of one National Women's Federation meeting reveal, entire villages were depleted of young women (seventeen to twenty-four years old) who packed their meager belongings and moved to the city. This moved local peasantmen to pen a collective letter addressed to no less a persona than Chairman Mao himself. In it, they complained that there were no young women left to marry in the village: Could the Chairman possibly take care of this matter by sending women to them?[21] Such preference for urban life continued during the early 1960s, as well, when there was a large movement of urban workers and students to rural areas.[22] One 1963 report from Shanghai noted a startling rise in divorce claims filed by men and women whose spouses had been sent down to the countryside. These workers, the report complained, "do not sufficiently appreciate the importance of agricultural labor" and use "material things and money as the only basis of marriage."[23]

Such appreciation for money led to desires that were clearly not in accordance with the state's plan to segregate the revolutionary community from its nonrevolutionary counterpart. According to state ideology, workers should want to marry other workers because they engaged in manual labor and were therefore members of the revolutionary classes. But workers apparently had other things in mind, such as living a more prosperous life. As a result, those who had clout in the post-1949 marriage market were people who had been financially successful in the *pre*-Communist era, even though many of them were now identified as belonging to an inferior group. Like women's preference to live in cities, the desire to marry a member of the former "exploiting classes" irked party investigators. In 1955, for example, a female worker in Beijing's Yi Li Food Company reluctantly married a cadre in the Public Security Bureau. In complete disregard for the state's political boundary markers, this worker told the interviewers that she regretted *not* marrying a capitalist. Had she married a man of means, she thought, she would have been able to "ride in the car and hire servants."[24] Concurring with these assessments was a report from the Shanghai Trade Union, which griped that factory workers "are not clear about the distinction between 'friend' (*pengyou*), 'comrade' (*tongzhi*) and 'lover' (*airen*). Couples go to one or two movies, and then decide to marry. The man sees someone else and forgets about the first woman."[25]

21 "Quanguo fulian huiyi jilu," Jiangsu Provincial Archives (JPA hereafter), 1956.

22 On this campaign, see Thomas P. Bernstein, *Up to the Mountains and Down to the Villages: The Transfer of Youth from Urban to Rural China* (New Haven, Conn.: Yale University Press, 1977).

23 "Bufen zhigong huixiang hou fasheng hunyin jiating jiufen he zisha shijian" (Incidents of suicide and marriage disputes occurring after workers return to the countryside), *Funü qingkuang fanying*, no. 7 (December 1963): 1–3.

24 BMA 84-3-30 (January 1955), p. 24.

25 SMA C1-2-611 (1951), p. 3.

Rural women were also interested in improving their lives, even if this came at the expense of good politics and undermining the state's goal of more politically correct relationships. Reports from the 1960s criticized peasant women for making excessive demands on prospective marriage partners, such as for gold earrings and rings, quilts, and apartments. According to the report, "women will agree to marry only after receiving all of this." State investigators criticized young women for refusing to marry (good class) peasants unless there was absolutely no other alternative and for seeking to marry into "bad class" landlord families because they were more "polite" than poor peasants and had been successful in making money in the past; in Yunnan Province, "good class" soldiers were also undesirable because "they might die in war."[26]

Rural CCP officials, who may have had more incentives to marry a "good class" poor peasant than "bad class" landlords and rich peasants, also placed economic over politically defined measures of virtue and desirability. Landlord families, even though they had much of their property and land holdings confiscated and had been reduced to the lowest political status, still seemed to have retained their reputation as those most capable of making money in the future. In Yunnan province, a female CCP official surnamed Wu agreed to marry a landlord's son. When the party branch tried to persuade her to break the engagement, Wu defiantly said: "I'm definitely getting married, even if it means no longer being a party member." Wu expressed no remorse for her marriage: "Even though his class status is bad, he's still an honest guy."[27]

As the above paragraphs show, the party was largely unsuccessful in creating hard boundaries between people (on the basis of who belonged to the revolutionary classes) as they went about forming personal relationships. For many, the old status hierarchy that placed high value on wealth and reputation was more salient than a potential partner's political credentials. Marriage selection has been portrayed more or less as the result of self-interested, pragmatic calculations in which women and men sought to use marriage to advance themselves materially and in social status (which was often coterminous with achieving urban identity). This finding, though somewhat novel in the literature on Maoist China, would not surprise people who work within rational choice approaches to decision making, as well as those using Darwinian-inspired accounts of mate selection.[28] The emphasis on "choice," or "selection," however, may obscure more about the

[26] "Guanyu hunyin wenti de qingkuang fanying" (Marriage Problems), *Funü Qingkuang Fanying* (August 1965), Chuxiong Prefectural Archives (CXA hereafter) 16-85-B1, p. 36; CXA 16-77-B1 (1963), p. 57; For Jiangsu, see JPA 1898 (April 1965), p. 14.

[27] CXA 16-82-B1 (November 1964), p. 57.

[28] See Richard Posner, *Sex and Reason* (Cambridge: Harvard University Press, 1992), chaps. 5–6; Robert Wright, *The Moral Animal: Evolutionary Psychology and Everyday Life* (New York: Pantheon, 1994), pp. 93–107.

way relationships are often formed than it illuminates. In everyday life, as we all know, people marry not only after calculating their "objective" interests, but also after feeling sexual desire at first sight, becoming obsessed with beauty, and falling in love. As much as the Communists wanted people to think about potential spouses' political identity and the new boundaries they erected between people,[29] innate human sexuality and sexual impulse proved to be a more powerful force in shaping relations between the sexes.[30]

Throughout the Maoist period, and contrary to most of the literature on this subject, state investigators charged with chronicling marriage and divorce practices among ordinary Chinese citizens in urban and rural areas were struck by the extent to which passion, rather than state-designated political boundaries, shaped social interactions. Such descriptions show up in actual divorce cases, where they might be expected to be found given the fact that divorce is often the end of a longer period of marital strife, as well as in the more routine bureaucratic reports on everyday marriage issues. Such reports frequently referred to the "chaos" (*luan*) of sexual relations (such as adultery, sex with multiple partners, swapping wives, or perhaps even passion more generally), especially in "small firms where party organizations were weak."[31] In a Beijing factory, for instance, one investigation revealed that in a one-month period, there were fifteen out-of-wedlock pregnancies among 300 female workers; another complained that underage married women had sex six to seven times, sued for divorce, and then killed their infants because they could not afford to raise them.[32] The high incidence of multiple sexual partners figured prominently in investigation reports. In a Shanghai factory, one woman "had at least eight lovers"; another woman

[29] In 1962, *China Youth* magazine cautioned, "Before a man and a woman get married, they should thoroughly understand each other. One must make a careful analysis and judgment of the political stand, ideological quality, attitude toward labor, habit of living, disposition and likes and dislikes." Cited in Elizabeth Croll, *The Politics of Marriage in Contemporary China* (Cambridge: Cambridge University Press, 1981), p. 42.

[30] Unfortunately, the literature on social life in China pays scant attention to this, emphasizing, for reasons that are still unclear to me, the powerful role of ritual, community surveillance, and the highly "restrained," unemotional nature of courtship, especially among peasants. "One of the most important constraints [on marriage] is the attitude that relationships between men and women ought to be regulated by the strictest sort of puritanical decency," write anthropologists Jack and Sulamith Potter. Emotions, they add, "are not thought of as significant in social relationships." See *China's Peasants: The Anthropology of a Revolution* (Cambridge: Cambridge University Press, 1990), pp. 182–3. Chinese who have written about their experiences in the PRC during the 1950s and 1960s echo such views. Jianying Zha, author of *China Pop*, similarly describes the 1950s and 1960s as a period when the CCP "systematically eradicated all palpable signs of bodily interest and institutions of carnal pleasure...sex practically vanished from sight in Chinese culture." See *China Pop: How Soap Operas, Tabloids, and Bestsellers are Transforming a Culture* (New York: New Press, 1995), p. 139.

[31] SMA C31-2-417 (1955), p. 9.

[32] BMA 84-3-30 (1955), p. 24; DCA 11-7-212, p. 27.

"had affairs with three men, all married: every day one goes and another comes to take his place."[33] In a quilt factory in Beijing, one woman had had nine boyfriends, but during the New Year festivities she was seen with yet another man. Several days after the party, she moved into his room.[34] Other Beijing workers went on dates to Tianqiao, a public area long the center of traveling theater in Beijing, to listen to local opera performances. After the opera, they went to the movies or sports arena, and then returned home to have sex.[35]

Interestingly, the state's own rhetoric sometimes offered workers a justification for their open displays of affection. At the same time that the party was interested in good-class individuals marrying other good-class individuals, it simultaneously called for "free love" marriages (i.e., not arranged or coerced) and for more "open social interaction among men and women," in order to reduce the level of sexual inequality in society. This "multivocality" was not lost on ordinary citizens, who proved quite capable of using the state's own language to justify their own desires. For instance, in some cases, workers had sex in full daylight and in front of other people. But if they were discovered and admonished by an official, they were reported to be "unafraid" and retorted that they were only following the Party's own call for "open social interaction among men and women."[36] In Beijing, for instance, one report from 1954 noted, women workers held the view that the PRC's Marriage Law, which called for relationships to be based on "free love," meant that you can "have sex with whomever you please."[37] As state officials discovered to their dismay, "political language," once learned, was a powerful weapon to justify behavior that did not quite fit political or social orthodoxies.

Peasants were also no strangers to love (or lust-)- based relationships. Such passions, and the short-term, ad hoc relationships they brought about, were a major irritant to critics investigating marriage practices in the countryside. In the Beijing suburbs, for instance, a 1954 party report on the marriage situation there made it a point to complain that a certain woman surnamed Wang "has slept with 4–5 men, and the village party secretary has already slept with her twice." In other rural areas, the report continued, "some women publicly live together with 3–4 men." The result, according to the report, was "chaos" in marital relations and the birth of many out-of-wedlock children.[38]

[33] SMA C31-2-417 (December 1956), p. 42.

[34] DCA 11-7-212 (1954), p. 27.

[35] DCA 1-1-141, p. 34; BMA 101–412, pp. 20–1. For a very perceptive study of the role of Tianqiao in Beijing social and political life, see Madeleine Yue Dong, "Juggling Bits: Tianqiao as Republican Beijing's Recycling Center," *Modern China* 25, no. 3 (1999): 303–42.

[36] SMA 84-3-28 (1954), p. 20.

[37] Ibid.

[38] BMA 84-3-28 (October 1954), pp. 45–6.

The mid-1950s expansion of mutual aid teams into cooperatives and the concomitant politicization of the countryside apparently had little effect on peasant marriage and sexual practices or the language peasants used to justify their relationships. In 1956, the Jiangsu Women's Federation complained that in several counties, women "flirt with three men at a time," trick men into giving them engagement gifts and then "refuse to talk to them again," marry only for money without any regard for the age or political class of their spouse, and "divorce after using up all their husbands' money," sometimes only a few days after marriage.[39] A 1958 article by a law student on the causes of divorce in the countryside pointed out a bit condescendingly that in "some backward rural areas," peasants "misunderstand the meaning of marriage freedom and marry on the basis of fleeting moments of passion." Two months later, he complained, they "petition for divorce," telling the judge: "I didn't know that he was 10 years older than me," or "I didn't know that s/he was married and already had children."[40]

As these reports show, it is quite clear that the state-erected political boundaries were not necessarily accepted as legitimate, proper, or desirable by many ordinary citizens. If one goal of the Chinese state was to create all sorts of boundaries between people (based on class) or around them (such as recommending a certain preferred method of courtship), this goal proved elusive. This was not for lack of trying, as the extensive documentation of investigations into family and sexual matters in and of itself testifies to a commitment of state resources. Rather, evidence of "chaotic" relations, interclass relationships and shot-gun marriages reveals a social vibrancy immune to state policies and ideologies. Despite campaigns, despite political study sessions, production drives, and the like, intimate life in China continued pretty much as it had before the revolution. In the realm of domestic space, therefore, labels issued by the state were not necessarily labels acted on by ordinary people.

The State in Public Spaces

One possible objection to the argument laid out above is that even though the state committed resources to changing the way people went about getting married and divorced, this issue was not a high priority. Moreover, changing intimate behavior is far more difficult than changing other sorts of social interactions or economic transactions, if only because the former are often not directly supervised by a state official. My case would be strengthened if I could show that such behavior also vexed state officials in more public and even official spaces and during activities that were subject to greater state

[39] JPA 35 (1956), pp. 29–30.

[40] Fei Yuke, "Luetan chuli nongcun diqu hunyin wenti de tihui," *Zhengfa Xuexi* 5–6 (1958): 57.

supervision. Below I consider several of these sorts of spaces – ranging from ballrooms to mediation sessions to courts – to try to determine the extent to which state-created boundaries moved beyond policy proclamations and propaganda tracts and actually shaped the way ordinary people behaved.

First, let us take a look at state efforts to create more orderly and regimented forums for courtship and entertainment. Much as modern states have been interested in ordinary citizens' sexual practices, they have also promoted certain life-styles, usually ones that reduce the risk of instability and encourage greater productivity. In the United States, the flurry of films about "mental hygiene" in the 1950s (which tried to teach teenagers about proper dating practices, sexually transmitted diseases, manners at home, and the like), was testimony to the state's (and businesses') interest in producing a stable home front and citizens capable of fighting the Cold War on the technological front. For the modern state and industry, unsupervised leisure time and unregulated space were associated with crime, licentiousness, delinquency, and low productivity. Maximum productivity and social stability could be maintained by channeling free time into organized activities, such as clubs and sports groups, and by designating spaces for approved social interaction (chaperoned proms, community festivities in town halls, etc.).[41] At least officially, Mao's views regarding leisure were similar to those in the capitalist countries he railed against in public speeches and documents.[42] Maoist opposition to leisure for leisure's sake was also based on a class analysis of Chinese society. Leisure was suspect because of its association with wealth, "decadent" urban living, and the disparagement of manual labor. The natural outgrowth of these views toward leisure was the attempt to regiment time and space, much as society generally was said to have been organized and regimented in work units or villages or else rather rigidly divided into "urban" and "rural" sectors owing to the household registration system.[43]

Intentions, however, are not the equivalent of outcomes, and it would be a mistake to deduce the latter from the former. In its attempt to regiment and to politicize space and time, the Chinese state encountered many of the obstacles that frustrated industrialists in the early stages of European industrialization.[44] In the West and in China, many workers in emerging industries were peasants or farmers, whose idea of leisure was not shaped by an industrial conception of time nor by Communist collectivist ideology. In villages, leisure time and space were shaped more by natural cycles of agriculture

41 On this point, see Shaoguang Wang, "The Politics of Private Time: Changing Leisure Patterns in Urban China," in Davis et al., eds., *Urban Spaces in Contemporary China*, p. 150.

42 Ibid., p. 152.

43 Ibid., pp. 153–4.

44 See E. P. Thompson, "Time, Work-Discipline and Industrial Capitalism," *Past and Present* 38 (1967): 56–97.

than regimented by political or economic power: Peasants might go to hear local opera at the township or county seat, sit around and smoke and gossip, or play cards and gamble. Such practices moved into the urban setting as peasants became "workers" without adopting a suitably "proletarian" cultural esthetic and identity (e.g., a commitment to Spartan living).

In China in the 1950s, the dance floor was where both the regime's production quotas and ideological goals regarding political relationships often foundered. Dance parties in China were not U.S.-style "sock hops," but rather events that were organized by work units and supervised by state officials. Social interactions within this state-supervised space were expected to be orderly, in part to ensure that night-time dancers would be able to get out of bed the following morning. As it turned out, however, dance parties were not as regimented as the regime hoped. In late 1954, a party report on the marriage situation in a Shanghai factory complained that there were "very many illicit affairs" among workers. Workers, it appears, were a bit too fond of dancing and would take off early from work and wander about the city frequenting various places of entertainment until the wee hours of the night, often with the assistance of pedicab drivers. The next morning, some were unable to show up on time for work.[45] In Shanghai's Number One Cotton Mill, some party officials likewise complained that workers were "irresponsible toward love," because they "wanted to have a good time," "chose boyfriends at random," and "left work to go to dancing." One woman in the factory reportedly "specialized in making friends," taking time off from work to go dancing, sometimes as often as six times a week. Other workers in the factory followed her example.[46] These sorts of relationships met the ire of state officials, who had hoped the relationships between the sexes would be a bit more orderly, civilized, and politically motivated. In a 1957 speech to workers, a Women's Federation official complained about "flash marriages: couples go to eat, to a movie, to a dance, and in their passion get married.... Some take longer, but when they court the only thing they talk about is food, drink, and entertainment, not each others' thoughts."[47]

The dance floor to be sure, was not the only public space where people failed to comport themselves according to official prescriptions for proper behavior. Archival evidence reveals similar instances in more official forums, such as mediation sessions and courtrooms. Mediation, for example, was promoted by the state as both a cost-cutting measure (since petitioners would not have to leave their villages and lose work hours to go to court) and a culturally appropriate method for resolving interpersonal disputes; such a view was often repeated to me by Chinese officials, who claimed that "we Chinese,

[45] SMA C31-2-228, p. 45.
[46] SMA C1-2-1443, p. 17.
[47] DCA 6-1-36, p. 10.

unlike you Westerners, do not sue at the drop of a hat." Until recently, much of the secondary literature on Chinese law and comparative dispute resolution took such statements at face value, arguing that mediation in the PRC drew on a deep historical wellspring of noncontentious, harmony-seeking methods of dispute resolution.[48] On the ground, however, the situation was often quite different. In a village in Yunnan province, for example, two male mediators vividly captured their dilemma: "Mediating," they said, "is just like whipping a mule: You whip the mule and it farts, stinking you up. You try to mediate and everyone will be angry with you." Another complained, "When you mediate... both sides threaten you, and each other, with murder or suicide. How can we possibly find a solution?" Unable to reconcile disputing parties, mediators adopted the pragmatic strategy of sending cases to courts and letting judges deal with the hassle. Courts, of course, were not pleased by this and complained that village mediators were sending cases their way "as soon as there's a conflict in the village."[49]

If mediation did not exactly proceed according to state plan, neither did court proceedings. As physical spaces, courts in China hardly have the sort of institutional gravitas of Her Majesty's court in England or a wood-paneled, chandeliered court in Connecticut or Boston. Nevertheless, it was expected that court petitioners accord the space some measure of institutional aura, even if they did not have to wear suits or their best clothing to file a petition. Litigants, on the other hand, had something else in mind: venting their anger in the presence of authority and getting their problem solved. Few appeared to care much about proper decorum or proper legal procedures. In Yunnan, for instance, women from the Yi minority who came to sell their produce at the county seat developed a penchant for "dropping in" on other people's hearings and cheering for one side or the other, raising such a racket that the proceedings had to be suspended. This was called *kan renao*, or "getting in on the fun." Some took advantage of the opportunity to sue for divorce themselves, often without their husband being present in the courtroom. Local officials who happened to see the Yi women in court were very concerned: "They're not coming to listen to cases or policy. They all want to divorce!" Soon a small controversy developed between court and township officials over the issue of "whether or not Yi women love suing for divorce."[50] Unfortunately, comments from the proverbial "peanut gallery" were not the only problem, as petitioners themselves were often disposed to airing their family's dirty laundry in front of the judge and other officials. The language

48 Jerome A. Cohen, "Chinese Mediation on the Eve of Modernization," in David Buxbaum, ed., *Traditional and Modern Legal Institutions in Asia and Africa* (Leiden: E. J. Brill, 1967); James Wall and Michael Blum, "Community Mediation in the People's Republic of China," *Journal of Conflict Resolution* 35, no. 1 (1991): 3–20.

49 CXA 11-4-14B-1, pp. 141 and 126.

50 CXA 16-27-A1 (February 1957), p. 2.

tended to be quite sexual and explicit, with wives and husbands trading barbs about each other's sexual performance and physical endowments. To make court proceedings more "civilized," higher level courts instructed that their subordinate units individualize hearings for plaintiffs if they persisted in discussing their sex lives or spouses' illicit affairs.[51] An etymological analysis of the ideographs for the phrase "getting a divorce" in Chinese provides further testimony of the decibel level of Chinese court proceedings, at least in working class and rural areas. In Chinese, the word for divorce is "*li hun.*" However, documents rarely used a neutral term such as "get" a divorce or "go" to court. Instead, the popular phrase was *nao lihun*; *nao*'s primary meaning is "to make a loud noise," "raise a racket," "create a disturbance," and "vent one's anger."

All of these reports about peasants' heading to court to sue for divorce or dropping in on court sessions just for the fun of it, are, I think, particularly interesting, considering that they occurred during the late 1950s, a period when the household registration system was supposed to have been rigorously enforced. As I pointed out earlier, the household registration system was another example of the Communist regime's attempt to create artificial boundaries between people. What was open and free space before (at least in the sense that people could move freely in it) became, with the onset of the household registration system, bounded space: One needed special documents to move about the countryside, and such documents were rationed by the state.[52] These documents, according to William Lavely, were "usually impossible to obtain."[53] But here again one would be wise not to put too much stock in what the state says it is doing or hopes to be accomplishing. As Joel Migdal notes in Chapter 1, the state tries to "induce people to see its parts as integrated and acting in conjunction with one another." This "image of the state" is often abetted by scholarship that does not look far enough below the surface and attributes all sorts of outcomes to "the" state as if it were a monolithic entity. But, here again, in our "extreme case" of a "strong" state erecting boundaries between people and places, there are many signs that even a national household registration could not hold down society and that space, rather than being bounded and serving only political purposes, could be used by society to break away from boundaries as well.

51 Ibid., pp. 36–7.

52 Vivienne Shue similarly maintains that opportunities for residential and occupational mobility were "close to zero after the Great Leap Forward . . . [as] the welfare of each individual must increasingly have come to be regarded as permanently tied to the welfare of that person's village or commune." See Vivienne Shue, *The Reach of the State: Sketches of the Chinese Body Politic* (Stanford, Calif.: Stanford University Press, 1988), p. 49.

53 William Lavely, "Marriage and Mobility under Rural Collectivism," in Rubie S. Watson and Patricia Buckley Ebrey, eds., *Marriage and Inequality in Chinese Society* (Berkeley: University of California Press, 1991), p. 290.

Records from rural archives in the 1950s and 1960s attests to people's ability to cross state-mandated spatial boundaries, just as they transgressed those based on class. Marriage and economic transactions (to the extent that these can be considered separately) seem to have been most affected. During the famine resulting from the Great Leap Forward, for example, there was a dramatic increase in the number of divorces in rural China.[54] In part this was because the post-leap famine strained family relations, as competition for scare resources pitted young against old and spouses against each other.[55] But family tensions were partially alleviated by women's willingness to flout state-mandated restrictions on movement through space. Compilers of the Kunshan County (Jiangsu Province) gazetteer attributed divorce to the fact that some women "blindly ran away" (*mangmu wailiu*) because of economic hardship.[56] In spite of the household registration system, women left their villages and returned to their natal homes, which were some distance away. From there, the road to divorce was not long.

Rural space was not only a resource (or refuge) to escape from the result of disastrous state policies, but also an economic resource. In cities, space was easier to control thanks to the establishment of work units, residence committees, and the like. The countryside, however, was less easily governed (one rural official remarked, "The countryside is like an open-air factory: They're both hard to manage"[57]). Despite the household registration system that was intended to demarcate clear boundaries between rural and urban areas, boundaries between them remained porous. Probably the best example of this was the black market in urban women that developed in the Shanghai region in the early 1960s. The terms of trade were simple: Cities lacked the good food that villages had, while villages lacked women, as many women abandoned the countryside for the city. The Shanghai Women's Federation reported that working-class urban women were being traded to Zhejiang in return for culinary delights. According to their investigation, most of the women transferred to Zhejiang were between seventeen and twenty-one years of age and already on the periphery of urban society: Most did not have household registration in the city, frequently moved between city and countryside, lacked stable employment, or were failing at school. To ensure that they would remain in the countryside and not return to the city, organizers of this marriage market (often comprised of an older female and seven or eight associates) used black market connections to procure products that rural men would be able to use to satisfy the material demands of their

[54] On this, see Neil J. Diamant, *Revolutionizing the Family: Politics, Love, and Divorce in Urban and Rural China, 1949–1968* (Berkeley: University of California Press, 2000), chap. 6.

[55] Edward Friedman, Paul Pickowicz, and Mark Selden, *Chinese Village, Socialist State* (New Haven, Conn.: Yale University Press, 1991), p. 240.

[56] *Kunshan xian zhi* (Kunshan county gazetteer) (1990), pp. 546, 566.

[57] Songjiang County Archives 8-1-37 (November 1964), p. 139.

new spouses. In the meantime, the Zhejiang men hoarded products that were strictly rationed in urban areas after the Great Leap, such as grain, oil, paper, and selected fruits and vegetables.[58]

These urban-rural trade networks continued well into the 1960s. Rural women moved to the city and tried to assume urban identities (despite the household registration system), while rural men attempted to acquire urban panache by marrying an urban woman (even though she might be only several years' removed from being a peasant, as many workers were). Spatial boundaries were porous, and identity was in flux. There were many holes in the state's edifice, and people found different ways to move through them in their pursuit of economic opportunity and social status.

Conclusion

As this chapter has shown, unorthodox sexual, marital, and economic behavior was a hallmark of the Maoist years. For many, state-established boundaries between groups were not fixed; politics was *not* more important than love or life; and institutions and "the party" did not produce awe, reverence, and obedience. Internal space that was set off and expected to generate new politically and culturally palatable forms of behavior (particularly in courtship) was used by local actors to pursue goals that did not always mesh with those of the state. While the stereotypical image of China during this period is one of heightened social regimentation and a society that more or less marches in lock-step to the beat of the state's drummer, this essay emphasizes *fluidity* both between classes and between spaces, as well as a social vibrancy and feistiness that often rendered politically inspired boundary markers obsolete and confounded more ideologically inclined state officials.

Unfortunately, it would be premature to conclude that these sorts of boundary crossings persisted throughout the entire Maoist period. While the emphasis on "politically correct" marriages and proper courtship procedures did not appear to take hold in the 1950s and early to mid-1960s, during the Cultural Revolution (1966–76) it is quite apparent that membership criteria for group belonging tightened. A "bloodline" theory of class emerged (which restricted membership in the early Red Guards to those whose fathers belonged to the "red" classes), and officially designated enemy groups (landlords, capitalists, and their progeny, whose identity was also determined at birth) suffered a great deal. Probably not coincidently, this internal fortification of group identity through the reification of revolutionary bloodlines was accompanied by the full-blown emergence of a "cellular" economy in

[58] "Linong funü zhong yi zuo jieshao ren wei huangzi cong zhong huoli weifan hunyinfa de qingkuang fanying" (Lane and Alley women violate the Marriage Law by becoming intermediaries under false pretenses and reaping a profit), *Funü Qingkuang Fanying*, (November 15, 1963), in SMA C31-2-906, pp. 131–3.

which villages were virtually roped off from cities and other communities, as well as China's near-complete diplomatic isolation. Interestingly, there is also substantial evidence that many of the politically incorrect marriages of the 1950s among the Communist elite came back to haunt them during the Cultural Revolution's witch hunt. When Mao called on Chinese youth (organized as Red Guards) to criticize members of the Communist Party, many of them focused on marriage- and sex-related boundary-crossing offenses. Youthful Red Guards criticized high-placed Communist officials and even People's Liberation Army marshals for marrying women with suspicious political backgrounds, engaging in multiple affairs, and even attending dance parties with beautiful women surrounding them, this in addition to the more traditional litany of political crimes (opposing Chairman Mao, etc.). As one Red Guard publication noted of Mao's heir-apparent Liu Shaoqi, who married a beautiful daughter of a high-ranking Nationalist official:

> Liu Shao-ch'i [Shaoqi] chose to establish ties with this wicked family by marriage. It can be seen that he has long ago ceased to be a communist cadre and a true communist. He is a simon-pure favorite of the bureaucrat-bourgeoisie, the protector of the bourgeoise, and the No.1 revisionist chieftain of China.[59]

Marshall He Long, a dashing People's Liberation Army (PLA) officer, was accused of even greater sexual impropriety. On these grounds, He Long was a relatively easy target, having been married and divorced nine times. Divorce, however, was not his only "misdemeanor." According to a Red Guard account, He Long had the gall to brag publicly about his sexual conquests: "Should I invite all my past concubines to dinner," he proudly said, "they could make a table!" His other "crimes" included carrying away any young and beautiful girl he saw in the street during his days "as a bandit" (before joining the PLA), lusting after Cantonese women (because they had "curved eyebrows and high cheekbones"), hiring a mistress of a Nationalist army officer to teach him dancing during his tenure in Yunnan in the early 1950s, dancing and then sleeping with Cultural Work Troupe members during the antibandit campaigns in the Southwest, consorting with prostitutes, and always discussing women. "After Liberation," they charged, "he was addicted to dancing" and "playing cards," never taking along Chairman Mao's collected works on any of his numerous trips.[60]

Liu, He, and many others accused of such "boundary-crossing" marriage and sex-related crimes during the 1940s and 1950s, did not survive the Cultural Revolution.

59 "A Glimpse of the Wicked Family," in U.S. Consul General – Hong Kong, *Selections from Chinese Mainland Magazines*, no. 574 (1967): 4. The article was translated from the Canton paper *Ba-er-wu zhan bao* (August 25th Battle News). For further documentation on these sorts of critiques, see Diamant, *Revolutionizing the Family*, chap. 7.

60 "Collection of Materials against Ho Long," in U.S. Consulate General – Hong Kong, *Current Background*, no. 859 (August 1968): 5, 25–6.

In PRC history, however, periods of extremely restrictive notions of group membership and spatial boundary setting are the exception rather than the rule. Looking at the reform period (1978–), we can see the reemergence of pre–Cultural Revolution tendencies in full force. Now, close to 100 million peasants move to and from cities as part of a so-called floating population; political class status is not a very important criterion in selecting spouses; and family structure is becoming more and more fluid with increasing divorce rates and the reemergence of de facto bigamy and polygamy (where wealthy men support one or two permanent girlfriends in addition to their de jure wives). While this may be less surprising during the reform period because the state has allowed for the emergence of a "private sphere," it is striking that such contemporary trends are not entirely dissimilar from state-society relations during the 1950s and the early to mid-1960s, a period when the state was far more intrusive and ambitious. Now, as then, many people are engaged in multiple forms of border crossing and refuse to accept state-mandated boundaries as meaningful or relevant to their lives.

10

Gender and the Reproduction and Maintenance of Group Boundaries

Why the "Secular" State Matters to Religious Authorities in Israel

Patricia J. Woods

The boundaries of identity, so to speak, are constructed much as are territorial boundaries.

Rebecca Kook[1]

The reality in Israel is that we are men of the law.

Interview with Rabbi R. Klein, Rabbinical Court of Beer Sheva, 1997

The Jewish People lives through its family.

Interview with Eli Suissa, former Minister of the Interior and Minister of Religion, Shas Party, 1997

As noted throughout this collection, the fundamental project of the nation-state has been to make the spatial logic of the state's territorial boundaries coterminous with the boundaries of the nation. The difficulties, and often the failures, of this task have been noted by many.[2] In some cases, as demonstrated by Basson in this volume, membership in the nation has been defined racially; mixed-race individuals and groups have presented a serious challenge to the conception of both nation and territorial state. Other studies in

I am grateful for funding support from the National Science Foundation Dissertation Grant (no. 9906136), Social Science Research Council International Dissertation Research Fellowship program, Social Science Research Council Near and Middle East Pre-Dissertation Program, the Dorot Foundation, and the University of Washington Near Eastern Languages and Civilization Department. The Department of Political Science at the Hebrew University of Jerusalem provided me with important scholarly and material support during part of this research, as did the Department of Socialogy and Anthropology at Tel Aviv University during another part of this research. I am also grateful to the participants of the Boundaries and Belonging project for formative comments and suggestions through the course of the project.

1 Rebecca Kook, "Dilemmas of Ethnic Minorities in Democracies: The Effect of Peace on the Palestinians in Israel," *Politics and Society* 23, no. 3 (September 1995): 309–36.

2 See, e.g., E. J. Hobsbawm, *The Age of Extremes: A History of the World, 1914–1919* (New York: Vintage Books, 1996), and *Nations and Nationalism since 1780: Programme, Myth, Reality* (Cambridge: Cambridge University Press, 1994).

this volume have noted the prevalence of transnational citizenship (Conant), supraterritorial nationalism (Watts), and modes of identity that place their foundations not on a nation-state but on a "universal community of believers beyond the nation-state" (Arat). Migdal has pointed out that while we generally like to see territorial boundaries as solid, as social scientists we are best served if we see them as constantly in flux. Indeed, this state of constant flux applies to territorial as well as to social maps.

In the case of Israel, state religious authorities have, indeed, sought to define the nation in a way that will allow it to be coterminous with the nation-state. Their primary project to this end has been to homogenize the Jewish community[3] so that all Jewish Israelis can be included in a properly Jewish nation-state.[4] To achieve this goal, they have sought to fix the boundaries of the community (who is in and who is out) through institutions that regulate certain practices. As in Diamant's work on China, the institutions are those laws that regulate marriage and divorce. In the Israeli case, religious authorities have succeeded in regulating marriage and divorce through laws that define the rights and responsibilities of the parties in highly gendered terms. But more than that, they have sought to regulate many types of public behavior along gender lines as well. These practices are used to divide community members from noncommunity members in a manner aptly defined by Migdal in the introduction to this collection and by Douglas's framework in her work on purity (including dietary laws in ancient Israel) and group boundaries.[5] The rewards of following these practices are community membership not in a neighborhood or village but as full members in the nation-state.[6] The sanctions against those who do not follow can be (more

[3] What is meant by community varies, of course, according to who is defining the community. For some Israelis, "the community" would mean all Israeli Jews, whatever their religious persuasion. For others, "the community" would mean all Israeli citizens, Jews and Arabs. For Haredi and Haredi-leumi, or Haredi-leaning religious Zionists (discussed further below), who constitutes "the community" is complex. On the one hand, only Jews who are defined as Jews according to Jewish religious law, *halakhah*, are part of the Jewish community. On the other hand, the whole of the Israeli Jewish community could be – and *should* be – Jews according to *halakhah*. Indeed, by this view, in order to create and reproduce a properly Jewish state, all Jews in Israel *must* be Jews, *halakhically*.

[4] For more on state homogenization projects, see, esp., Benedict Anderson, *Imagined Communities* (New York: Verso, 1991); and Ernst Gellner, *Nations and Nationalism* (Oxford: Blackwell, 1983). It is important to note, as is mentioned below in the text, that others have engaged in homogenization projects in Israel. However, they have done so on secular or other terms.

[5] Mary Douglas, *Cultural Bias* (London: Royal Anthropological Institute of Great Britain and Ireland, 1978), and *Purity and Danger: An Analysis of Concepts of Pollution and Taboo* (London: Penguin Books, 1970).

[6] For more on the differences between citizenship in the state of Israel and membership in the nation-state, see, esp., Yoav Peled, "Ethnic Democracy and the Legal Construction of Citizenship: Arab Citizens of the Jewish State," *American Political Science Review* 86, no. 2 (June 1992): 432–42; Yoav Peled and Gershon Shafir, "The Roots of Peacemaking: The

often for women) exclusion from the institution of marriage for both the adult and future offspring. In the case of Israel, marriage and divorce laws, together with gendered regulations of public behavior, are used, literally, to constitute the community. Thus, exclusion from state-sanctioned marriage has serious implications for belonging.[7] It is the regulation of these institutions that produce, reproduce, and maintain the community's boundaries that is the reason many religious official who are part of the Haredi (ultra-Orthodox) community, which generally disapproves of the secular state, have joined the state. Boundaries, in this sense, are social – and through the state have become political – rather than territorial.

The question that gave rise to the investigation in this essay is the new participation, by the 1970s, of Haredi Jews within the wide religious bureaucracy of the Israeli state.[8] At the establishment of the state of Israel, the Haredi communities did not approve of the secular state, most refusing to ally with it. These communities were in favor neither of the new state's liberal democratic principles nor its appeal to secular legal principles. They held that the establishment of Israel was the province of God alone and could be brought only through the coming of the Messiah. Establishing the state was, therefore, an act of extreme human arrogance. The relationship between Haredim (plural of Haredi) and state institutions was further complicated by a diaspora history in which Jewish communities had to work hard to protect themselves against the interests of (especially Christian) rulers. Jewish communities tried to maintain some level of communal autonomy from Christian kings and states.[9] In the modern period, and in Israel in particular, Haredi communities have advocated against the incorporation of Jews into modern technological society, modern social institutions, or modern political institutions. That is, a long legacy has discouraged Haredim from joining many aspects of the "modern world," but particularly the

Dynamics of Citizenship in Israel, 1948–93," *International Journal of Middle East Studies* 28 (1996): 391–413; Kook, "Dilemmas"; Sammy Smooha, *Israel: Pluralism and Conflict* (Berkeley: University of California Press, 1978).

[7] A number of immigrants from the former Soviet Union and Eastern Europe whom I interviewed reported feeling pushed out of the community because their divorce was not recognized by religious authorities, barring any future offspring from marriage within the state, or because their parents' marriage or divorce was questionable, making them not officially Jewish. This is the subject of deep pain for those involved, as noted in many Israeli TV newscasts on the topic.

[8] Menachem Friedman, "The Chief Rabbinate – A Dilemma Without a Solution," *Medina, Mimshal V'Yahasim Beynleumiyim* 3 (1972): 118–28 (in Hebrew).

[9] In the Muslim world, and especially the Ottoman Empire, this autonomy was formalized and protected by laws giving Jews formal status as (usually second-class) citizens with communal autonomy, usually with regard to personal status law but sometimes other areas as well. This protection of autonomy meant it was usually easier in the Muslim world for Jewish communities to defend themselves against the interests of the ruling population when those interests came in conflict.

modern state. Indeed, most Haredi leaders still advocate a "Torah state," or theocracy.[10]

Haredi communities have continued to maintain their own rabbinical courts since the establishment of the state of Israel. They have maintained their own educational systems, albeit partially funded by the state.[11] They have lived in semi-cloistered communities; women in particular have been encouraged not to engage in business or social relations outside Haredi neighborhoods.[12] The extreme cultural and institutional isolation has been noted by many. In fact, it has been understood as one of the defining characteristics of the Haredi community in Israel. However, by the late 1990s, there was a notable trend toward more participation in modern commerce and certain forms of technology. Haredi women, men, and families regularly visit the most secular of modern sites of commerce: large malls that now mark the outskirts of many Israeli cities.[13] A new "Haredi Center for High-Tech Training" was established and, as of September 2000, had placed 1,200 former yeshiva students in high-tech firms in Israel.[14] Haredi women, too, have entered the work force within Haredi neighborhoods and have begun to use computer technology as a way to telecommute, allowing them to work from home.[15]

[10] Interview with Johnathan Rosenblum, founder of Am Ahad, an English-language lobby and public relations organization for the Haredi community, Jerusalem, May 2000. On Haredi disapproval of the establishment of the state, see Charles S. Liebman, *Religion, Democracy, and Israeli Society* (New York: Routledge, 1997); Tom Segev, *1949: The First Israelis* (New York: Henry Holt, 1998); Howard M. Sachar, *A History of Israel from the Rise of Zionism to Our Time*, 2nd ed. (New York: Knopf, 1996); Mitchell Cohen, *Zion and State: Nation, Class and the Shaping of Modern Israel* (New York: Columbia University Press, 1992); Amnon Rubinstein, *The Zionist Dream Revisited: From Herzl to Gush Emunim and Back* (New York: Schocken, 1984).

[11] See, e.g., Leslie Sebba and Varda Shiffer, "Tradition and the Right to Education: The Case of the Ultra-Orthodox Community in Israel," in *Children's Rights and Traditional Values*, Gillian Douglas and Leslie Sebba, eds. (Brookfield: Ashgate/Dartmouth, 1998).

[12] Tamar El-Or, *Educated and Ignorant: Ultra-Orthodox Jewish Women and Their World* (Boulder, Colo.: Lynne Rienner, 1994).

[13] On changes in Haredi communities in Israel toward participation in modern commerce and some forms of modern technology, see Yair Sheleg, *The New Religious Jews: Recent Developments among Observant Jews in Israel* (Jerusalem: Keter, 2000), p. 136 (in Hebrew); and Oded Hermoni, "The Ultra-Orthodox Discover High-Tech," *Haaretz*, September 11, 2000.

[14] Hermoni, "The Ultra-Orthodox."

[15] Sheleg, *New Religious Jews*, p. 174. Sheleg argues that a new ideology emphasizing a Haredi woman's role as supporting her husband's religious studies has led to this development, whereby women have entered paid employ, including work with computers. This paid work has typically remained within Haredi neighborhoods; work with computers allows a new freedom for women to work from home. Interview, Yair Sheleg, May 2000. The use of computers is interesting in the Haredi community, given statements by Haredi leaders against computers. (See, e.g., Adam Heilman, "Counterattacking the Computer Busters," *Haaretz*, December 4, 1998: "The religious court of the Haredi Congregation, associated with the

Before this new opening trend, as early as the early 1970s, Haredim began to join the wide religious bureaucracy of the Israeli state. They joined as rabbinical court judges; as members of the central rabbinical authority, the Rabbinate; and sometimes as administrative personnel and political appointees within the various ministries of the state. Given all of the historical, religious, and cultural factors encouraging Haredim to avoid the state, why have they joined it in large numbers so that the religious bureaucracy, once controlled by (then generally moderate) religious Zionists, is now mainly in command of Haredim and Haredi-leaning religious Zionists, who tend to have more conserving positions on religious change? One factor hinted at above is a general, although not decisive, opening of Haredi communities to modern technologies, markets, and institutions. These cultural factors cannot by themselves, however, explain why Haredim have joined the state religious bureaucracy in such large numbers. For Haredim began to join the state – in a decisive movement – long before the wider cultural opening trend noted in the 1990s. Indeed, their joining the state may have been significant in the later opening of Haredi communities to some aspects of the modern world, whereas the reverse is not likely given the timing of events.

The question remains, What led Haredi religious authorities to enter the "secular" state as early as the 1970s? I argue, based on interviews with religious officials in Israel, that Haredi and Haredi-leumi (defined below)[16] officials have entered the state as a matter of strategy to produce, reproduce, and maintain the type of society they envision as the "right" Jewish (and Israeli) society. They have a certain vision for the society and that vision requires institutional backing. The strategy, in this case, serves ideology. Many in Israel have argued that religious officials are motivated primarily by interests of money and power.[17] I argue that money and power serve their primary motivation: the creation, reproduction, and maintenance of a certain kind of Jewish society, which they seek to maintain through control of institutions. In a world of nation-states, the only way to control those institutions is through the state. The state is the only game in town. It is the central institution through which policies can be implemented, laws can be written and changed, and social visions can be enacted. What is even more important in this case is that religious institutions were incorporated into the state at its establishment. This incorporation has meant that any religious

United Torah Judaism Knesset faction, ruled last month that computers have the capacity to 'bring the Evil Inclination in by the back door'").

16 As discussed below, Haredi-leumi Jews are Haredi-leaning religious Zionists who, as scholars such as Liebman and Cohen have noted, have begun to converge with Haredim along both religious and political lines. See Charles Liebman and Asher Cohen, "A Case of Fundamentalism in Contemporary Israel," in Liebman, *Religion, Democracy and Israeli Society*, p. 57.

17 In relation to control of education funds, see, e.g., Sebba and Shiffer, "Tradition and the Right to Education."

constituency wishing to influence religious policy *must* join the state. Thus, despite a general distrust of the "secular" nation-state on the part of many, religious officials have felt compelled to join the state and use its authority to support their agendas. The social vision of religious authorities involves a specific notion of the Jewish People and requires the regulation of those institutions that constitute that community, namely, gendered marriage and divorce law and gendered regulation of religious participation.

In the following section, I outline the main groups that make up the religious communities in Israel, explaining why it matters that Haredi and Haredi-leumi religious authorities have joined the state. In the final section, I present evidence from interviews with religious officials indicating why they believe religious institutions and religious officials must be part of the state.

Who Are The Religious Communities in Israel?

Whether analyzing attitudes of "the orthodox" toward the peace process or the role of "the Orthodox" in the religious-secular conflict (now being fought out largely in the Israel High Court of Justice),[18] the Jewish religious

[18] This conflict, which I call the religious law conflict, has been fought out primarily in the Israel High Court of Justice – and from there, periodically, in the streets and media – consistently for at least fourteen years. Hints of the conflict were seen in earlier High Court cases, such as the Benjamin Shalit case of 1969, but before that were usually argued in parliamentary or executive fora.

The institutional conflict between the secular High Court and religious authorities emerges from a deep rift between certain religious and secular segments of the Israeli population. As of 1996, some 50 percent of Israeli Jews cited their primary identity as "Jewish"; 40 percent cited "Jewish" as their secondary identity; 47 percent listed "Israeli" as their first choice; 44 percent listed "Israeli" as their second choice. According to Arian, approximately 40 percent of the Israeli public is "determinedly secular"; 25 percent are either Orthodox or ultra-Orthodox; and the remaining 35 percent fall between those poles (Asher Arian, *The Second Republic: Politics in Israel* (Chatham, N.J.: Chatham House, 1998), p. 10). A survey conducted in 1993 found that 79 percent of the Israeli Jewish population was religiously observant to some extent; 14 percent were "strictly observant" (most likely corresponding to Orthodox and ultra-Orthodox); 24 percent were "observant to a great extent"; and 41 percent were "somewhat observant." The last two categories most likely correspond to people who would label themselves "traditional." It also found that 67 percent of the population either approved of the current place of religion in public life (51 percent) or wanted more religion in public life (16 percent). Meanwhile, 42 percent of the sample answered that there should be a separation between religion and state ("definitely yes," 25 percent; "yes," 17 percent); 39 percent said there should not be a separation ("definitely no," 16 percent; "no," 23 percent) (ibid., 10).

What these surveys suggest is that a high percentage of the Israeli Jewish population identifies strongly with Judaism, even if one's level of practice is moderate or low, and even if one could be called "secular" in terms of use of modern technology, social, and political institutions. My interviewees who were pro–High Court as well as those who were pro–religious establishment suggested to me that the conflict over religion in the state is being fought out on the margins; only the extreme secularists or the extreme religious were fighting

communities in Israel have often been treated as made up of only one or two groups. References to "the Orthodox" in these contexts generally include religious Zionists and Haredim within the account, but typically do not specify either. Significant changes in the Jewish religious community of Israel over the past three decades indicate a need for a new understanding of the relationship between religious groups. On the one hand has been a dearth of evidence about differences between these communities, as well as which community is involved in which political conflicts. On the other hand, there has been a certain lack of specificity even within the religious communities of Israel. Of my interviewees, who fall anywhere from the most strict (Haredi) to relatively open to changes in gender roles and participation in modern institutions (modern Orthodox), all referred to themselves simply as "Orthodox."[19]

Historically, the religious communities of pre-state Israel were broken into three groups: the Mizrahi movement;[20] the Haredi community, represented by groups such as Agudat Israel; and the Ottoman Orthodox Jewish community.[21] The Haredim were usually understood to be Ashkenazi in origin, antistate, anti-Zionist, in favor of strict interpretations of Jewish religious law (*halakhah*), and against incorporation of Jews into modern technology or modern institutions (social or political). By the end of the 1950s, the number of Jews of Middle Eastern origin (*mizrahi* Jews, not related to the mostly Ashkenazi prestate Mizrahi movement) was greater than those of European (Ashkenazi) origin. The Shas party, established to protect the interests of the *mizrahi* community, by the 1980s became a very powerful player in Israeli politics. In addition to its ethnic affiliations, it is a party whose leaders are Haredim. Thus, by the 1980s, the term "Mizrahi Haredim" began to be used by scholars and by the Israeli population.

about the issue. (Each suggested that the other side represented a marginal group.) What appears from these surveys, however, is more disturbing for Israeli stability. While those who are mobilized on the issue are certainly small in number, the population at large is itself split on the proper role of religion in the state. More recent surveys support the notion that the Israeli population is split on the relative significance of religion for them. Arian found that in the 1996 elections, among Benjamin Netanyahu (rightist Likud Party) voters, 68 percent identified first as Jewish, whereas among Shimon Peres (leftist Labor Party) voters, 66 percent identified first as Israelis (ibid., p. 9).

19 Reform and Conservative leaders whom I interviewed referred to themselves specifically as Reform or Conservative.

20 The Mizrahi movement was a prestate (non-Haredi) Orthodox movement in Israel that eventually became a political party. It was mainly composed of Ashkenazi Orthodox Jews. See, e.g., Segev, *1949*; Cohen, *Zion and State*; Rubinstein, Zionist Dream; Avraham Avi-Hai, *Ben Gurion State-Builder: Principles and Pragmatism, 1948–1963* (Jerusalem: Israel Universities Press, 1974).

21 On Ottoman Jewry in Palestine, see Michelle Campos, "Ottomanism, Zionism and the Young Turk Revolt of 1908 in Palestine: A View from the Local Sephardi and Maghrebi Community," paper delivered at Association for Israel Studies Conference, Tel Aviv University, May 2000.

Much has been written about the radicalization of some religious groups in Israel after the 1967 war. Barzilai, Sprinzak, Ravitzky, and others have noted the rise of religious radical groups such as that of Kahane and his followers, who mobilized on the issue of land settlement in the newly Occupied Territories of the West Bank and Gaza.[22] These lands contained many sites holy to Jews. Kahane and others saw the acquisition of these territories as a religious signal that Israel could begin to develop a biblical "Greater Israel," which by some accounts extended over the entire Levant and even northeast into Ancient Mesopotamia (now Iraq). Significantly, a large part of the religious communities who were radicalized included religious Zionists, who had previously been fairly moderate on security and other political issues. After the 1967 and 1973 wars, politically moderate religious Zionists became a minority.[23] The remainder set on a course that led them closer and closer to Haredi positions on modernity, gender roles, and religious institutions. Indeed, some scholars have noted a "convergence" between this group of religious Zionists and Haredim, religiously and politically.[24] By the early 1980s, the term "Haredi-leumi,"[25] and its acronym in Hebrew, Hardal, was coined by a religious-Zionist youth group leader who disapproved of this development.[26] Hardal has the double meaning in Hebrew of "mustard"; the term was intended to be disparaging, but has reportedly been embraced by religious Zionists of this religious-political position.

While a segment of the religious Zionists who had always been willing to participate in the state moved closer to Haredi religious and political positions, another change began to occur in Haredi communities (particularly in Ashkenazi Haredi communities, which had been more isolated from the larger Jewish community than had been the Mizrahi Haredim). As early as the early 1970s, Haredi rabbis began to join the Rabbinate and rabbinical courts in notable numbers.[27] This trend continued; some have noted that by the end of the 1990s, the majority of the Rabbinate and rabbinical court judges were Haredim.[28] Haredi rabbis regularly run for the two Chief Rabbi

[22] Gad Barzilai, *Wars, Internal Conflicts, and Political Order: A Jewish Democracy in the Middle East* (Albany: State University of New York Press, 1996); Ehud Sprinzak, *The Ascendence of Israel's Radical Right* (New York: Oxford University Press, 1991); Aviezer Ravitzky, *The Roots of Kahanism: Consciousness and Political Reality* (Jerusalem: Shazar Library, Institute of Contemporary Jewry, Vidal Sassoon International Center for the Study of Antisemitism, Hebrew University of Jerusalem, 1986).

[23] Interview, Livka Luvitch, founding member of the Women's Forum, a (mainly modern) orthodox women's organization, Nire Etzion, June 2000.

[24] Liebman and Cohen, "A Case of Fundamentalism," p. 57.

[25] Literally, "Haredi nationalist."

[26] Liebman and Cohen, "A Case of Fundamentalism," p. 58.

[27] Friedman, "Chief Rabbinate."

[28] Very little has been written about this topic, probably because it is difficult to find statistics on the religious makeup of rabbinical institutions in Israel. Interviews with people on various sides of the religious law conflict, however, indicate that a majority of rabbinical

positions in the country. In fact, the two current Chief Rabbis in Israel are Haredim who, according to some critics, "consider themselves subordinate to the Haredi rabbis."[29] The trend of Haredi participation in state religious institutions is noteworthy for many reasons, including its implications for the state.

Haredi communities have maintained a high level of communal independence within the state, using their own rabbinical authorities to determine *kashrut* (dietary law) observance and food standards, to manage local conflicts as well as marriage and divorce hearings, to run religious facilities, and to administer religious schools.[30] And yet Haredi rabbis took it upon themselves to enter into the paid service of a state whose very establishment was, theologically, disapproved of as an act of humans pretending to stand in God's stead. Why would religious officials and leaders enter a secular state of which many disapproved? In the remaining pages, I present the answers that religious officials in Israel – Haredi and Haredi-leumi – gave to me. Their reasons go to the heart of the nature of the Jewish state, the nature of the Jewish community, the question of who will be part of the Jewish community, and who is empowered to define the terms that resolve the answers to each of these questions. The desire to define, to maintain, and to control the institutions that reproduce social boundaries between Jew and non-Jew, between "real" Jew and "non-real" Jew, drive Haredi as well as Haredi-Leumi participation in the state.

These boundaries, in turn, define who is a member of the nation in contrast to who is a citizen of the state. Kook[31] has argued that membership and citizenship are different in the Israeli context. Membership in the nation requires Jewishness, while citizenship in the state is open to non-Jews, such as Arabs, as well. I am arguing that religious authorities seek to homogenize the Jewish Israeli population so that all Jewish Israelis will be Jewish in *halakhic* terms. Those not Jewish in terms of *halakhic* religious institutions incorporated into the state would not be full members of the nation. Thus, religious authorities have sought to define the parameters of national membership in

court judges and members of the Rabbinate in the 1990s were Haredim. Interview, Yair Sheleg, Jerusalem, May 2000; interview, Uri Regev, Jerusalem, March 2000. Asher Cohen and Charles S. Liebman have noted this trend in "The Struggle among Religious Zionists over the Issue of a Religious State," in *Religion, Democracy and Israeli Society*. See also Friedman, "Chief Rabbinate."

29 Shahar Ilan, "Chief Rabbis of No One," *Haaretz*, September 6, 2000. Ilan notes the significance of the coming election (2003) of the Chief Rabbis, in which both "national-religious" (or Haredi-leumi) and Haredi candidates are running. Ilan argues that a Haredi win "will mark the final severance of religious Zionism from the Chief Rabbinate" but does not note the religious and political convergence between those two groups.

30 Interview, Rabbi Menachem Porush, former head of Agudat Israel, Jerusalem, December 1999.

31 Kook, "Dilemmas."

more specific terms than have been previously institutionalized or codified. The stakes are nothing less than defining the nation-state.

Why Join the State?

Gender and Group Boundaries

In interviews in the late 1990s, religious officials presented strikingly similar accounts of what is at stake in keeping religious institutions within the state. The first reason that religion must be part of the state, according to these officials, was the need for centralized authority in religious marriage and divorce law. As the language used in interviews indicates, the central concern with marriage and divorce law was to ensure that the boundaries of the community remain intact. This concern with group boundaries was expressed through the idea of one unified (I will say, homogenized) nation and through the desire to identify "real Jews" from "non-real" Jews.

The concern with a unified community has not been unique to the religious establishment. Early Zionist leaders of the state, such as David Ben-Gurion, Israel's first Prime Minister, also expressed concern with unity.[32] In fact, Ben-Gurion's primary concern was to unify the Jewish community under the auspices of a strong state that would ultimately be a secular and secularizing state. Zionists leaders at the establishment of the state and religious officials in the 1990s envisioned dramatically different communities. The institutional forms that would be required to produce that particular unified community also varied dramatically. Indeed, the social vision and resultant institutional demands of the religious communities is at the heart of the conflict between religious and secular elements now being fought in a virulent, ongoing battle in the Israeli courts. Thus, religious authorities are highly aware that their efforts have vigorous opponents, giving more urgency to their agenda. The urgency of this unification (or homogenization) comes through in the words of Eliyahu Ben-Dahan, the Director General of the Rabbinical Courts of Israel:

> The State of Israel is a country to which Jews from all around the world have gathered. Every individual has absorbed the culture of the place [of origin]. When the State of Israel was established, the intention was to establish a new state that would unify everyone [the Jewish people], and would turn them into a single body, into one people.[33]

In this formulation, as in Ben-Gurion's, the *unification* of the Jewish people goes beyond the goal of providing a place for all Jews to become "normal" in the international sphere through the creation of a nation-state,

[32] Avi-Hai, *Ben-Gurion.*

[33] Interview, Rabbi Eliyahu Ben-Dahan, Director General of the Rabbinical Courts of Israel, Jerusalem, August 1997.

as envisioned by the "father of Zionism," Theodore Herzl.[34] As with Ben-Gurion, and indeed almost all European ethno-nationalist formulations of his time,[35] this religious unification, too, required a high level of homogenization. Homogenization has been a critical part of nation-building projects from the earliest conceptions of nationalism. Both Anderson and Gellner cite literacy and education as a central route to homogenization into a singular nation.[36] Language and literacy were important to the Israeli nation-state building project, as organized and managed by early Zionist leaders. But for the religious establishment in Israel, the community is built, unified, and its continuity assured primarily through the institution of family. As Eli Suissa, former Minister of Religion and Minister of Interior, put it, "The Jewish People lives through its family."[37] In terms of institutions, this emphasis on family means marriage and divorce laws.

Identity as a Jew, according to Jewish religious law (*halakhah*), is determined through the mother; restrictions on her marriage and kosher conception are extensive. These are restrictions that Douglas would call restrictions in service of the boundaries of the group (rather than those of grid, which set the hierarchy of relations between individuals in the community).[38] If a woman has a child with one man while she is, technically or in practice, married to another man, there are severe sanctions against that child.[39] The child is considered a *mamzer*, literally a bastard, who cannot marry within the Jewish community or participate in certain rituals. The sanction continues for ten generations. Almost every religious official I spoke with emphasized that without religious marriage and divorce laws, Israel would be split into different "nations" (*Amim*), one the product of kosher marriages, and one with children who could not marry Jews who are legitimate in the eyes of *halakhah*.

Marriage and divorce determine who is a Jew, who is inside and who is outside the community. Marriage and divorce laws determine who can marry whom, who can have children with whom, and whose children will be considered part of the community. Women who are unable to gain a divorce (these women are called *agunot*, or "chained") may not establish relations with a man or establish a family. Notably, in law and in practice, men who remain undivorced may start a new family in Israel without restrictions on

34 Theodore Herzl, *The Jewish State (Der Judenstaat)*, trans. Harry Zohn (New York: Herzl Press, 1970).

35 See Eric Hobsbawm on the treaties of Versailles, *The Age of Extremes: A History of the World, 1914–1919* (New York: Vintage Books, 1996), pp. 31–4.

36 Anderson, *Imagined Communities*; Gellner, *Nations and Nationalism*.

37 Interview, Eli Suissa, former Minister of Religion and Minster of Interior, Tel Aviv, August 1997.

38 Douglas, *Cultural Bias*.

39 A woman is technically still married if she is in the midst of divorce proceedings or if her husband refuses to give her the religious divorce paper, a *get*.

their children.[40] Several women whom I have interviewed were threatened with a negative decision in their divorce case if they established another relationship while waiting for the religious divorce paper, a *get*. A negative decision meant that they would never have a chance at a *get*, in turn prolonging their tied condition indefinitely. In some cases in Israel, a *get* involves years of waiting, sometimes beyond child-bearing age. Given the social and even state promotion of child bearing as women's national duty, waiting beyond child-bearing age can create severe emotional turmoil for women.[41] The structural situation of women in Jewish divorce law in Israel challenges principles of equality across gender lines, making it a prime arena for conflict between secular courts and religious officials.[42]

According to Rabbi Ben-Dahan:

> If we were to behave in Israel such that personal status law was not defined by *halakhah*, we would create two peoples (amim). For, it is clear that the Orthodox could not marry secular Jews that did not marry according to *halakhah*, and certainly not with their children. Because *we would not know who they are*. Maybe the marriage was okay; maybe there is a problem [according to *halakhah*]. Therefore, within a few years we would have two peoples here. *We want to create here one people*. [Emphasis added]

Plia Albek,[43] former Assistant State Attorney, suggested the same reason that religious personal law is critical to the Jewish state:

> If we did not have religious marriage laws, the Israeli society would be split into at least two groups, Jews, and people who are not really Jews, *halakhically*. . . . I would never be able to allow my daughter to marry an Israeli. Who knows who his mother

[40] Under *halakhic* law, a man who is not divorced may be remarried if he has the signature of 100 rabbis. In practice in Israel, a man who is not divorced may start a new family without getting remarried; as long as the woman partner has no *halakhic* restriction binding her, his children from this new union will have no restrictions placed on them. By contrast, if a woman who cannot gain a divorce begins a new relationship and has children, her new children will be "bastards" with lesser rights within the community for ten generations. One of those lesser rights is that they can marry only other "bastards." They are also not counted in certain religious rituals.

[41] Nira Yuval-Davis, "National Reproduction and 'the Demographic Race' in Israel," in *Women-Nation-State*, Nira Yuval-Davis and Floya Anthia, eds. (London: Macmillan, 1989). See also Yael Yishai, *Between the Flag and the Banner: Women in Israeli Politics* (Albany: State University of New York Press, 1997).

[42] For discussions of conflicts between the existing religious personal status laws and women's rights in Israel, see, e.g., Charles Leibman and Eliezer Don-Yehya, *Religion and Politics in Israel* (Bloomington: Indiana University Press, 1984), 24; Martin Edelman, *Courts, Politics, and Culture in Israel*. (Charlottesville: University Press of Virginia, 1994), 65; Philippa Strum, "Women and the Politics of Israel," *Human Rights Quarterly* 11 (1989): 485; for one rabbinic criticism of *halakhic* decisions that conflict with women's rights, see Eliezer Schweid on Rabbi Haim Hirschensohn in *Democracy and Halakhah* (Landham, Md.: University Press of America, 1994), pp. 64–5 and 72–4.

[43] Interview, Plia Albek, Jerusalem, July 1997.

was? We can do research, but how far back could you go? Maybe the problem is with the great-grandmother and there is no longer a record. If we did not have religious personal law here, we would never be able to be *certain* that one Jew could marry another. I would have to send my daughter to Switzerland to marry within the Orthodox community there.... What is the point of having a Jewish state if I have to send my daughter to Switzerland to find an Orthodox Jew?

Menachem Porush, the leader of Agudat Israel for thirty years, also cited Jewish marriage and divorce laws as critical to the Jewishness of the state. Across the board, there seemed to be a concern with the unity of the people and with unifying the people through religious law, in both the associational and the conscriptive senses.[44]

Entering the state serves several instrumental purposes for religious authorities, all of which serve the larger ideological goal of creating, reproducing, and maintaining the social boundaries of the community. One such purpose is to put the law of the land behind religious officials, to give legal bite to their decisions in an age of secular nation-states in which religious proclamations have little remaining authority. Rabbi R. Klein[45] asserted the significance of the connection between Judaism and the state in helping women in divorce cases. Klein is a rabbi in the Rabbinical Court in Beer Sheva who, once or twice a year, flies around the world to hunt down men who have refused to give their wives a divorce paper (a *get*). By all accounts, his searches take him to the far corners of the earth. His concern with women's plight in divorce law in Israel is evident in his chosen work:

If these [religious marriage and divorce laws] were not legal under the state law, it would be a catastrophe. I will tell you why. In the whole world, in Europe, in America, in Australia, the laws of Israel, the laws of Jewish marriage and divorce, are not part of the [civil] law....

Israel is the only place that says, "You, Rabbi Klein, can make a *get*, but you cannot take money from people for it, because you live by our salary." I get a salary from the state. Rabbi Ben-Dahan also. All of us. Because what we do is legal. It says, in my opinion – and I am speaking from experience – a woman in the United States wants

44 Wald and Shye define associational identity in Israel as that indicating personal commitment to religious organizations and implying voluntary immersion in a social network (Kenneth Wald and Samuel Shye, "Religious Influence in Electoral Behavior: The Role of Institutional and Social Forces in Israel," *Journal of Politics* 57, no. 2 (May 1995): 495–508). Others in identity politics have emphasized ascriptive identity, in which the identifier is ascribed to the individual or group from outside the self. In the Israeli case, both types of identification occur (see, e.g., Iris Marion Young, *Justice and the Politics of Difference* (Princeton, N.J.: Princeton University Press, 1990)). Here I am using the term "conscriptive" to denote that for those who do not identify with these particular religious institutions or practices, not only is an identity being ascribed, but *specific practices are being required* before that official, ascribed identity can go into force.

45 Interview, Rabbi R. Klein, Rabbinical Judge, Rabbinical Court, Beer Sheva, Israel, August 1997.

to divorce. Why? Because her husband beats her, does not give her money, goes with other women. What can she do? She can go to the state and register to receive a civil divorce paper.... But that is not enough for a woman [to be free] to marry someone else. She needs a kosher *get*. According to the Jewish, Orthodox *halakhah*, she needs a kosher *get*. And a non-Orthodox woman needs a kosher *get* just as much, because if she does not receive one, her children will be *mamzerim* [plural of *mamzer*], and her children will give her a host of troubles all her life, because they will ask her, always: "Why did you make us *mamzerim*?" So, she can go to a rabbi and the rabbi in America will write what she tells him and will send an invitation to the husband [to discuss the divorce]. The husband does not come. He doesn't care. The rabbi cannot do a thing.

The reality in Israel is that we are men of the law. If the same husband receives an invitation from me and he does not come, he is already tied: by the scruff of his neck, he's going to jail. The second time, I do not need any favors from him. The police bring him to me.

Klein made the argument that the state authority vested in rabbinical courts gives him a power to support women, and anyone with legitimate claims, that rabbis in other countries do not have. While it has been noted that the situation of women in religious law in Israel is highly problematic from a civil rights perspective, Klein presents an interesting twist on the way that many secular critics in Israel see the situation: the religious establishment pushing religion into the state, thus taking power away from the state, and all the while hurting groups such as women.

Klein saw the connection between Judaism and the state as growing out of the needs of the people and as giving the needed institutional backing to create the justice that the great rabbis envisioned. Without the state, the social world that rabbis such as Klein want to protect and build would be at peril. He involves himself in the state because in the contemporary world, the only way to assert the legitimate authority to enforce the decisions of rabbinical court judges is through the state. And yet, historically speaking, rabbis have not usually been part of state authority; as noted previously, many Haredi communities objected to the establishment of the Israeli state altogether. Thus, in a real sense, allying with the state is a calculated choice. But the instrumental ends serve the social vision. To complicate matters further, as mentioned before, *the very incorporation of religious institutions into the state made it imperative that all religious constituencies seeking influence in religious matters likewise incorporate themselves into the state*. The incorporation of religion into the state, in a real sense, forced the hand of religious authorities, even those opposing the state.

Religious authorities' need for the state in the contemporary world is obvious in Klein's example of the U.S. woman who cannot use any sort of state authority to push her husband to give her a divorce (our conversation did not include the new New York laws). Without the state behind rabbis, rabbis would have no power to enforce the laws that they see as defining and reproducing the values and norms that make Israel a Jewish society.[46] They could not protect and reproduce the boundaries of the community without state support. And this is the first goal: Protect and reproduce (literally, through marriage and divorce laws) the boundaries of the community. Involvement in the state is a strategic necessity in a world of nation-states, in a world where local rabbis no longer have teeth of their own without police or other state offices behind them. To this day, rabbinical courts have only the status of mediators in nonreligious matters, even within Haredi communities, whose members turn almost exclusively to rabbinical courts.[47] But in those tightly knit communities, communal authority and sanctions remain strong enough that rabbinical authority is ensured. Were there no state backing in marriage and divorce law for the wider population, the nightmare of Suissa, Ben-Dahan, Albek, Porush, and Klein would come to pass: Israel would be a state of Jews who are Jewish according to orthodox *halakhah* and Jews whom these officials would not call Jews at all. Albek would have to send her daughter to Switzerland to find an Orthodox Jew to marry. In Suissa's words:

> From our perspective, as religious people, we see great significance in the notion that the religion should be connected with the state. From our perspective, there is a unity [between religion and state]. What is the difference between Judaism and the rest of the world? – this is what we believe as religious people – that the Jewish state must be connected to Jewish symbols, to Jewish elements. To the Torah, to the *halakhah*, to the tradition. On Yom Kippur [the Day of Reckoning], we fast. The state must be closed.... We do not want to have a separation between religion and state. We want there to be a connection and an integration between the two. As such, we have a place in the Knesset as religious people, we want to have influence in the Knesset and the government. It is a Jewish state. We want it to remain Jewish, that the state will have signs visible to the outside that it is a different state. That is why we do what we do.

Suissa's words reflect a view of the state, again, as emerging from the needs of "the people":

> Because the state is connected to religion, the mayor of a city cannot say, "I only deal with electricity in the streets, with sewage...." *There are people. The people are Jewish.* There are others, but in the main, they are Jewish. *And if the majority*

46 Most religious officials I talked to were quick to recognize the existence of non-Jewish communities in Israel. Indeed, they emphasized the rights of all communities to religious autonomy. But at the same time, there remains a tendency in Israel to use "Israel" as a stand-in for "Jews," correcting that definition only periodically with terms such as "the Jewish community in Israel" or "the Arabs in Israel" or "Arab-Israelis" or, more rarely, "Palestinian-Israelis." The religious officials I spoke with also tended to talk about Israel as "Jews" or even "the Jews," while the next moment talking about other religious communities within the state.

47 Interview, Menachem Porush, Jerusalem, December 1999; interview, Yair Sheleg, Jerusalem, June 2000.

> *are Jewish, there must be an indication* [of that], so the mayor of the city also takes care of Jewish issues. A mayor is thus turned into a little Minister of the Interior. As such, he must also give religious services. If I am Minister of the Interior and also Minister of Religion, and a mayor is also a little minister of interior and a minister of religion, then it all works out fine. But if he has a problem with religion as such: local councils – how are local councils administered – again, the connection. [Emphasis added]

Suissa appealed to both the central power of the state and majority rule on several occasions in an interview with me.[48] In talking about Reform and Conservative Jews' battle to enter public institutions, he argued:

> They are maybe two thousand people in the state. They want to force themselves upon us. Overseas, they are many, but we do not tell them what to do. Here, this is a Jewish state. There is an official Rabbinate. The Rabbinate has authority over *kashrut*. Because it is a Jewish state. They cannot come and force themselves upon us in our house. Do not try to make us live like you.

This appeal to the central authority of the state to make the case for the legitimacy of "Orthodox" Judaism in Israel cannot be overemphasized.[49] Suissa was quite aware of the importance of state religious institutions in *maintaining* just that legitimacy. He was strongly against allowing Reform and Conservative Jews into local religious councils, which make decisions

[48] This appeal to majority rule may sound at odds with an understanding of the ultimate source of authority as divine. In fact, there is a notion similar to majority rule in traditional Jewish legal thought (and practice). Menachem Elon, in his work on Jewish law and communal authority in Jewish history, notes that rule of the public was always dependent on public consent. The public consented to be ruled but could not ignore the rights of the individual. The individual, on the other hand, had needs that must be respected, but s/he was also subject to the rules and laws of the whole. See Elon, "Communal Authority and the Relationship between the Individual and Society in Hebrew Law," *Yearbook of Halakhah, Israeli Thought, and Problems of Judaism* (1978): 209–37 (in Hebrew). In a sense, the community acted as a court: "the good people of the community" were to address the needs of the whole as well as the needs of the individual, but the community was "not to hear those who have the status of lawbreakers (or at least certain kinds)." See Elon, "Jurisdiction and Power in the Jewish Community," *Yearbook on Hebrew Law* 3–4 (1976): 7–34 (in Hebrew). The community, following principles ultimately of divine source, could set laws that would govern the community. Who was empowered to define those rules was a select group within the community (not unlike other cases in which a select group is enfranchised, such as white, male landowners in the early United States, or male-only franchise elsewhere). Thus, a form of majority rule existed – rule by a consensus of leaders and scholars – but it was not a simple majority of the whole community.

[49] Surveys throughout the 1990s show an increasing openness to Reform and Conservative streams in Judaism on the part of Jewish Israelis. It does not appear that this trend is due only to the increase in Jews from the former Soviet Union, as it appears to reflect a wide range of the Israeli public.

on matters of religious administration:

He who believes in the Torah and in religion must guard it. Therefore, we think that there is no place for them [Reform and Conservatives] in religious councils. The religious council has to give services related to religion, one of which is the need to guard it and to make sure that, for example, people do not open stores on Sabbath. How can a member of a religious council who desecrates the Sabbath, who does not believe in Sabbath at all, go and vote in favor of closing stores on Sabbath? It does not stand up to reason. Therefore, we say that he is not appropriate for this forum: "You are against this forum."

Internal Group Restrictions and Gender Roles: Marking In Group as Out Group

Gender is a critical and central issue in these officials' concerns with maintaining authority within the state as well as continuity within the community. In 1997, Ben-Dahan presented a neutral to positive position on the incorporation of the first woman, Leah Shakdiel, into a local religious council in the late 1980s:

[Shakdiel] entered the local council in the end. But that was a completely different issue [than Reform and Conservatives]. She is Orthodox. In her case, religious men said it would not be pleasant for them to sit with a woman and argue with her over issues. If a woman was there, it would not be modest. Here, Leah Shakdiel accepts the *halakhah*.

Shakdiel, on the other hand, remembered that at the time (1988), she was not at all welcomed in the religious council, even after the High Court ruled that she must be allowed to be a member:

They would schedule meetings at hours that were completely impossible for child rearing because the obvious assumption was that they were not involved in child rearing. They have this slave at home who does it, and so they can do whatever they want. They would keep information away from me because they had this perception of women as being pure, and "you don't need to know all of the details." Meanwhile, I'd say to them, "If you don't give me the details it means you are disempowering me, you are leaving me out of the game." And they had a hard time knowing what to do with that because they were very much aware of the fact that the games that they were playing were dirty games, and they didn't know how to include me in that. Even when they wanted to enlist my support in one of the dirty games they were playing against other men, they didn't know how to do it because it's not done with the women.[50]

She noted that it was the religious Zionist (Haredi-leumi) National Religious Party (NRP) that initially barred her participation, not Shas, as has since been written in local newspapers. "I am suddenly quoted as someone who was

[50] Interview, Leah Shakdiel, Jerusalem, July 1997.

barred from serving in the religious council by Shas. Nobody remembers that it was the NRP who barred me."[51]

In other areas relating to women within the religious fold, religious officials have not been as quick to acquiesce to change. Regarding the Women of the Wall (WOW), a group of modern Orthodox, Conservative, and some Reform women who have been fighting for the right to pray at the Western Wall of the Temple mount since 1989, Ben-Dahan first denied that they were Orthodox women. In fact, their (unsanctioned) behavior itself has been used to define them as out-group:

> Who said that they are Orthodox?... There are rules for the Orthodox. If a person is Orthodox, he has rules and he has the *halakhah*. Let anyone come and say they have one Orthodox rabbi who allows them to pray, women and men together.

But, of course, the WOW seek to pray as only women. Ben-Dahan went on to make an interesting distinction between what is allowed in one's ("private"?) community synagogue and what is allowed at the site most holy to all of Judaism:

> The Women of the Wall want to pray with *tfillin*. They want to make a *minyan* of themselves, with a Torah Scroll and everything. At the Kotel [the Western Wall], this is not acceptable. If it is done at their own synagogues, no one would say a thing to them.

In fact, the majority of WOW do not seek to pray as a *minyan*, something allowed only for men. But the WOW do seek to pray as a group, out loud (something considered immodest by some Haredim), with a Torah Scroll, and with certain other rituals allowed only to men.

When the Women of the Wall held their *Rosh Khodesh* [new month] prayer session at the Western Wall on June 4, 2000, their first after the High Court asserted their unequivocal right to pray there in on May 22, 2000, a handful of Haredi men and women responded with angry protest, letting all know that none of this was acceptable. The Women of the Wall were called "Egypt," "Amalek," "Christians," "missionaries," destroyers of the People of Israel – in short, the worst enemies, everything most *outside* the boundaries of the Jewish people. One Haredi woman, in particular, physically pushed herself against some Women of the Wall. When a policewoman tried to intervene, the Haredi woman yelled at her:

> You are guarding the Christians! You are not guarding Jews. You're not guarding the People of Israel! It's forbidden for them to be here! You're taking their side. You're taking their side! Don't be on their side. You are not okay. It's forbidden for you to be on their side. This is not a place for shows! This is a holy place. This is a place for

[51] Ibid.

the People of Israel. Not for Christians. It wasn't even like this in Egypt! Phooey – dirt on you all![52]

One excerpt from my notes from that event illustrates the chasm seen by many Haredi and Haredi-leumi Jews between themselves and Jews whom they see as breaking internal restrictions enough to put them outside the boundaries of the community:

A young ultra-Orthodox woman approaches the women's section. She stands behind the WOW for a few minutes, seeming to determine from bystanders what, exactly, is going on. Suddenly, she walks past the WOW. She says with a quiet voice that is full of gentle, heart-felt devotion: "Women, the Messiah is *coming*! The Messiah is *coming*! You should be ashamed" and one other sentence that was a curse or a warning of the evil that would befall them, but I didn't hear the exact words. Five or ten minutes later, presumably after her prayers at the Wall, she walks out past the WOW. She says, with an equally gentle, devoted, and pained voice: "God doesn't hear you. My lady! God *doesn't hear you.*"[53]

Gender regulations within religious practice mark the boundaries of the community by marking those who are outside it. By calling the WOW Christians, Amalek, Egypt, and other historical enemies of the Jewish People, they are marked as outside the Jewish People altogether. The pained admonition that God literally does not hear the prayers of the WOW is the most extreme form of placing them outside the boundaries of the People of Israel.

Shakdiel was considered a member of the "religious community," as a modern Orthodox religious Zionist woman. The WOW typically are considered outside the religious fold because most Israelis believe they are Reform women, not Orthodox of any kind. The Reform and Conservative movements in Israel, however, are considered completely outside Judaism to the point of being heretical. Ben-Dahan presented the changes brought by Shakdiel's integration into a previously all-male world of religious councils as positive in comparison with the major threat to one coherent state religious authority presented by a Reform woman (whom he considered not a real Jew) entering a religious council:

Here, Leah Shakdiel accepts the *halakhah*. But here [in the case of Joyce Brenner, a Reform woman elected to religious council in Netanya], it is not only an issue of modesty. She [Brenner] says, "I do not accept your *halakhah*." Let's say the religious council decides that there should be more *kashrut* supervisors, or more observance of Sabbath. She can say, "I am against giving money to *kashrut*." It's like a Trojan horse.

[52] Author's notes taken at the Women of the Wall prayer session, June 4, 2000, at the Western Wall of the Temple Mount.

[53] Notes from the author's research notebook, observations of the Women of the Wall Rosh Khodesh session, Western Wall of the Temple Mount, Jerusalem, June 4, 2000.

Indeed, like those in the religious establishment today, it is the intention of Reform and Conservative activists to become part of religious institutions in order to represent their different views of the Jewish People and of *halakhah* and to make changes in religious institutions accordingly. It is equally the intention of current religious authorities to keep that from happening, to protect religious institutions from non-Orthodox change. So again we see an awareness on the part of religious officials of the importance of religious institutions, and state authority behind those institutions, in maintaining the kind of community they seek to protect and reproduce.

Conclusion

I have emphasized the word "reproduce" because it is important to understanding the processes through which religious officials seek to maintain the boundaries of the community in perpetuity. This maintenance is accomplished through religious marriage and divorce laws that ensure that the literal reproduction of the community is done in a kosher manner that creates a community of "Jews" who are Jews by Orthodox *halakhah*. As has been noted by much literature on the topic, the word "reproduce" highlights well the central role of gender and gender roles and norms in this program to protect the nation, the nation-state, or in my terms, following Douglas, the boundaries of the community.[54] After an initial battle, the Orthodox and ultra-Orthodox officials were willing to concede to Shakdiel entering the religious council. The reason was that she was a Jew who followed Orthodox *halakhah* and thus should not be expected to challenge the basic goal of maintaining the community through *halakhah*. Reform and Conservative Jews were another story altogether. In interviews with Ben-Dahan and Suissa, one of the first issues raised in conversations about Reform and Conservative Jews – whether the topic was religious councils or praying at the Western Wall – was gender: gender norms and what in their eyes were gender perversions. The following is Ben-Dahan's first reaction to my question

[54] See, e.g., Jacqueline Stevens, *Reproducing the State* (Princeton, N.J.: Princeton University Press, 1999); Valentine M. Moghadam, ed., *Gender and National Identity: Women and Politics in Muslim Societies* (London and New Jersey: Zed Books Ltd., and Karachi: Oxford University Press, 1994); John Stratton Hawley, ed., *Fundamentalism and Gender* (New York and Oxford: Oxford University Press, 1994); Suad Joseph, "Elite Strategies for State Building: Women, Family, Religion and the State in Iraq and Lebanon," in *Women, Islam and the State*, Deniz Kandiyoti, ed. (Philadelphia: Temple University Press, 1991); Afsaneh Najmabadi, "Hazards of Modernity and Morality: Women, State and Ideology in Contemporary Iran," in Kandiyoti, ed., *Women, Islam and the State;* Lesley Caldwell, *Italian Family Matters: Women, Politics and Legal Reform* (London: Macmillan, 1991); Yuval-Davis, "National Reproduction and 'the Demographic Race' in Israel," in *Women-Nation-State*, Nira Yuval-Davis and Floya Anthia, eds. (London: Macmillan, 1989); Kumari Jayawardena, *Feminism and Nationalism in the Third World* (London: Zed Books, 1986).

about his response to the Reform and Conservatives in general:

Whoever wants to pray, you are welcomed. But they [Reform and Conservatives] do not want to pray. They want to make a provocation. For example, at the Kotel, there is a *mekhitza* [a separator] between women and men, and they want to enter with men and women together. They want to pray together. It was explained to them that this is a holy place, we do not accept [this behavior]. But they want to do it *davka* [just in order to do it, as if to be petulant]. No one will bother them any time they come alone. They want to pray together and the *halakhah* is against that.

When I asked a similarly general question to Suissa, he immediately responded:

They wanted to put a Reform woman in the religious council in Netanya, and I said no [as Minister of the Interior]. It is a problem of religious conscience. Because of that, I think that the court [High Court of Justice] should not have decided in this case. Without reference to all the politics around the case. I announced that I would not sign. So, the Prime Minister took my jurisdiction, the right and authority from me, and he signed. Now, we are making a bill that would not allow Reform Jews to enter religious councils [to be elected]. Why? Because our position is that the religious council must take care of religion. What is religion? To keep Sabbath, to eat kosher. The Reform do not do this. The Reform marry men with men. Women with women. *Goy* [non-Jew] with Jew. Together. According to the religion, this is forbidden.

Marriage, gender roles, and community boundaries all appear as critical in Suissa's analysis. While he mentioned Sabbath and *kashrut* first, the prescient examples he raises have to do with gender and community: They marry men with men, women with women; they marry *goys* with non-Jews. Like Ben-Dahan, Suissa argued that the point of the Reform is to act as a sort of Trojan horse against the existing state power of the current religious establishment:

And it is why they come to the religious councils. Would I go to a church – perish the thought – and make myself a member of a church? I would not, because I do not believe in it. If I am against it, then why should I go there? The Reform do not believe in the religion. They do things against the religion. They desecrate the Sabbath. They eat on Yom Kippur. So they cannot be members of a religious council. To be on the inside and work against it? It's absurd.

When early Zionist leaders agreed to incorporate religious institutions in the state, seeking what was really the appropriation of religious authorities, they led the state to the unintended and ironic consequences of the increased political salience of religious authorities. For the average citizen, the most common interaction with the state outside the military is through identity registry, marriage (ceremony and registry), divorce (at least part of legal proceedings and registry), and other personal status issues. All of these come under the jurisdiction of religious authorities, making religious authorities key state actors in the everyday lives of citizens.[55] Moreover, religious authorities, as members of the state, have used state authority in the performance of their offices and in the pursuit of their social vision.

Interviews with religious officials in Israel show that they give high priority to participating in the state, despite the fact that they disapprove of the principles of general law on which it is founded. They disapprove of any law that would supersede divine authority. It is from divine authority that they see religious marriage and divorce law, as well as gendered regulation of religious practice, as emerging. At the center of concern is the creation, reproduction, and maintenance of group boundaries, those boundaries that illustrate who is part of the Jewish People and who is not. I have argued that the entrance of religious officials into the state is, indeed, strategic. And yet using the state is a strategy that serves the primary goal of transforming the society into the vision they have of the Jewish People. Strategy serves ideology. It should not be a surprise that a group that does not subscribe to the Enlightenment principles from which individual self-maximizing emerged as an ideal would be motivated by their religious ideology rather than the seeking of power itself. Religious officials absolutely seek power. There is no question about that. But it is not power for power's sake. It is state power in order to create and enforce the institutions necessary to create and to reproduce their vision of society, God's Jewish People.

Marriage and divorce law protect the boundaries of the community through the regulation of reproduction and defining of offspring, *halakhically*, as Jews or not. I emphasize the "or not" side of the equation, for defining in-group always results in someone defined as out-group. In the case of Israel, a proportion of the Israeli community who consider themselves very much to be Jews stands to be defined as outside the Jewish People if religious authorities are successful in some of the battles mentioned herein. The proportion is even higher since the immigration of approximately 800,000 former Soviet Jews in the 1990s, many of whom are considered non-Jews by religious authorities.

The regulation of gender boundaries is of critical importance in marriage and divorce law as well. A woman who cannot get a kosher divorce from her husband can never have more children legally, *halakhically*. If she does, her children will be considered *mamzerim* for ten generations. In a state with no civil marriage, that is a great restriction to put on a child. It means, quite literally, that her children will not be able to marry within the Jewish community in Israel. A man who cannot acquire a divorce, on the other hand, may have children with another woman, provided that she herself is *halakhically* free. The gendered aspects of these regulations are notable

[55] Religious authorities define "who is a Jew" for identity cards. All citizens of Israel must carry identity cards. Driver's licenses are not used, as they are in the United States, as the primary identity card.

because of this difference. The laws seek to regulate with whom women can reproduce. They regulate men as well, but with far fewer restrictions or repercussions. Thus, the crossing of gendered marriage and divorce laws is inherently tied to the regulation and reproduction of the boundaries of the community.

Regulation of religious practice – worship as well as participation in religious institutions – is another tool used within the community to determine who is a "real Jew" and who is not. Gender roles are extremely important as such a marker. Viewed by religious officials as within the community, Leah Shakdiel was eventually accepted as a representative on her local religious council. Once she was allowed to be a representative, however, she faced a great battle to get information and to be allowed to be a real participant on the religious council. The WOW, on the other hand, have not been accepted at all, despite High Court rulings in their favor. Their crossing of gender boundaries, by performing rituals traditionally limited to men, has won them such epithets as "Amalek," "Egypt," and "missionaries." All of these terms define the WOW as outside the community; as a Haredi women at the WOW Rosh Khodesh session in June 2000 exclaimed: "These are not the People of Israel!" The regulation and reproduction of just who is counted as the People of Israel and members of the nation-state of Israel is, for Haredi and Haredi-leumi communities, dependent on the participation of religious officials in a state that will enforce their institutions and their vision.

PART V

BEYOND THE STATE

Transnational Forces and the Challenge to the State

11

Passports into Credit Cards

On the Borders and Spaces of Neoliberal Citizenship

Matthew Sparke

> We have included in our design the necessary technological platforms to ensure that the card will have a useful life of approximately five years. Most importantly for commercial users today, it will sport the ubiquitous magnetic strip which the government will not use, making it completely available to the commercial sector. We have also included a microchip in the design as we will require some of the available storage space for automated inspections. We will make the remainder of the chip's storage available to our commercial partners. We think this is especially significant because of the recent announcement by Visa, MasterCard and Europay of their joint specification for chip-based credit cards. To further the appeal of this idea to the commercial sector, we will also allow cards prepared by our partners to display the logo of the partner. This would create in the mind of the card holder an instant link between our high technology application and the sponsoring corporation. Just think of the possibilities for a frequent traveler pulling out a card bearing the IBM or United Airlines logo, for example. Now potentiate that image by seeing the card as a charge card, an airline ticket, a medium by which you access telecommunications systems, an electronic bank, and/or any other card-based application you can conceive.
>
> Ronald Hays[1]

These plans for a new kind of passport using credit card and biometric technology are not the plans of a banker, a commercial web systems designer, or some other corporate planner. They are plans developed by a Seattle-based Immigration and Naturalization Service (INS) officer in the United States Department of Justice. Specifically, the plans are for a card that can be used by frequent cross-border travelers in order to secure for themselves

[1] Ronald J. Hays, "INSPASS: INS Passenger Accelerated Service System," paper written on January 4, 1996, that was published on a now inactive web page of the Department of Justice. For reasons that are no doubt connected to the argument for public-private partnerships put forward here by Hays, his paper in now available on the site of the "Biometric Consortium" at http://www.biometrics.org/REPORTS/INSPASS.html (accessed August 12, 2002).

fast track border crossings based on preclearance. The cards will, in this vision, contain biometric information such as digitized hand-print data that will allow machinery installed at border checkpoints to ascertain whether the cardholder is in fact the person with the precleared record. Coordinating with selected foreign partners as well as collaborating with business, the plans for the card anticipate a remarkable future where borders are effectively to be policed by credit card machines owned by private companies. It is a world in which precleared cardholders come and go as they please across multiple borders irrespective of their nationality (so long as they are from a country that has joined the system) and dependent only on whether they are carrying their card. The various insignia of national identity that are today inscribed on specific national passport covers would in this world be replaced by the corporate logos of transnational corporations. And the class-organized, transnational world of credit card transactions, along with all their liberating and constraining market-mediated contradictions, would seem to come to eclipse the more equalized world of belonging regulated in the second half of twentieth century by the serial sameness of national passports.[2] This is a view of the future, then, where the ambiguities of state control and state protection associated with passports would appear to be transcended by the ambiguities of corporate control and free market flexibility afforded by credit cards.[3] As such, the vision outlined by Hays is of more than mere technical, bureaucratic, or local interest. It is symptomatic of a significant transformation of citizenship under the political-economic regime of market-based governance commonly called "neoliberalism."

Neoliberalism is a useful bracket term for the dominant political commonsense of our time. It brackets together the policy-making commitments to free trade, privatization, price stability, and deregulation popularized in the west by Ronald Reagan and Margaret Thatcher, exported to much of the rest of the world by the International Monetary Fund, World Bank and World Trade Organization, and now repackaged anew as some sort of "Third

[2] As Jane Caplan and John Torpey note in their survey of the history of modern identity cards, "the adoption of the passport regime in international travel is intimately tied to the development of citizenship rules." Jane Caplan and John Torpey, "Introduction," in Jane Caplan and John Torpey, eds., *Documenting Individual Identity: The Development of State Practices in the Modern World* (Princeton, N.J.: Princeton University Press, 2001), 3.

[3] On the ambiguities of state-society relations associated with passports, Torpey glosses Max Weber as follows: "As the documentary expression of modern states' efforts to monopolize the 'legitimate means of movement,' the passport concentrates in itself the enormous increase in modern states' control over individual existence that has evolved since the nineteenth century. At the same time, in a world in which documentary attestation of identity is generally required for the legal traversal of state boundaries, passports facilitate people's movements. In addition passport ensure that their bearers may avail themselves of the protections that states may provide in an uncertain and potentially hostile world.' John Torpey, "The Great War and the Birth of the Modern Passport System," in Caplan and Torpey, eds., *Documenting Individual Identity*, 256–57.

Way" by the likes of Tony Blair, Jean Chretien, and Gerhard Schroeder. The transformative impacts of this dominant policy-making regime on citizenship have been significant, but to understand them better we need particular concrete cases through which to examine the changes. The argument in this chapter is that the re-regulation of borders and the related redevelopment of border regions provide just such opportunities for empirical study. Underpinned by popular neoliberal assumptions about the benefits of privatization and entrepreneurial policy making, and forced through in part because of globalizing capitalism's need for speedy and flexible cross-border movement, the re-regulation of border controls involves shifts in how citizenship is both policed and imagined. Likewise, regional redevelopment plans for border regions in areas that come under continental free trade agreements commonly reflect the same increasing influence of market-oriented concepts of citizenship. In the Pacific Northwest of the United States, the actual plans of Hays are yet to be fully implemented. Instead, they need to be seen as part of a longer term set of trends in border re-regulation, trends that have involved two fast track border crossing systems known respectively as the "PACE lane" and "NEXUS." These border re-regulation innovations need in turn to be examined in the light of specific border region redevelopment patterns. The aim in this chapter is to flesh out some of these broader trends, thereby exploring more concretely the remaking of citizenship portended in the vision articulated by Hays. While the episodic story of border re-regulation has to attend to the tidal changes in federal legislation in Washington, D.C., the account of border region redevelopment plans has to be more localized, and in this respect it is the regional developments on the Pacific Coast between the United States and Canada – the district for which Hays has been an INS commissioner – that will be the main focus.

After 9/11, it may seem anachronistic to be discussing North American efforts to soften borders and speedup border crossing. It may also seem a strange stretch to connect such border re-regulation to the more geographical issue of border region spaces and their redevelopment. Both of these concerns can be answered together because they both centrally relate to the ways in which the emerging neoliberal norms of citizenship appear to depend on new forms of class-based inclusion and exclusion that have actually been intensified, at least in terms of border practices, since the crisis in confidence in U.S. "homeland" security. Long before the attacks on the World Trade Center and the Pentagon, the concept of facilitating fast border crossing for business traffic on the West Coast was always twinned with security concerns about catching criminals and potentials terrorists. In turn, this bifurcated vision of border re-regulation also always went hand in hand with the new regional redevelopment ideas for the region. These ideas are examined at length later, save to note here that they have been organized around the international promotion of a postnational cross-border regional concept that the local politicians, planners, and think-tanks like to call "Cascadia." As a cross-border region, Cascadia is imagined politically, economically, and culturally as a kind of neoliberal utopia destined for growth and prosperity as a gateway of global-local commerce and as a homeland for managerial class elites. It is the exclusivism of this vision that explains why it is necessary to consider the wider geographical issues surrounding cross-border regional redevelopment in conjunction with the re-regulation of the border. The events of 9/11 have simply intensified this exclusivism along with the attendant patterns of recoding and reimagining citizenship. The resulting reimagination of the border and cross-border region presents us with a space where distinctions are made between travelers less on the basis of their nationality and more on the basis of whether they appear to be good for "economic security" or whether they can be deemed a threat to "political security." As a consequence of 9/11, then, the impetus to increase security has come together with the enduring planning vision of a business-friendly cross-border region. The result, as we see below, involves increased plans and practices of re-regulating the border that aim simultaneously at easing obstacles for business traffic while strictly securitizing everybody and everything else.

There are, of course, many complex contradictions involved in combining neoliberal freedoms with increased political security. These contradictions are telling, and much like the changing border regulations they produce and the border-region politics in which they unfold, they reveal a great deal about the contemporary transformation of citizenship. By examining them through their effects on the grounding of new assumptions about citizenship in cross-border space, the primary goal of this chapter is to register some of the complex ways in which citizenship is being recodified in an area where neoliberal commitments to public-private partnerships and free market solutions are well entrenched. My broader goal is to connect the particular reimagination of space and citizenship in Cascadia with global tendencies toward new geographical visions of community and belonging that center on nodes and networks. By highlighting the contrasts between these visions and older geographical imaginations of belonging in territorially discrete nation-states, I seek ultimately to contribute to the wider debate over how elite postnational citizenship – what the anthropologist Aiwha Ong calls "flexible citizenship" – is coeval with significant transformations to the territoriality and borders of the modern nation-state.[4] While Ong herself examines the

4 Aiwha Ong, *Flexible Citizenship: The Cultural Logics of Transnationality* (Durham, N.C.: Duke University Press, 1999). The flexible citizenship in which Ong is most interested is that of wealthy ethnic Chinese business managers who have purchased multiple passport along with many other social and political rights associated with multiple national citizenships, all with a view to securing business advantages, real estate deals, and/or family security through elite education. Clearly, though, there are many other forms of cosmopolitan belonging in the current era, not all of them privileged with the official imprimatur of state citizenship. This is a point that the anthropologist James Clifford has made extensively, as do many of the other contributions to Pheng Cheah and Bruce Robbins, eds., *Cosmopolitics: Thinking and Feeling beyond the Nation* (Minneapolis: University of Minnesota Press, 1998). See, esp.,

ways in which Chinese managerial elites have effectively purchased multiple citizenship and multiple passports, this study highlights tendencies that have the potential to transcend the whole regime in which national citizenship is codified and policed through national passports. Before I turn to the empirical material itself, though, a little more needs to be said about my theoretical and terminological starting points.

Citizenship and the Symptoms of Neoliberalism

In dealing with the diffuse and perspectival stuff of cultural norms and geographical imaginations, my method has of necessity to be open-ended and qualitative. The focus is not on the numbers of people crossing the border, on how many are actually being processed by the new border technologies, or on the technical specificities of any one particular plan, such as that of Hays. The chapter is much more concerned with what the general innovation of new border policing strategies and new cross-border visions tell us about the changing shape of dominant assumptions about citizenship. The word "ideology" could be used here, but it is not, because of its misleading associations with deliberately false or propagandistic representations. That said, the main concern of the chapter is with changing *ideas* about citizenship and with the ways that these are complexly, yet powerfully, interwoven with real, practical changes in how the border between Canada and the United States is being managed. For the same reason, the case-study material here is presented as a symptom or, more precisely, as a set of symptoms of a wider set of changes. It is not a representative sample of all the borders in North America, still less of all the borders in the world. But it is a border that provides us with a remarkable window on to how citizenship is being reimagined, recodified, and, therefore, remade in an era when laissez-faire, free-market capitalism has become globally dominant.

Conceptually, my starting point is the sociologist T. H. Marshall's famous mid-twentieth-century work on citizenship and social class.[5] In this work Marshall's main concern is with how the commitments to equality that are central to modern ideals of citizenship have been historically squared with ongoing class inequalities between actual citizens. To answer this question, he argues that it is necessary to distinguish among three different forms of citizenship that became increasingly differentiated in the context of

James Clifford, "Mixed Feelings," in ibid., 362–70. Following Clifford, I would argue that we need to study the *discrepant* forms of cosmopolitan culture as they take form in differently rooted global routeways, whether they be the plush aisles of red carpet in business class or the barbed-wire borderlands of the U.S.-Mexican desert. Obviously, then, this chapter's attempt to chart the elite model of flexible citizenship reflected in the re-regulations and reimaginations of the Canada-U.S. border by no means illustrates all of the challenges to traditional national norms of citizenship in the era of neoliberalism.

[5] T. H. Marshall, "Citizenship and Social Class," in Gershon Shafir, ed., *The Citizenship Debates: A Reader* (University of Minnesota Press: Minneapolis, 1998), 93–112.

modernity: civil citizenship (involving freedom of access to markets, the right to sell one's labor, and the right to the protection of private property and contracts under the law), political citizenship (involving the rights to vote and run for office), and social citizenship (involving rights to education and other services aimed at securing a basic standard of living). Surveying the English experience, Marshall suggests that the formative historical periods for each of these types of citizenship followed one another consecutively, with civil rights expanding widely in the eighteenth century, political rights in the nineteenth, and social rights in the twentieth. In the first two of these three phases Marshall argues that the underlying tension between the equalizing implications of citizenship and class inequality shaped the subsequent expansion of rights. Social citizenship emerges thus in the twentieth century as a countervailing force against class inequality, but then, Marshall concludes (in an argument that reflected his 1960s interest in the development of the United Kingdom's welfare state), seemed set to be at continual odds with the ongoing class pressures of capitalist society. The historical details and transferability of the evolutionary account to other contexts are questionable, as too are the adequacy of Marshall's categories in light of feminist and postcolonial critiques of the normative white western man of property who stands at the center of most modern formulations of rights-bearing citizenship.[6] But these concerns noted, Marshall's concern with the fundamental tension between capitalist class dynamics and social citizenship, his sensitivity to the differentiation of the different forms of citizenship, and his basic argument that their distinct histories overlay one another serve as a useful heuristic for approaching the question of what is happening to citizenship today under neoliberalism. Most particularly, as the geographers Sallie Marston and Katharyne Mitchell have argued, Marshall's attention to how eighteenth-century civil citizenship was associated with the liberal repudiation of interventionist government helps to explain how a certain sort of *retreat* to civil citizenship is now coincident with the entrenchment of neoliberal policies.[7]

[6] For the feminist critiques, see Sallie Marston, "Who Are 'the People'? Gender, Citizenship and the Making of the American Nation," *Environment and Planning D: Society and Space* 8: 449–58; Nancy Fraser and Linda Gordon, "Contract versus Charity: Why Is There No Social Citizenship in the United States?," in Shafir, ed., *Citizenship Debates*, 113–27; and Eleonore Kofman, "Rights and Citizenship," in John Agnew, Katharyne Mitchell, and Gerard Toal, eds., *A Companion to Political Geography* (New York: Routledge, forthcoming). For a wonderful and powerfully critical review of how citizenship in the West was systematically imagined by liberal thinkers (such as Mill) in a way that assumed the necessary denial of citizenship rights to the inhabitants of European colonies, see Uday Singh Mehta, *Liberalism and Empire: A Study in Nineteenth Century British Legal Thought* (Chicago: University of Chicago Press, 2000).

[7] See Sallie Marston and Katharyne Mitchell, "Citizens and the State: Contextualizing Citizenship Formations in Space and Time," in Clive Barnett and Murray Low, eds., *Spaces of Democracy* (London: Sage, 2002).

With the increasing dominance of laissez-faire, market-based models of governance it seems we are witnessing the progressive erosion of national citizenship rights and the wholesale transformation of the constitutional qualities of social, political, and even, in some ways, civil citizenship. In this respect it must be recalled that Ronald Reagan, the grandfather of neoliberal economic policy, described the expansion of market based governance as having a *constitutional* impact. In announcing the Canadian-U.S. Free Trade Agreement, for example, Reagan described the neoliberal trade and investment charter as "a new economic constitution for North America."[8] This was no verbal slip. As Stephen Clarkson and many other critics have since noted, the constitutionalism of the free trade agreement amounted to a bill of rights for continental businesses, giving them expansive movement rights and enabling them to relocate production sites or threaten to do so, thereby winning tax and other regulatory concessions from local governments. In this context, citizens have been left able to vote in formal elections, but their elected governments have been strait-jacketed by trade law and obliged to curtail certain social programs and environmental protections. As a result, the meaning and quality of political and social citizenship has been eroded.

North American free trade is just one example of neoliberalism at work, and it needs emphasizing that the constitutional capacities of trade agreements have their governmental effects only in a worldwide context wherein global competition for business investment and growth has becomes a primary force shaping public policy.[9] As the political scientist Stephen Gill explains, it is the combination of all these forces that has systematic world-shaping effects, effects that comprise a regime Gill calls "disciplinary neoliberalism."[10] This disciplinary regime is further buttressed, the anthropologists Jean and John Camaroff remind us, by neoliberalism's naturalization as an

[8] Quoted in Stephen Clarkson, "Constitutionalising the Canadian-American Relationship," in Duncan Cameron and Mel Watkins, eds., *Canada under Free Trade* (Toronto: James Lorimer, 1993), 3.

[9] Neoliberalism, therefore, is more than just a quasi-constitutional outcome of signing trade agreements into law (as some free trade protesters sometimes suggest). It is just as much a product of the more global pattern of accelerated economic interdependency and the norms of free trade it has brought with it – often more simply dubbed "globalization." There is a systematic way in which neoliberalism in this sense has been progressively locked into transnational place ever since the oil crises and the collapse of the Bretton Woods system at the start of the 1970s. Although much of the subsequent development of the Uruguay GATT round and the final formation of the WTO has been labeled "Americanization" by critics, the United States – and especially local government within the United States – often remains just as susceptible as smaller economies to the structural force of this emerging free-trading regime.

[10] Stephen Gill, "Globalisation, Market Civilisation, and Disciplinary Neoliberalism," *Millennium: Journal of International Studies* 24, no. 3 (1996): 399–423. Gill describes disciplinary neoliberalism further as being "institutionalized at the macro-level of power in the quasi-legal restructuring of state and international political forms: the 'new constitutionalism.' [This] can be defined as the political project of attempting to make transnational

apolitical logic. Thus, they claim, "there is a strong argument to be made that neoliberal capitalism, in its millennial moment, portends the death of politics by hiding its own ideological underpinnings in the dictates of economic efficiency: in the fetishism of the free market, in the inexorable expanding needs of business, in the imperatives of science and technology."[11]

The arguments about neoliberalism made by Gill, the Camaroffs, and many others oblige us to reflect again on how exactly the differentiated development of citizenship charted by Marshall is being transformed. An initial, schematic response would be to argue that social, political, and civil citizenship rights are being undermined in the reverse order of Marshall's original narrative of their formation. Thus we see cutbacks and/or privatization of state social services (because of the new emphases on fiscal discipline, price stability, and market-based governance), followed by the attrition of meaningful electoral rights (because of money in politics and the increasing leverage of markets and trade agreements over elected governments), followed in certain countries by the eclipse of even civil rights as legal protections for ordinary workers are eviscerated and increasing numbers of people are incarcerated, expelled, or, as in the United States, executed. Clearly, this reversed schema risks reproducing Marshall's own evolutionary teleology, and one way in which to begin nuancing such an account of citizenship in the current era is to address the ways in which certain sorts of rights are not being destroyed but rather *transnationalized*. This is certainly true of the types of economic rights that Marshall put at the center of civil citizenship. The rights to move freely between markets and be protected wherever by the rule of law are clearly being expanded transnationally as free trade regimes around the world are effectively entrenching a series of quasi-constitutional protections for everything from patents on intellectual property to cross-border movement freedoms for business professionals. But here Marshall's attention to class remains of the utmost importance. It is, after all, largely the wealthy business classes, or what the sociologist Leslie Sklair calls the "transnational capitalist class," for whom the prospects of transnational civil citizenship appear most real.[12] Indeed, in the United States the prospects of a more mass generalization of these rights to others seems ever more remote as post-9/11 security concerns and the widespread escalation of anti-immigration politics become increasingly dominant. It is precisely against the backdrop of these antithetical imperatives that the developments in border policing and territorial imagination in the so-called Cascadia region need to be situated.

liberalism, and if possible liberal democratic capitalism, the sole model for future development. It is therefore intimately related to the rise of market civilization" (p. 412).

[11] Jean Comaroff and John Comaroff, "Millenial Capitalism: First Thoughts on a Second Coming," *Public Culture* 12, no. 2 (2000): 322.

[12] Leslie Sklair, *The Transnational Capitalist Class* (Oxford: Blackwell, 2001).

The account begins next with a detailed examination of the various plans to provide expedited crossing for frequent travelers across the 49th parallel on the West Coast. These plans have now gone through a number of metamorphoses, and the changes and the political struggles they have provoked reveal a great deal about the array of clashing forces shaping the codification of citizenship at the border. After relating this account of legal and institutional innovation, we turn next to the cultural geographical imagination of Cascadia as the regional space in which the movement to "bulldoze the border" has developed. Lastly, in the conclusion the aim is to connect these empirical accounts to the larger theoretical questions concerning the emergence of flexible citizenship and the disarticulation of the nation-state in the contemporary era.

From PACE-ing the Border to the NEXUS of Business and Security

At a conference on Cascadia and tourism in Seattle in 1996, the United States INS chief responsible for the border with Canada at Blaine prefaced his update on expedited crossing lanes with a tellingly curt description of the approach to belonging deployed by border guards. "There are basically just two main types of bordercrossers," he explained, "those that go in primary processing and those that go in secondary. If you are in primary our chief aim is to get you across the border as fast as possible, ideally in a matter of seconds. If you are in secondary," he went on, "we really don't care how long it takes.' What he meant by "secondary" were all those cases for which longer periods of questioning become necessary on the basis of the primary border guard's assessment. People put into secondary at the Blaine crossing have to wait for a longer period of questioning in INS offices behind the curbside booths. They can be asked to provide further documentation, they can have their car searched, and they can even be strip-searched themselves, but, whatever the scope of the interviews and interrogations, they can expect to have their border crossing considerably delayed, if not halted altogether. Meanwhile, the INS chief underlined, the service focuses much of its energies on speeding up the crossings of those in primary. At the conference, this commitment to speeding up primary processing was received with warm applause by the assembled audience of coach tour and cruise operators, who were eager to emphasize that anything the INS could do to further ease congestion at the border would be good for their businesses. They understood that the service had an important responsibility to stop, as one manager put it, the "bad guys," but they, the folks in business suits, the "good guys," needed all the help they could get to make the border-crossing experience less time consuming and less of a burdensome friction on business.

This kind of pressure to make borders more permeable for the "good" flows (all the while distinguishing them and separating them from control of the "bad") has been a perennial puzzle of border management since the first development of border control posts. However, the definition of the "good" and the "bad" in terms of business and the starkness of the bifurcation between them would seem to reflect the contemporary impact of neoliberalism on citizenship and the definition of belonging in North America. Becoming an American citizen may help one to win a place in primary, but it is not a necessary condition, let alone a sufficient condition of belonging there. Frequent travel, business travel, vacation travel, or some mixture thereof are weighed, too, and thus inclusion inexorably becomes more and more about having capital or thinking of territory and belonging in terms of capital. Indeed, the division between primary and secondary processing would seem to provide a border checkpoint corollary of the dual labor market effect that is often discussed by economic analysts of so-called post-Fordist flexibility.[13] It divides a necessary and integral core population from a contingent and externalized marginal population. The fact that migrants to the United States constitute a crucial part of the contingent labor market population serves only to further underline the substantive connections and overlaps between these economic and political definitions of belonging. Of course, on the border there are often individual cases of mistaken identity, poor paperwork, and abusive and unprincipled enforcement, but the fundamental division of border-crossers into two groups of primary and secondary is the basic way in which the checkpoint serves to manage belonging.

Efforts to expedite "primary" travel across the 49th parallel on the Pacific Coast developed throughout the 1990s. Soon after the implementation of the Canadian-U.S. Free Trade agreement in 1989, local business elites started pushing for a fast fast track system at the border, and over the next two years their hopes were realized with the establishment in 1991 of the Peace Arch Crossing Entry, or so-called PACE lane. While some security-minded border guards came to joke about PACE standing for "Paraphenalia and Contraband Express," the INS was nevertheless rigorous in implementing the new program.[14] The first year of the its experimental implementation was 1992, and by the fall of that year, American officials had approved 19,000 PACE applications. After the initial enthusiasm for the project, the numbers of applicants fell. However, by the end of 1999, some 27 percent of southbound vehicles across the 49th parallel at the West Coast crossings were using the PACE lane. Before its immediate demise following 9/11 in 2001, it had almost 190,000 enrollees. By that point, the PACE program had expanded to more Washington/British Columbia border checkpoints and had become the dedicated commuter lane (DCL, in INS parlance) with the largest number of enrollees in North America.

[13] David Harvey, *The Condition of Postmodernity* (Oxford: Blackwell, 1989).

[14] Noted in Douglas Ward, "Using Fast Lane Is in the Cards," *Vancouver Sun*, June 27, 2002, p. A4.

The system the PACE lane established was quite simple, with nothing like the high-technology, biometric, and credit-card features of the system that Hays came to outline in 1996.[15] Applicants could go through a screening process and then, if they passed, be issued a decal for their cars that showed they were entitled to drive in the PACE lane when they came to the border. This lane had lines much shorter than all the other lanes, and the likelihood of a long verbal interrogation by the border guard was considerably reduced. So long as applicants were American or Canadian citizens, and so long as they were prepared to pay the relatively small fee to purchase PACE lane membership, the application process was not especially burdensome. And the result, as the promoters of Cascadia liked to point out, was an important step toward the larger dream of "bulldozing the border" for business traffic. Thus under the radical-sounding section title "bulldoze the checkpoints" of their report on the economic potential of the cross-border region, two influential Cascadian boosters argued that PACE "should be more widely promoted and expanded, eventually leading to even more open borders between the United States and Canada."[16]

All the PACE lane really did was to entrench further and to encode bureaucratically the divide between primary and secondary. It gave the primary population who traveled across the border frequently the chance to buy the additional flexibility they needed to cross the border fast, all the while guaranteeing them a certain degree of protection from the likelihood of being trapped by delays or erroneous assignments to secondary. In a sense, then, the PACE lane merely stripped away the superficial sense of equality that used to emerge from the common experience shared by primary and secondary populations alike of waiting in line to be interviewed at the checkpoint. An illustrative equivalent of this transformation within nation-states such as the United States might be found in the way in which valet parking takes away the forced equality of searching for parking spots in busy city centers. With rarely a lineup at all in the PACE lane, those who signed up as members could follow the equivalent of a red carpet up to the border and proceed onward

[15] However, it should be noted that there were already in the mid-1990s other operational systems that were far more technologically advanced than PACE. The most notable among these was the SENTRI (Secure Electronic Network for Traveler's Rapid Inspection) network put into place on the border with Mexico at San Diego. However, given its location and its purpose of distinguishing precleared travelers from ordinary Mexico-U.S. border crossers, the acronym SENTRI is a telling militaristic contrast to PACE.

[16] Paul Schell and John Hamer, "Cascadia: The New Binationalism of Western Canada and the U.S. Pacific Northwest," in R. Earle and J. Wirth, eds., *Identities in North America: The Search for Community* (Palo Alto, Calif.: Stanford University Press, 1995), 148. The terminology of bulldozing had been carried forward from an earlier piece by Paul Schell, "Bulldozing Borders," *The New Pacific* (Summer 1990): 5–10. It should be noted that Schell later went on to become mayor of Seattle; during his tenure, his vision of bulldozing checkpoints was radically revisited by anti-WTO protesters. Schell's neoliberal response was to call in the National Guard and impose curfews on downtown Seattle.

with almost as little trouble as crossing a line between two provinces or two states. The flexibility enjoyed by PACE lane members interestingly paralleled Ong's more general account of flexible citizenship. Such flexible citizenship, she argues, "refers to the cultural logics of capitalist accumulation, travel, and displacement that induce subjects to respond fluidly and opportunistically to changing political-economic conditions."[17] As we see below, the Cascadian cultural logics and discourses that lay behind the PACE lane also concerned capitalist accumulation, travel, and displacement. Moreover, they also have been articulated with a view to providing the envisaged Cascadian elite with all the border-crossing fluidity they might need to seize on the synergies and codevelopment opportunities presented by the vision of an emergent cross-border political economy. However, unlike the decentered and hybrid discourses and practices that are the focus of Ong's ethnography of Chinese business managers, the PACE lane was a bureaucratic innovation of the state, and as such, its emergence, maintenance, and more recent replacement by the NEXUS system need to be understood in terms of the contradictory political directives of the state.

Not unlike North American free trade itself, and notwithstanding the associated bulldozing rhetoric, border deregulation through fast track lanes actually requires more regulation, more policing, and more bureaucratic processing at the border in order to make the same border more permeable for the properly codified cross-border flows. The PACE lane also required more international support and coordination, with the Canadian government developing its reciprocal CANPASS program to expedite the reverse frequent traveler flows into Canada across the same border. As a result of this relationship to state regulations and interstate agreements, the institutional evolution of the PACE lane was actually quite tumultuous. After its initial success and after being hailed in 1995 as a step toward a complete bulldozing of the border, the PACE lane suffered a heavy legislative blow the following year in 1996 when the politics of anti-immigration clashed directly with the politics of economic flexibility. The focus of this clash was the passage of the Immigrant Responsibility and Illegal Immigration Reform Act, a Republican-sponsored piece of legislation that ultimately came to be signed by President Clinton. This clash, like the PACE lane and associated plans such as those made by Hays, must be examined as symptoms of the evolving assumptions about citizenship in the United States in the 1990s.

The politics involved in the 1996 legislative struggles can be seen summarily in terms of the tension between an emphasis on interdicting "bad flows" and an emphasis on expediting "good flows." But the contentious ground of this dispute in Congress was not between Republicans and Democrats and certainly not directly between immigrants' rights representatives and business representatives. Instead, the dispute largely took place

[17] Ong, *Flexible Citizenship*, p. 6.

within the Republican party itself between politicians more keenly focused on trade and development issues and those more exercised by a conservative, anti-immigrant nationalism. Pulled together under the leadership of Newt Gingrich, these feuding elements within the party together shaped the drafting of the Immigrant Responsibility and Illegal Immigration Reform Act (IRAIIRA). As well as condensing the tensions dividing Republicans, this act was also profoundly animated by Gingrich's own trademark fascination with technological futurism. Indeed, technology was turned to in the act as the very means through which to combine strict interdiction with accelerated flow facilitation. The result, nevertheless, was a piece of legislation that represented a practical disaster for PACE lane advocates. "It's more than a slap in the face," a key Cascadian visionary told a reporter. "It would bring business between Canada and the United States to a grinding halt."[18] However, such practicalities were not noticed at the time as the bill was pushed through Congress in a giant omnibus legislative package at the end of a long session. It was not until after a pliant President Clinton signed the act into law that the problematic and self-defeating aspects of the legislation started to become apparent.

From the perspective of PACE lane supporters and advocates of dedicated commuter lanes on other parts of the 49th parallel, the particular offending part of the act was Section 110.[19] This section became infamous insofar as it threatened – had it ever been implemented – to create instantly the worst and slowest moving traffic jams ever experienced on the U.S. border with Canada. On the West Coast, the resulting tailbacks of traffic were anticipated to stretch all the way back to Vancouver from Blaine. They clearly would have made it impossible for anyone, whether they had PACE decals or not, to get even close to the border in a hurry. Uniformity and equality would have returned through the slow-moving sameness of congestion. The main reason for the expected delays was that the section demanded that *all aliens* entering and *exiting* the United States would have to file arrival and departure records. The rationale for this demand was the concern that many illegally resident aliens in the United States were coming in on legal visas and then simply overstaying. The idea behind the act was to keep bureaucratic track of all such aliens, thereby enhancing the capability of the INS and law enforcement agencies to track down those overstaying their visas. For PACE lane advocates, the problem with this whole section lay in the targeting of so-called aliens, a word long used in the United States to designate the status of foreignness against which U.S. citizenship and belonging is defined.

[18] Alan Artibise, quoted in L. Pynn, "Without Politicians, Cascadia Is Just a Dream," *Vancouver Sun*, November 12, 1997, p. A1.

[19] For a useful overview of the controversy, see Theodore Cohn, "Cross-Border Travel in North America: The Challenge of U.S. Section 110 Legislation," *Canadian American Public Policy* 40 (October 1999): 1–70.

Although some local Washington State representatives such as Republican Jack Metcalf did not seem to realize this as they voted for the act, the wording "aliens" therefore meant that the law would apply to Canadians, even if it was racist fear about undocumented immigration from Mexico that was a driving force behind the legislation.[20] With Canadians thereby covered by the section, the act effectively condemned the northern border to the likely delays that would be created as each and every Canadian citizen filled in the entry-exit forms at the border.

In response to the IRAIIRA the Canadian government went into a high gear lobbying effort to repeal Section 110. They wanted the northern border and Canadians to be excepted from the stringent demands of the act. But to this the Mexican government added its own criticisms of Section 110, arguing moreover that one NAFTA signatory should not be treated any differently from another. These intergovernmental complaints were then also complemented by Cascadia's promoters and many other neoliberally minded groups from northern border states across the United States whose view of Canadians was and is as business partners, not potential illegal aliens.[21] A lobby group entitled "Americans for Better Borders" was also formed, supported chiefly by the big auto companies and other transnationals such as Eastman Kodak, with vested interests in moving goods quickly across the border. These lobbies had good connections with business-oriented Republicans and Democrats, and it was not long before legislative amendment ensued. Section 110 was first put on hold, and then finally, in the early summer of 2000, it was rewritten so as to be completely harmless to the status quo. Like the Canadian government, Cascadia's promoters heralded this as a success, but as they did so few noticed and none acknowledged publicly that in many ways Section 110 (along with a number of other key parts of the 1996 act) actually represented a form of congressional response to the call to expand the PACE program and other forms of expedited, preclearance-type, passport processing.

To pick just one example of the pro-PACE lane rhetoric, here is more of the plea made by the Cascadian visionaries quoted above. Calling for a new border regime based on coordinated data-management, or what they called "one stop passport control," Schell and Hamer argue:

> Ideally, a continental North American clearance someday would make one-stop passport control available for overseas guests, and within the continent would make access between British Columbia and Washington, for example, as easy as access between Oregon and Washington today.[22]

[20] Steve Wilhelm, "Future Border Procedures Concern Trade Advocates," *Puget Sound Business Journal*, October 16, 1997, p. A6.

[21] Joel Connelly and Michael Paulson, "U.S., Canada Say Border Law Would Create Havoc," *Seattle Post-Intelligencer*, May 19, 1999, p. A3.

[22] Schell and Hamer, "Cascadia," 143.

Obviously, the predicted impact of Section 110 was the complete reverse of this vision. Highlighting this reversal in his critique, Senator Patrick Leahy of Vermont summarized the problem perfectly: "This is not Checkpoint Charlie," he said. "This is the largest unguarded frontier in the world."[23] However, a closer look at the wording of the act itself reveals how it was actually built on the same vision of technological facilitation, preclearance data-base management, and dual-tier processing that underpinned dedicated commuter lanes such as the PACE lane:

SEC 110. AUTOMATED ENTRY-EXIT CONTROL SYSTEM
(a) SYSTEM. Not later than 2 years after the date of the enactment of this Act, the Attorney General shall develop an automated entry and exit control system that will –
(1) collect a record of departure for every alien departing the United States and match the records of departure with the record of the alien's arrival in the United States; and
(2) enable the Attorney General to identify, through on-line searching procedures, lawfully admitted nonimmigrants who remain in the United States beyond the period authorized by the Attorney General.[24]

Running through this section, as well as through the act more generally, is an emphasis on technological solutions. The entry and exit control system would be *automated*, the section dictated. Perhaps it was for this reason that the drafters of the legislation were not worried by concerns about long delays. The technology, even though there was no budget to pay for it in the act, would somehow solve the problems by creating a dual system for border crossers, thereby speeding up the movement of legitimate travelers while enabling a foolproof process for identifying, detaining, and deporting the illegal. Collecting all departure records might in earlier times have created enormous problems, but another techno-futuristic part of the act – Section 104 – saw this as easily addressed through new high-tech biometric systems. These systems, which were already being tested in 1996 at various U.S. airports, effectively represented a further technologization of the sort of preclearance system installed with PACE.

It was in this context that Ronald Hays made his pitch for the high-technology biometric, public-private partnership, credit card solution outlined in the epigraph at the start of this chapter.[25] Hays suggested that biometric systems would simply accelerate fast track services by providing one-to-one automated inspections by machines at border checkpoints. The machines would determine whether a card holder of a preclearance card actually was the person who had been precleared by making a one-to-one

[23] Quoted in G. Frandsen, "Tighter Entry Rules Could Snarl the Border," *Seattle Times*, November 25, 1997, p. A5.

[24] *United States Code Congressional and Administrative News*, 1996, 104th Cong., 2nd Session, vol. 3, Public Laws 104–208 to 104–325.

[25] Hays, "INSPASS."

match. A digitized hand or voice print encoded on a chip on the card would be matched by the machine by a reading of the card holder's hand or voice at the border. Automated in this way, the biometric systems promised to be extremely quick. Adding a further neoliberal gleam to this promise of technological efficiency and speed, Hays's description of INS planning also highlighted how the preclearance lane cards and the automated checking machines would actually be owned and maintained by private companies. He acknowledged that this would be a significant change in accepted government practice, but with a view it seems to communicating with the neoliberal revolutionaries in Congress, he noted that this was very much in line with the whole emphasis on "reinventing government."

The idea of the INS turning to private industry to operate an automated inspection system would have been considered radical, and undoable, just a few years ago. Today it fits in perfectly with the "reinventing government" strategy that stresses the development of effective ways to control costs and improve the delivery of governmental benefits and services. To quote William Plamondon, chair of the Facilitation/Reduction of Barriers subcommittee of the recently completed White House Conference on Travel and Tourism: "[w]e must draw upon the individual strengths of the public and private sectors and form a partnership that will encourage people to come to the United States."[26] Building on this logic, then, Hays argued for three guiding axioms in the development of the new border technologies. "The partnership the Immigration and Naturalization Service is considering is based upon three key ideas," he explained. The INS should be the gatekeeper, not the operator, of the system; the card should contain a variety of technological platforms for maximum flexibility; and the card should have a commercial plus a governmental identity.

The resulting vision of passports turned credit cards turned globalized badges of corporate belonging seems the very apotheosis of the neoliberal model of civil citizenship. If one follows the logic all the way, it is a vision not of discrete national passports combined with credit-card functionality, but rather of a wholly new one-world passport for jet-setting border crossers. While credit cards are already in many ways a medium for demarcating economic citizenship and belonging around the world, the neoliberal vision aims at linking this realm of emergent economic citizenship *directly* with the realms of political and social citizenship. The whole corporate model here has a neat symmetry as a border regulation policy vision and discourse, and so it is not hard to see why such ideas appealed so much to the Gingrich Republicans.

However, when this vision and discourse were converted into legal code in the IRAIIRA, the contradictions between its border-crossing reconceptualization of access and belonging and the still extant system of nationally

[26] Ibid.

defined and bordered citizenships came rudely to the fore. Here, then, is an example of the limits as well as of the effectiveness of neoliberalism as a force restructuring the meaning of citizenship. Just as transnational corporations still cohabit with nation-states in many ways, so, too, do policies benefiting the transnational capitalist class have to be implemented and worked out in a world of nation-states and national politics where neoliberal interests are often dependent for their advancement on the support of neoconservative nationalists. These contradictory tendencies came to light in yet another way in 2000 when, after having been saved from the specter of Section 110, the PACE lane went on to become a victim of neoliberal budget cuts.[27] It was not long after recovering from these threats in 2001 that the whole PACE system was closed as an immediate border securitization response to the attacks of 9/11.

The instant results of the state of high security at the border after 9/11 were monumental delays. INS and customs agents implemented so-called Code Red antiterrorism operations that involved inspecting individually all private vehicles, trucks, and buses.[28] Reporting on the resulting traffic jams, the New York Times noted that in some areas the wait times lasted nine hours or more.[29] The economic consequences of these delays on the Ontario-Michigan border between Detroit and Windsor were still larger than those on the West Coast because of the "just-in-time" production systems run by the auto companies moving parts and vehicles across the border. Not surprisingly, the INS and customs were asked to rectify this situation immediately and, according to U.S. Commissioner of Customs, Robert Bonner, were able to use "smart border enforcement" strategies to quickly bring the waiting times back to normal.

The customs service immediately went to work with the auto manufacturers, the state of Michigan, and operators of the bridges and tunnels in Detroit to develop a plan to ease waiting times while maintaining a high level of security. "We implemented a comprehensive plan in a day"; within a few days, waiting times were nearly back to normal, and just-in-time inventory systems were again operating with predictable regularity.[30]

Although the economic stakes and the speed of the response were less rapid on the West Coast, the same discourse of smart border enforcement

[27] See Meg Olson, "Pace Lane Office Opens after Summer-Long Closure," *The Northern Light*, November 2, 2000.

[28] Later the National Guard was also sent to do support work at the border, too, creating the further impression of a state of high alert and fortification. However, to combat the concern that this was sending a negative message toward America's largest trading partner, Attorney General John Ashcroft emphasized that the guard was there "to help facilitate the border not fortify the border." Quoted in Meg Olson, "National Guard Impact on Border Waits Remain Unclear," *The Northern Light*, December 6, 2001.

[29] Anthony dePalma, "Slow Crawl at the Border," *New York Times*, October 21, 2001, p. A1.

[30] Robert Bonner, "The Customs Patrol," *Washington Post*, February 16, 2002.

and the same emphasis on working with business ultimately came to guide policy. However, in this context, the PACE lane with its simple car decals and low technology identification process was seen to be not smart enough. Once closed, it stayed closed, notwithstanding significant economic impacts and reverberating complaints.

Some of the complaints about the PACE lane's demise are worth quoting here because they provide a good illustration of the sense of entitlement to fast lane privileges evinced by the business community. "The PACE program was very beneficial to people and business, and I was one of them," said a local developer of a resort in Birch Bay to a reporter. "Our visitors are down 67%."[31] Across the border in Canada, Darcy Rezac, president of the Vancouver Board of Trade, told another reporter the same story. "The PACE system was a godsend to many of our members," he said. "Many members said it changed their lives and that they simply won't do business now in the U.S. because of the lengthy delays at the border."[32] Rick Turner, president of International Aviation Terminals, echoed the same theme: "The lack of a fast-lane system has made travel between the Lower Mainland and Washington state quite inconvenient, time-consuming and costly."[33] As these complaints multiplied, a forum was convened in November in a northern Washington resort to discuss the problems. At this meeting, many other voices reiterated the same sense of loss and frustration among the business community. Ken Hertz, for example, the executive vice president of Trillium Corporation, complained that the border economy was being hurt by the "regulatory mentality" of the INS and customs and by what seemed to him to be the inaction of the state's congressional delegation. "We're in an economic disaster, and not enough attention is being paid to it."[34] Hertz need not have worried, however, because by then the local U.S. Representative Rick Larsen was already attempting to nudge the federal authorities to make allowances. After visiting the border towns in October and observing their plight, Larsen immediately wrote to the INS commissioner asking for the PACE lane to be reopened. "In light of the economic paralysis now gripping these towns," he said, "I would like to suggest action can be taken to increase traffic without sacrificing the safety of our border.... Participants have paid for [the PACE lane].... They would still be subject to inspections but in effect could jump the line."[35] Here the place of the PACE lane in the transition from passport to credit card becomes clear again. PACE participants have paid for the privilege of flexible citizenship, the representative implies. They should be

[31] Meg Olson, "PACE Reopening Unlikely," *The Northern Light*, November 1, 2001.

[32] Ward, "Using Fast Lane."

[33] Ibid.

[34] Quoted in John Stark, "Security Stifles Fast Lane Plans," *The Bellingham Herald*, November 28, 2001.

[35] Meg Olson, "Larsen Asks INS to Reopen Tighter PACE," *The Northern Light*, October 11, 2001.

allowed to "jump the line," he proceeds to insist, not as traditional citizens but as consumers who have paid for a particular set of transnational rights.

Larsen's pleas to reopen the PACE lane did not prevail, but they, alongside all the criticisms of the cross-border business community, laid the argumentative groundwork for the new smart border enforcement system that has now come to take the place of PACE. Another step in this direction was made on December 12, 2001, when Canada and the United States signed the so-called Smart Border Declaration. With this, the two governments declared their commitment "to collaborate in identifying and addressing security risks while efficiently and effectively expediting the legitimate flow of people and goods across the Canada-U.S. border."[36] The central aim of the declaration, then, was to entrench further a dual-tiered approach to border management and thereby finesse the contradictions between the new emphasis on increased security and the ongoing concern with reducing frictions on business. John Manley, the Canadian Minister of Foreign Affairs, made clear that from his perspective, security and efficiency would thereby somehow become one. "We have agreed to an aggressive action plan that will allow the safest, most efficient passage of people and goods between our two countries, as part of our ongoing commitment to the creation of a Smart Border." Emphasizing the technological sophistication of the new plans, Manley went on: "This action plan will enhance the technology, coordination and information sharing that are essential to safeguard our mutual security and strengthen cross-border commerce for the world's largest binational trading relationship."[37] Governor Tom Ridge, who had been appointed director of the new Office of Homeland Security shortly after 9/11, echoed the same mantra of combining efficiency and security with his own supporting comments on the declaration. "On behalf of President Bush," he said, "I was pleased to visit Canada to meet with Minister Manley and senior Canadian officials to discuss how to build a smart and secure border that allows the free flow of people and goods between our two countries. We look forward to working together to achieve real time real solutions as quickly as possible."[38] Five months later, President Bush himself repeated the same dual goals as he signed into law the Enhanced Border Security and Visa Entry Reform Act of 2002. "I'm honored today," he said, "to sign a bill that is an important step in an effort to secure our border, while promoting trade and commerce."[39]

As a result of the Smart Border declaration, of the new law signed by President Bush, and of all the efforts surrounding them, the old PACE lane on the British Columbia-Washington State border came to be replaced on

[36] Canada-United States Smart Border Declaration, http://webapps.dfaitmaeci.gc.ca/minipub/Publication.asp? Filespec=/Min_Pub_Docs/104780.htm (accessed December 12, 2001).

[37] Ibid., p. 1.

[38] Ibid.

[39] See the White House web-site records at http://www.whitehouse.gov/news/releases/2002/05/20020514-4.html (accessed August 13, 2002).

June 26, 2002, by the new NEXUS system.[40] Visiting the NEXUS enrollment center on July 1, Representative Larsen explained in the now familiar dualistic Smart Border rhetoric that "NEXUS is going to help us insure [*sic*] a more secure border while insuring [*sic*] trade and tourism can continue."[41] Like the PACE and CANPASS systems, and yet joined together as a bureaucratic bridge between Canadian and U.S. governmental functions, NEXUS now allows for the same fast track border-crossing experience with little of the normal customs and immigration questioning. It is also based on preclearance, but unlike the prior systems it operates on the basis of photo-ID and biometric "proximity cards." NEXUS members crossing into the United States on the dedicated lane carry the card in their car, and as they approach the border it relays all their enrollment data – including fingerprints, photo ID, name, date of birth, and so on – to an antenna and from there to a border guard's computer screen. This is by no means the complete apotheosis of automation and corporatization envisaged by Hays, but it clearly represents another step in that direction. It also very directly illustrates the ways in which the dual track, "primary" and "secondary" partitioning of cross-border traffic, lives on after the PACE lane, not just in terms of the dualistic Smart Border discourse, but also very practically in the new hardware of border checkpoint policing. Thus, while the immediate impact of 9/11 was to interrupt the neoliberal dream of bulldozing the checkpoints and to lead to considerably increased federal attention on the border, this attention also led, in the end, to increased spending on technology and, through this, to the installation of a technical fix to the problem of combining neoliberal commercial freedoms with the heightened American emphasis on so-called homeland security.

The Cascadian Space of Neoliberal Selfhood

Changing modes of regulating the border and expediting fast cross-border flows clearly give us a number of examples (in terms of both discourses and practices) of how citizenship is being policed in new ways by the state. The history of the PACE lane and the emergence of the successor NEXUS system help thus to illustrate what Marston and Mitchell describe as the contextual contingency of state citizenship formations. "In the era of "fast" capitalism," they say,

> with a constant movement of bodies and capital across state borders, it became clear that the state could not and was not interested in guaranteeing the general

[40] The application materials for NEXUS are on a Canadian government website at http://www.ccra-adrc.gc.ca/customs/individuals/nexus/menu-e.html (accessed on August 13, 2002).

[41] Quoted in Meg Olson, "Nexus Tweaking Should Speed-up Enrollment Process," *The Northern Light*, July 4, 2002.

rights of citizenship to all those within its territorial borders. Citizenship protection, in terms of its entitlements and obligations, became increasingly uneven, selective and fragmented, not related to territory per se, but more explicitly to economic considerations. The state thus extended citizenship rights to some but not others, i.e. to those who could bring various kinds of advantages to particular state sectors either economically or in terms of state legitimacy. State protection waxed and waned depending on historical and geographical context, and citizenship itself thus began to be perceived as a strategic category that was neither universal nor timeless, but rather one that was easily and often manipulated.[42]

The use of the past tense here might be read as overly hopeful, but it underlines the point that historically changing state policies produce changing citizenship formations over time. The case of changing border enforcement policies would seem to offer an illustrative case in point. However, the story of border re-regulations related here is not just about explicit state policies. It is also about the regulatory micropractices of government and their effective production of new forms of subjectivity. These are the circulating relations of power, selfhood, and statehood that the philosopher-historian Michel Foucault once called "governmentality."[43] In terms of governmentality, then, the evolving systems of border control reveal a great deal about a moment in which it would seem that the processes of producing and disciplining national subjects are being increasingly morphed into processes and disciplinary strategies that support the production and circulation of more mobile transnational subjects. In this respect, it can be further noted that the shifts that are made manifest in the changing border regime are broadly coincident with the consumerization of citizenship that the Foucauldian sociologist Nikolas Rose associates with the marketization of disciplinary practices

[42] Marston and Mitchell, "Citizens and the State," 28.

[43] Interestingly, at the close of his famous piece on governmentality, Foucault identifies in what he says is "a very global, rough and inexact fashion" three modalities of governmentality that correspond at least thematically, if not temporally, with Marshall's three phases of citizenship. "First of all, the state of justice, born in the feudal type of territorial regime which corresponds to a society of laws – either customs or written laws – involving a whole reciprocal play of obligation and litigation; second, the administrative state, born in the territoriality of national boundaries in the fifthteenth and sixteenth centuries and corresponding to a society of regulation and discipline; and finally a governmental state, essentially defined no longer in terms of its territoriality, of its surface area, but in terms of the mass of its population with its volume and density." Michel Foucault, "Governmentality," in Graham Burchell, Colin Gordon, and Peter Miller, *The Foucault Effect: Studies in Governmentality* (Chicago: Chicago University Press, 1991), 104. This quotation is worth noting, because like Marshall's account, it begs the question of what is happening today in a world where the territoriality of the nation-state has been both eclipsed and undercut by a host of globalizing economic dynamics. Just as the evolution from PACE lane to NEXUS points toward a postnational form of neoliberal civil citizenship, it might also be offered as a story of the changing geographical organization of governmentality in a world where Foucault's "governmental state" (i.e., the welfare state) is in decline.

under neoliberalism.[44] Rose suggests that this new regime is distinguished, too, by discourses and practices through which the dominant model of self-hood becomes that of the calculating business enterprise. The day-to-day ability to cross the border in a fast lane would appear thus to represent just one more example of the entrepreneurial citizen self on the move. The question to which I now turn concerns what geographical models of belonging, or what imagined communities, to use Benedict Anderson's phrase, help to ground and to secure this calculating entrepreneurial citizen's transnational world.[45] This question is important not only because it helps to explain some of the energies and personal investments that lay behind the agitation for the PACE lane and NEXUS, but also in its right as a way of fleshing out more clearly the wider ramifications of a neoliberal reimagination of citizenship.

According to Aiwha Ong, "The capability of entrepreneurial figures to manipulate and transform borders into value of trade and production has ... reconfigured the spaces and demographics of American citizenship."[46] Ong, however, does not offer any geographical examples of what these reconfigured spaces might look like. The neoliberal concept of Cascadia, I submit, provides just such an example. To quote again from Paul Schell and John Hamer, the Cascadian promoters who argued for the expansion of the PACE lane in 1995, the vision of Cascadia begins from a conceptual revaluation of the border as an "open border" of trade and transnational capital flows. "The lines imposed over 100 years ago have simply been transcended by contemporary cultural and economic realities," they thus assert.

> Cascadia is organizing itself around what will be the new realities of the next century – open borders, free trade, regional cooperation, and the instant transfer of information, money and technology. The nineteenth- and twentieth century realities of the nation-state, with guarded borders and nationalistic traditions are giving way.[47]

44 Rose prefers to use the term "advanced liberalism," but his argument about how the infiltration of market and accounting concepts have also helped to refashion citizens as consumers still seems congruent with the account of neoliberal border control policies outlined here. See Nikolas Rose, *Powers of Freedom: Reframing Political Thought* (Cambridge: Cambridge University Press, 1999).

45 Anderson himself is evidently no fan of the new scholarly enthusiasm for all things transnational. That said, his robust arguments in the second edition of *Imagined Communities* about the abstract logoization of political and disciplinary space in the modern nation-state help to undergird the seriousness of the question about what kinds of territorial logics might underpin new forms of deep horizontal but yet transnational community. Benedict Anderson, *Imagined Communities: Reflections on the Origin and Spread of Nationalism*, rev. ed. (London: Verso, 1991). For his skepticism about transnationalism, see Benedict Anderson, "Nationalism, Identity, and the World-in-Motion: On the Logics of Seriality," in Cheah and Robbins, eds., *Cosmopolitics*, 117–33.

46 Aiwha Ong, "Latitudes of Citizenship," in Alyson Brysk and Gershon Shafir, eds., *People Out of Place: Globalization and the Citizenship Gap* (New York: Routledge, forthcoming).

47 Schell and Hamer, "Cascadia," 141.

Exploring further evocations of this millenial postnational vision will make it possible to examine in more detail the inclusions and exclusions of the resulting neoliberal imagined community.

The core concept to which all the Cascadian visionaries have returned over and over again is that of the cross-border region as a geographical embodiment of the free-trade neoliberal times and, as such, as a kind of postnational homeland for a managerial neoliberal elite. A good example in this respect is the almost spiritual evocation of Cascadia that appeared in the *B.C. Business Magazine*. Illustrative of the assumptions circulating around notions of the entrepreneurial citizen self, the magazine asserted that "Cascadia is neither a place nor a feeling. It's a rite of passage, a sign of maturity. To seek this braver, newer world, a British Columbian would look not on a map, not in his shrivened or competitive heart, but in his bank account – economic man's most sacred place."[48] This placeless, accounting logic is telling for more reasons than just its virile brave new world heroism. It is also reveals a model of Cascadian belonging based squarely on the economic bottom line, a vision of citizenship as entrepreneurial calculation. For Charles Kelly, the Canadian publisher of a magazine called *The New Pacific* that became the major organ of pro-Cascadian writing before it went defunct, this vision had necessarily to be understood in geographical terms as a new regional order. The cross-border region as a place of business has necessarily, he suggests, to be considered as a place also of political reorganization:

> People in the greater Northwest are moving to establish some semblance of a regional order. Movement on the political scene represents a public realization that business is more and more looking to cross border opportunities. The shift, from business transactions to policy formation, makes official what many in industry and small business have known for some time – there must be greater cooperation if the region is to both compete in international markets and harmonize the area's sometimes conflicting and counter productive policies and regulations. The benefits in the long term are obvious. In all probability, the New Regional Order will have more staying power than the much hyped New World Order.[49]

As a sign of the attendant model citizenship in this new regional order, Kelly's arguments were accompanied by another development he initiated as publisher of *The New Pacific*. He ran a flag competition in the magazine, offering a $2,000 prize for the winning design of a flag for Cascadia. A flag was duly chosen and, with its array of lurid colors, provided the Cascadian promoters with their own postnational emblem of "banal nationalism."[50] However, the

[48] B. Buchanan, untitled essay, *B.C. Business*, September 1992, pp. 36–37.

[49] C. Kelly, "Midwifing the New Regional Order," *The New Pacific* (Spring 1994): 6.

[50] The phrase is that of Michael Billig, who argues for a reconsideration of the power of songs, flags, and other everyday taken-for-granted symbols in attempts to come to terms with the hegemony of nationalism. Michael Billig, *Banal Nationalism* (London: Sage, 1995).

uses to which this flag were put, including doing service as a banner above a booth for small "Cascadian" software firms at the Las Vegas Comdex show, were not the typical nationalist uses at all. The flag was not meant to fly above government buildings or to become part of an official seal. Far from it; Kelly, like all the other economically oriented promoters of Cascadia, insisted on the region's nonnational, indeed nonstate-like character. "We're not talking about political union here," he told one reporter. "We both have capitals 3,000 miles away that don't consider our interests a priority."[51] It is these kinds of pronouncements that further illustrate the neoliberal model of citizenship and belonging embedded in the Cascadian idea.

In part, the statement about not creating a political union served and serves as a protection against accusations of either breaking up or making colonizing incursions into Canada. Yet the main reason for insisting on Cascadia's nonstate-like character relates to the other supplementary argument through which the region has been promoted as an embodiment of globalization. This argument is that the region also somehow embodies the political spirit of globalization: chiefly, the spirit of the neoliberal dogma of smaller, less interventionist government. As a corollary, then, to the spatial supposition that suggests that Cascadia's eclipse of the 49th parallel enables it to capitalize on the benefits of free trade, this argument asserts that because British Columbia, the westernmost province in Canada, and Washington and Oregon States have all shared a similar experience of historical alienation from faraway federal capitals, they are all also inclined toward a distrust of big government. Bruce Agnew, for example, the director of the Cascadia Project at the Discovery Institute, put it like this: "We are finding borders and national government policies increasingly irrelevant and even crippling."[52] Or in the words of David Johnson, U.S. Consul to Vancouver and a participant in the some of the early 1990s meetings on Cascadian cooperation: "This area is unified by a common hatred of their central governments."[53] No wonder then that the new flag was not meant to fly above a new Cascadian state house. And no wonder, too, that perhaps the other most significant promotional use of the Cascadia name and concept has not been to launch a movement for more meaningful regional democracy but rather to brand a regional stock fund, the Cascadia Equity Fund, managed by the Aquila investment firm.[54]

51 R. Gilbert, "Erasing National Borders to Build a Trade Region," *Christian Science Monitor*, July 20, 1992, p. 9.

52 Quoted in V. Schodolski, "Northwest's Economy Defies National Borders," *Chicago Tribune*, August 1, 1994, p. 1.

53 Jim Francis, "Cascadia Isn't Just for Dreamers Anymore," *Sunday Oregonian*, September 20, 1992, pp. R1–R4.

54 G. Halverson, "Regional Road Maps Guide Some Mutual Funds," *Christian Science Monitor*, October 8, 1996, p. 11.

The Cascadian visionaries have over time gone beyond writing op-ed pieces in newspapers and business journals. While the PACE lane remains one of their signal success stories, they have nonetheless been tireless in developing other concrete plans for cross-border codevelopment. The following list of policy goals of the self-appointed Cascadia Planning Group not only give a sense of these more practical plans, but also reveal how such plans fall into line with the wider common practice of neoliberal governance. "Co-operation in a corridor context has numerous, clear advantages," the document notes under the heading of "cooperating regionally to compete globally":

- It is an effective way to add leverage to investment strategies. The rationalization of functions corridor-wide and corridor-long can eliminate redundant activities and site them in the most cost-efficient, least disruptive locations.
- Corridor coalitions on border, trade and environmental issues can raise the Cascadia Region's profile as a competitor for funding and can achieve collateral benefits such as improvements that serve local users as well as through traffic, and border and gateway (port and airport) staffing that encourages commodity flow through congested areas.
- A Corridor context can also create an idea sharing forum that offers leverage in innovative, comprehensive use of non-capital solutions: intelligent transportation systems, telecommuting, regulatory harmonization, work rules and hours of operation at key facilities.
- Corridor co-operation can create a larger, more secure financial base that allows access to funding under the most favorable conditions. The benefits include stronger credit ratings, use of the full-range of current and evolving financial mechanisms and public-private partnerships, and the possibility of a distinctive Cascadia Corridor Corporation as a focal point for organizing the financial resources that support major investments. The result of corridor cooperation can make Cascadia one of the world's premier, cross-border regions, and define new economic, social and environmental realities for the 21st Century.[55]

This bulleted list not only illustrates the practical connections that the visionaries see between their constructions and such material matters as credit ratings and easing congestion at the border. In addition, the list of the advantages said to accrue from the critical mass and leverage of cooperation is also clearly shot through with telling appeals to the neoliberal common denominators of entrepreneurial governance. Thus eliminating redundancy, increasing cost efficiency, regulatory harmonization, and public-private partnerships are all there, as is the still more basic neoliberal inclination toward seeing all global life as one giant struggle for the survival of the fittest, which is to say, the most "premier." Ironically – and especially so given the previously noted tendency to trace Cascadia's neoliberal credentials back to a history of western alienation – much of this strategic cooperation argument

[55] *Cascadia Planning Group*, "British Columbia-Washington Corridor Task Force," mimeo (January 1999), pp. 3–4.

is aimed precisely at the very federal governments of which Cascadians are so supposedly suspect. In the area of federal transportation funding, for example, the Cascadia Planning Group believes that applying cooperatively as a binational region will lend more credibility to its proposals for road improvements and a high-speed rail development among Vancouver, Seattle, and Portland. Nevertheless, such appeals for federal resources from D.C. and Ottawa – just like the appeals for PACE lane expansion and more funding for facilitative border guards – are not envisioned in terms of national democratic governance and belonging. They are all about attracting more private capital, more entrepreneurial innovation, and what might be called more neoliberal settlement in the region.

Given the Cascadian plans already listed, it should not be too hard to imagine the sorts of citizens given pride of place in the new regional order of Cascadia. Basically, they include just two main groups: hi-tech business entrepreneurs and monied travelers. To address the former first, the visionaries tend to argue that the business entrepreneurs will spring naturally from the binational Cascadian earth in much the same way as the mountains and streams that give the region its name. Dori Jones Yang, a writer for *Business Week*, came away from the region with the following impression:

> Across the Pacific Northwest, from Burnaby to Boise, from Corvallis to Calgary, high-tech companies have sprouted up like mushrooms in a rain forest, emerging from the lush soils of the region and attracting an inflow of technical talent from across the continent. Cascadia is not yet the heart of the technology world. But as the glow in Silicon Valley fades, it's right where the high-tech sun is rising. And it has what many regions wish they could replicate: a natural environment where entrepreneurs thrive and techies long to live.[56]

This message of regional boosterism basically seeks to sell Cascadia as the perfect place from which hi-tech business can be conducted: perfect not just because of the position of the region or its cross-border synergies, but also because it provides a postindustrial ludic landscape, filled with all the environmental amenities that will enable the new masters of the hi-tech universe to thrive and to feel as if they really belong. No matter if this belonging is inaccessible to the many people who make products for these people elsewhere around the world. The true Cascadian citizens are a privileged elite who like to live locally while profiting globally. Here, for example, is another description of what one contributor to a coffee-table book on Cascadia describes as the business "pilgrims" to the region:

> [Cascadians] have seen idealistic, if feckless, communism fall, sensible but uncaring capitalism triumph, and the dawning Information Revolution threaten to wreak as much social havoc in the twenty-first century as the Industrial Revolution did in the nineteenth. They know where they want to spend the next few decades of change,

[56] Doris Yang, "Magic Mountains," *The New Pacific* (Autumn 1992): 19–23.

and it's the same sort of place that a lot of other smart people are starting to crave: a pleasantly isolated region rich with food, water and plenty of natural resources, where they can find a good job and a nice life. That's why, although compromises will be made and growing cities will sprawl alarmingly, the dominant ethic of this region will continue to revolve around environmentalism. The New Ecotopians have seen the rest of the world. In fact they help run it. And now they've moved to the suburbs – Cascadia, that is – they'll do whatever has to be done to keep its troubles away from their neighborhood.[57]

Belonging in Cascadia, in these comfy compromised terms, thus becomes envisioned in much the same way as belonging in a suburban gated community. Writ large as a cross-border landscape with hi-tech business campuses, golf courses, shopping malls, and nicely manicured gardens, the neoliberal citizenry are provided with a space through which they can move easily across borders all the while they rest assured that their regionalized idyll will remain undisturbed.

It would be wrong, though, to suggest that outsiders are prohibited from belonging in this bulldozed-borders vision of Cascadia. The key is bringing in money. Thus, as well as advertising its multicultural credentials as a site for Pacific Rim business, the promoters also make much of the possibilities of Cascadia as a tourism destination. The large coffeetable book in which Sutherland's comments appeared, for example, was also marketed as part of a wider campaign to attract more tourists to the region.[58] The book contains page after page of glossy photos of the region, from the cities to the wilderness areas, each time playing up the similarities north and south of the border and, throughout, advertising Cascadia as an attractive vacation destination. In addition to just one picture book, though, the campaign to bring more tourists to the region has been developed for over a decade now under the banner of another Cascadian slogan, "The Two-Nation Vacation." A pamphlet for travel agents designed as part of this campaign and circulated in 1997 put the following gloss on how tourists can thereby find their own way of belonging in the binational landscape:

Cascadia, gateway to the Pacific Northwest and the Two-Nation Vacation, consists of the American states of Washington and Oregon and the Canadian province of British Columbia. It's an advantageous location of international tourism and trade.... There's something magnetic here for a certain kind of soul... one who appreciates natural beauty, limitless recreational opportunities, and the vibrant blend of international influences that have produced Cascadia's diverse culture and thriving economy. Many people have decided to call this region home which is a decision you'll understand once you see Cascadia for yourself.... Washington, Oregon

[57] Jim Sutherland, "Natural Selection," in M. Beebe, *Cascadia: A Tale of Two Cities, Seattle and Vancouver, B.C.* (New York: Harry Abrams, 1996), 40–43.

[58] Beebe, *Cascadia.*

and British Columbia. That's where Cascadia is. But once you've experienced this magical place, its going to be somewhere else as well. It'll be in your heart and on your mind . . . forever.[59]

In this vision, the vector of regional belonging becomes almost entirely switched around. Cascadia itself becomes an object, magical or otherwise, that can belong to you, the tourist. It is the ultimate commodification of belonging, all framed with new age appeals to natural beauty, diversity, and special magnetism. Insofar as the advertisement represents a certain commercialized sense of the regional self (itself based in part, it should be noted, on a certain sort of denial of commercialization), it also helps to illustrate how the entrepreneurial citizen-subjects of the cross-border space imagine Cascadia as a neoliberal homeland.

Conclusions

Borders, states, and societies are mutually formative – borders shape what they contain and are shaped by them – but border research undermines lazy assumptions that "state" and "society," "state" and "nation," or "state" and "governance" are synonymous or territorially coterminous. Instead of becoming redundant in a "borderless" world, the increasing differentiation, complexity and contradictions of political borders make border research more important and more revealing of wider social change.[60]

As I hope I have now shown, borders and border spaces can indeed reveal much about wider patterns of social change. The above theoretical argument of James Anderson and Liam O'Dowd is well made in this respect because it underlines how much of the revelatory quality of border region transformation stems from the ways in which it helps unsettle assumptions about the spatial congruence of state, society, nation, and governance. In an era of neoliberal governance that is mediated by both national-state governments and various transnational forms of effective government (including trade agreements and global institutions such as the World Bank), it seems vital to abandon these assumptions while at the same time tracking the ways in which forms of national-state policy making still shape citizenship and belonging on the ground. With a view to doing just this, this chapter has explored the history of the PACE lane and NEXUS, as well as the development of the concept of Cascadia. The aim has not been to argue that fast border crossing and the concept of a cross-border region embody the so-called borderless world. This is what the neoliberal promoters do themselves. Instead, by examining the statements of these promoters and their uneven success in developing and then maintaining a system of fast border crossing, the purpose of the

59 Undated pamphlet.

60 James Anderson and Liam O'Dowd, "Borders, Border-Regions and Territoriality: Contradictory Meanings and Changing Significance," *Regional Studies* 33, no. 7 (1999): 594.

chapter has been to highlight the changes as symptoms of mediated and yet persistently emergent neoliberal tendencies. In this conclusion, I reflect further on what these tendencies tell us about changing state-society relations and the much commented-on "disarticulation" of the nation-state. Clearly, as many of the other chapters in this volume show, international borders and border spaces are by no means the only useful empirical entry point into these questions. And so it is also worthwhile to consider here why exactly borders can be as illuminating as Anderson and O'Dowd aver.

Much of the recent flurry of writing about borders in the social sciences and humanities has built on the basic insight that they offer revealing research windows through which to examine the changing meaning of citizenship and statehood in an era marked by the end of the Cold War, global migration, and intensified political and economic interdependencies.[61] As conspicuously tangible and observable zones, borders provide spatial laboratories where the grand abstractions of "globalization," "global civil society," and "the network society" can be compared with the empirical reality of what is actually happening on the ground.[62] Of course, as soon as such research is pursued very far, though, the epistemological conceit that the border is in fact a simple ground where all the abstract flows and ties become visible is exploded. Borders, too, are complex abstractions, particularly insofar as they underpin the representation and consequent imagination of nation in cultural and social life. So while they do indeed function as practical checkpoints where land is fenced, goods counted, and people stopped, labeled, and sometimes killed, borders also exist as part of the complex mental mapping of nation-states disseminated in media as varied as weather maps and school textbooks.[63]

[61] For a useful recent survey of the ways in which border research speaks to questions about migration and othering, see Henk Van Houtum and Ton Van Naerssen, "Bordering, Ordering and Othering," *Tijdschrift voor Economische en Sociale Geografie* 93, no. 2 (2002): 125–36.

[62] See, e.g., Heikki Eskelinen, Illka Liikanen, and Jukka Oksa, eds., *Curtains of Iron and Gold: Reconstructing Borders and Scales of Interaction* (Aldershot: Ashgate, 1999); Thomas Wilson and Hastings Donnan, eds., *Border Identities: Nation and State at International Frontiers* (Cambridge: Cambridge University Press, 1998); and Liam O'Dowd and Thomas Wilson, eds., *Borders, Nations and States: Frontiers of Sovereignty in the New Europe* (Aldershot: Ashgate, 1996).

[63] Some of the most useful recent research on changing border regimes has drawn attention to precisely these questions of cultural and political representation. For example, Eve Darian-Smith's careful investigation of the reterritorializations wrought by the building of the Channel Tunnel between Kent and Nord-Pas de Calais richly testifies to the contradictions between the transnational economic imperatives driving the cross-channel project and the old English state formations and their constituencies who, she shows, have been so culturally disoriented by the tunnel and the attendant EU plans for regional transformation (Eve Darian-Smith, *Bridging Divides: The Channel Tunnel and English Legal Identity in the New Europe* (Berkeley: University of California Press, 1999)). In this case, the border has certainly not disappeared between the United Kingdom and France, but the capacity for the channel to function in the United Kingdom as an absolute endpoint for both national mental maps and legal regulation is shown by Darian Smith to have been profoundly disrupted. She argues thus that the

As Anssi Paasi has clearly argued in the terms of Anthony Giddens's structuration theory, this means that international boundaries lie at the heart of a reciprocal territorial dynamic between the socio-political production of space and the spatial production of society and politics.[64] Borders are the practical products of the nation-states on which they retroactively bestow an abstracted and imagined idea of contained coherence. Moreover, these reciprocal ties extend beyond the relays between representing and inspiring nationhood. As well as providing the cartographic outlines for the socio-cultural imagination of nation, borders also faciliate the more disciplinary mental-mapping of the state itself as a contained and containing abstract apparatus. In this way, they help give the "idea" of the state its abstracted coherence as a state *apart* from society, all the while practically enabling state officials to go about the more messy, quotidian work of managing and policing membership *in* society.[65] Borders, then, are hybrid sites where the reciprocal ties between the social and cultural definition of belonging to a nation and the bureaucratic regulation of belonging to a state – ties that form the very basis of modern citizenship – are worked out and written out in space. They are places, in fact, where the generative geography dissembled by the space-spanning hyphen in "nation-state" is actually inscribed on the earth. It is primarily because of this, I think, that borders provide especially useful sites from which to examine and nuance claims about the touted disarticulation of the nation-state.

Channel Tunnel as a practical reterritorialization of the border has also served as a condensation point for English anxieties about European integration and the associated cultural politics surrounding changes to the norms of the nation-state. (See also Matthew Sparke, "Chunnel Visions: Unpacking the Anticipatory Geographies of an Anglo-European Borderland," *Journal of Borderland Studies* 15, no. 1 (2000): 2–34.) In another study of a case where the border really has disappeared, Daphne Berdahl's book on German reunification shows how detailed ethnographic attention to the territorial legacy of the former international boundary also preempts lazy assumptions about wholesale deterritorialization. In so doing, it opens up useful insights on the unevenness of citizenship and the divergent meanings of belonging in the newly reunited Germany, as well as showing how the mental maps of the Kella community – the former East German village that is the focus of the study – continued to be regulated by the legacies of the fencing and military checkpoints that overshadowed it for so long. See Daphne Berdahl, *Where the World Ended: Re-unification and Identity in the German Borderland* (Berkeley: University of California Press, 1999).

64 Anssi Paasi, *Territories, Boundaries and Consciousness: The Changing Geographies of the Finnish-Russian Border* (New York: Wiley, 1996), 27.

65 See Chapter 1. I should note that my own formulation of these relations here builds simultaneously on the arguments of James Scott and Timothy Mitchell. Both are especially attuned to the geography of state formation, but while Scott tends to anthropomorphize the state that "sees" spatially, Mitchell offers a corrective attention to how spatial organization embues the state with an aura of all-seeing-ness. See James Scott, *Seeing like a State: How Certain Schemes to Improve the Human Condition Have Failed* (New Haven, Conn.: Yale University Press, 1998); Timothy Mitchell, "The Limits of the State: Beyond Statist Approaches and Their Critics," *American Political Science Review* 85, no. 1 (1991): 77–96; and Mitchell, *Colonising Egypt* (Cambridge: Cambridge University Press, 1989).

In terms of claims about disarticulation, there are actually very few scholars that are willing to echo Kenichi Ohmae's famously arrogant arguments about a borderless world and the coming end of the nation-state.[66] Indeed, it seems an almost ritualistic gesture of the general texts now being written on globalization to strawman Ohmae as a tendentious extremist against whose claims the more sober reflections of social science are reflected in all their scholarly rigor.[67] However, what these general texts still share with Ohmae is an attention to the ways in which national territoriality is today being undermined, loosening the hyphenation of nation and state and leading to a variety of new geographical configurations of state authority and the eclipse or at least the deterritorialization of the nation as a dominant terrain of cultural and political identity formation. Scholte in fact defines contemporary globalization on the basis of its "supraterritoriality" and "deterritorialization." In the more anthropological and culturally sensitive literatures on global networks, this particular concern with disarticulation and the resulting transformation of citizenship is still more strongly expressed. Thus in his book on the "Cultural Dimensions of Globalization," Arjun Appadurai writes of the nation and state that "the hyphen that links them is now less an icon of conjuncture than an index of disjuncture."[68] For Appadurai, such disjuncture is made manifest most strongly in the emergence of what he calls "ethnoscapes," the flows of people across international borders along with the subsequent development of new border-crossing forms of diasporic consciousness and identity. This is more than jargon mongering, and the notion of ethnoscapes – along with Appadurai's related concepts of transnational media-scapes, finance-scapes, techno-scapes, and ideo-scapes – all help to elucidate some of the factors that have led to such concrete developments as the PACE lane and Cascadia. However, what Appadurai and other scholars of identity formation tend to ignore is the way in which such forms of deterritorialization are both mediated by existing state practices and coupled with new types of *re*territorialization. He therefore pays scant attention to how emergent norms of cross-border belonging are mediated by the transformation and re-regulation (not dissolution) of traditional borders.

Appadurai's omission, of course, is exactly what this chapter has sought to address. In doing so, I used the title "Passports into Credit Cards" because it seemed to capture the zeitgeist tendencies and underlying hopes of the Cascadian visionaries. Clearly, the actual plans that Hays laid out have still yet to be realized, and the uneven and unfinished developments that

[66] Kenichi Ohmae, *The End of the Nation-State: The Rise of Regional Economies* (New York: Free Press, 1995).

[67] See David Held, Anthony McGrew, David Goldblatt, and Jonathan Perraton, *Global Transformations: Politics, Economics and Culture* (Stanford, Calif.: Stanford University Press, 1999), and Jan Art Scholte, *Globalization: A Critical Introduction* (New York: Palgrave, 2000).

[68] Arjun Appadurai, *Modernity at Large: Cultural Dimensions of Globalization* (Minneapolis: University of Minnesota Press, 1996), p. 39.

have led so far from PACE to NEXUS illustrate how the neoliberal vision of postnational citizenship has been consistently frustrated by stubbornly national state practices. That said, I conclude here by noting that the evidence from the Canada-U.S. border on the West Coast does nonetheless point toward an increasingly incongruent spatial organization of civil citizenship vis-à-vis national-state practices. While social and political citizenship remain framed (and increasingly constrained) by national territorial logics, it seems clear that the emergence of fast-track border crossings and the associated vision of postnational Cascadian belonging point toward a delinking of elite managerial citizenship from the territorial confines of the nation-state. They are examples of a shift toward a limited form of transnational citizenship for the transnational capitalist class, a sense of citizenship animated by an entrepreneurial sense of self and enabled by a neoliberal regime of state transformation and transnational state making.[69] To quote one last time from the plans outlined by Hays, "none of this is blue sky thinking. Its power comes from the linking together in a unique way of already existing ideas. The technological, commercial, and governmental timing are right."

The timing may be right, but from the perspective of the increasingly large numbers of critics who challenge the neoliberal world-view, the politics, the ethics, and the social implications of neoliberal citizenship are all wrong. To end, then, on a different note, I would like to ask whether it is possible to think about other forms of transnational citizenship that move beyond the credit card model, forms of political and, perhaps one day, even social citizenship that create freedom of safe movement for everybody irrespective of whether they prequalify for platinum, gold class, or all the other red-carpet, VIP club fast-capitalist privileges. Sites such as the Port Allegre World Social Forum offer an obvious starting point for building such a future, but many other evocations of alternative "transnationalism from below" already exist. I close with one example from the writing of Bharti Mukherjee, whose character Jasmine (in the novel of the same name) describes a specter haunting not Europe but the transnational neoliberal world:

> There is a shadow world of aircraft permanently aloft that share air lanes and radio frequencies with Pan Am and British Air and Air India, portaging people who co-exist with tourists and businessmen. But we are refugees and mercenaries and guest workers, you see us sleeping in airport lounges, you watch us unwrapping the last of our native foods, unrolling our prayer rugs, reading our holy books, taking out for the hundreth time an aerogram promising a job or space to sleep, a newspaper in our language, a photo of happier times, a passport, a visa, a laissez-passer. . . . We ask only one thing: to be allowed to land; to pass through; to continue. . . . What country?

[69] For further elaboration of what I mean by transnational state making, see Matthew Sparke, *Hyphen-Nation-States: Critical Geographies of Displacement and Disjuncture* (Minneapolis: University of Minnesota Press, forthcoming).

What continent? We pass through wars, through plagues. I am hungry for news, but the discarded papers are in characters or languages I cannot read. The zig-zag route is the straightest. I phantom my way through three continents.[70]

This is a piece of fiction, but it evokes the many experiences and spaces that lie beyond the neoliberal imagination. Alert to these alternatives, a truly smart border policy needs to begin imagining more global, more democratic, and more inclusive models of citizenship.

[70] Quoted in Van Houtum and Van Naerssen, "Bordering, Ordering and Othering," 133.

12

Contested Boundaries

Citizens, States, and Supranational Belonging in the European Union

Lisa Conant

Introduction

In the contemporary European Union (EU), the European Parliament includes a Belgian citizen representing an Italian constituency and an Italian citizen representing a Belgian constituency. A national court's reference to the European Court of Justice (ECJ) allowed a British citizen to circumvent nationality requirements and become a student teacher in Germany. Ongoing legal challenges opened the vast majority of public sector employment to Europeans on the basis of their qualifications rather than their nationality. Even the citizens of nonmember countries that are associated only with the EU successfully invoke ECJ legal interpretation; Algerians and Moroccans have been convincing the highest French courts to grant supplemental pension benefits that the national administration refused to "export" to nonresidents. Yet against all this transnational activity, less than 2 percent of Europeans reside outside their home country within the EU, and an even smaller fraction work in another EU Member State. Both EU institutions and national courts respect states' rights to restrict "sensitive" public service posts, including positions in prisons and the military, to their own nationals. And EU Member States unanimously agreed to limit a long list of social welfare benefits to residents within their territories, with the approval of the ECJ.

I thank Joel Migdal and participants in the "Boundaries and Belonging" workshops at the Jackson School of International Studies during 1999 and 2000 for feedback. I also thank Bruno de Witte, Miriam Aziz, and the participants of the "European Forum" in February 2001 for comments. I am grateful for financial support that enabled me to undertake the research in this project, which includes funding from the Robert Schuman Centre for Advanced Studies at the European University Institute, Berlin Program for Advanced German and European Studies of the Freie Universität Berlin and Social Science Research Council, and the European Community Studies Association and the Ford Foundation (grant number 940-0466 to ECSA). Conclusions and mistakes are mine and not those of the sponsoring institutions.

Such discrepancies suggest that shifts toward a more European basis for belonging coexist with enduring commitments to national and territorially bounded communities. Indeed, formal advances toward a supranational community of Europeans have persistently coincided with efforts to preserve national distinctions and to resist EU encroachments. Over the course of nearly fifty years of regional integration, a striking range of economic, social, and political rights has developed to accommodate transnational interactions among individuals. Many of these rights are most commonly associated with national citizenship in liberal democratic states. The explicit declaration of European citizenship itself appeared in 1992. What is equally striking, however, are gaps in the content of European rights, official practices that diverge significantly from formal legal obligations, and the limited extent to which individuals try to exercise those rights that transgress traditional boundaries between national societies.

This chapter examines the interactions that produce foundations for a supranational form of belonging yet simultaneously preserve the national character of societies within the EU. National governing elites, migrants, and EU institutions have been creating the basis for the emergence of a European society. But the struggles between these actors and the responses of broader publics reflect that the process of reconstructing boundaries and belonging remains contested. Patterns of conflict and cooperation indicate that identification with Europe and commitments to achieve a genuine community of Europeans are shallow.

National governments initially pursued regional integration in order to promote peace and prosperity on a continent plagued by devastating wars. For the original Member States, the Second World War discredited purely national solutions to European problems and made national preservation appear dependent on cooperation. Joint control over coal and steel resources, along with market integration, were means to link (West) German interests to Western Europe and to encourage economic growth and modernization. The exchange and regulation of industrial and agricultural goods dominated the early integration agenda. Visions of European nation building were largely absent, and arrangements to enable labor migration were a mere sideshow that owed their existence to the anticipation of labor shortages.

The European legal provisions that Member States adopted to facilitate labor migration did resonate with a small minority of individuals, who migrated across borders to take advantage of economic opportunities outside their home states. Migrants' experience in their new host states revealed major problems with the implementation and interpretation of their European rights. Supranational institutions then served as allies in migrants' efforts to enforce their rights against states. Member States had endowed supranational institutions with enforcement mechanisms in order to protect themselves from the negative consequences of other states' cheating. Supranational institutions used these enforcement mechanisms to act on their mandates to promote the European interest and to expand their own institutional competencies. The European Commission, which oversees the administration of European law and prosecutes violations of it before the ECJ, can use its control over infringement proceedings as a source of pressure to shift the meaning and scope of European provisions. The ECJ, which resolves EU legal disputes, used its authority as the ultimate interpreter of European law to create a system of enforcement that protects *individuals* from the negative consequences of states' cheating. In this system of legal recourse, individuals realize their European rights before national courts. National courts refer disputes about European law to the ECJ, which interprets the relevant EU provision in a preliminary ruling. The national court then uses the ECJ's interpretation to decide the case. This multilevel system results in the enforcement of European law by national courts against national administrations.

The legal struggle between migrants and Member States offers the ECJ the opportunity to expand a European foundation for belonging. Broad judicial interpretation of narrow provisions on labor mobility has created rights that Member States never intended to honor, and it has extended these rights to populations of beneficiaries that national governments certainly intended to exclude. Some of the most controversial ECJ case law involves the extension of legal rights beyond citizens of EU Member States to the resident third country nationals of particular states formally associated with the EU: Algeria, Morocco, Turkey, and Tunisia. Yet even as the ECJ builds a set of European rights, it also respects the primacy of national loyalties in some instances. Limited by the parameters of Member State agreements, the ECJ maximizes opportunities for interaction among Europeans but stops short of any effort to challenge forms of exclusion that are linked to core national commitments.

Those ECJ rulings that expand European legal entitlements can involve political and financial liabilities for multiple Member States. Responses to these unanticipated developments, however, cannot be explained simply in terms of cost-benefit calculations. National governments have resisted some European rights that bore few costs but that challenged traditional notions of belonging. A recurring tendency to emphasize residence in the provision of social welfare benefits prioritizes territorial communities over those linked by national citizenship, without any necessary cost advantages. And despite parallel financial burdens related to social welfare benefits for EU nationals and associated third country nationals, resistance to new entitlements has been strongest in the case of associated third country nationals, who remain largely unrecognized as members of a community of "Europeans."

Official resistance to migrants' claims suggests that national governments remain firmly committed to national communities. Loath to disobey the ECJ flagrantly, national governments usually resist legal obligations indirectly. National administrations obey individual judgments while they refrain from altering their practices. Such evasion can persist for long periods in the absence of sustained legal pressures.[1] The European Commission's prosecution constitutes one possible source of such pressure. The other includes relentless litigation before national courts, which increases the costs of evasion and may convince administrations to come into conformity to avoid constant legal challenge.

That neither source of sustained legal pressure is readily available reflects further gaps in the commitment to a supranational community of Europeans. The European Commission does not have sufficient resources to investigate evasive practices exhaustively. As a result, it must rely on private complaints to identify possible infractions, and it must choose among the battles it wishes to fight. Relative to larger issues of European competitiveness and the interests of large firms, migrants rarely make the cut. Many officials dealing with social issues within the European Commission may be genuinely committed to the rights of individual Europeans. Yet most collective efforts by the European Commission to ameliorate the situation of migrants seem to be responses to a distinct lack of popular enthusiasm for European integration and the prospect that future cooperation might fail to win domestic ratification as a result. The first significant efforts to publicize migrant rights followed the ratification crises of the 1992 Treaty on European Union.[2] The European Commission's recent report on the need for a European system of legal aid for cross-border disputes followed the identification of endemic problems associated with individual access to European rights in a large-scale survey, pursued in the context of the negotiation and ratification of the 1997 Amsterdam Treaty.[3]

The plight of migrants before national courts further points to a fundamental lack of identification with other Europeans within civil society itself. Migrants face many obstacles to litigation. Insufficient knowledge about European rights, the limited number of lawyers specialized in the legal concerns of migrants, the lack of class actions and legal aid in the European legal system, and the sheer financial costs associated with litigation all prevent migrants from independently generating meaningful legal pressures. Organizational support could help migrants to overcome many of the burdens associated with litigation. Organizational resources facilitate awareness, the coordination of promising claims, and forum shopping for the national judges most receptive to an expansive interpretation of European

[1] Lisa Conant, *Justice Contained: Law and Politics in the European Union* (Ithaca, N.Y.: Cornell University Press, 2002), chap. 3.

[2] Examples of this effort include the "Europe Direct: Dialogue with Citizens" web page (http://europa.int/citizens), information pamphlets, and the toll-free telephone Signpost Service (0800 581591).

[3] Antoine Fobe, "Donner une assistance juridique aux citoyens par-delà les frontières," Forum sur la cityonneté européenne, 30 October 2000, Paris; Commission of the European Communities, *Green Paper on Legal Aid in Civil Matters: The Problems Confronting the Cross-Border Litigant*, COM (2000) 51 final (9 February 2000).

legal rights. However, the national orientation of most labor and citizen organizations is typically unsympathetic to the situation of migrants. Migrant organizations themselves tend to represent particular expatriot ethnic communities and rarely are transnational in membership. Small networks of legal professionals demonstrate their commitment to a supranational conception of belonging by pursuing migrants' rights before national courts and the ECJ. However, even these few individuals and organizations that help migrants appear to be primarily committed to universal rights, rather than to regionally contingent forms of belonging. Most who aid migrants assist individuals facing discriminatory treatment within their community, regardless of whether they are of EU origin. These patterns of civic organization, along with persistently low levels of intra-EU migration, indicate that national societies remain uninspired by the prospect for a supranational community of Europeans.

Finally, on some occasions where legal pressures effectively challenged quiet forms of evasion, national governments engaged in more active forms of resistance to maintain traditional social boundaries. Member States acted unanimously to overrule a line of ECJ case law in order to limit payment of particular social security benefits to residents within their borders. In response to the accretion of rights for associated third country nationals, Member States preempted the ECJ's ability to extend these rights to new populations by collectively eliminating all measures that confer individual rights in the newer association agreements with states of the former Communist bloc. Germany also sought to preempt ECJ interference by abandoning a proposal for a new social program that might have been subject to European legal obligations and by carefully constructing the operation of another social program to restrict access de facto according to traditional territorial criteria. These responses to the ECJ's efforts to construct a more European basis for belonging demonstrate that Member States continue to privilege national and territorial communities over any potential European society.

The chapter proceeds in three sections: First, I discuss the extent to which European law reflects an effort to restructure boundaries and the basis for belonging within the EU. Next, I trace how this process has been contested, identifying the evasive practices and overt confrontations associated with efforts to dismantle traditional boundaries and conceptions of belonging. Finally, I evaluate how individuals and civil society have responded to evolving legal obligations. The dominant pattern of interaction among these actors suggests that any new European foundation for belonging remains thin.

European Law: The End of Nationality and Territory as a Basis for Belonging?

European rights that facilitate labor mobility erode the importance of territory and nationality as criteria for inclusion in communities that enjoy equal treatment with respect to employment, residence, social welfare benefits, and taxation. The advent of European citizenship also confers a few supranational political rights, creating a polity that transcends national boundaries to a limited degree. Yet in this section I argue that the historic lack of a broader commitment to the development of a transnational European society is evident from the gaps and restrictions associated with EU legal provisions. Both Member States and the ECJ have refrained from challenging central features of national exclusiveness as European rights have evolved. The checkpoints where individuals find themselves interrogated about whether they belong have largely ceased to be connected to the territorial boundaries between Member States. Instead, individuals find their European and national credentials under scrutiny well inside national borders when they apply for public sector jobs, social and medical assistance, social security benefits, admission to higher education, tax exemptions, and the right to vote. At these checkpoints, the markers that identify those who belong remain intimately connected to national origin, economic status, and the location of permanent residence.

The national citizens of Member States owed their first rights to move freely between member countries to the expectation of labor shortages and the potential economic benefits of greater labor mobility. As a result, early European treaty provisions limited free movement rights to those who worked, established businesses, or provided services.[4] The first regulation on labor rights even limited the authorization to work in another Member State to situations involving an insufficient number of national workers.[5] This explicit protection disappeared by 1968, leading to the creation of a formally open labor market in the private sector.[6] In this new regional market, Member State nationality served as the core marker of the right to cross borders to participate in the economy of another Member State.

Yet an exception for the public service simultaneously restricted transnational employment rights.[7] The public service exception allowed Member States to ensure that their own citizens served the national community in fields encompassing communications, culture, education, energy, health care, scientific research, and transportation. Migrant challenges to this exclusion resulted in over twenty years of litigation about the appropriate definition of public service.[8] The ECJ's definition significantly narrowed the public service exception, but it nonetheless preserved exclusive access for posts that

4 Articles 48, 52, and 59 of the Treaty Establishing the European Economic Community, 25 March 1957 (EEC).

5 Ruth Nielsen and Erika Szyszczak, *The Social Dimension of the European Community* (Munksgaard: Handelshøjskolens Forlag, 1993), 37.

6 Council Regulation 1612/68/EEC of 15 October 1968, *Official Journal of the European Communities* II (1968): 475.

7 Article 48 EEC, para. 4.

8 *Giovanni Sotgiu v Deutsche Bundespost* C-152/73, (1974) *European Court Reports* (E.C.R.): 153.

presume "a special relationship of allegiance to the State and reciprocity of rights and duties which form the foundation of the bond of nationality."[9] Subsequent ECJ case law consistently recognized the importance of national ties in the performance of particular occupations. Meanwhile, a stream of ECJ decisions denounced nationality requirements for employment in public health care, education, and civilian research as well as essentially commercial services related to culture, transportation, and public utilities.[10] Despite the claims of Member States, the ECJ did not consider any of these areas to require a core commitment to the state or its national community. The European Commission followed the ECJ's lead. After a series of cases had reinforced a narrow reading of the public service exception, the European Commission made a formal announcement that this exception to the free movement of workers remained justifiable only for high state offices, the judiciary, armed forces, and police and tax authorities.[11] Together, the ECJ's definition of public service and the European Commission's interpretative guidelines simultaneously expanded migrant access to public sector employment and retained exclusive criteria for those occupations that demand national loyalty.

Productive economic status, whether in the private or in the public sector, historically served as the key marker signifying the right to reside in another Member State. EU provisions did not extend residence rights to those who are not active in the economy until 1990, when commitments to abolish frontier controls intensified as part of the effort to complete the internal

[9] *Commission v Belgium* C-149/79, (1980) E.C.R. 3881.

[10] *Commission v Belgium* C-149/79, (1982) E.C.R. 1845; *Commission v France* C-307/84, (1986) E.C.R. 1725; *Deborah Lawrie-Blum v Land Baden-Württemberg* C-66/85, (1986) E.C.R. 2121; *Commission v Italy* C-225/85, (1987) E.C.R. 2625; *G. B. C. Echternach v Minister van Onderwijs en Wetenschappen* C-389/87, (1989) E.C.R. 723; *Annegret Bleis v Ministère de l'Education Nationale* C-4/91, (1991) E.C.R. I-5627; *Association de Soutien aux Travailleurs Immigrés (ASTI) v Chambre des employés privés* C-213/90, (1991) E.C.R. I-3507; *Volker Steen v Deutsche Bundespost* C-332/90, (1992) E.C.R. I-341; *Volker Sonntag v Hans and Elisabeth Waidman* C-172/91, (1993) E.C.R. I-1963; *Pilar Allué & Coonan v Università degli studia di Venezia* C-33/88, (1989) E.C.R. 1591 and C-259/91, (1993) E.C.R. I-4309; *Commission v Belgium* C-37/93, (1993) E.C.R. I-6295; *Adrianus Thijssen v Controledienst voor de Verzekeringen* C-42/92, (1993) E.C.R. I-4047; *Ingetraut Scholz v Opera Universitaria di Cagliari and Cinzia Porcedda* C-419/92, (1994) E.C.R. I-505; *Guido van Poucke v Rijksinstituut voor de Sociale Verzekeringen der Zelfstandigen and Algemene Sociale Kas voor Zelfstandigen* C-71/93, (1994) E.C.R. I-1101; *Ioannis Vougioukas v Idryma Koinonikon Asfalisseon (IKA)* C-443/93, (1995) E.C.R. I-4033; *Commission v Greece* C-290/94, (1996) E.C.R. I-3285; *Commission v Luxembourg* C-463/93, (1996) E.C.R. I-3207; *Commission v Belgium* C-173/94, (1996) E.C.R. I-3265; *R. O. J. Grahame and L. M. Hollanders v Bestuur van de Nieuwe Algemene Bedrijfsvereningeng* C-248/96, (1997) E.C.R. I-6407; *Kalliope Schöning-Kougebetopoulou v Freie und Hansestadt Hamburg* C-15/96, (1998) E.C.R. I-47; *Commission v Greece* C-187/96, (1998) E.C.R. I-1095; *Commission v Spain* C-114/97, (1998) E.C.R. I-6717.

[11] Commission, Communication, *Official Journal of the European Communities* C-72 (13 March 1988): 2.

market. And national governments limited this right to migrants with sufficient wealth and social insurance to provide for their own needs.[12] Even the formal realization of free movement and residence rights for all Europeans through the Treaty on European Union (TEU) in 1992 still depends on financial independence in practice. EU Member States are not about to welcome any migrant who is dependent on social and medical assistance (public assistance or "welfare"). EU provisions exempt social and medical assistance from their scope of obligations. The European Convention on Social and Medical Assistance, an achievement of the Council of Europe, establishes very limited reciprocal rights for the nationals of all but two EU Member States. Individuals qualify for medical and social assistance outside their home country only by having been legally resident in a host state for five to ten years, depending on their age. Continuous long-term residence and close ties within a territory are the key markers of belonging at this checkpoint. Those Europeans who fail to meet these criteria face potential deportation, where their "true" home country must assume responsibility for their needs.[13] Otherwise, EU Member States care only for those Europeans who demonstrate a clear entitlement to live among the national community. Such entitlement derives primarily from previous residence that was independent of social and medical assistance.

Migrants challenge their exclusion from particular social welfare benefits by disputing distinctions between social assistance and social security in EU provisions. EU cooperation on social welfare measures has always been confined to the aggregation, coordination, and export of benefits that individuals become entitled to largely through their status as workers.[14] Labor mobility could be viable only if workers were not penalized for crossing borders to pursue employment and returning "home" to retire. As a result, productive economic status gains migrants access to all potential social security benefits and any other "social and tax advantages" granted to national citizens within a Member State. Economic activity also signals the right to equal treatment for members of the migrant's family, regardless of their nationality.[15] Through participation in the market, migrants and their families become eligible for full integration into their host communities.

[12] Council Directive 90/364 EEC, *Official Journal of the European Communities* L-180 (13 July 1990): 26; Council Directive 90/365/EEC, *Official Journal of the European Communities* L-180 (13 July 1990): 28; Council Directive 93/96 EC, *Official Journal of the European Communities* L-317 (18 December 1993): 59.

[13] European Convention on Social and Medical Assistance, 11 December 1953, Article 7.

[14] Article 51 EEC and Council Regulation 1408/71/EEC of 14 June 1971, *Official Journal of the European Communities* II (1971): 416.

[15] Council Regulation 1408/71/EEC and Council Regulation 1612/68/EEC; *Württembergische Milchverwertung-Südmilch-AG v Ugliola* C-15/69, 1969; *Pieter Marsman v Rosskamp* C-44/72, 1972; *Michel S. v Fonds National de Reclassement Social des Handicapés* C-76/72, 1973; *Donato Casagrande v Landeshauptstadt München* C-9/74, 1974; *Sotgiu* C-152/73, 1974; *Angelo Alaimo*

The ECJ's expansive interpretation of both social security and social advantages has significantly broadened migrant rights to equal treatment within national communities. Member States' failure to provide definitions for social security and social assistance in EU provisions left the ECJ free to construct its own categories, which typically led to the classification of borderline benefits as social security.[16] Meanwhile, an absence of a definition for "social and tax advantages" led the ECJ to rule that migrants are entitled to all advantages "which, whether or not linked to a contract of employment, are generally granted to national workers primarily because of their objective economic status as workers or by virtue of the mere fact of their residence on the national territory."[17] As a result of this ECJ case law, many social welfare benefits intended for national citizens and residents must be provided to migrants who are neither citizens nor residents. No longer a mere temporary factor of production, currently or previously active migrants and their families command the support of virtually all community structures.

Despite this expansive interpretation, however, the ECJ simultaneously recognizes a distinction between social assistance and social security that respects fundamental differences in the obligations that states have toward national citizens and migrants. According to the ECJ, social assistance encompasses legislation designed to provide benefits to those in need, where eligibility is dependent on an element of individual assessment such as means

v French Republic C-68/74, 1975; *Anita Cristini-Fiorini v Societé Nationale des Chemins de Fer Français* C-32/75, 1975; *Vito Inzirillo v Caisse d'Allocations Familiales de l'Arrondissement de Lyon* C-63/76, 1976; *Patrick Kenny v Insurance officer* C-1/78, 1978; *Diamante Toia-Palermo v Caisse Regionale d'Assurance Maladie de Lille* C-237/78, 1979.

16 *Helmut Heinze v Landesversicherungsanstalt Rheinprovinz* C-14/72, 1972; *Allgemeine Ortskrankenkasse Hamburg v Landesversicherungsanstalt Schleswig-Holstein* C-16/72, 1972; *Fossi* C-79/76, 1977; *Paulin Gillard v Directeur Regionale de la Sécurité Sociale de Nancy* C-9/78, 1978; *Renzo Tinelli v Berufsgenossenschaft der Chemischen Industrie* C-144/78, 1979; *Even* C-207/78, 1979; *Allgemeine Ortskrankenkasse Mittlefranken v Landesversicherungsanstalt Ober- und Mittelfranken* C-818/79, 1980; *Tamara Vigier v Bundesversicherungsanstalt für Angestellte* C-70/80, 1981; *Castelli* C-261/83, 1984; *Hoeckx* C-249/83, 1985; *Angelo Camapana v Bundesanstalt für Arbeit* C-375/85, 1987; *Luciana Costa-Mazzier v Ministre de la Prevoyance Sociale* C-39/74, 1974; *Odette Callemeyn-Verbeke v Ministre de la Prevoyance Sociale* C-187/73, 1974; *Epoux Fracas v Belgian State* C-7/75, 1975; *Inzirillo* C-63/76, 1976; *Rita Frilli v Ministre de la Prevoyance Sociale* C-1/72, 1972; *Castelli* C-261/83, 1984; *Caisse Régionale d'Assurance Maladie de Paris v Giuseppina Biason* C-24/74, 1974; *Caisse Régionale d'Assurance Maladie Rhône-Alpes v Anna Giletti-Tomagno, Giardini, Tempar and Severini* C-379–381, 385/85 and 93/86, 1987; *Commission v France* C-236/88, 1990; *Commission v France* C-307/89, 1991; *Piscitello* C-139/82, 1983; *Roger Stanton Newton v Chief Adjudication Officer* C-356/89, 1991.

17 *Ministère public v Even* C-207/78, 1979; *Francesco Reina v Landeskreditbank Baden-Württemberg* C-65/81, 1982; *Carmella Castelli v Office National des Pensions pour Travailleurs Salariés* C-261/83, 1984; *Ministère public v Mutsch* C-137/84, 1985; *Sarl Prodest v Caisse Primaire d'Assurance Maladie de Paris* C-237/83, 1984; *Maria Frascogna v Caisse de Depots et Consignations* C-157/84, 1985; *Joszef Deak v Office National de l'Emploi* C-94/84, 1985; *Vera Hoeckx v Openbaar Centrum Voor Maatschappelijk Welzijn Kalmthout* C-249/83, 1985.

testing but not on periods of employment, affiliation, or insurance.[18] Such social assistance falls outside the scope of EU obligations and, therefore, will not be exported to follow a migrant's movement across national boundaries. Migrants' qualification to receive such social assistance from a host state will also be dependent on the long-term residence requirements of the European Convention on Social and Medical Assistance. Migrants from or in Austria and Finland, the two EU member states that are not parties to this convention, will also find themselves without any entitlement to social assistance.

By contrast, the ECJ categorizes as social security any "legislation which confers on the beneficiaries a legally defined position which involves no individual and discretionary assessment of need or personal circumstances."[19] Migrants can coordinate and export these benefits regardless of further cross-national migration, and residence of any period will entitle them to such benefits provided by a host state. While these rulings blur distinctions between migrants and national citizens, they also recognize a sphere in which a national community may provide only for itself, that is, the assistance available to those in "need," who hold no other entitlement to care. And although the ECJ rejects the notion that Member States can categorize their own benefits definitively,[20] the ECJ has nonetheless refrained from challenging Member States' efforts to eliminate export requirements for a set of borderline benefits likely to fall under the judicial definition of exportable social security. Here, the ECJ has recognized the legitimacy of limiting benefits that are linked to a particular social environment to residents of the state granting the benefit.[21] For these benefits, which are primarily designed to provide a minimum standard of living for particular categories of persons, such as the elderly or disabled, the marker of belonging is permanent resident. Those who leave the immediate community lose their right to such supplemental income support.

EU nationals hold the widest range of entitlements to these economic and social rights, but third country nationals gain access in a limited range of circumstances, further blurring the criteria of belonging in European society. Being the family member of an EU national formally marks an individual as entitled to equal treatment as a European, but only if the EU national has exercised his or her European legal rights by crossing national boundaries to engage in economic activity in another Member State. The perverse

[18] *Paola Piscitello v Istituto Nazionale della Previdenza Sociale* (INPS) C-139/82, 1983.

[19] *Carlo Fossi v Bundesknappschaft* C-79/76, 1977; *Piscitello* C-139/82, 1983; *Hoeckx* C-249/83, 1985.

[20] *Hoeckx* C-249/83, 1985.

[21] Council Regulation 1247/92 of 19 May 1992, *Official Journal of the European Communities* L-136 (30 June 1992); *Kelvin Albert Snares v Adjudication Officer* C-20/96, (1997) E.C.R. I-6057; *Vera Partridge v Adjudication Officer* C-297/96, (1998) E.C.R. I-3467.

result is that the third country spouses and children of EU nationals employed outside their home states will have more European rights than the third country family members of EU nationals who remain active only in their home states. The migrants' family will possess the right to reside with the migrant, conditional rights to remain permanently in the host state, admission to the educational system on the same conditions as nationals of the host state, the right to work, and access to all social security benefits and other social advantages.[22] None of these derived European rights applies to the families of EU nationals who remain in their home countries. Here, exclusively national rules on immigation apply, which often exclude third country family members from access to many of these rights.

The accretion of European rights among a set of associated third country nationals has been one of the most contentious developments for Member States. Association agreements between third countries and the EU articulate conditions of cooperation, with the general intention to foster economic exchange and development. Association agreements with Algeria, Morocco, Tunisia, and Turkey also include references to the nondiscriminatory treatment of nationals from these countries who work within the EU.[23] The inflow of workers from these associated states was important to European economies from the 1960s through the mid-1970s, when most of these agreements were adopted. The last agreements with any of these countries that mention equal treatment for workers include Turkish agreements from 1980, after which unemployment replaced labor shortages and demand for less skilled labor declined. Accords with Turkey, which were designed to facilitate potential membership, include the most extensive provisions concerning conditions of employment, access to education, and residence.[24] Accords with Algeria, Morocco, and Tunisia, which were concluded

22 *Massam Yvonne Dzodizi v Belgium* C-297/88 and 197/89, 1990.

23 The Accord of Ankara of 1963, *Official Journal of the European Communities* L-217 (29 December 1964): 3687; The Supplementary Protocol to the Association Agreement between the EEC and Turkey of 1970, *Official Journal of the European Communities* L-293 (29 December 1972): 68; Decision No. 1/80 of the Association Council of 19 September 1980 (not published); Decision No. 3/80 of the Association Council of 19 September 1980, *Official Journal of the European Communities* C-110 (25 April 1983): 60; Association Agreement between the EEC and Morocco of 27 April 1976, adopted by Council Regulation 2211/78 of 26 September 1978, *Official Journal of the European Communities* L-264 (27 September 1978): 2; Association Agreement between the EEC and Tunisia of 26 April 1976, *Official Journal of the European Communities* L-265 (27 September 1978): 2; Association Agreement between the EEC and Algeria of 26 April 1976, adopted by Council Regulation 2210/78 of 26 September 1978, *Official Journal of the European Communities* L-263 (27 September 1978): 2.

24 An interview with a legal adviser, Bundesministerium des Innerns, Bonn, 25 January 1996; "Gesetz zu dem Europa-Abkommen vom 16. Dezember 1991 zur Gründung einer Assoziation zwischen den Europäischen Gemeinschaften sowie ihren Migliedstaaten und der Republik Polen," *Bundesgesetzblatt* 1993 Teil II, Bonn (26 August 1993) 1316, 1322.

after the adoption of European regulations on social security coordination, include the strongest provisions concerning equal treatment in social security.

Migrant demands to realize these provisions challenged the exclusionary practices of national administrations and created the opportunity for the ECJ to extend European rights to resident workers from these countries. In disputes that arose over the application of these provisions before national courts, the ECJ claimed the competence to interpret all of these association texts as European legal measures.[25] By ruling that particular provisions of these agreements have legal effects, the ECJ created rights for Turks, Moroccans, Algerians, and Tunisians that are enforceable before national courts.

ECJ interpretation of these association texts has simultaneously conferred and denied a complex variety of rights. ECJ decisions that particular provisions from Turkish accords were insufficiently precise or reliant on further implementing measures denied Turkish nationals the right of free movement as workers and nondiscriminatory access to some social security benefits.[26] In these respects, Turks remain excluded from the community of mobile Europeans who enjoy access to employment and portable social security across the EU. However, the ECJ's case law on Decisions of the Association Council significantly expanded Turks' employment and education opportunities and granted exceptional European residence rights. On the basis of Turkish nationals' participation in the labor market, the ECJ granted the right to renew existing work permits, to switch employers, and ultimately to apply for any position in the labor market. The ECJ also created specific rights regarding access to employment by the relatives and children of Turkish nationals legally working within the EU.[27] Finally, the ECJ's linkage of the right to work with the right to reside created a legal right of residence for Turkish nationals. This introduction of a right to residence based on European law privileges Turkish nationals relative to all other third country nationals, who are exclusively subject to national measures on residence for periods longer than ninety

[25] *R. & V. SPRL Haegemann v Ministre des Affairs Économiques* C-181/73, (1974) E.C.R. 449; *Meryem Demirel v Stadt Schwäbisch Gmüd* C-12/86, (1987) E.C.R. 3719; *S. Z. Sevince v Staatssecretaris van Justitie* C-192/89, (1990) E.C.R. I-3461; *Kazim Kus v Landeshauptstadt Wiesbaden* C-237/91, (1992) E.C.R. I-6781; *Z. Taflan-Met, S. Altun Baser, and E. Andal-Bugdayci v Bestuur van de Sociale Verzekeringsbank te Amsterdam* and *O. Akol v Bestuur van de Nieuwe Algemene Bedrijfsvereniging* C-277/94, (1996) E.C.R. I-4085; *Bahia Kziber v Office National de l'Emploi* C-18/90, (1991) E.C.R. I-199; *Zoubir Yousfi v Kingdom of Belgium* C-58/93, (1994) E.C.R. I-1353; *Zoulika Krid v Caisse Nationale d'Assurance Vieillesse des Travailleurs Salariés* (CNAVTS) C-103/94, (1995) E.C.R. I-719; *Hallouzi-Choho v Bestuur van de Sociale Verzekeringsbank* C-126/95, (1996) E.C.R. I-4807; *Greece v Commission* C-30/88, (1989) E.C.R. 3711; *Hayriye Eroglu v Land Baden-Württemberg* C-355/93, (1994) E.C.R. I-5113.

[26] *Demirel* C-12/86, 1987; *Akol* C-277/94, 1996.

[27] *Eroglu* C-355/93, 1994.

days.[28] With respect to residence, then, Turks with a solid record of labor market participation belong to Europe more than any other "foreign" group.

Meanwhile, the ECJ's conferral of legal effects to provisions of the association agreements with the Maghreb states grants nondiscriminatory access to social security schemes relative to host state nationals. As a result, Moroccan, Algerian, and Tunisian workers and their families essentially are entitled to the full range of social security benefits granted EU nationals under existing regulations.[29] In one case, the ECJ granted derived rights to the spouses of this set of third country nationals that it had previously denied the spouses of EU nationals.[30] To avoid the situation in which third country nationals would enjoy protection superior to that of EU nationals, the ECJ overturned its previous decision, granting the broader entitlement to EU nationals as well.[31] In this instance, inclusion of a group clearly on the edge of the community led to the expansion of rights among those more widely accepted as Europeans.

ECJ legal interpretation in this area poses the greatest challenge to traditional conceptions of boundaries and belonging in the EU. Association agreements, which Member States found expedient at one time and whose application they fully intended to control, now provide the foundation for legal claims among individuals who are not the national citizens of any EU Member State. Migrants from countries conventionally considered to be outside Europe are formally entitled to be treated as Europeans in important, if limited, spheres of life. Belonging, not unlike the case of EU nationals, ultimately depends on national citizenship and economic status. Member States' decisions to limit the exportability of particular social welfare benefits, and the ECJ's acceptance of this, has rendered belonging dependent on permanent residence for many associated third country nationals as well.

The evolution of European political rights has trailed the development of economic and social rights and remains characterized by fundamental gaps in the extent to which Europeans belong to any supranational political community. The national citizens of Member States acquired their first "European" voting rights when direct elections to the European Parliament began in 1979. The selection and representation of Members of the European Parliament (MEPs) became truly supranational after the 1992 TEU

[28] *Kus* C-237/91, 1992; Treaty of Amsterdam, 1997; Denis Martin, *La libre circulation des personnes dans l'Union Européenne* (Brussels: Bruylant, 1994), 325–62.

[29] *Kziber* C-18/90, 1991; *Yousfi* C-58/93, 1994; *Krid* C-103/94, 1995; *Hallouzi-Choho* C-126/95, 1996.

[30] *Hallouzi-Choho* C-126/95, 1996; *Kermaschek v Bundesanstalt für Arbeit* C-40/76, (1976) E.C.R. 1669.

[31] *Cabanis-Issarte* C-308/93, 1996; Noreen Burrows, "Non-discrimination and Social Security in Co-operation Agreements," *European Law Review* 22 (1997): 166–9.

granted EU nationals the right to vote and to stand as a candidate in these elections in the Member State of residence, regardless of their nationality. The TEU linked this right to the introduction of the concept of "European citizenship." The other important political right this European citizenship confers is the right to vote and to stand as a candidate in municipal elections where one resides. Meanwhile, the right to vote in national elections remains regulated by national rules that typically restrict this right to citizens, regardless of their residence. Member States can also impose minimum residence periods to qualify for voting rights in municipal and European Parliament elections in the event that "foreign" EU nationals constitute a disproportionately high (defined as 20 percent) percentage of the local population.[32] Trust in European citizens apparently remains dependent on their being a small minority or long-term residents. The supranational basis for European citizenship is also very shallow: Individuals must be the nationals of an EU Member State to be European citizens, and this nationality is determined exclusively according to the national laws of each Member State. The 1997 Treaty of Amsterdam explicitly declares that European citizenship complements rather than replaces national citizenship, confirming two layers of belonging that preserve national distinctions.

Protection of more fundamental human rights in the EU has been limited and indirect, based primarily on the Council of Europe's European Convention on Human Rights and the national constitutional traditions of the Member States. The ECJ has incorporated human rights principles from both of these sources in its case law. Member States confirmed the European Community's respect for human rights in the preamble to the 1986 Single European Act (SEA), recognized the two traditional sources of human rights protections in the TEU, and extended the ECJ's jurisdiction over these areas to EU actions in the Treaty of Amsterdam. By the conclusion of the negotiations for the Nice Treaty, Member States also announced an "EU Charter of Fundamental Rights," but this charter is merely a political declaration that carries no legal force. National constitutions and the Council of Europe's Convention have protected most Europeans' basic human rights relative to their own national governments. But protection against the actions of the EU itself has been much more precarious, traditionally dependent on the ECJ interpreting non-EU texts on fundamental rights and subject to extremely restrictive standing rules. Rights to petition the European Parliament and the right to contact the new European Ombudsman help Europeans to resolve their grievances toward EU institutions but are hardly a substitute for a set

[32] Article 19 of the Treaty of Amsterdam; Council Directive 94/8/EC of 19 December 1994, as amended by Council Directive 96/30/EC of 13 May 1996; Council Directive 93/109/EC of 6 December 1993 as summarized by European Communities, "Citizenship of the Union," http://europa.eu.int/scadplus/leg/en/lvb/123026.htm, http://europa.eu.int/scadplus/leg/en/lvb/123025.htm.

of legally binding rights relative to the EU. Freedom from the state, among the first political rights to emerge in liberal democratic states,[33] may be the last right Europeans achieve as citizens of the EU.

Realizing the Supranational Community? Discrepancies between the Idea and Practice of European Belonging

The idea of European rights as a set of rules that demonstrate a broader basis of belonging diverges from national practices that retain traditional boundaries between communities. Although most national governments eventually rescinded nationality restrictions on most public sector employment, they avoided making these necessary legislative changes for nearly twenty years and continue to evade obligations associated with EU nationals' access to public sector employment today. And despite consistent reinforcement of migrants' legal rights, national administrations continue to limit access to many social welfare benefits on the basis of territorial and national criteria. Member State responses reflect the extent to which national governments fail to recognize migrant EU nationals and associated third country nationals as members of a community of Europeans who deserve equal treatment.

Public Servants, Public Sector Employment, and the Contested National Bond

Member States have been reluctant to honor the implications of ECJ case law that granted all EU nationals access to most fields of public sector employment. Evasion prevailed during the decade after the ECJ issued its narrow definition of the public service exception to the free movement of workers in 1980. Two years after this initial suit against Belgium, the Belgians unsuccessfully defended the status of canteen staff and gardeners as public servants. To justify their restrictive employment practices under European law, they essentially had to claim that those in these positions, among others such as plumbers and electricians, somehow required the national bond or were closely connected to the exercise of official authority. The French apparently thought that French nurses had more need of the national bond than Belgian nurses, whose status as public servants had been denied four years before the French lost their case at the ECJ. The French also seemed to think that their high school teachers required more of a national bond than student teachers in Germany, where the ECJ had denounced nationality requirements six years earlier. Italians suffered from a similar delusion that the foreign language instructors in universities somehow qualified under the public service exception. Such evasion persisted after the European

33 T. H. Marshall, *Citizenship and Social Class* (London: Pluto, 1992).

Commission issued its recommendation on this issue in 1988, designed to promote free movement in areas that would clearly fall outside the range of legitimate protection. Member States ignored the European Commission's guidelines, and the ECJ continued to hear a stream of disputes about nationality clauses in sectors that it had opened to EU nationals well into the 1990s.[34]

As the steady trickle of migrant challenges to exclusionary practices persisted, the European Commission initiated a systematic program of prosecution. Ten Member States faced formal infringement proceedings by July 1990. The only two Member States without apparent violations were Ireland and the Netherlands.[35] The Member States' response to these legal pressures was largely cooperative. With the exception of Luxembourg, which initially replied that "it did not envisage taking any special measures of the kind desired,"[36] all targeted Member States proposed reforms to align their official practices with the European definition of public service. By late 1994, Belgium, Denmark, France, Germany, Italy, Portugal, Spain, and the United Kingdom amended domestic legislation to abolish nationality conditions for at least some categories of public sector employment.[37] French and German reforms were not confined to fields targeted by the European Commission but abolished nationality requirements for employment across broad fields of public service.[38] Yet Germany also continued to reserve appropriate public service positions for German citizens alone.[39] And the French opening did not eliminate all potentially questionable restrictions, as demonstrated by continuing infringements against French discrimination in shipping and water transport.[40] The United Kingdom rescinded one of its few public sector restrictions – abolishing nationality requirements for certain categories of researchers – to meet European obligations.[41] Greece introduced a proposal to open public sector employment to EU nationals but did not adopt it.[42] The ECJ subsequently denounced remaining restrictions in Greece

[34] Refer to note 11 for the citation of these cases.

[35] Martin, *La libre circulation des personnes*, 61.

[36] *Commission v Luxembourg* C-473/93, 1996.

[37] Commission, "Twelfth Annual Report on Monitoring the Application of Community Law – 1994," *Official Journal of the European Communities* C-254 (29 September 1995): 35.

[38] Commission, "Fourteenth Annual Report on Monitoring the Application of Community Law – 1996," *Official Journal of the European Communities*, C-332 (3 November 1997): 30; Décret no. 94 of 16 February 1994; the Tenth Public Service Amendment Act of December 1993; Commission, "Twelfth Annual Report on Monitoring the Application of Community Law – 1994," 35; Martin, *La libre circulation des personnnes*, 61.

[39] Deutscher Beamtenbund (DBB): *Handbuch für den Öffentlichen Dienst in Deutschland 1995* (Bonn: DBB Verlag GmbH, 1995), 62.

[40] Commission, "Fourteenth Annual Report on Monitoring the Application of Community Law – 1996," 89.

[41] Order no. 1221 of 12 May 1991; Martin, *La libre circulation des personnes*, 62.

[42] Martin, *La libre circulation des personnes*, 61.

and Luxembourg, and the European Commission continued infringement proceedings.[43]

Despite all this reform and prosecution, however, the European Commission continued to identify obvious violations in national restrictions on positions that have nothing to do with the exercise of official authority, such as tourist guides and cellists, in addition to positions already deemed open: language assistants, public education, university instruction, postal delivery, telecommunications, radio and TV broadcasting, airlines, shipping, surface transport, urban and regional transport, civilian research, medical care, and the distribution of water, gas, and electricity.[44] Most of these infringements targeted Luxembourg, which had insisted that it would not amend its legislation, as well as two of the usual suspects: Belgium and Greece. Yet the European Commission also had to use infringement proceedings to combat ongoing evasion in Member States that had already adopted legislative reform to open public sector employment to EU nationals, including France, Italy, Spain, and the United Kingdom.[45] The ECJ consistently denounced blanket nationality restrictions throughout these infringement proceedings.[46] Reforms in Belgium ultimately depended on the Belgian Conseil d'État's (Council of State) declaration that European provisions on the free movement of workers were supreme to contrary provisions of the Belgian constitution.[47] Vigilant prosecution has been critical to extinguish restrictions in the other two laggards since Luxembourg relented only after the European Commission decided to pursue a daily penalty payment of 14,000 euro for continued noncompliance, and Greece still faces a referral for a daily penalty payment of 57,400 euro.[48]

Migrant legal challenges and prosecution by the European Commission continue to identify lingering evasion. Long established and repeated ECJ prohibitions against discrimination in pay and working conditions for EU nationals employed in the public sector of a host state fail to induce changes

43 *Commission v Greece* C-290/94, (1996) E.C.R. I-3285; *Commission v Luxembourg* C-473/93, (1996) E.C.R. I-3207; Commission, "Fourteenth Annual Report on Monitoring the Application of Community Law – 1996," 88–9.

44 Commission, "Thirteenth Annual Report on Monitoring the Application of Community law – 1995," Com(96) 600 final, 29 May 1996, 121–8, 137–43; Commission, "Fourteenth Annual Report on Monitoring the Application of Community Law – 1996," 87–91 and 95–7.

45 Commission, "Fourteenth Annual Report on Monitoring the Application of Community Law – 1996," 87–91, 95–7.

46 *Commission v Luxembourg* C-473/93, 1996; *Commission v Belgium* C-173/94, 1996; *Commission v Greece* C-290/94, 1996.

47 Commission, "Fourteenth Annual Report on Monitoring the Application of Community Law – 1996," 202.

48 Commission, "Seventeenth Annual Report on Monitoring the Application of Community Law – 1999," COM (2000) 92 final (23 June 2000): Introduction, 11, 44.

in official practices.[49] After opening much public sector employment to EU nationals, Member States began to discriminate against migrants by disregarding their experience in the public sector of other Member States. Cases in 1997 and 1998 indicate that the Dutch, Greek, and German governments expected that they could ignore professional experience or periods of employment from other Member States even though the ECJ had denounced such discrimination in an Italian case in 1994.[50]

The contradictions among national governments' long-term evasion, eventual willingness to reform restrictive legislation, and simultaneous evasion regarding other forms of discrimination suggest a number of problems with European commitments. Resistance could potentially be attributed to a tendency to use public sector employment to absorb national labor during periods of high unemployment or to the traditional importance of fields such as education to national socialization. Yet national governments did not face any real threat of being inundated by "foreign" applicants. Very few EU nationals have ever been interested in exercising their right to work outside their home states, in either the public or private sector. The likely pool of qualified "foreign" candidates is minuscule in most fields of public sector employment, which is evident from both the low levels of migrant employment in those states with relatively open public sectors and the lack of opposition to reform by public sector unions in states with traditionally discriminatory hiring practices.[51] National governments simply could not be bothered with the hassle of legislative reform in order to help a small set of migrants, who would not even be able to register their gratitude by voting in national elections. Persistent prosecution and migrant legal challenges, which held the potential for EU fines and financial liability in national courts by the early 1990s, undoubtedly changed most governments' attitudes toward the burden of legislative reform.[52] Keeping a few migrants out of public sector employment was certainly not worth recurrent legal recriminations, with their potential for financial penalty. As a result, national governments eliminated most restrictions that had been clearly established as violations. Meanwhile, they left other remaining discriminatory practices intact, waiting for serious legal pressures to emerge.

49 *Sotgiu* C-152/73, 1974; *Commission v Italy* C-225/85, 1987; *Allué* C-33/88, 1989 and C-259/91, 1993.

50 *Scholz* C-419/92, 1994; *Grahame and Hollanders* C-248/96, 1997; *Commission v Greece* C-187/96, 1998; *Schöning-Kougebetopoulou* C-15/96, 1998.

51 Conant, *Justice Contained*, chap. 6.

52 Under Article 171 of the TEU (Article 228 of the Amsterdam Treaty), the ECJ may impose a financial penalty on states that have failed to comply with previous rulings. National judges may also order states to pay financial damages for breaches of European law in the aftermath of the ECJ's case law on state liability, which began with *Frankovich and Bonafaci v Italy* C-6,9/90, (1991) E.C.R. I-5357.

Migrants, Residents, and Contested Access to Social Welfare

ECJ interpretation on nondiscriminatory access to social welfare benefits has been subject to enduring resistance by national governments. In the case of social and tax advantages, resistance manifests itself primarily as an evasive effort to exclude nonnationals from support conventionally offered to residents. Meanwhile, more active opposition to the export of social security benefits appears to privilege those individuals who remain within the state's territory. These contradictory trends are united in their effort to exclude nonnationals, who are least likely to meet the qualifying conditions attached to many social and tax advantages and are most likely to migrate after retirement or the onset of a disability.

With respect to social and tax advantages, the consistent and extensive ECJ case law denouncing virtually all forms of discriminatory treatment faces quiet evasion. Similar to the stream of parallel disputes over public sector employment, migrants generate a series of challenges that illustrate how national governments ignore prior judicial prohibitions against discrimination in the conferral of all social and tax advantages.[53] This trail of ECJ cases results largely from disputes over qualifying conditions, which frequently act to exclude nonnationals. National governments control access to benefits by attaching qualifying conditions without regard to the situation of migrants. When faced with a claim of discriminatory access, national administrations defend their rules in the hope that restrictions will escape censure. Yet any anticipation that qualifying conditions will fall outside the scope of ECJ interpretation on social or tax advantages is generally unjustified. Steve Peers observes:

> Indeed, it is very clear that measures are still usually classified as "social advantages" by the Court even if they are only available to residents meeting certain conditions.... In the Court's practice, government measures will be classified as

[53] *Ann Florence Reed v Minister van Justitie* C-59/85, 1986 *Pietro Pinna v Caisse d'Allocations Familiales de la Savoie* C-41/84, 1986 (I) and *Pietro Pinna v Caisse d'Allocations Familiales de la Savoie* C-359/87, 1989 (II); *Sylvie Lair v University of Hannover* C-39/86, 1988 *Annunziata Matteuci v Belgium* C-235/87, 1988; *Commission v Greece* C-305/ 87, 1989; *Lopes da Veiga v Staatssecretaris van Justitie* C-9/88, 1989; *Commission v Germany* C-249/86, 1989; *Klaus Biehl v Administration des Contributions* C-175/88, 1990; *URSSAF v Le Manoir* C-27/91, 1991; *Elissavet Paraschi v Landesversicherungsanstalt Württemberg* C-349/87, 1991; *Allué* C-33/88, 1989 and C-259/91, 1993; *V. J. M. Raulin v Minister for Education and Science* C-357/89, 1992; *M.J.E. Bernini v Minister for Education and Science* C-3/90, 1992; *Noushin Taghavi-Iannino v Ministre des Affaires Sociales* 243/91, 1992; *Carmina Di Leo v Land Berlin* C-308/89, 1990; *Commission v United Kingdom* C-279/89, 1992; *Commission v Belgium* C-326/90, 1992; *Commission v Belgium* C-300/90, 1992; *Hanns-Martin Bachmann v Ministre des Finances* C-204/90, 1992; *Commission v Luxembourg* C-111/91, 1993; *Maria Chiara Spotti v Freistaat Bayern* C-272/92, 1993; *Hugo Schmid v Minister van Sociale Voorzorg* C-310/91, 1993; *Ingetraut Scholz v Opera Universitaria di Cagliari* C-419/92, 1994; *John O'Flynn v Chief Adjudication Officer* C-237/94, 1996; *Commission v Belgium* C-278/94, 1996.

"social advantages" if they are available to workers as workers, to residents as residents, *or* to specified classes of persons as specified classes of persons, unless the class of person in question is defined by a criteria [*sic*] inherently and inseparably related to nationality of a Member State. Since there are a paucity of such measures, the test . . . laid out in *Even* has been met consistently except for military-related benefits.[54]

In addition to the trail of individual challenges, the European Commission's 1997 report on the application of European law identified many overt and covert forms of national discrimination related to traditional social and tax advantages. The European Commission targeted potential and established violations in Belgium, France, Germany, Greece, Luxembourg, the Netherlands, Spain, and the United Kingdom. Much of this discrimination affects access to conventional advantages: access to employment for migrants' children, supplementary allowances for large families, early retirement schemes for frontier workers, study grants for workers, pension transfers, income tax, nonresident taxation, and social welfare benefits and services.[55] This enduring pattern of legal challenge is consistent with Member States' efforts to evade legal obligations. National administrations continue to apply discriminatory practices, which periodically inspire individual litigation before national courts or prosecution by the European Commission. However, unlike the situation with public sector employment, legal challenges have remained sporadic. Formal prosecution has been piecemeal, falling short of the systematic enforcement effort that the European Commission engaged for public sector employment.

With respect to social security benefits, national governments supplemented evasion with more active forms of resistance to avoid their obligations to export particular types of social security. Evasion prevailed in this area until the European Commission prosecuted a longstanding French violation, which inspired the French government to negotiate an amendment to the existing European regulation in order to exempt particular benefits from exportation. In this case, national governments legislated unanimously in the Council of Ministers to overrule the ECJ's categorization of portable social security, creating a list of special noncontributory benefits that need not be exported. Meanwhile, ECJ case law on exportability contributed to the failure of one popular social measure and the careful design of another in Germany, where leaders sought to preempt ECJ interference.

ECJ judgments first classified a set of noncontributory Belgian benefits as social security, even though the relevant allowances were supplemental income support that seemed similar to social assistance. The ECJ's classification qualified the benefits for export, which Belgium contested as inappropriate.

[54] Steve Peers, "'Social Advantages' and Discrimination in Employment: Case Law Confirmed and Clarified," *European Law Review* 22 (1997): 164.

[55] Commission, "Fourteenth Annual Report on Monitoring the Application of Community Law – 1996," 28–9, 87–91, 93.

Meanwhile, the French recognized that a set of their benefits was analogous to the exportable Belgian benefits, but they continued to administer their benefits according to purely national criteria, which included residence and nationality conditions.[56] Even when a preliminary ruling identified French supplemental pensions as an exportable social security benefit in the 1974 Biason case,[57] the French authorities admitted no obligation to rescind restrictive national criteria. The French held that *Biason*, considered relevant only to the specific case, lacked consequences for the general administration of benefits. The French then sought to solidify their position in discussions to amend the existing European regulation.[58]

Over a decade later, the French faced a further set of individual challenges related to supplemental pensions in the 1987 Giletti case.[59] Once again, the ECJ required exportation and the French refused to reform their legislation or to issue new orders to institutions administering the funds.[60] The European Commission pursued infringement proceedings against France, challenging the refusal to export and French nationality conditions before the ECJ in 1990 and 1991.[61] Meanwhile, in the 1991 Stanton Newton case,[62] the United Kingdom attempted to defend residence conditions for a mobility allowance whose criteria clearly fell under the ECJ's definition of social security. The European Commission cited the entire European case law on noncontributory benefits of mixed type and prevailed before the ECJ.[63]

Having definitively lost before the ECJ, national governments retaliated by successfully orchestrating legislative overrule. Within a year of the British preliminary ruling and direct ECJ condemnation of French law, the Council of Ministers reached unanimous agreement to amend the existing European regulation in order to exempt a set of special noncontributory benefits of mixed type from the export requirement associated with social security.[64] Legislative overrule of the ECJ is conventionally considered to be next to impossible wherever unanimity is necessary because the interests of at least one Member State are likely to coincide with the ECJ, leading to a veto that

[56] *Costa* C-187/73, 1974; *Callemeyn* C-187/73, 1974; *E. Fracas* C-7/75, 1975; *Inzirillo* C-63/76, 1976; *Frilli* C-1/72, 1972; *Biason* C-24/74, 1974; *Giletti and others* C-379–381, 139/82, 1983; *Commission v France* C-236/88, 1990; *Commission v France* C-307/89, 1991; Françoise Roger, "Europe et fonds national de solidarité," *Retraite et Société*, no. 4 (1993): 43–8.

[57] *Biason* C-24/74, 1974.

[58] Roger, "Europe et fonds national," 48.

[59] *Giletti and others* C-379–381/85 and 93/86, 1987.

[60] Roger, "Europe et fonds national," 49–51.

[61] *Commission v France* C-236/88, 1990, and *Commission v France* C-307/89, 1991.

[62] *Stanton Newton* C-356/89, 1991.

[63] Ibid.

[64] Council Regulation 1247/92 of 19 May 1992, *Official Journal of the European Communities* L-136 (30 June 1992).

maintains judicial interpretation.[65] Yet this argument assumes the existence of contending national interests or competition between democratic constituencies. The ease with which Member States reached unanimous agreement in this case reflects the sorry position of migrants within the EU. Migrants, who are effectively excluded from the national polity in their host states, cannot generate any countervailing pressure on host governments themselves. Even the loyalty of sending countries to their emigrant nationals is shallow: Although Spanish consular offices provide legal representation for some of their nationals' disputes in other Member States, Spain refrained from exercising its veto rights to help a sizable group of migrant Spaniards in one instance. And national governments did not need to worry about offending any domestic constituency by excluding migrants from particular social security benefits. The Member States overturned the ECJ with secondary legislation in this instance, which did leave them vulnerable to judicial overrule on the basis of the treaty, which is considered the supreme source of European law. However, a migrant challenge with this precise claim failed to convince the ECJ as well. The ECJ chose to legitimate the linkage of particular benefits to permanent residence within the community granting the benefit, regardless of the discriminatory effect this would have on migrants.[66]

During this process of legislative overrule, the German government refrained from exempting any particular German benefits from export. Since it could not predict the negative outcome of the anticipated treaty-based challenge to the revised regulation, the German administration instead structured domestic programs in order to preempt ECJ interference. Germany had been spared the need to export supplemental income schemes largely due to criteria associated with qualifying conditions and the administration of benefits through local and regional (*Land*) authorities. As a result, German leaders felt confident that existing German programs for social assistance would retain their status as social assistance and would avoid exportation obligations. The German government then took precautionary steps to ensure that proposals for two new social benefits, which concerned a supplemental

[65] Fritz Scharf, "The Joint-Decision Trap: Lessons from German Federalism and European Integration," *Public Administration* 66 (Autumn 1988): 239–78; Andrew Moravcsik, "Preferences and Power in the European Community: A Liberal Intergovernmentalist Approach," in *Economic and Political Integration in Europe: Internal Dynamics and Global Context*, eds. Simon Bulmer and Andrew Scott (Oxford: Blackwell, 1994), 69–70; Mark Pollack, "Delegation, Agency, and Agenda Setting in the EC," *International Organization* 51 (Winter 1997): 118–19; Karen Alter, "Who Are the 'Masters of the Treaty'?: European Governments and the European Court of Justice," *International Organization* 52 (Winter 1998): 136–42; Alec Stone Sweet and Thomas Brunell, "Constructing a Supranational Constitution: Dispute Resolution and Governance in the European Community," *American Political Science Review* (March 1998): 66.

[66] *Snares* C-20/96, 1997; *Partridge* C-297/96, 1998.

pension scheme and long-term care insurance, would not result in further export obligations.

The German government abandoned its initiative for a supplementary pension scheme, the Fink Modell, despite the substantial support this program enjoyed from both Social and Christian Democrats. The Fink Modell was designed as a means to supplement the income of retirees who fell below the level that normally qualifies a resident for social assistance, relieving poor pensioners of the stigma of standard social assistance programs. German leaders opposed exportation of this type of benefit because they intend it as a means to assist individuals in coping with the cost of living in Germany,[67] which was essentially the objection that the French, Belgians, and British had to the exportation of their supplemental income programs as well.[68]

The cancellation of the Fink Modell represents a preemptive action: The prospect of future ECJ interference altered the course of German policy making. A country that traditionally promotes a high level of social protection abandoned a preferred new benefit scheme in order to avoid the imposition of extraterritorial obligations. This reaction, a choice to restrict the expansion of social protection rather than to be compelled to export it, reflects a frustrating dilemma for those committed to improving social welfare. Ostensibly "progressive" case law contributed to a distinct lack of progress for poor pensioners within Germany. It is precisely such ECJ case law that has invoked the ire of high-level German politicians, from former Social Minister Norbert Blüm to former Chancellor Helmut Kohl. German leaders called for "judicial restraint" and assailed the ECJ for overlooking the practical and financial consequences of its judgments.[69] Yet the resistance to export requirements across Member States also reflects a fundamental lack of commitment to provide a minimum standard of living for Europeans. The cost of living certainly varies across Member States and the associated countries whose nationals are entitled to social security, but the generosity of richer states need extend only to those migrants who "earned" their right to social

[67] Peter Clever, "Sozial Sicherheit im Rahmen der europäischen Integration," *Die Angestellten Versicherung* (7 August 1992); Peter Clever, "Grundsätzliche Bemerkungen zur Rechtsprechung des EuGH," *Die Angestellten Versicherung*, no. 2 (1993b): 71–5; "Vor allem armen Rentnern helfen," *Kölner Rundschau* (19 December 1988); Thomas Link, "Finks Rentenrisiken," *Die Welt* (19 December 1988); Manfred Zuleeg, "Die Zahlung von Ausgleichszulagen über die Binnengrenzen der Europäischen Gemeinschaft," *Deutsche Rentenversicherung*, no. 10 (1988): 621–9; interviews with two legal advisers in the Federal Labor Ministry, Bonn, 17 and 22 January 1996.

[68] Roger, "Europe et fonds national," 44, 47; British observations in *Stanton Newton* C-356/89, 1991.

[69] Willi Rothley, "Bonn will das EC-Recht untergraben," *EG Magazin*, no. 1–2 (1993): 38; "Europäischer Gerichtshof: Kampfansage an die Unabhängigkeit," *Handelsblatt* (26 November 1992): 34.

security through prior contribution to the national economy. But no such magnanimity extends to these migrants.

In the case of long-term care insurance (*Pflegeversicherung*), German officials hoped to preempt the exportability of benefits by categorizing program benefits to fall outside European export obligations. The German Care Insurance Law (*Pflegeversicherungsgesetz*) defined all of its benefits as "benefits in kind," which are not subject to export obligations under European law. Social security programs offering benefits in kind must provide services for resident EU nationals as long as they have been insured against the relevant risk in a social security scheme of any other Member State. By contrast, social security programs that offer direct "cash benefits" must export payments to entitled recipients, regardless of their residence. German care insurance offers both direct payments to institutions providing care and "care allowances" to individuals who receive care from family members in their own homes. Direct payments to institutions providing care clearly function as a benefit in kind, but care allowances look suspiciously similar to traditional cash benefits. By labeling care allowance as a benefit in kind, however, Germany avoided the burden of covering care for migrants who have worked and paid social security contributions in Germany but live in another Member State.[70] Once again, German policy making responded to ECJ decisions, but the intent was to avoid standard European legal obligations. Rather than yielding to European prohibitions against territoriality and national discrimination, Germany structured its rules to confine benefits within national boundaries.

In this case, however, migrants' challenges to their obligation to pay contributions for a benefit from which they would be excluded led the ECJ to strike back. The ECJ ruled that German care allowances possess features similar to cash benefits, regardless of their classification in domestic legislation as benefits in kind.[71] Similar to its position on European definitions of public service and social security, the ECJ imposed its European definition of a cash benefit, with all of its export obligations. As a result, individuals working in Germany but living elsewhere must pay contributions, but they also have a legal right to export care allowance abroad.

Although Germany's individual effort to territorialize benefits failed, the collective success of Member States in confining particular benefits within their borders, along with a broader trend to emphasize local provision of services, may ultimately have the unintended consequence of convincing

[70] "Pflegeversicherungsgesetz," *Sozialgesetzbuch* XI (introduced 1 January 1995); *Bericht der Beauftragten der Bundesregierung für die Belange der Ausländer über die Lage der Ausländer in europäischen Staaten* (Bonn: December 1995); *Manfred Molenaar and Barbara Fath-Molenaar v Allgemeine Ortskrankenkasse Baden-Württemberg* C-160/96 (1998) E.C.R. I-843.

[71] *Molenaar* C-160/96, 1998.

migrants to remain in a host state that they would otherwise leave after retirement. The end costs to the government might be the same as if migrants had left the national community and exported their benefits. The ultimate cost of these policy decisions may even be greater than the costs of exportation because migrants choosing to remain would qualify as long-term residents for social and medical assistance, and their demand on this assistance would be likely only to increase with age and distance from family members in the home state. National governments rely on migrants' stronger attachment to their home countries and unwillingness to remain permanently within a host community when they anticipate they will save a dime with their export restrictions.

Evasion may triumph in this area because the European Commission has not committed itself to any systematic effort to prosecute discriminatory practices. Unlike the case of public sector employment, institutional support for migrants' legal entitlements to social welfare benefits has not materialized. The European Commission has even cautioned against expansions in statutory social benefits, arguing that the costs of social protection schemes can have a negative effect on employment and growth.[72] National governments, meanwhile, show no signs of a growing European commitment to greater social equality. Member States have demonstrated their intention of maintaining firm control over social security coordination by continuing to require unanimity, despite the broad expansion of qualified majority voting since the SEA in 1986.[73] Interests in social security cooperation were always linked tightly to the interest in promoting labor mobility. With the recent and exclusive exception of highly skilled labor, any interest in labor mobility diminished shortly after Member States laid solid foundations for equal treatment in European provisions due to the shock of the oil crisis and the recession and unemployment that followed. Economic decline and restructuring during the 1980s increased unemployment and contributed to large-scale redundancies among migrant workers, in particular. Recent discussions about the potential need for an active labor immigration policy in both national and EU contexts narrowly focus attention on the emerging information economy's demand for highly skilled technical workers and the lack of homegrown talent.[74] Once again, economic status appears as the core marker of belonging for those outside traditional national communities.

72 Commission, *White Paper on Growth, Competitiveness, and Employment*, Supplement 6/93 (Luxembourg: Office for Official Publications of the European Communities, 1993), 124, 136.

73 Treaty of Amsterdam (17 June 1997).

74 Ralph Atkins, Thomas Hanke, and Cordula Tutt, "German Minister Calls for More Flexible Laws in Immigration Rethink," *Financial Times*, 26 September 2000; Deborah Hargreaves, "EU Launches Immigration Plan," *Financial Times*, October 2000.

Third Country Families, Associated Nationals, and Contested European Membership

Perhaps the clearest manifestation of the contested nature of European belonging is evident in conflicts over the place of non-EU nationals in European society. Discriminatory practices toward migrant EU nationals, although endemic with respect to public sector employment and social welfare benefits, pale in comparison to the exclusion that third country nationals experience within the EU. The European legal rights enjoyed by third country nationals encounter the most pervasive and intense official resistance. Yet these peripheral migrants find allies not only in the ECJ, but also in national courts and domestic organizations committed to the individual rights of everyone resident in their communities. It is in the treatment of third country nationals that struggles within the state appear most contradictory and membership in European society most confused. In addition to flagrant evasion, conflict over third country nationals' European rights generates bizarre paradoxes. National governments find themselves forced to treat the third country family members of EU migrants better than the third country family members of their own national citizens. Meanwhile, the nationals of associated states with no likely prospect of EU membership, such as Algeria and Morocco, have more European entitlements than the nationals of more recently associated states that are slated to enter the EU within this decade, such as Poland and Hungary.

Realizing the European rights of migrant EU nationals' families remains among the most persistent problem areas, particularly if dependants are third country nationals. Although migrants' families enjoy rights to equal treatment regardless of their nationality, national administrations frequently treat these individuals as if they were simply foreigners without any special legal rights.[75] Of course, these individuals could be treated as "regular" foreigners if they were merely related to the host state's own citizens. The 1986 Gül case[76] exposes both a clear violation of a basic right under European law and the contradictory position of third country family members in European society. German authorities tried to restrict a Cypriot physician, Gül, from obtaining a regular permit to practice medicine in Germany. Married to a British national working in Germany, Gül had received a temporary permit to practice medicine while training as an anesthesiologist in Germany. European law explicitly provides spouses of employed EU migrants with

[75] Interviews with a legal adviser, Groupe d'Information et de Soutien des Travailleurs Immigrés (GISTI), Paris, 22 February 1996; with a representative from the European Trade Union Confederation, Brussels, 6 March 1996; with a representative of the Euro Citizen Action Service (ECAS), Brussels, 7 March 1996; with a representative of the Bund der Spanischen Elternvereine, Bonn, 23 January 1996; with a representative of the Bundesarbeitsgemeinschaft der Immigrantenverbände, Bonn, 24 January 1996.

[76] *Emir Gül v Regierungspräsident Düsseldorf* C-131/85, 1986.

access to employment and does not exclude them from particular professions. Spouses of migrant workers must simply demonstrate that they have the appropriate qualifications. Since Gül completed a German anesthesiology residency, he satisfied these requirements. Nonetheless, German officials claimed that European law did not provide the right to work in a particular profession such as medicine, insisted that non-EU nationals receive only temporary permits, and argued that renewal was not desirable because many German physicians were unemployed. The German observations even attempted to connect restrictions on the freedom of movement due to public health grounds to the public health sector, even though these exceptions are clearly designed to restrict the movement of diseased individuals rather than the movement of physicians. The Germans lost the case on all grounds.[77] Yet had Gül been married to a German citizen who had always worked in Germany, the German government would have been legally justified in its restriction.

Member States have also responded to ECJ case law on the legal rights of associated third country nationals with evasion and preemptive acts that have produced a similar paradox. National governments contest the very principle that association agreements are part of the European legal order that confers enforceable rights.[78] As a result, national administrations make the most strenuous efforts to evade these migrants' legal claims. In response to challenges, national governments have complied with individual decisions and avoided reforms to accommodate the rights of associated third country nationals. Furthermore, the Member States acted unanimously to preempt future judicial expansion of individual rights by eliminating measures for the equal treatment of migrants in all new association agreements.

With respect to evasion, Germany distributed ECJ case law granting residence and employment rights to Turkish nationals to competent authorities with instructions to interpret the legal decisions as restrictively as possible. Authorities should respond favorably only to instances with virtually identical factual conditions, which results in the need to bring new legal challenges for broadly parallel situations.[79] As a result, national courts have been busy resolving over 200 disputes related to these rights.[80] The French response to ECJ decisions that grant equal treatment in social security to associated third county nationals from Morocco and Algeria was almost identical to its handling of the export of supplemental income benefits for EU nationals. French authorities first ignored the implications of the ECJ's 1991 *Kziber* ruling,[81]

[77] *Gül* C-131/85, 1986.

[78] Christoph Schumacher, "Soziale Sicherheit für Drittstaatsangehörige und Assoziierungs/Europa-Abkommen," *Deutsche Rentenversicherung*, no. 10–11 (1995): 687, 689; Roger, "Europe et fonds national," 66.

[79] Interview with a legal adviser, Bundesministerium des Innerns, Bonn, 25 January 1996.

[80] *Juris* search, 5 December 2000.

[81] *Kziber* C-18/90, 1991.

which originated from a Belgian court. The French continued to refuse to rescind their general exclusion of associated third country nationals after an Algerian national successfully appealed for a supplemental income benefit from the French Cour de Cassation in 1991, who ruled according to the ECJ's *Kziber* decision without making any reference to it. French authorities treated these judgments as individual cases that lacked consequences for administrative practices writ large.[82] The French administration continued to resist reforms after a French court received a preliminary ruling on the case of an Algerian national in 1995.[83] French authorities ordered the offices distributing supplemental income benefits to provide benefits only to those individuals who initiated proceedings in French courts.[84]

Such evasion is formally legitimate under European law because ECJ decisions officially apply only to the parties addressed by specific rulings. However, what is striking about this instance of evasion is that France was also defying its own constitutional court. Different agents of state power are acting against each other here. In January 1990 the Conseil Constitutionnel had declared unconstitutional the denial of supplemental income schemes to nationals who have no special bilateral social security rights. This decision affects all foreigners in France, not just associated third country nationals.[85] In response to what they saw as an egregious breach of the law, organizations that assist migrants helped bring over eighty-nine cases for associated third country nationals before French courts. At least fifty-nine of these decisions accorded benefits, while fourteen rejected the applications.[86] Meanwhile, the French administration remained content to consider specific cases as they proceeded through courts, awarding benefits under particular judicial orders for individual applicants.[87] In response to criticisms of this practice, French officials observed that the extension of social security rights to associated third country nationals would have strong, damaging implications for public finances.[88] But the French state acted against itself yet again, when the Conseil d'État, which is essentially an extension of the national administration itself as the supreme administrative court, denounced such administrative practice as an abuse of power and annulled the relevant administrative orders.[89]

[82] Roger, "Europe et fonds national," 63–68.
[83] *Krid* C-103/94, 1995.
[84] "Condition d'attribution du Fonds National de Solidarité," no. 347 and 365, 1994 and 1996; *Lettre-circulaire* no. 169–95, 1995.
[85] Collectif des Accidentés du Travail (CATRED) et al. 1994, 3.
[86] Ibid., 27–9.
[87] Roger, "Europe et fonds national," 68.
[88] "Condition d'attribution du Fonds National de Solidarité aux étrangers non ressortissants d'un État membre de la CEE," no. 347, 1994.
[89] Conseil d'État, no. 174219 174220 176805 ¼ SSR, Groupe d'Information et du Soutien des Travailleurs Immigrés et Association "France Terre d'Asile," 14 January 1998.

In addition to this evasion, Member States collectively preempted ECJ intervention in this area for all new association agreements with third countries. Most notably, the Member States eliminated migrant rights in association agreements with Central and Eastern European countries, including those scheduled for eminent EU membership. Member States refrained from including provisions for the equal treatment of migrant workers from prospective EU members such as Poland, the Czech Republic, Slovakia, Hungary, Bulgaria, Romania, and Slovenia. The one exception includes the existence of an individual right of establishment, so newly associated nationals may start their own businesses in the EU.[90] The EU apparently welcomes entrepreneurs, but not any potential competitors in the labor market. The Member States even revoked nondiscrimination measures from a cooperation accord with Yugoslavia in 1991.[91] These actions are the national governments' collective response to the ECJ's interpretation of accords with Turkey, Algeria, Morocco, and Tunisia.[92] The Member States have certainly made their distaste for the ECJ decisions clear. They have also rendered the citizens of Eastern and Central Europe less European than the citizens of states many would classify in the Middle East. Of the four states with association agreements conferring migrant rights, only Turkey is a potential future member of the EU. And Turkey is virtually guaranteed to be granted membership later than countries in Central Europe. Such preemption is hardly a warm welcome to prospective EU nationals.

The European Commission has not extended much of a welcome to associated third country nationals, either. Instead of advocating that the ECJ confer legal effects on social security measures in the accords with Morocco, Algeria, and Tunisia, it argued for the necessity of further (intergovernmental) measures of the Association Council.[93] And despite rampant evasion of consistent ECJ legal interpretation, the European Commission has bothered to prosecute only one likely infringement in this field, a case against France regarding social security benefits for Algerians, Moroccans, and Tunisians.[94] Yet the European Commission did make one constructive proposal related to all third country nationals' rights within the EU: It suggested the rather minimalist humanitarian idea of extending social security benefits to cover urgent medical care for *insured* third country nationals who are briefly

[90] Martin, *La libre circulation des personnes*, 376–484.

[91] Roger, "Europe et fonds national," 68.

[92] Schumacher, "Soziale Sicherheit," 692; Elspeth Guild, *A Guide to the Right of Establishment under the Europe Agreements* (London: Baileys Shaw & Gillet, 1996); Martin, *La libre circulation des personnes*; European Trade Union Institute, *The Association Agreements between the European Community and Poland, Hungary, and Czechoslovakia: A Trade Union View* (Brussels: European Trade Union Institute, 1992).

[93] *Kziber* C-18/90, 1991; Roger, "Europe et fonds national," 66.

[94] Commission, "Fifteenth Annual Report on Monitoring the Application of Community Law – 1997," *Official Journal of the European Communities* C-250 (10 August 1998): 42.

visiting a second Member State. Even this the Member States rejected.[95] Apparently, national governments would rather let third country nationals drop dead abroad than concede that social security coordination for third country nationals is covered under legally enforceable European provisions.[96]

In summary, Member States have responded to the ECJ's efforts to abolish national discrimination among Europeans with considerable resistance. National governments persistently attempt to evade the broad application of European legal rights to migrants within the EU. When pressed to bring practices into line with ECJ interpretation, Member States have reacted by adopting measures to overturn or to preempt unwelcome migrant rights. These negative responses are consistent with patterns of interest to the extent that many legal entitlements entail financial costs while benefiting individuals who cannot even contribute to the reelection of national governments. Yet resistance also reflects the importance of traditional conceptions of identity, independent of overt economic or political interests, because (1) national governments long evaded and continue to evade virtually costless rights associated with public sector employment, and (2) they resist benefits for associated third country nationals to a much greater extent than benefits for EU migrants, despite parallel costs associated with rights for each population. As the European Court of Justice attempts to blur national boundaries by creating transnational European rights and obligations, Member States actively maintain and reconstruct territorial and national borders through their law, policy, and practice.

No Stake in Europe? Individuals and Civil Society between Nationalized and Universal Communities

The EU has the potential to create a European foundation of belonging for a population of approximately 300 million EU nationals. Yet individuals have not been very responsive to their European entitlements throughout the history of integration. Only a tiny minority of EU nationals has ever exercised the free movement rights that provide them equal access to opportunities available in other Member States. According to the most recent census figures, only 4.9 million EU nationals live in a Member State other than the country whose nationality they possess, and only two million of these migrants are employed.[97] With the exception of substantial Italian

95 *Official Journal of the European Communities* C-242, 1995: 7.

96 Herwig Verschueren, "EC Social Security Coordination Excluding Third Country Nationals: Still in Line with Fundamental Rights after the *Gaygusuz* Judgment?," *Common Market Law Review* 34 (1997): 991–2.

97 Commission, *Social Europe*, DG-V – no. 2/93 (Luxembourg: Office for Official Publications of the European Communities, 1994), 31, and Commission, *The Demographic Situation in the European Union: 1994 Report*, DG-V – COM (94) 585, (Luxembourg: Office for Official Publications of the European Communities, 1995), 67.

migration in the early days of European integration, most intra-EU migration flows are limited to border regions.[98] Expectations of large-scale migration from other southern Member States were never realized. This is partly due to delayed implementation of the free movement rights of workers from poorer new member countries such as Portugal and Spain. Free movement of goods, whether intentional or not, then tends to substitute for migration within the EU. Meanwhile, migration from nonmember countries generally has outpaced migration of EU nationals.[99] The population of associated third country nationals who possess explicit European legal rights, at 4.15 million, alone almost matches the population of migrant EU nationals. This group of non-EU nationals includes residents of Turkish (2,300,000), Moroccan (1,000,000), Algerian (600,000), and Tunisian (250,000) nationality.[100] Combined, the two populations of migrants who legally belong to Europe total approximately nine million, which constitutes slightly less than 3 percent of the entire population base within the European Union.

This migrant population, to the extent it is organized at all, is overwhelmingly organized in the form of associations representing single ethnic groups. Associations of migrants of the same national origin organize cultural and social activities and provide assistance to each other primarily in the form of general information about housing, employment, and vocational training within local communities.[101] Very few associations have a genuinely transnational membership. Exceptional cases include the European Union Migrants Forum and Euro-Citizen Action Service. Moreover, of the tiny minority of associations that provide legal assistance to migrants, virtually all provide this assistance without regard to the migrant's national origin. EU nationals do not hold a privileged position, except with the Euro-Citizen Action Service and the recently launched Free Movement Solidarity Fund. Otherwise, those who provide legal counsel to migrants deal predominantly with asylum, human rights, third country immigrants, and racism.[102] The small numbers of lawyers and associations that bother to help migrants overcome

98 Thomas Straubhaar, "International Labour Migration within a Common Market: Some Aspects of the EC Experience," *Journal of Common Market Studies* 27 (1988): 50–1.

99 Ibid., 56–7.

100 Commission, *The Demographic Situation: 1994 Report*, 68.

101 European Union Migrants Forum, *The European Union Migrants' Forum Proposals for the Revision of the Treaty on European Union at the Intergovernmental Conference of 1996* (Brussels: EU Migrant Forum, May 1995); Inter-regional Trade Union Committee, *Draft Political Call by the ITUCs to the ETUC, the Affiliated Confederations, the European Institutions, and States* (Brussels: European Trade Union Confederation, 14 July 1994); Euro Citizen Action Service (ECAS), *Draft ECAS Blueprint for a Chapter on European Citizenship in the Revised TEU* (Brussels: ECAS, 1996); Groupe d'Information et de Soutien des Travailleurs Immigrés (GISTI), *Les étrangers et le droit communautaire* (Paris: GISTI, September 1995).

102 Centre d'Information et d'Études sur les Migrations Internationales (CIEMI), "Migrants, solidarité, droits de l'homme, recherche/documentation," *Répertoire des Associations Immigrées et de Solidarité dans l'Union Européenne*, 10th ed. (Paris: CIEMI, June 1994).

exclusion appear to be committed to the equal treatment of all individuals within their communities. Most attempt to enforce universal rights, rather than the particular rights of those with European credentials.

The resource constraints faced by these associations suggest that mobilizing civil society behind the equal treatment of migrants is difficult. Few organizations possess the resources to deploy litigation at all. Groups that have supported litigation to help migrants in the EU include the Immigration Law Practitioners' Association (ILPA) of London and Groupe d'Information et de Soutien des Travailleurs Immigrés (GISTI) in France. The Spanish Consulates have supported some litigation on behalf of migrant Spanish nationals as well. Litigation is usually very challenging for nongovernmental organizations to carry out. GISTI relies overwhelmingly on volunteers and has limited resources to pursue litigation. Simply finding lawyers with sufficient expertise in European employment and social security rights constitutes a major problem.[103] The financial base of the new Free Movement Solidarity could be wiped out in a single case if appeals through one of the more expensive national legal systems were involved: Available funds for the period from November 2000 to April 2001 consisted of 32,226 euro, with an additional potential reserve of 12,394 euro. Litigating a case to its ultimate conclusion in the United Kingdom can cost upwards of 40,000 pounds, which are worth more than euros. The paucity of organizational resources reflects the traditionally marginal position of migrants: Migrant labor is concentrated in basic manufacturing in Germany; the trade services industry, construction, and public works in France; and basic services, excluding public administration, in the United Kingdom.[104] Meanwhile, most labor organizations and civic groups that represent individual interests focus on national communities and have not yet engaged transnational or migrant issues seriously. In this respect, civil society in Member States remains overwhelmingly nationalized.

Employers are a potential champion of migrant rights, since nondiscrimination measures expand the potential pool of qualified candidates. However, European employers in both the public and private sectors have remained relatively uninterested in promoting the free movement of workers. Serious interest in greater labor mobility has a very narrow focus on highly qualified labor.[105] This does not generate much political pressure for reform because

[103] Interviews with a legal adviser of Groupe d'Information et de Soutien des Travailleurs Immigrés (GISTI), Paris, 22 February 1996; with a legal adviser of the Union of Industrial and Employers Confederations of Europe, Brussels, 6 March 1996; with a representative of the European Citizens Action Service, Brussels, 7 March 1996; with a representative of the Bundesarbeitsgemeinschaft der Immigrantenverbände, Bonn, 24 January 1996; with a representative of the EU Migrants Forum, Brussels, 4 March 1996; with a representative of the Bund der Spanischen Elternvereine, Bonn, 23 January 1996.

[104] Organization for Economic Cooperation and Development, *Trends in International Migration: Annual Report 1994* (Paris: OECD, 1995): 40, 85.

[105] Ibid., 126.

highly qualified workers and their employers can generally be easily accommodated through piecemeal exceptions to existing practices. Demand for lower skilled labor, where most migrant male labor has been concentrated, has been declining in Europe over the past two decades. Decline and restructuring in manufacturing and mining sectors, as well as volatility in the construction sector, has contributed to increasing unemployment among migrant male workers. Laid-off migrant workers, who are generally older and experienced only in manual and unskilled jobs, have little hope of finding employment. The better qualifications of a second generation of "migrant" workers manifests itself in the increasing employment of foreigners across most sectors of the economy, including those once dominated by nationals. However, these young "migrants" still are unemployed at higher rates than young nationals, partially due to discrepancies in educational attainment between the children of migrant workers and nationals.[106]

These trends in the labor market coincided with increasing migration within and into Europe. Increasing migration among EU nationals from 1988 to1990 was followed by increasing migration of third country nationals into the European Union. The number of third country nationals increased suddenly, growing by more than 1.5 million people from 1990 to 1992. During this period Germany admitted eight times more foreigners, both EU citizens (160,000) and non-EU nationals (800,000), than other Member States. Nationals of Central and Eastern Europe account for 25 percent of this increase (over 200,000 people).[107]

With continuing high unemployment levels in Europe, the plight of new migrants attracted little sympathy. Member States have largely responded to the upsurge in migration with a policy of closure toward third country nationals. Although current EU nationals are not directly affected by these restrictive policies, reforms reflect official orientation toward migrants, in many cases migrants who are citizens of Central and Eastern European states who will be EU nationals in the near future. During the 1990s all EU Member States, with the exception of Denmark and Sweden, legislated major changes in their domestic migration regimes. Belgium, France, the Netherlands, and Spain tightened regulations concerning the entry and residence of foreigners. Italy, the Netherlands, Portugal, and Spain created new measures to identify and to reduce illegal migration and employment. German investigation of suspected illegal employment and abuse of unemployment benefits among foreigners intensified from the early 1990s.[108] Austria, Belgium, Finland, France, Germany, Luxembourg, the Netherlands, Portugal, Spain, and the United Kingdom adopted more restrictive asylum procedures. In the German case, asylum reform required constitutional amendment. All of

106 Ibid., 40–1.
107 Commission, *The Demographic Situation: 1994 Report*, 69.
108 OECD, *Trends*, 89–90.

these legislative reforms expedite the identification of fraudulent claims, illegal residence, and underground employment, and they strengthen measures to deport foreign offenders.[109] The practical effect of these measures has been substantial: German recognition rates for asylum applications fell from a high of 29 percent in 1985 to approximately 3 percent by 1992.[110]

At the EU level, intergovernmental cooperation focuses overwhelmingly on security issues that frame the need for a common migration policy in terms of criminality. As a result, evolving EU provisions, many of which escape review by national and European legal institutions, concentrate on means of policing and control.[111] The growing electoral successes of far-right parties, most notably Jörg Haider of the Austrian Freedom Party and Jean-Marie Le Pen of the French National Front, are the darkest manifestations of antiforeigner sentiment in Europe. Although other EU Member States denounced the inclusion of Haider's party in the Austrian government and Le Pen was soundly beaten in the second round of the 2002 French presidential elections, the widespread increase in domestic restrictions on migration and preliminary EU efforts to exclude third country nationals more effectively reflect an official effort to restrict membership in European society.

In conclusion, neither states nor societies within the EU are responding enthusiastically to the opportunity to construct a genuinely European foundation for belonging. The exclusion of many migrants from their legal entitlement to equal treatment reflects a significant discrepancy between what ECJ justices and national officials consider to be appropriate practice. The ECJ created rights that national governments never intended to honor, and reactions of evasion, overrule, and preemption prevail as a result. Moreover, even the ECJ and European Commission refrain from challenging core forms of national belonging. Meanwhile, few individuals seize the opportunity to transgress traditional boundaries and to integrate themselves within a transnational community of Europeans. Even fewer bother to work with others to achieve their common rights as Europeans. The supranational European society is elusive and will remain so until someone cares to build it.

109 Ibid., 43–5.

110 Ibid., 89–90.

111 Virginie Guiraudon, "European Integration and Migration Policy: Vertical Policy-making as Venue Shopping," *Journal of Common Market Studies* 38 (June 200): 260.

13

Boundaries of the Nation-State and the Lure of the Islamic Community in Turkey

Yeşim Arat

Crosstalk
I cannot redraw all the borders of myself
however they divide and separate
I cannot unlearn all the markers of MY WORLD
whatever their origins (or destinations)
there's always residue
what I can't excise
I carry borders and markers wherever I am
Local or global here or there
I cannot talk across them all always

Ailbhe Smyth, "Borderline Crosstalk," in *Knowing Feminisms* (1997)

This chapter is about the attempt to "redraw borders" of ourselves, "unlearn" markers of our world, and "talk across" borders and markers. I focus on the Turkish Islamist attempt to construct an alternative community to that of the nation, by using the tool of the nation-state. In its inception, the Turkish nation-state established its borders and authority in opposition to the religious groups that prevailed in the country. The secular nation-state redrew the boundaries of Islam in public space in its struggle to claim its territorial hegemony. Ironically, in contemporary Turkey, the Islamist groups used the public space and the political democracy that the nation-state legitimized within its territorial boundaries to herald the Islamist call. The translocal solidarities and norms that Islamists appealed to could best be cultivated in the context of the political arena the nation-state needed to legitimize its secular rule. Ultimately, the Islamists in Turkey who envisioned crossing territorial boundaries of the nation-state could hope to realize their own political ambitions within these borders they criticized. The Islamist Welfare Party manipulated the dialectical interplay between the sense of belonging to the nation-state and the sense of belonging to the larger universal community of Islam to enhance its position and pursue its interests within the parameters of the nation-state. The Islamic constituency, in turn, manipulated the markers of its Islamic identity, thus fitting into the local context and attempting to "talk across" borders.

After a brief look at the historical loci of tensions between Islam and the state in Turkey, I turn to contemporary politics and the Islamist Welfare party (1983–98). I examine the discourse of the Welfare party on transnational Islamic solidarity and trace the implications of this discourse on the Kurdish constituency and the head-scarved Islamist women. Based on my research on Islamist women of the Welfare party, I point to the contradictions that the boundary markers of the Islamist and secular discourses generate at the level of the individuals who attempt to redefine their identities within the parameters of these discourses. Islamist women who were brought up within the confines of the secular nation state selectively choose the Islamist markers of their identity as they cover their heads and refuse to abide by many other allegedly Islamic dictates. In the context of the secular nation state, the Islamist attempt to construct an alternative community by using the framework of the secular nation-state is, in turn, permeated by the norms and values of the former.

The Heritage of Contestation: Universal Islam and the Local State

Ottomans bequeathed to the Republican Turks the heritage of conflict between allegiance to the state and allegiance to Islam. Islam, as a world religion, upheld the ideal of world hegemony, even though it could never realize it in practice.[1] It has been claimed that "Islam was not merely a religion; it was a nationality, a political community, a civilization."[2] In theory, Islam could not be divorced from the state if the rulers were true Muslims. In practice, it could. In theory, the sultans were bound by the Shariat and could be removed from power for violating it by the highest religious authority in power, the Seyh-ül-Islam (Sheik of Islam). In practice, the sultans were powerful enough to dominate the Seyh-ül-Islams and allowed secular Western legal codes, especially penal and commercial codes, to coexist with the religious code. Furthermore, Islam had a universal appeal, but the state was territorially bound. The feeling of belonging to the universal Muslim community had to be realized in and circumscribed by an allegiance to the territorially bound state.

Ottoman sultans accommodated this tension by allowing Islam to legitimize their patriarchal rule. In turn, they assumed the responsibility of expanding Muslim rule through their military conquests. When the power of

[1] Bryan Turner, "Review Essay: Citizenship and Political Globalization," *Citizenship Studies* 4, no. 1 (2000): 83.

[2] Niyazi Berkes, *The Development of Secularism in Turkey* (Montreal: McGill University Press, 1964), p. 268.

the Ottoman state deteriorated, the Ottoman sultans did not hesitate to manipulate the universal appeal of Islam and the Muslim community to generate internal and external support. For example, against emerging nationalisms within the empire, they appealed to religion to maintain the empire. Religion was used to preserve the political community within its established territorial boundaries.

After the establishment of the republic in 1923, the founding fathers endorsed the newly rising secular ideology of nationalism within the newly drawn and, compared with the Ottoman Empire, much shrunken territorial boundaries of the state. The new republic severed all ties with the multiethnic, religiously sanctioned Ottoman Empire[3] to become a secular westernizing nation-state. The basis of allegiance to the state changed. The first article of the 1921 constitution declared that sovereignty belonged to the nation unconditionally and replaced Islam as a principle of political legitimacy.

The founding fathers were keen on enacting their idea of the nation-state as a secular homogenous body united with ideology of Turkish nationalism. They initiated a series of institutional and legal reforms to disestablish Islam and to separate religious institutions of the state from those of society.[4] In 1924 the institutions of the Caliphate was abolished. The position of Seyh-ül-islam and the Ministry of Religious foundations had similar predicaments. In their place, the General Directorate of Religious Affairs and the General Directorate of Pious Foundations were instituted. The Law on the Unity of Education outlawed religious education and brought all educational institutions under control of the Ministry of Education. In 1926 a new civil code was adopted from the Swiss code. The new code was critical not merely in providing the basic framework for male female equality in the polity, but also in dismantling the power of the Shariat over political and social life. By and large the secularizing reforms were and remain unprecedented in the Muslim world.

Despite the efficiency and authoritarianism with which the secularizing reforms were carried out to establish the secular nation-state, the state elites were also reluctant to divorce themselves from the attractiveness of religious ties to reinforce nationalist solidarity. In practice, even among the highly unified political elite that led the reforms, there were fractures and divergences from a concept of secular nation-state where citizens were tied to the state with feelings of civic belonging. Religion crept in the secular

3 Bernard Lewis, *The Emergence of Modern Turkey* (London: Oxford University Press, 1976); Metin Heper, *The State Tradition in Turkey* (Walkington: Eothen, 1985); Çağlar Keyder, *State and Class in Turkey* (London: Verso, 1987); İlkay Sunar, "State, Society and Democracy in Turkey," in V. Mastny and R. C. Nation, eds., *Turkey between East and West: New Challenges for a Rising Regional Power* (Boulder, Colo.: Westview, 1996).

4 Binnaz Toprak, *Islam and Political Development in Turkey* (Leiden: E. J. Brill, 1981); Andrew Davison, *Secularism and Revivalism in Turkey* (New Haven, Conn.: Yale University Press, 1998).

nationalist constructions of citizenship. Article 88 of the 1924 Constitution stated that the people of Turkey, regardless of their religion and race, were in terms of citizenship to be Turkish. Yet, in practice, being Muslim was a cause for positive discrimination. Non-Muslims were discriminated against with a number of policies. In the population exchange that took place between Greece and Turkey, religion became the criterion to define nationality when Turkish-speaking members of the Orthodox Church in Central Anatolia were sent to Greece; when Orthodox Christian Gagauz Turks from Romania sought to settle in Turkey, they were not allowed.[5] Muslim Albanians and Bosnians who were not of Turkish background were admitted, however.[6]

Being a Muslim was a cause for positive discrimination in nationalist state policies besides population exchange. Non-Muslims became victims of a heavy wealth tax after World War II. Christians and Jews were not admitted to military schools. In 1930, non-Muslim personnel of Turkish Railways were laid off. The ideal of a secular nation-state, which adhered to a concept of civic nationalism, was, in practice, undermined with the temptation of a Muslim heritage that could reinforce or foster Turkish nationalism. Yet the state maintained its control over how religion would fit into the boundaries of its primarily secular nation-state.

Islamist Ascendance

The struggle of the competing political elites to contain and to control Islam and/or to manipulate it to promote their political power continued in the context of the socio-economic and political development in the country. Over time and over this struggle, the Muslim constituency gained more political power and public opportunities for social mobility. Boundaries within which Islamists operated and the platforms to which they carried Islam expanded over time as "concessions" given to them critically influenced who ruled. Those who had only Quranic courses to propagate Islam had access to Prayer Leader and Preacher Schools (İmam Hatip Okulları) with the advent of the Democrat party in the 1950s. By the end of the 1960s, an Islamist party came on the political stage to compete for political power. The party was closed, then established under a different name, played a key role in the coalitionary governments of the 1970s, and was closed again in the 1980 military intervention. However, by the end of the 1980s and in the 1990s, Islamist intellectuals, Islamist bourgeoisie, Islamist banks,

[5] Kemal Kirişçi and Gareth Winrow, *The Kurdish Question and Turkey* (London: Frank Cass, 1997).

[6] Kemal Kirişçi, "Disaggregating Turkish Citizenship and Immigration Practices," *Middle Eastern Studies* 36, no. 3 (July 2000): 1–22.

and Islamist radio and TV channels proliferated in the public domain. The Islamist Welfare party, founded in 1983 after the military intervention, received 21.4 percent of the national vote in the 1995 elections and became the major coalition partner of the government in power between July 1996 and June 1997.

There were various internal and external reasons as to why the Islamists gained power and why the political elites could use Islam to enhance their electoral strengths. Rapid socio-economic change and the internal mass migration from rural to urban areas provided the major base for Islamist support in the peripheral regions of the metropolitan cities.[7] The inability of the traditional political parties to mobilize the migrant masses or those disenchanted with the system was linked to the inability of the secular Republican nation-state ideology to meet their needs. Some argued that the Kemalist secular nation-state ideology lacked the poetry and the fervor to mobilize these masses by appealing to hearts as well as minds.[8] Others claimed that this official ideology was captive to its authoritarian legacy and could generate neither political nor economic liberalism to respond to these newly emerging heterogeneous demands.[9] Failure of the Kemalist nation-state to meet the needs of the changing population accounted for the attractiveness of Islamism and the rise of the Islamist Welfare party.

External factors beyond the nation-state were also crucial in contributing to the lure of the Islamist call. In the context of a globalizing world where economic and communication networks undermined national boundaries, the Islamist call could reach far with more allure. The revolution in Iran, which challenged the supremacy of the West, incited people's imagination of the larger glorious Islamic community. The Iranian-based Hizbullah (Party of God) physically infiltrated the country beyond borders. Non-Turkish Islamist intellectuals, such as Mawdudi and Sayyit Kutb, were widely translated into Turkish and had a significant impact on Turkish youth.[10] Turkey began to play an active role in Islamic organizations. The number of Turkish pilgrims going to Mecca increased dramatically into ten thousands physically crossing territorial boundaries to recreate them in solidarity with Muslims from other countries. As the Islamist press mushroomed, news of the Islamic world from Iran to Afghanistan, beyond the territorial boundaries of the nation-state spread to ignite the loyalties of Turkish citizens to Islam.

7 Binnaz Toprak, "Surviving Modernization: Islam as Communal Means of Adaptation," *Il Politico* 56, no. 1 (1991): 147–161.

8 Şerif Mardin, *Religion and Social Change in Modern Turkey* (Albany: State University of New York Press, 1989).

9 Çağlar Keyder, "Whither the Project of Modernity?," in Sibel Bozdoğan and Reşat Kasaba, eds., *Rethinking Modernity and National Identity in Turkey* (Seattle: University of Washington Press, 1997).

10 "Türkiye'de İslami Hareket," *Girişim* (March 1990): 8–40.

The Nation-State and Its Islamic Criticism

Islamist intellectuals and ideologues were critical in promoting Islam, radicalizing the Welfare party, and expanding its constituency.[11] In an era of globalization where traditional ties of citizenship based on affiliation with a territorial state weakened,[12] Islamists in Turkey were ready to offer an alternative bond of allegiance cross-cutting territorial boundaries and competing with secular ties of citizenship. Similar in some ways to secular critiques of the nation-state in the West, they challenged the viability of the territorially bound nation-state, propagating, instead, the political community of Islam, the ummah[13] that cut across national boundaries. Unlike advocates of cosmopolitan democracy or world order model projects who had more inclusionary visions of global orders and, instead, more reminiscent of Samuel Huntington, who prophesied a clash of civilizations, many Islamist thinkers envisioned the world as a bipolar structure divided between Christianity and Islam. I focus on the prominent Muslim intellectual Ali Bulaç to elaborate a strong Islamist criticism of the nation-state. Bulaç's vision turned Huntington's vision upside-down, replacing the status of Islam with Christianity, and retained his essentialism.

Bulaç, much like Samuel Huntington, argued that, "from a cultural, political, social and metaphysical perspective, today's world is a bipolar world just as it was before. Now, one of the poles is Western liberalism and Christianity, while the other is Islam."[14] Within these two competing realms, nation-states are anachronistic institutions that need to be and are being surpassed. According to Bulaç, nation-states are anachronistic because they cannot accommodate difference. Different identities, ethnic, or religious groups can not coexist within the logic of the nation-state, which recognizes only a monolithic ethnic or religious group. A modern nation-state can allow for Christian, Buddhist, or Muslim schools or educational institutions to operate in its territory, but it does not allow for free and oppositionary spaces where alternative lives can be led (according to the dictates of these religions).[15] Many different ethnic groups and even more numerous different language-speaking groups aspiring for nation-states of their own only means millions of people cutting each other's throats.[16] Ethnic cleansing in

[11] Haldun Gülalp, "Political Islam in Turkey: The Rise and Fall of the Refah Party," *The Muslim World*, January 1999, p. 32.

[12] Richard Falk, "The Decline of Citizenship in an Era of Globalization," *Citizenship Studies* 4, no. 1 (2000): 5–17; Daniele Archibugi et al., eds., *Re-imagining Political Community* (Stanford, Calif.: Stanford University Press, 1998).

[13] "Ummah" is the Arabic word for Islamic political community.

[14] Cited in *Girişim*, March 1990, p. 13.

[15] Ali Bulaç, *Modern Ulus Devlet* (Istanbul: Iz yayıncılık. 1998), pp. 433–44.

[16] Ibid., p. 16.

Bosnia-Herzegovina or Caucasia are his proofs. Nation-states aim to assimilate and annihilate everyone in their homogenizing melting pot.[17]

According to Bulaç, the authoritarian, homogenizing nation-state is a development that needs to be "overcome." The larger socio-economic and political integrations among communities whose social structures, histories, beliefs, geographies, and interests overlap attest to this need on the part of many nation-states. This integration, he argues, is not a return of nationalism but, to the contrary, the return of the ummah epoch that involves unification around a higher, more inclusionary identity.[18]

For a Muslim, the issue of overcoming the nation-state is particularly significant. Bulaç contests the legitimacy of the totalitarian nation-state for the Muslims, because God has ordained His will to be realized through the community of believers under the leadership of an imam or the caliph, who follows the Prophet. The imam is expected to be chosen from within the ummah and to establish an Islamic state based on a contract. The imam receives his legitimacy to enforce the Shariat from the consensus (biat) generated within the ummah. The totalitarian nation-state can accommodate neither the different interpretations and different sects recognized within Islam nor the right to life of different religious communities to live according to their laws and customs, whereas Bulaç claims (without explaining how) that an Islamic state can.

According to Bulaç, appropriating the nation-state would not solve the problem for Muslims, either. It would merely undermine the natural Islamic community. The nation-state was established to bring about a secular welfare state and society that it could not deliver. The attempt to Islamicize the modern state would allow the state to swallow Islam or alienate it. Nation was invented and imagined by the modern state. As such, Bulaç argues, it was not real, the way family, community, and the ummah were. The family, the community, and the ummah are thus essentialized without being explained.

The political community of Muslims, the ummah, essentialized as the only "real," "uninvented" polity, is also seen as a necessary base for a "genuine" democracy. Because, for a Muslim, the religious community is the only legitimate and natural community that could organize through a state, different religious, cultural, or political blocs could come together and sign a contract[19] to generate real democracy. Bulaç goes on to argue that according to this contract, the individual would have the right to choose which community to belong to. Each community would declare the basic rules and norms according to which they would organize their communal lives such that the individuals could make conscious choices. The different communities would specify how to regulate public and administrative matters or rights and

[17] Ibid., p. 17.
[18] Ibid., p. 18.
[19] Ibid., p. 134.

responsibilities in the contract they make.[20] The example of the Medina pact contracted by the prophet Mohammed among Muslims, Jews, and pagans is behind the model Bulaç depicts.

Bulaç's model has its problems. There is no guarantee of individual rights and liberties in a model of a society where it is ultimately the communities to which one belongs that define the predicament of the individuals. The relationship among the different communities that are expected to draw up a contract is also problematic. Ultimately, a set of rules enforced by the powerful might have to dictate the terms of such a contract. It is also unclear how within the Muslim community different understandings of Shariat are to be accommodated if the communal rules are as uniform and totalistic as Bulaç claims they are to be. Under these circumstances, it is unclear how a democracy can function.

Despite questions one could raise about this model, it is important that for the Muslim intellectual the sense of belonging that the nation-state aims to generate and the boundaries within which this belonging is to be nurtured are seriously challenged. Accordingly, the Muslim intellectual encourages the believer to think beyond the boundaries of the nation-state and nurtures the sense of belonging to the Islamic community claimed to be the sole base of political power. Even though it is very questionable how the Islamic political community will uphold diversity and plurality, it is in the name of these concepts and in opposition to a totalitarianism that prevents diversity that the boundaries of the nation-state and the feelings of belonging to it are contested. Especially considering the strict rules and laws of the religious community and the strict boundaries that define the parameters of a Muslim community, the consensual democracy that the ummah practices is bound to be limited in scope. It is bound to be one that discourages deviance and difference of opinion and assumes homogeneity, much as consensual democracies in nonreligious contexts do. Nonetheless, the legitimacy of the modern nation-state is seriously contested.

The Welfare Party between Islam and the Nation-State

While the nation-state might have been radically criticized from a theoretical Islamic perspective, in practice the Islamists had to define their lives within its confines. The Welfare party was the political party that aimed to appeal to the religious sentiments of the population in its pursuit of power within the nation-state. As a political party within the secular Turkish republic, the Welfare party could not propagate an Islamic state. The second article of the constitution defines the state as a secular one. Article 14 prohibits the propagation of religious and sectarian cleavages or the use of basic rights and liberties to form a state order based on these concepts.

[20] Ibid., pp. 134–5.

The Welfare party, founded in 1983 after the 1980 military intervention and closed by a constitutional court decision in 1998, formally had to observe these rules. The party program of 1983 stated that it was prepared in accordance with the understanding that "the Turkish Republic was before anything else loyal to Atatürk nationalism which meant that all its individuals are united in pride, joy and predicament in a spirit of national solidarity and a sense of justice."[21] The party program promised to promote cultural and moral development in the country, but underlined that this would be accomplished with an eye to national characteristics and specifities.[22] On the whole, the party program focused on practical matters and the development strategies of the party.

In practice, the Welfare party explicitly used Islam as its reference point. The medium of party politics prevailing in the country helped the Islamists and the Welfare party that channeled their interests to promote an Islamist vision among the citizens of the secular nation-state. Consequently, tension regarding the boundaries of Islam within the secular republic became inevitable. The party appealed to its local constituencies with a discourse of Islamic belonging beyond the borders of the nation-state. Thus the boundaries of the nation-state were contested as the party trespassed those borders at the discourse level. However, the appeal to Islamic belonging beyond the nation-state threatened not merely the physical boundaries of the nation-state, but also the secular laws that governed it. The party's appeal to the Kurdish constituency as Muslim brothers transgressed the code of secular Turkish nationalism. Its call to the head-scarved women as good Muslims challenged the exclusive nature of Turkish secularism. In both cases, secular laws of citizenship and belonging to the nation-state were contested.

The Welfare Party and the Borders of the Nation-State

The Welfare party program stated that the party aimed to maintain good relations with all countries and especially the neighboring ones. It was added on benignly that, if possible, relations with countries that had historical and cultural ties to the party would be particularly emphasized with regard to mutual material and moral benefits to both.[23]

However, over time, the party explicitly advocated strengthening ties with the Muslim countries, rather than the European ones. The chairman of the party, Necmettin Erbakan, proposed five steps that the party would take in this direction. First, Muslim countries and communities would establish their own Muslim Countries' United Nations Organization. He argued that there were forty-six independent Muslim nations and about as many Muslim

21 *Refah Partisi Programı* (Ankara: n.p., 1983), pp. 5–6.
22 Ibid., p. 7.
23 Ibid., p. 31.

communities in the world. When these eighty countries and communities established their United Nations, he argued, not "might" but "right" would reign and about 1.5 billion Muslims would collaborate among themselves and exert their weight on the world scene as one body.[24] Second, parallel to NATO, Muslim countries would establish their defense cooperation organization and produce their own armaments with their own division of labor. When need be, they would gather under one command and prevent injustice if perpetrated against Muslims. Third, a "Muslim countries Common Market Organization and Union" would be established. Thus, "within the 1.5 billion people Muslim world, goals of economic cooperation within one market, establishment of giant corporations, fast technological development and prevention of exploitation would be achieved." Fourth, The "Muslim countries Common Money Unit" would be established. "The Muslim countries and communities of 1.5 billion people" would thus replace the dollar that they now used to trade between themselves. These Muslim countries now kept huge dollar reserves, even though the dollar was an instrument of "modern imperialism" and thus served "imperialism" and "Zionism." In case the Muslim countries began using their own unit of money, those powers that served "imperialism" and "Zionism" would begin using the money of the Muslim countries as reserve. Finally, a "Muslim Countries Cultural Cooperation Organization" would be established. This organization would facilitate the cooperation among universities, institutes, and research centers in Muslim countries and promote collaboration in the fields of science and technology. In the words of Erbakan, "when Muslim countries and communities take these steps, they will have the power to protect the order which upholds justice [also meaning "God"] against the unjust aggression of imperialism and Zionism."[25] He argued that Turkey's duty is to be the vanguard of the "Just Order" against "Imperialism" and "Zionism" in the changing new world.

In this five-step proposal, there is no mention of the ummah per se, but a political Islamic community is explicitly advocated. Erbakan's model is formed after a Western or a European one. The yearning to replace the European Common Market or the European Monetary Unit with a Muslim one is all too obvious. Less obvious, perhaps, are the differences between the two unions. A political community where Islam is the common bond is different from one where the joining parties like nation-states make a secular contract. To the extent that Islam is an explicitly political religion that dictates the terms of social, economic, as well as political life, the difference is stark. In a religious community, God's laws or those laws that the powerful claim as God's laws prevail, while in a secular community, human will does.

[24] Necmettin Erbakan, *Türkiye'nin Meseleleri ve Çözümleri* (Ankara: n.p., 1991), pp. 32–3.
[25] Ibid., pp. 32–5.

Erbakan's vision is that of a bipolar world just like the one Ali Bulaç depicts where the significance of national boundaries erode. Along with Muslim countries, Muslim communities are also included in this new Islamic political community that is projected. In other contexts, Erbakan has simply referred to the "Union of Muslim Communities," rather than countries.[26] To strengthen the boundaries of this bipolar world, an attempt is made to portray the other as the enemy, the "imperialist" who exploits, or simply the "Zionist." It is claimed that institutions such as the United Nations protect the interests of Zionism and imperialism and act against the interests of Muslim countries and communities. The interests of "imperialism" and "Zionism" are assumed to overlap, without conflict.

Within this dichotomous world, the Muslim side represents "justice" or "just order that upholds the right." The word "justice" according to Islam is an attribute or a name of God, hence a metonym for God. The "other side" represents "force" or "the order of oppression that upholds force."[27] The "other side" is also seen in primarily religious terms. In the election manifesto that was prepared for the December 1995 general elections when the party received the largest number of votes, the "other order" was also explicitly named as a Christian one. The electoral manifesto stated that Turkey's place was not the Christian union based on the Treaty of Rome, which was established on the advice of Pope Pius XII, that is, the European Union, but rather the "World Muslim countries union."[28] In short, God marks the new boundaries of the political community Erbakan advocates. The nation-state of Turkey within this conception is relevant insofar as it can play a leading role to precipitate the union of Muslim countries and communities. He further argues that this is what all Muslim countries want.[29]

Erbakan's religious borders are not merely projected outside the boundaries of the Turkish nation-state but begin within Turkey. He argues that within Turkey there are only two parties: one of Justice, again used as a metonym for God, and the rest. The rest are all the same. These are all parties of savage, interest-seeking capitalism. All are for the European Union, which means, in Erbakan's words, that "we should break away from the Islamic world and unite with the Christians, form a single state, let them make our laws, let them operate us. The mission of these parties is to crush the nation and pay interest to the west and its collaborators."[30] Erbakan thus projects the good and the bad on to this dichotomous world he begins creating within Turkey and expands outside its borders.

26 Necmettin Erbakan, *Refah Partisi 4. Büyük Kongre Açış Konuşması* (Ankara: n.p., 1993), p. 8.
27 Ibid., p. 35.
28 *Refah Partisi 24 Aralık 1995 Seçimleri Seçim Beyannamesi* (Ankara: n.p., 1995), p. 29.
29 Erbakan, *Türkiye'nin Meseleleri ve Çözümleri*, p. 36.
30 Erbakan, *Refah Partisi 4*, p. 15.

Transgressing Secular Turkish Citizenship: The Welfare Party and the Kurds

There were opportunities as well as pitfalls for the party in extending this image of "us" against "them" within Turkey. In its appeal to the Kurdish constituency in Turkey, the Welfare party deftly benefited, for a limited time, from the discourse of Islamic solidarity encompassing multiple communities and ethnicities. With the guerrilla war that the Kurdistan Workers' Party initiated, in the early 1980s, to seek autonomy from the Turkish state, Kurdish nationalism flared up. To the extent that traditional Kurdish identity was intrinsically tied to religious identity,[31] any articulation of Kurdish interests necessitated a recognition of religious identities. The Welfare party thus used the opportunity to cultivate this religious link to the Kurdish community and appealed to Islam, which trespassed national borders to accommodate different sects and ethnic communities. The nation-state eventually set the limits to how far the Welfare party could cultivate this bond by trespassing nationalist borders.

Religious sheiks had played an important role in the political life of the Kurdish tribes particularly after the nineteenth-century reforms in the Ottoman empire undermined the influence of the local Kurdish emirs. The sheiks who had religious legitimacy appeared on the Kurdish scene as the new political actors who could mediate between tribes in conflict and maintain peace, which the secular Ottoman administrators could not.[32] Over time, the religious sheiks became the political leaders who instigated revolts and were critical in defining Kurdish identity against the Ottomans and later the Republican state. As the Republican state secularized, the Kurds felt their ties to the new state weaken. It has been claimed that the famous Kurdish revolt of 1925, the Sheik Said revolt, exhibited a symbiosis of religious as well as nationalist causes and was precipitated by the removal of the Caliphate in 1924.[33] The Republican state was committing double treachery from the perspective of the Kurds. The new state did not merely undermine religious ties of solidarity to the Kurds, but it also deviated from aspirations of civic citizenship with which it had originally intended to relate to its citizens and, instead, began cultivating Turkish nationalism. When the Kurdish nationalist aspirations erupted in the 1980s, the Turkish state failed to reach its Kurdish population within a politically liberal framework of civic citizenship.

At this point, the Welfare party was ready to fill in the vacuum created by the Turkish state and the "other" political parties. The party, which advocated an Islamic Union among all the Muslims of the world, advocated the same message to the Kurds. Unlike most other parties, the Welfare party

[31] Mesut Yeğen, "The Turkish State Discourse and the Exclusion of Kurdish Identity," in Sylvia Kedourie, ed., *Turkey: Identity, Democracy, Politics* (London: Frank Cass, 1996).

[32] Ibid., p. 219.

[33] Ibid., p. 221.

separated the issue of terrorism, which was instigated by the PKK uprising, from the Kurdish question and argued that the latter prepared the grounds for the former while the former made the solution to the latter more difficult. The Welfare party argued as follows:

> We know from history that our region of which Kurds are also part of has been administrated by large states and empires. Without doubt, Kurds are part of the Islamic geography and Islamic world of this region. Even though some of their leaders are inclined to European, American or other powers, the heart of the Kurdish people beat in the Islamic world. Consequently, no regional choice can be envisioned and have a chance for realization without taking into consideration the Islamic factor. We believe that legal equality and cooperation that will be established among us brothers will bring a satisfactory solution to the Kurdish problem. . . . The solution is not the establishment of new national states and carving new pieces, but rather uniting pieces, and moving towards a new whole which does not depend on racism.[34]

The party thus rejects the formation of a new Kurdish state, one of the worst fears of the Turkish nation-state, at the same time as it underplays Turkish nationalism and implicitly criticizes its policies as racist. Instead, Islamic brotherhood and historical religious links are underlined: "For centuries we have always been one and together, we have fought all our wars together as one heart and one body."[35] Similarly, formation of a separate state is vehemently criticized: "The West and all countries are removing the boundaries between themselves to become one state and society and the outside powers want to divide us, to exploit and victimize us." It is assumed that the West is one unified whole and the active enemy and separatism is a Western ploy.

The Kurdish policy of the Welfare party and the discourse of Islamic brotherhood, which downplayed belonging to the nation-state, paid off. The party became the strongest in the southeastern Kurdish region. In the 1994 local elections and the 1995 general elections, the Welfare party would get 27.3 percent and 27.2 percent of the total votes, respectively, in eighteen provinces where people whose mother tongues were Kurdish constituted more than 15 percent of the population. Its closest rival, the pro-Kurdish HADEP, would get only 19.5 percent of the votes in the 1995 general elections in which it participated.[36]

Yet this policy of advocating Islamic solidarity and underplaying Turkish nationalism, at least in the particular way it was done, provided not merely opportunities for strengthening the party but also undermining it. The Welfare party strategy was an intrinsic threat to the nation-state and a double-edged sword. On the one hand, the recognition of Kurdish ethnic identity by the party meant that Turkish nationalism was threatened. On the other hand, cultivation of religious ties with the Kurds threatened the secular ties

[34] Erbakan, *Refah Partisi* 4, p. 38.
[35] Ibid., p. 39.
[36] Kirişçi and Winrow, *The Kurdish Question*, 147.

of citizenship that the Kurds as much as any other ethnic group were to develop with the nation-state. In 1998, the party was closed for exploiting religion in politics and undermining secularism. Necmettin Erbakan was sentenced to a one-year prison sentence because of the way he advocated Islamic solidarity in a speech he made in 1994 in Bingöl, a province with a substantial Kurdish population. In that particular case, Erbakan claimed once again that there were only two parties in this country, the Just and the Vain. In his own words: "That which represents the Just represents the faith of my brothers from Bingöl. The infidel will make our laws.... For centuries the children of this land began school by pronouncing the name of God. You came and deposed the name of God. In its place, you put in 'I am a Turk, I am right.'[37] ... When you claim this, then the Muslim child with Kurdish origin has the right to say 'Well, you see, I am a Kurd and I am more right than you.' ... We will not be slaves to the Christians.... We shall establish the World Islamic Union."[38] This particular speech was found to be in violation of Article 312 of the Turkish Penal Code, which prohibited provoking people into hatred and enmity by promoting differences in class, race, religion, and region. Erbakan was found guilty of provoking people into enmity and hatred by exploiting religion. The Muslim population of the country was divided into believers who followed the Welfare Party and the nonbelievers who followed other parties. To the extent that the Kurds followed the Welfare party in Muslim solidarity, their ethnic identity, which threatened the conception of a homogenous state, could be recognized. Yet the nation-state was keen to set the boundaries that could be trespassed and where its conception of nationalism could be criticized.

Transgressing Secular Turkish Citizenship: The Welfare Party and the Head-Scarved Women

Islamist discourse aimed to appeal not merely to the Kurds, but also to the women who covered their heads as a dictate of Islam. The Islamists appealed to the Kurds in Islamic solidarity and in recognition of the Kurdish ethnic identity. Their appeal to women who covered their heads in observance of Islam was in recognition of their Islamic identity or in recognition of the Islamic law, deemed above the secular law of the Republic. Thus the secular law of the nation-state was trespassed in defense of religious law in pursuit of power that could be realized only within the nation-state. Transgressing boundaries was not an uncomplicated matter. Women aimed to talk across the boundaries of the secular nation-state as well as the boundaries of Islam. Both the party and the head-scarved constituents had to live with the

[37] The reference is to the pledge elementary school children have to repeat every morning and that aims to install Turkish nationalist values.

[38] *Milliyet*, July 6, 2000, p. 22.

"residue" of established borders as they engaged in a process of redefining boundaries and constructing new boundary markers.

Even though the Republican nation-state never passed a law that banned head covering for women, as it had done regarding the traditional fez for men, there was a dress code for civil servants (statute no. 2413) that required them to "dress like their partners in civilized nations of the world." Women, particularly those in developed urban centers, gradually adopted Western dress codes.

As Islam gained more economic and political power in the public realm, female students who were influenced by the Islamist call began coming to universities with their heads covered. Head scarves marked the boundaries of their newly acquired Islamist identity and heralded the fact that they were going to transgress the boundaries of nation-state secularism. Beginning in 1982, a series of bans on head covers was passed and repealed. The process involved not merely the council of higher education, but also the legislature, the president, and the judiciary. In 1984, the council of state rejected a court case that aimed to have the ban removed, and in 1989, the constitutional court ruled that the use of head covering in the universities was unconstitutional. The issue was taken even to the European Human Rights Commission when a university administration, obeying regulations, refused to prepare the diplomas of two graduating students who insisted that pictures showing them wearing head scarves be used in their diplomas. The commission ruled in favor of the university administration and the state.

The Welfare party advocated the rights of women to cover their heads in public institutions and universities. The party in its 1983 program underlined the importance of civic liberties, particularly that of liberty of conscience and religion, and criticized the principle of secularism, as understood by the state, to be an enemy of religion. The program defined secularism as a principle that would protect freedom of conscience and religion from any kind of intrusion.[39] In practice, the party heralded the rights of female students to cover their heads in public institutions, which was what the party understood from civil liberties and explicitly advocated thereafter.

The Welfare party argued that the believers were oppressed by the secular state when Muslim women were not allowed to cover their heads as Islam dictated. The party prepared a proposal to democratize the constitution, which basically entailed lifting the ban on head scarves.[40] To advocate their case, ironically, they referred to European examples and elaborated how the French, who referred to "laicism" in their constitution, expanded the meaning of the term to allow for religious freedoms and living according to one's religious dictates.[41] References to French laicism were ironic, because the

39 *Refah Partisi Programı*, p. 8.

40 Erbakan, *Refah Partisi* 4, p. 79.

41 Ibid., p. 80.

practice of laicism in France has meant the suppression of religious expression of Muslims, particularly the wearing of head scarves in French public schools. In 1989, when three Muslim girls attending public school north of Paris refused to take off their scarves in school, they were duly expelled. The French authorities argued that "the mission of the public schools was to neutralize religious difference."[42] Turkish laicism was similar to French laicism in both theory and practice. A deeper layer of irony lay in the need the Islamists felt when they tried to legitimize their case in the context of the secular nation-state and referred to the French and the Europeans, the infidels they tried to liberate themselves from and establish a union against.

Yet dictates of Islamic law were difficult to reconcile with the laws of the secular state without transgressing boundaries of the latter. In its verdict against head covering of students in public schools, the constitutional court defended the boundaries of the statist concept of secularism. The court argued that "in a laicist order, religion is prevented from politicization and becoming an administrative device, and kept in its real respectable place in people's consciences."[43] The boundaries of secularism were thus clearly delineated according to the courts or the state. Religion belonged to the private realm, the "respectable place in people's consciences." Similar to the argument of the French about the need "to neutralize religious difference" in public schools, the Turkish courts ruled against religious laws shaping public space.

The European Human Rights Commission supported the decision of the higher Turkish courts. The commission maintained the right of the secular state to restrict religious practice, consistent with the citizen's right to equal treatment and religious freedoms. This restriction would "allow students of different beliefs to coexist."[44] Particularly in countries where the majority of the population belonged to a particular religion, it was argued, exhibition of symbols of this religion could be a cause of pressure on those who did not practice this religion. The assumption in the commission's reasoning was once again that head scarves were symbols of Islamic belonging that had to be contained within the private realm.

According to the Welfare party, Islamic law was universal and dictated over the lives of the believers. Turkish state courts argued that Islamic laws defied and transgressed their secular universal laws. Civil liberties could be defended within the parameters of secular law. However, they had to be defined clearly. Enforcing a dictate of religion on secular public space was

[42] Quoted in Katherine Pratt Ewing, "Legislating Religious Freedom: Muslim Challenges to the Relationship between 'Church' and 'State' in Germany and France," *Daedalus* 129, no. 4 (Fall 2000): 41.

[43] "Yükseköğretim kurumlarında kılık kıyafet ile ilgili mevzuat ve hukuki değerlendirmeler" (Statutes and legal assessments regarding dress codes in higher educational institutions), pamphlet issued by the Council of Higher Education in 1998, p. 3.

[44] Ibid., pp. 7–8.

a transgression of secular boundaries. Perhaps most critically, head covers were not simple signs of being Muslim. They were boundary markers of not merely Islamic identity but Islamic law, which endorsed other injunctions. To the extent that they were dictates of Islamic law and that those who covered themselves claimed they wanted to obey Islamic law, the same law also stated that there be polygamy, unilateral divorce, and so on, dictates that were prohibited by the secular personal code of the state. Islam was a religion that was not easy to privatize, and that is what the Republican nation-state had aimed to do. In other words, it was difficult to disaggregate insistence on head covering from other dictates of Islam that aimed to organize private as well as public life. Wearing the head scarf was not like wearing a cross, which was not a dictate of religious law. Islam as a religion had its elaborate system of law that threatened to engulf the secular state unless the practice of those laws could be restricted to the private realm.

Many women were trapped in their allegiance to Islamic law and their allegiance to secular liberal norms. They wore their head scarves as boundary markers of their Islamic identity; however, implications of their head scarves were complicated. In a study I conducted on Welfare party Women's Commissions, many women who covered their heads wanted to practice Islamic law.[45] They covered their heads because they believed that Islamic law dictated they do so. However, they were also raised in a secular nation-state and confined by its laws. They took the civil liberties that the secular state guaranteed for granted. None would come out in public and claim that she would like to see an Islamic state. Yet neither would they come out in public, in defense of the basic secular legal framework to ensure the Republican state that their head covering was merely an act of personal devotion and that they would like to preserve the separation of state and religion. They wanted to construct their own Islamic community, with its political and public implications, at the same time as they wanted to preserve the liberties and freedoms that the secular nation-state guaranteed.

The solutions that Islamist women came up with reflected their secular backgrounds and Islamic aspirations. Some of these women wanted to practice Islamic law to the extent that it dictated head covering, but were reluctant to adopt its other dictates, such as polygamy and unilateral divorce. They had come to value their personal autonomy, which was guaranteed under the secular personal status code of the nation-state. These women argued that times had changed, and under the circumstances of the day, certain Islamic dictates could not be practiced. They thus relied on contextual and sociological explanations to define the boundaries of their new Islamic community.

Others chose to focus on the "essential Islam," as they defined it. They claimed that Islamic dictates such as polygamy would not be an issue if Islam was practiced as it should be. Islam dictated fairness. A good Muslim would

45 Yeşim Arat, *Political Islam in Turkey and Women's Organizations* (Istanbul: TESEV, 1999).

make sure to treat his wife fairly and would not remarry in case he was unfair to his first wife. Those who gave similar arguments also recognized the undesirability of polygamy and were in fact apologizing for bad Islamic practices with a reference to "real" Islam.

Some focused on the "essential contractual nature" of Islamic marital practices and argued that the condition of monogamy could be written into an Islamic marriage contract. Western notions of equality prescribed by secular law codes had infiltrated their moral frameworks. With different arguments, they tried to adopt head scarves selectively as boundary markers of Islamic identity and Islamic law. They thus hoped to have their new Islamic universe overlap with the boundaries of their secular nation-state.

The idiosyncratic Islamic constructions of belonging in the context of a secular nation-state are reflected in public opinion surveys as well. Obedience to Islamic law contradicts obedience to secular codes of the nation-state; yet those socialized within the secular context want to have both or rather to expand the parameters of the secular framework at the same time as they retain its features that allow for their autonomy. In a survey conducted in February 1999 with a representative sample of Turkish electorate, 21.2 percent responded positively to a question that asked whether they want to have a religious state based on the Shariat. Further probes showed how peculiar this desire was. Asked whether they thought that those guilty of adultery should be punished according to Quranic dictates, only 1.4 percent of the same group responded positively.[46]

Conclusion

The Islamists challenged the boundaries of the nation-state with their call for universal Islamic solidarity. Yet their call to reach beyond the territorial boundaries of the nation-state primarily aimed to appeal to their local constituency, within the boundaries of the nation-state, and to solve their specific problems. Thus, theirs was a construction of belonging that competed with that of the nation-state and that originated and aimed to succeed within the nation-state. The universal Islamist call was geared for political gains within the boundaries of the nation-state and was structured to succeed by using the political apparatus of the nation-state.

This Islamist challenge contained both opportunities for success as well as risks within the nation-state. The Welfare party, which manipulated this Islamist call, walked a tightrope. It could lure both the Kurds and the head-scarved women with the universalistic Islamic call to increase its electoral strength. Yet in both cases the party transgressed the boundaries within which the legal framework of the nation-state could accommodate it. The rhetoric of Islamic solidarity that surpassed ethnic boundaries strained the

[46] Ali Çarkoğlu and Binnaz Toprak, *Türkiye'de Din, Toplum ve Siyaset* (Istanbul: TESEV, 2000).

nationalist boundaries of the state. The rhetoric of head scarf as an Islamic dictate that needed to be recognized in the context of religious freedoms strained the secular boundaries of the state. The nation-state ultimately could not tolerate the competing construction of belonging that the Welfare party cultivated.

The constituents, at least among the head-scarved women who had to define themselves between these rival modes of belonging that the state and the Islamists offered, tried to pick and choose from the alternatives. Because they had to live with the "residue" of the "markers" of these two worlds, they imbued old markers with new meanings as they picked and chose. Thus the head scarf meant (even though this meaning was not recognized by the state) that the woman who wore it belonged to an Islamic community, but that she did not necessarily accept polygamy or unilateral divorce as the boundary markers of Islam. Within these competing constructions of belonging to a secular and an Islamic world, the woman with the head scarf selectively defined the boundary markers of her community.

The Islamist attempt to construct a community rival to that of the nation-state within the nation-state and by using the nation-state was marked by a tension that could not be accommodated by the nation-state. Yet the lure of a universal Islam cross-cutting boundaries of the nation-state challenged ethnic as opposed to civic understandings of citizenship. It exposed and perforated the boundaries of official secularism. Finally, it allowed a group of citizens to construct their own realms of belonging by picking and choosing the boundary markers of their own Islam, which simultaneously reflected the boundary markers of their secular nation-state.

PART VI

CONCLUSION

14

Conclusion

Béatrice Hibou

Over the past decade, forms of state power and the relations between the state and society have been apprehended in terms of both their complexity and their potential fluidity. The most recent studies establish a point of convergence, highlighting transformations in frontiers of power; the complexity of the state and the ambivalent nature of its specific manifestations; and the porosity and mobility of national, social, and political boundaries and social formations, whatever their origins. Likewise, these works underscore the plurality of identities and the fact that seemingly contradictory affiliations are not necessarily mutually exclusive. While the state-society opposition still structures prevailing modes of analysis in centers of power, and most notably in the heart of world financial institutions and the "international community," it is nonetheless recognized among scholars as being reductionist and hence of little utility in efforts to outline actual modalities of power. To reiterate Joel Migdal, "The state's being simultaneously a part of society and apart from society" (Introduction) is now a generally accepted axiom.

The introduction to this book and the chapters that follow all confirm this thought: The plurality of affiliations are not systematically opposed, since they intersect and articulate with one another, and the fluidity of socio-political frontiers makes questions about the centrality or marginality of the state futile, if not sterile. The chapters herein avoid this impasse, inquiring instead into the ways in which we can conceptualize and understand the multiple nature of the logics of power. These interrogations and demonstrations are, of course, not entirely novel, since much work has been completed on this topic with respect to specific themes (e.g., identities, citizenship, or modes of regulation) or specific geographical regions (e.g., Sub-Saharan Africa, North Africa, Asia, the European Union). The originality of the two-year collaborative effort published herein resides in the comparative perspective put

Translated by Janet Roitman, CNRS-MALD, Paris.

forth through a series of heterogeneous examples. These span from the eighteenth century to the present, from United States to Europe, making detours through the Middle East and Asia, from the biggest empires to the smallest states, from linguistic considerations to questions of religious identity and topics of citizenship, from territorial limits to social, political, and cultural boundaries. This volume does not seek to impose yet another complex and subtle analysis of one or another concrete situation. Instead, it invites the reader to engage in a more global reflection on state practices, their interactions with other social logics, and, in the end, the frontiers of power. The first lesson we can draw from this reflection is the necessity to relativize the supposed exceptional nature, or at least the novelty, of our era. The various examples presented herein tend, indeed, to point out the banal quality of the alleged singularity of present-day globalization. The historical cases (Kasaba and Stein on the Ottoman Empire, Kemp on Israel, Basson on the United States, Lawson on Canada, and Diamant on China) demonstrate the multiplicity and ambivalence of state practices, the complexity of power relations, and the ambiguity inherent in articulations between various social groups or modes of affiliation. In that sense, they situate the question of continuity and rupture for the contemporary cases (Burma by Callahan, the Kurdish movement by Watts, Israel by Woods, Europe by Conant, and Turkey by Arat).

A comparative reading of these different chapters and the introductory argument inspire three considerations – among many other possible ones – that all turn around the problem of conceptualizing the exercise of power in its multiple modalities. It goes without saying that the elaboration of this problem forces me to iron out the different approaches, modes of understanding, and interpretations put forth by the contributing authors. But it is also obvious that, over the tortuous path through time, field of application, and space, a certain convergence in manners of apprehending the frontiers of power emerges.

First, all the preceding chapters underscore that the fluidity of the frontiers of power, the plurality of its modes of exercise, as well as the complexity of the state and the ambivalence of its manifestations should not be construed as exceptions or specificities born of contemporary "globalization." To the contrary, these qualities characterize all human organizations and institutions. The preeminence of analyses that account for this complexity and that reject dualist and globalizing explanations is, perhaps, what is in fact new about the contemporary period. Thus all the chapters claim or show that it is not possible to conceptualize the state as a coherent unit, which is a fiction today as much as it was in the past. The state apparatus is fragmented and multiple (Migdal and Lawson)[1] and there are wide gaps between

[1] Atul Kohli, Joel Migdal, and Vivienne Shue, *State Power and Social Forces: Domination and Transformation in the Third World* (Cambridge: Cambridge University Press, 1994).

laws, discourse, intentions, and concrete practices (Diamant, Conant, and Arat). Moreover, and perhaps more important, empirical observations of the exercise of power suggest the impossibility of locating and clearly identifying what the state is (Kasaba, Stein, Watts).

These factors do not necessitate more complex analyses of the state and power simply in response to the so-called increased complexity of present-day situations. Rather, such complex approaches are the only ones that allow us to account for the multiplicity of logics that are not necessarily homogenous – or even contradictory – at the heart of power itself. State practices are by definition ambivalent; their paradoxical nature is often denoted according to a presupposition of unity and coherence. Kemp, Callahan, and Lawson show how discourses and nationalist behavior (whether Israeli or Burmese today, or Canadian during the last century) result in both the inclusion and exclusion of various populations. Integration of these populations takes place through concomitant transformations in citizenship, on the one hand, and practices of control and surveillance, on the other. However, at the same time, exclusion takes place through the construction of a specific category: the "dangerous population." The logics of differentiation and assimilation are thus concomitant and not opposed or mutually exclusive.

The recent resurgence in social science literature of the subject of the plurality of referents and frontiers of power is perhaps only a reflection of a greater sensitivity to the multiple and ambivalent nature of state interventions and the logics of state. To take up the example reviewed by Kasaba, policies for the sedentarization of populations in the Ottoman Empire were not defined by a precise and clear boundary between nomads and sedentary peoples, and such policies did not necessarily seek to move that line of distinction. The modalities for the exercise of Ottoman power were fluid and indecisive, founded simultaneously on movement and stability, repression and co-optation, intimidation and negotiation, control and accommodation. They were reflections, most notably, of the fact that interactions – between nomads and sedentary people, between state power and local communities – were much more imprecise and ambiguous than current vocabulary and representations suggest. All the chapters in this volume indicate, more or less explicitly, the impossibility of conceptualizing state practices and modalities for the exercise of state power in terms of coherence. Referring to the example of "mixed blood" populations in the United States, Basson depicts the contradictions inherent in public interventions that aimed to define citizenship according to race. Kasaba emphasizes the importance of contingent negotiations and, in consequence, the coexistence of multiple logics that are not necessarily homogeneous with regard to policies for territorial control. And again, referring to the Ottoman Empire, Stein shows how multiple identities, which did not always have nationalist connotations, interacted without necessarily following a particular line of conduct. The complexity and incoherence of state practices, the state's limitless interactions with diverse actors of social life, and the contradictions and conflicts inherent in the multiplicity of modalities for the exercise of state power all demonstrate the fundamentally incomplete nature of state policy and, more generally, state interventions. All the contributors to this volume stress the point that absolute mastery of state policy is impossible and that globalizing or totalizing projects are utopian. Incompleteness and ambivalence are no doubt the master words of these chapters.[2]

The rich and complementary analyses put forth through these diverse examples point out, once again, the pertinence of Michel Foucault's work on the diffuse nature of power, the impossibility of apprehending power other than by observation of its effects and the manners by which its exigencies are assumed and represented. "Power is not an institution, and not a structure; neither is it a certain strength we are endowed with; it is the name that one attributes to a complex strategical situation in a particular society."[3] In that sense, not only are modalities for the exercise of power multiple and continually mutating, but power also does not have a totalizing capacity or a specific coherence. This is as true today as it was in the past. This intellectual tradition, which rejects all substantialist or normative visions of the state, can be found in certain works by Max Weber, who underscored, for example, the "inexhaustible limitlessness of the sensible and phenomenal world" and studied nonbureaucratic forms of state.[4] This tradition invokes Foucault (and especially his notion of power and related concepts, such as governmentality), as well as de Certeau and Paul Veyne. The latter are noted for their analyses of practices (or, in other words, "what people really do") and their respective methods.[5] For Veyne, the latter involves "[d]escribing in a positive manner and presupposing nothing else; that is, not presupposing the existence of a target or an object, a material cause, a type of conduct. Judging people by their acts and eliminating the eternal ghosts which are brought forth by language. Practice is not a mysterious moment, a basement of history, a hidden motor: it is what people do. If it is in some sense 'hidden,' and if we can provisionally call it 'the hidden part of the iceberg,' this is simply because it shares the destiny of the quasi-totality of behavior and universal history: we are often conscious of it, but we do not have a concept

[2] Bruno Jobert, "De la nécessaire incohérence de l'action étatique," in Bruno Théret, ed., *L'état, la finance et le social: Souveraineté et construction européenne* (Paris: La Découverte, 1995), pp. 223–37.

[3] Michel Foucault, *Histoire de la sexualité*, vol. 1: *La volonté de savoir* (Paris: Gallimard, 1976), in English, *The History of Sexuality*, vol. 1: *An Introduction* (New York: Vintage, 1990), p. 93.

[4] Max Weber, *Essai sur le sens de la "neutralité axiologique" dans les sciences sociologiques et économiques*, in Max Weber, *Essais sur la théorie de la science* (1917; Paris: Press Pocket, Plon, 1992), translation.

[5] Michel de Certeau, *L'invention du quotidien*, vol. 1: *Arts de faire* (Paris: Gallimard, Collection "Folio essais," 1980).

of it."[6] This approach puts the discrepancies between practices and discourse (or "image," in the words of Joel Migdal in the Introduction to this book), practices and conceptualization (or mental maps) at the heart of analysis, delineating, then, *bricolages* (to take up de Certeau's term). To be sure, state power appears, through this lens, confused, adulterated, or incoherent (as we see below), but this is the only way to enter into the details of its usages, its conduct, its manners of being, and its manners of understanding and acting in social and political spheres.

Corresponding, in some ways, to the intellectual tradition just described, the works of Lonsdale and Berman on colonial Kenya are a particularly useful reference for the perspectives put forth in the present book. By opposing state building and state formation, Lonsdale and Berman put forth a conceptual framework for understanding the complexities, incoherence, and fluidity demonstrated by the chapters under discussion. They "introduce a key distinction between 'state-building,' as a conscious effort at creating an apparatus of control, and 'state-formation,' as an historical process whose outcome is a largely unconscious and contradictory process of conflicts, negotiations, and compromises between diverse groups whose self-serving actions and trade-offs constitute the 'vulgarisation' of power."[7] In other words, state power is not constructed and conceived in a deliberate, coherent, and homogeneous manner. It is the fruit of an experience, anchored in history and made of tensions and compromises between different actors and social groups. This experience, which takes place unconsciously and heterogeneously, is what forms the state.

Berman and Lonsdale develop their argument through the study of the birth of the colonial administration in Kenya, from 1895 to 1905.

> State-building could not be a wholly destructive process. The British conquerors had to create a new high politics, a hierarchy of self interest, out of existing networks of authority. African leaders may have been forced to carry the unprecedented burdens, but they had also to be allowed new means to pursue old interests. Without obedient

[6] Paul Veyne, "Foucault révolutionne l'histoire," in Paul Veyne, *Comment on écrit l'histoire* (Paris: Editions du Seuil, 1978), p. 211, author's translation.

[7] Bruce Berman and John Lonsdale, *Unhappy Valley* (London: Longman, 1992), vol. 1, p. 5. In France, this distinction has been largely used by scholars affiliated to the research center CERI (Centre d'Etudes et de Recherches Internationales), Paris: for an analysis and a systematic problematization, see Jean-François Bayart, "A propos de *Unhappy Valley*," *Revue Française de Sciences Politiques* 44, no. 1 (February 1994): 136–39, and Jean-François Bayart, "L'historicité de l'état importé," in Jean-François Bayart, ed., *La greffe de l'état* (Paris: Karthala, 1996), pp. 11–39. For the use of this distinction in a concrete situation, see Béatrice Hibou, *L'Afrique est-elle protectionniste? Les chemins buissonniers de la libéralisation extérieure* (Paris: Karthala, 1996), for trade policy in African countries; see Yves Chevrier, "L'empire distendu: Esquisse du politique en Chine des Qing à Deng Xiaoping," in Bayart, ed., *La greffe de l'état*, pp. 265–395, for reforms in China; and see Romain Bertrand, "La tradition parfaite: Formation de l'état et imaginaire national en Insulinde coloniale," Ph.D. thesis, Institut d'Etudes Politiques de Paris, 2000, for nationalism in Indonesia.

followers they were useless to their new rulers as to their old communities. And it was not only African notables who found much that was familiar in the unknown. For the embryo state *was not only built*, as a deliberate means to contain and direct power for the benefit of few. It was also *formed out* of anonymous actions of many. In evading servitudes ancient and modern, the weaker members of African society used novel forms of association to regain old personal freedom. However unwillingly, the state protected these subversive young ways of common life and labour as much as it fostered fresh privilege. **State-formation (the vulgarisation of power), and state-building (its cultivation), were contradictory processes that complemented each other.**[8]

The theoretical references reviewed above shed a particular light on the texts assembled herein. As illustrated by Diamant on weddings in China, Woods on ultra-Orthodox Jewry in Israel, or Arat on Islamists in Turkey, the question is less one of determining how states react to and resist logics pursued by social forces outside the state. It is less a matter of understanding how the norms and the metaphorical as well as literal borders of the state are modified – or eliminated – through the effects of competition and conflict with other social norms. Rather, it is a matter of revealing or exposing, to take up a somewhat Foucauldian vocabulary, the multiple points of the exercise of power. Or to use terms closer to Lonsdale and Berman, this involves taking into account processes of the formation of referents and norms associated with the state. This process of state formation can be contrasted to processes of state construction, which nonetheless sustain and complete the former.

It seems clear that, for social science researchers of diverse intellectual traditions, power cannot be described as a substance nor defined in a clear, stable, and definitive manner; the exercise of power is everything but coherent, univocal, and predictable. But this conclusion forces us to note the extent to which functionalist and substantialist analyses prevail in contemporary spheres of power, and especially the international community. This is most manifest in the use of certain – often Manichean and simplistic – concepts, such as the now famous "governance," be it "good" or unqualified. It is indeed striking that, despite the plethora of refined analyses of state power produced in academe, international financial institutions, high-level administrators, and national leaders continue to approach the state in terms of its administrative apparatus and deliberate political programs. They are, in this sense, both victims of voluntarist illusions and blind to the plurality of modes of government and regulatory figures.

The second lesson to be drawn from this book is the necessity to go beyond analyses that simply note oppositions and conflicts, approaches that seek to identify the norm, the rule, or the law that predominates or that captures people's allegiances. In other words, this book underscores the need to go beyond questions formulated in terms of choices among competing

[8] Berman and Lonsdale, *Unhappy Valley*, p. 15, emphasis in original, boldface added.

norms, rules, and referents. Once having conceptualized the complexity of the exercise of power and the multiplicity of affiliations mentioned above, it is evident that one must also try to conceptualize the lack of choice, the management of multiplicity and complexity, and the absence of coherence rather than attempting, in a functionalist manner, to define a nonexistent coherence or choice.

Stein demonstrates this most clearly in her analysis of Sephardic Jews in the Ottoman Empire. At the turn of the century, Judaism was not put forth as a form of nationalism; the disposition associated with "being Jewish" was articulated with other allegiances (to the Ottoman Empire, to Europe, to other Ottoman millets, to "the modern"). And this did not imply a situation of choice, hierarchy, priority, or even contradiction. This manner of being "multivectored," this "multichromatic notion of community," "the slipperiness of the notion of belonging," to reiterate Stein, are in no way specific to the period or the Empire under study. For instance, Jean-François Bayart has shown that, in spite of "fictions of identity,"[9] globalization should not be apprehended as a struggle between western norms and local norms, between cultural identity and political identity, or between religious logics and state logics. Instead, it should be viewed as the articulation between different forms of affiliation and a plurality of referents and strategies, which are identity-related but also political. Likewise, numerous studies of the relationship between religion and politics have underscored the multiplicity and the intertwining of forms of legitimacy and modes of political historicity that are often assumed to be antithetical.[10] Woods demonstrates the inevitable coexistence in Israel, and even more, the complementary nature of secular and religious actors, logics, and aims. In her chapter and especially in her work on female Islamic organizations,[11] Arat suggests – in consonance with other studies of this question[12] – that

[9] Jean-François Bayart, *L'illusion identitaire* (Paris: Fayard, 1996), translated as *Fictions of Identity* (London and New York: Hurst and Columbia University Press, 2003).

[10] On Turkey, see Niyazi Berkes, *The Development of Secularism in Turkey* (London: Hurst, 1964); Nikki Keddie, ed., *Scholars, Saints and Sufis: Muslim Religious Institutions in the Middle East since 1500* (Los Angeles: University of California Press, 1972); Paul Dumont, "L'Islam en Turquie, facteur de renouveau?," *Les Temps Modernes* 456–57 (July–August 1984): 352–76; Robert Mantran, ed., *Histoire de l'Empire ottoman* (Paris: Fayard, 1989). On North Africa, see Mohamed-Hedi Cherif, *Pouvoir et société dans la Tunisie de H'usayn Bin 'Ali (1705–1740)*, 2 vols. (Tunis: Publications de l'Université de Tunis, 1986); Taoufik Bachrouch, *Le saint et le prince en Tunisie* (Tunis: Faculté des Sciences Humaines et Sociales de Tunis I, 1989); Abdellah Hammoudi, *Master and Disciple: The Cultural Foundations of Moroccan Authoritarianism* (Chicago: University of Chicago Press, 1997); Jocelyne Dakhlia, *Le divan de rois: Le politique et le religieux dans l'islam* (Paris: Aubier, 1998); Mohamed Tozy, *Monarchie et islam politique au Maroc* (Paris: Presses de Sciences, 1999).

[11] Yesim Arat, *Political Islam in Turkey and Women's Organizations* (Istanbul: TESEV, 1999).

[12] On Iran, see Fariba Adelkhah, *La révolution sous le voile* (Paris: Karthala, 1991); on Turkey, see Nilufer Goele, *Musulmanes et modernes* (Paris: La Découverte, 1993), and Jenny White,

the use of the veil cannot be analyzed as a challenge to the rules of the Republic or as a sign of the supremacy of allegiances to Islam over the secular state. It represents, rather, the articulation, in distinct and yet also concomitant times and spaces, of multiple allegiances, such as the – not necessarily incoherent or conflict-ridden – possibility of playing off of different identities, using different norms and rules, including those that are not convergent.

Due to a particular structure of power and the visibility of apparent contradictions at the heart of power, research on North African countries has illustrated the "cacophony" of power as well as its "useful" contradictions.[13] The latter coexist in spite of their incompatibility, as is made evident in the case of two principles of government – legality and allegiance – in Morocco.[14] These studies show with respect to the control of resources or the organization of religious life, for example, how contradictory political policies are dressed in the same forms of validity and significance. Furthermore, the sense of incoherence is also sometimes part of the political imaginary. The North African situation is, in my opinion, instructive with respect to other regions; it merits attention insofar as it proposes a particular approach: that is, not attempting to establish, at all costs, the coherence of state interventions, representations, and prevailing norms. Contrary to the view put forth by James Scott, the state does not seek, or at least does not only seek, to impose uniformity, to simplify, to standardize, and to render legible.[15] The state's vision can be incoherent and might not seek consensus with respect to discourse and practices. As Janet Roitman has shown with regard to the emergence of new figures of regulatory authority in the Chad Basin,[16] it is less useful to think in terms of oppositions and the substitution of one register by another

Money Makes Us Relatives: Women's Labor in Urban Turkey (Austin: University of Texas Press, 1994); on France, see Chalha Chafiq et Farad Khosrokhavar, *Femmes sous le voile: Face à la loi islamique* (Paris: Les Editions de Félin, 1995).

13 Dakhlia, *Le divan des rois*.

14 Béatrice Hibou, "Les enjeux de l'ouverture au Maroc: Dissidence économique et contrôle politique," *Les Études du CERI*, no. 15 (April 1996); Tozy, *Monarchie et islam politique au Maroc*.

15 James Scott, *Seeing like a State: How Certain Schemes to Improve Human Condition Have Failed* (New Haven, Conn.: Yale University Press, 1998).

16 Janet Roitman, "Le pouvoir n'est pas souverain: Nouvelles autorités régulatrices et transformations des États dans le Bassin du Lac Tchad," in Béatrice Hibou, ed., *La privatisation des états* (Paris: Karthala, 1999), pp. 163–96, translated as "Power Is Not Sovereign: New Figures of Regulatory Authority in the Chad Basin," in Béatrice Hibou, ed., *Privatizing the State* (London and New York: Hurst and Columbia University Press, 2003), and Janet Roitman, "New Sovereigns? Regulatory Authority in the Chad Basin," in Thomas M. Callaghy, Ronald Kassimir, and Robert Latham, eds., *Intervention and Transnationalism in Africa: Global-Local Networks of Power* (Cambridge: Cambridge University Press, 2001).

than to apprehend the logics that emerge from the compatibility inherent in different registers, between different boundaries, and between different forms of affiliation. The multiplicity and heterogeneity of the genealogies of factors that come into relationship render such a choice between registers impossible and exclude all unique forms.[17]

A very telling contemporary example of this is the ongoing formation of the European Union. In her chapter on legislation regarding migration and employment in the civil service, Conant demonstrates this point, indicating the coexistence of both national and European norms and referents. But we must go farther in our analysis, stepping beyond the terms established by ideas of resistance by member states (or their will to preserve national distinctions), the gap between European laws and official practices, and struggle over the process of the reconstruction of socio-political boundaries and affiliations. Recent studies of the European Union that are founded on in-depth and detailed empirical research show, to the contrary, that the complexity of the European dynamic, which both affirms and undermines individual states, has increased the margins of maneuver and the field of choice, thus multiplying allegiances. Research completed on certain regions of Europe,[18] on policy related to fishing rights,[19] on citizenship,[20] on multiple forms of

[17] For a similar analysis in the economic domain, see Jean-Yves Grenier, *L'économie d'ancien régime* (Paris: Albin Michel, 1996), on the French Ancient Regime. See also the works on the diversity of capitalism and importance of mixed forms in western Europe, with the French School of "Régulation." Michel Aglietta, *Régulation et crises du capitalisme* (Paris: Calmann-Levy, 1976); Robert Boyer, ed., *Capitalisme fin de siècle* (Paris: Presses Universitaires de France, 1986); Jacques Mistral, "Régime international et trajectoires nationales," in Boyer, ed., *Capitalisme fin de siècle*; Bruno Théret, *Régimes économiques de l'ordre politique: Esquisse d'une théorie régulationniste des limites de l'état* (Paris: Presses Universitaires de France, 1992), and "To Be or to Have: On the Problem of the Interaction between State and Economy and Its Solidarist Mode of Regulation," *Economy and Society* 23, no. 1 (1994). And in postsocialist countries, see Jean-Louis Rocca, "L'entreprise, l'entrepreneur et le cadre: Une approche de l'économie chinoise," *Les Études du CERI*, no. 14 (April 1996); David Stark and Laszlo Bruszt, *Postsocialist Pathways: Transforming Politics and Property in East Central Europe* (Cambridge: Cambridge University Press, 1998); and Antoine Kernen, *Le processus de privatisations à Shenyang, Chine Populaire* (Paris: Karthala, 2003).

[18] Andy Smith, *L'Europe politique au miroir du local: Les fonds structurels et les zones rurales en France, en Espagne et au Royaume-Uni* (Paris: L'Harmattan, 1995); Patrick Le Galès and Christian Lequesne, eds., *Le Paradoxe des régions en Europe* (Paris: La Découverte, 1997).

[19] Christian Lequesne, *L'Europe bleue: A quoi sert une politique communautaire de la pêche?* (Paris: Presses de Sciences, 2001).

[20] Etienne Balibar, "Une citoyenneté européenne est-elle possible?," in Bruno Théret, ed., *L'état, la finance et le social*, pp. 534–52; Jurgen Habermas, "The European Nation-State: On the Past and Future of Sovereignty and Citizenship," *Public Culture* 10, no. 2 (1998): 397–416; Patrick Weil and Robert Hansen, eds., *Nationalité et citoyenneté en Europe* (Paris: La Découverte, 1999); Jean-Marc Ferry, *La question de l'état européen* (Paris: Gallimard. NRF Essais, 2000).

capitalism,[21] on the enlargment of the Union,[22] or on the judicialization of politics[23] suggests that, in these contemporary processes, there is no question of the reconstruction of allegiances and socio-political boundaries in the heart of Europe. To the contrary, we are witnessing a new episode in the phenomenon of managing the multiple. That is, the game taken up by Europeans is not a zero-sum game.[24] These studies demonstrate quite clearly that European actors now have an increasing number of choices not so much due to the potential for subverting national laws, but because of the existence of different scales of intervention, national innovations, and plural allegiances, all of which are now more numerous, more open, and more easily accessed. European construction can thus not be analyzed in terms of fetters or even constraints. It is, above all, a matter of a process of translation, invention, interpretations, and comings and goings, as well as the pluralization of regulatory bodies and political, social, and identity-related referents. The European Union is history in the making and not that of national resistances and the reformulation of affiliations and boundaries according to a new European paradigm. This is also true for national borders. The ongoing debate over the physical limits of Europe (with the respective candidacies of Turkey and the Balkan states) underlines the impossibility of choosing between different referents in order to determine the seemingly incontrovertible factor of physical geography.

Apprehending and conceptualizing incoherence, multiplicity, and heterogeneity relativizes the power of analyses based on oppositions, dichotomies, and competition. This is not to say that such situations do not exist; we would not want to fall into the trap of a unitary explanation that refers to the principle of incoherence as an overriding modality. We must remember, as Migdal reminds us in the introduction to this book, that antagonistic situations, negotiations, and reconfigurations brought on by frontal or indirect confrontations have a certain continuity. Empirical studies have a tendency to explain given situations rather than to reveal the historical processes that give rise to such situations. Having said that, I would like to point out, following the contributions of Kasaba, Kemp, and Arat, another tendency that

[21] Michel Albert, *Capitalisme contre capitalisme* (Paris: Le Seuil, 1991); Théret, *Régimes économiques de l'ordre politique*; Robert Salais and Michael Storper, *Les mondes de production* (Paris: Editions de l'Ecole des Hautes Etudes en Sciences Sociales, 1993); Colin Crouch and Wolfgang Streeck, eds., *Les capitalismes en Europe* (Paris: La Découverte, 1996); J. Rogers Hollingsworth and Robert Boyer, eds., *Contemporary Capitalism: The Embeddedness of Institutions* (Cambridge: Cambridge University Press, 1997); David Coates, "Models of Capitalism in the New World Order," *Political Studies* 47 (1999): 643–60.

[22] François Bafoil and Béatrice Hibou, "Les périphéries de l'Union européenne," *Les Études du CERI*, forthcoming (December 2003).

[23] Renaud Dehousse, "L'Europe par le droit," *Critique internationale* 2 (January 1999): 133–50.

[24] Christian Lequesne , "Capteurs de quotas: La pêche européenne entre territoires et marché," *Critique internationale* 2 (January 1999): 121–32.

seems to be quite widespread in social science research: the overdetermination of oppositional logics, the construction of false dichotomies, and the assumption of situations of competition. Dichotomous thinking is perpetuated by a certain number of confusions and comparisons that are worth noting, especially since, as I indicated above, they help us better to decipher their power within the international community. Several mechanisms at work are worth presenting.

1. *Confusion between images and practices, as suggested by Migdal in his introduction.*[25]
2. *Confusion between discourses and practices, which is a related but distinct problem.* For instance, analyses of Islamist parties suggest that opposition and confrontation between religious referents and state-based referents are exacerbated by accounts of the rhetoric and discourses of such political parties (as opposed to the political practices) that are, in themselves, dualist.[26] In his chapter, Diamant shows that even in a "strong" state, such as China, one cannot content oneself with looking at state intentions and discourses; redrawing political boundaries is an unreachable goal.
3. *Abusive comparisons, such as the assimilation of respect for religious belief with cultural – and hence political – identity, which gives rise to the thesis of a "clash of civilizations."*[27] If, to the contrary, we attend to the subtlety of relations between different factors and domains (e.g., between a specific language or culture and nationalism, or between cultural identity and political identity), analyses in terms of oppositions, "shocks," and contradictions appear simplistic and, worse, instrumentalist.[28]
4. *Imprecise vocabulary and use of concepts.* By paying attention to the genesis and the historical signification of any particular notion, we can see that certain current oppositions are mere constructions. In this volume, Stein illustrates this point with reference to notions of right or belonging, showing that these notions date back to the Tanzimat period and have become an anachronism through analysis of a specific

[25] Jean-Pierre Olivier de Sardan, "A propos de la privatisation des états," *Revue Tiers Monde* 41, no. 61 (January–March 2000): 217–21; Joel Migdal, *State in Society: Studying How States and Societies Transform and Constitute One Another* (Cambridge: Cambridge University Press, 2001).

[26] Jean-François Bayart, "Republican Trajectories in Iran and Turkey: A Tocquevillian Reading," in Ghassan Salamé, ed., *Democracy without Democrats? The Renewal of Politics in the Muslim World* (London: I. B. Tauris, 1994), pp. 282–99; Fariba Adelkhah, *Étre moderne en Iran* (Paris: Karthala, Collection "Recherches Internationales," 1998), translated as *Being Modern in Iran* (New York: Columbia University Press, 2000); Tozy, *Monarchie et islam politique au Maroc.*

[27] Samuel Huntington, *The Clash of Civilisations* (New York: Simon and Schuster, 1992).

[28] Jean-François Bayart, *Fictions of Identity*; Stein, Chapter 3.

language (Ladino by Sephardic Jews) as an indicator of belonging. Kasaba shows that the opposition often assumed between nomads and sedentary peoples obscures the understanding of the politics of sedentarization carried out under the Ottoman Empire. And, in my own previous research, I attempt to show how analyses of state failure or state weakness are developed on the basis of a very particular and circumstantial concept of the state.[29] The latter is the so-called Weberian state, which is characterized by a strong and highly structured administrative apparatus; specific institutions, such as the law (symbol par excellence of state authority); continuous, bureaucratic, and homogeneous interventions in space; and so on. There are, as is now known, myriad examples demonstrating that univocal notions are often much more contingent than current usage implies. This applies to a wide variety of concepts, such as the peasantry,[30] the rule of law,[31] civil society,[32] participation,[33] efficiency,[34] and "good" or "bad" policy.[35] Moreover, authors such as Bayart have argued that hypotheses about the absence or importation of states in Africa rest on a very restricted definition of the state (the European state of the nineteenth century), which prevents us from apprehending the originality and

29 Béatrice Hibou, "Retrait ou redéploiement de l'état?," *Critique internationale*, no. 1 (1998): 151–68, and *La privatisation de états* (Paris: Karthala, collection "Recherches Internationales," 1999), translated as *Privatizing the State* (London and New York: Hurst and Columbia University Press, 2003).

30 M. Lahmar, *Du mouton à l'olivier: Essai sur les mutations de la vie rurale maghrébine* (Tunis: Cérès Editions, 1994).

31 John Ohnesorge, "The Rule of Law, Economic Development, and the Developmental States of Northeast Asia," in Christoph Antons, ed., *Law and Development in East and South East Asia* (Richmond: Curzon Press, 2002).

32 On the history of the concept and the process of oversimplification, see Sunil Kilnani, "La 'société civile,' une résurgence," *Critique internationale* 10 (January 2001): 38–50.

33 Lloyd M. Sachikonye, "From 'Equity' and 'Participation' to Structural Adjustment: State and Social Forces in Zimbabwe," in David B. Moore and Gerald J. Schmitz, eds., *Debating Development Discourse: Institutional and Popular Perspectives*, 178–200 (New York: St. Martin's Press and London: Macmillan, 1995).

34 Igor Kopytoff, "The Internal African Frontier: The Making of African Political Culture," in Igor Kopytoff, ed., *The African Frontier: The Reproduction of Traditional African Societies* (Bloomington and Indianapolis: Indiana University Press, 1987); Jane I. Guyer, "Wealth in People and Self-Realization in Equatorial Africa," *Man* 28, no. 2 (1993): 243–65; Sarah Berry, *No Condition Is Permanent: The Social Dynamics of Agrarian Change in Sub-Saharan Africa* (Madison: University of Wisconsin Press, 1993); Fillip de Boeck, "Domesticating Diamonds and Dollars: Identity, Expenditure and Sharing in Southwestern Zaïre," in Birgit Meyer and Peter Geschiere, eds., *Globalisation and Communal Identities* (Oxford: Blackwell, 1999).

35 James Ferguson, "From African Socialism to Scientific Capitalism: Reflections on the Legitimation Crisis in IMF-ruled Africa," in Moore and Schmitz, eds., *Debating Development Discourse*, pp. 129–48.

the historicity of state forms (which he develops with reference to the metaphor of the rhizome).[36]

5. *An ahistorical view, which, as we noted above, involves amnesia with respect to historical rootedness, often giving rise to false dichotomies.* Retracing the genesis of forces that seem, at any given moment, contradictory often sheds light on a common history that unites them. This is most forcefully elucidated by Stein and Arat with regard to Islam in Turkey. In spite of its rhetoric, the Ottoman Empire never managed political life according to the rules of Islam, just as the Turkish Republic was not constructed out of the negation of Islam.[37] Over the centuries, relations between two disparate sources of legitimacy and two referents were complex, and so it is impossible today to oppose Islamic parties and the secular state. In an entirely different context, Roitman argues that while new figures of regulation in the Chad Basin – or the "douaniers-combattants," who are essentially paid, underpaid, and unemployed military personnel who have entered into the business of the customs service in Chad and Cameroon – seem to defy the state and even eclipse its official power, they in fact share a common history and even common epistemological grounds with state power.[38] These new figures of authority are self-proclaimed customs officials and exercise such authority, in the form of systematic extraction, on local populations. However, they are part and parcel of the state apparatus, not only because they are, or once were, military personnel, but also because their modes of conceptualizing power relations are consonant with and do not confound forms of state power.
6. *Functionalist reasoning, which occludes certain modes of the exercise of power and, while distinct from state power, is part and parcel of one and the same political economy, the same imaginary, and the same political or economic subjectivity.* The example of smugglers presented by Migdal in the Introduction is very telling in this regard. Doubtless, smugglers can be presented as actors who violate the law and thus articulate or endorse norms and referents that are distinct from those associated with the state. However, they might simply express another manner of exercising power. This is suggested by Clancy-Smith in her study of smugglers and pirates in nineteenth-century

[36] Jean-François Bayart, *L'état en Afrique: La politique du ventre* (Paris: Fayard, 1989), translated as *The State in Africa: The Politics of Belly* (London: Longman, 1993); see also Hibou, *Privatizing the State*. On the thesis of "importation of the state," see Bertrand Badie, *L'état importé: Essai sur l'occidentalisation de l'ordre politique* (Paris: Fayard, 1992).

[37] See also note 10.

[38] Janet Roitman, "The Garrison-Entrepôt," *Cahiers d'Études Africaines* 150–152, XXXVIII-2-4 (1998): 297–329, and *Fiscal Disobedience: Governing Citizens in Central Africa*, forthcoming (Princeton University Press).

North Africa.[39] Such activities were not necessarily competing with the state; they were, instead, complementary to regular or official commerce. This scenario is confirmed in contemporary cases by both Janet Roitman and myself:[40] Smuggling and fraud in Africa is another way of managing "extraversion."[41] Actors who seem to make and impose their own laws, on the one hand, and those who subvert them, on the other, share the same conception of power and access to economic resources. Evidently, certain aspects of state authority are diminished by these alternative forms of power: for example, in its control and management of production or the control of customs receipts and financial resources. But state power is also strengthened or reinforced by these alternatives, as new sites of accumulation are generated through which rents are derived and social mobility is secured for marginal populations. Given these circumstances, one cannot conclude that smugglers and those engaged in fraud oppose the state and that their rules simply compete with those of the state.

These precautions are what make the difference between situations where oppositions really do exist and situations where negotiations, accommodations (to use Kasaba's expression), and cohabitation prevail. Such specifications in our conceptual apparatus should serve to weaken, most notably, analyses structured by the terms of resistance and conflict, such as those put forth by authors such as Gören Hyden or even James Scott. As Peter Geschiere has aptly demonstrated,[42] James Scott's *Seeing like a State* is flawed by a monolithic vision of the state, the failure to take into account its incoherence and oppositions between state and communities or between state uniformity and local diversity. This causes him to neglect the diversity and complexity of the articulation between state formation and the crystallization of local communities and to misunderstand the concomitant processes

[39] Julia Clancy-Smith, "The Maghrib and the Mediterranean World in the Nineteenth Century: Illicit Exchanges, Migrants and Social Marginals," in Michel Le Gall and K. Perkins, eds., *The Maghrib in Question: Essays in History and Historiography* (Austin: University of Texas Press, 1997).

[40] Janet Roitman, "Objects of the Economy and the Language of Politics in Northern Cameroon," Ph.D. dissertation, University of Pennsylvania, 1996; Hibou, *L'Afrique est-elle protectionniste?*

[41] For Jean-François Bayart, strategies of extraversion "compensate for difficulties in the autonomization of their power and in intensifying the exploitation of their dependants by deliberate recourse to the strategies of extraversion, mobilizing resources derived from their (possibly unequal) relationship with external environment" in order to turn them into "a major resource in the process of political centralization and economic accumulation." Bayart, *The State in Africa*, pp. 21–24, and "Africa in the World: A History of Extraversion," *African Affairs* 99 (2000): 217–19.

[42] Peter Geschiere, "Le social standardisé: L'état contre la communauté?," *Critique Internationale* 1 (October 1998): 60–65.

of globalization and the reinvention of the local or the production of localities.[43] Thus, strategies of resistance are often less systematic and widespread than is often claimed. As Kasaba shows with respect to nomads under the Ottoman Empire, mobility cannot be systematically analyzed as resistance to the state. To the contrary, the Ottoman Empire played off different logics, accommodating the movements of certain populations. Likewise, the simplicity involved in interpretations based on an opposition between the state and civil society has long been demonstrated, such a dichotomy being itself based on a reductionist view of the notion of civil society. Numerous studies now illustrate the complicit relations between state and society, as well as the direct links between state formation and communal forms of violence or the synergy involved in creating uniformity and the invention of difference.

Finally, beyond my first two points – the complex, multivocal exercising of power and the existence of multiple, seemingly contradictory allegiances of people – the third lesson to be drawn from the chapters of this volume is the multiple significance of boundaries. These often reveal practices engendered by "the center" and, more generally, of the state, barriers and separations, as well as practices of mediation and points of fusion.

Recent scholarship on borders is a manifestation of the recognition that boundaries are central sites, or privileged spaces of observation of fluid and moving forms and of the continuous formation of social and political practices, as well as state practices. Basson illustrates this point in her presentation of "mixed blood" populations, a group even more marginal than the American Indians because they are situated beyond the cultural and political boundaries defined by the state. The legal and juridical interventions and, more generally, their socio-political treatment underscore the importance of race as a referent in the formation of American citizenship. Basson shows how litigation, problems raised by marginal groups, and their demands have even contributed to the increasing centrality and primacy of racial criteria in political practice, which reveals the nature of the North American state, its priorities, and its ambiguities. This is also true for Burma, as described by Callahan, who demonstrates how peripheral and excluded regions are in fact central for the junta in power. In fact, such regions are in no way ignored: The description of policies with respect to minorities indicates not only the government's preoccupation with such populations (control, fear of an opposition), but also the most important modalities for state intervention (the invention of tradition and cultural marking, language, and administrative standardization, all of which involve more than simply development programs).

[43] Arjun Appadurai, *Modernity at Large: Cultural Dimension of Globalization* (Minneapolis: University of Minessota Press, 1996); Meyer and Geschiere, eds., *Globalisation and Communal Identities.*

On this same subject, the chapters assembled here all speak to the centrality of margins and the place of marginal persons, thus responding to recent work on that theme.[44] Studies of Sub-Saharan and North Africa again illustrate this point. The ambiguous status of smugglers, pirates, "protégés,"[45] strangers, mulattos, and indigenous peoples or allogenes has offered and still offers numerous possibilities to local populations, including social and economic advantages.[46] The main reason for this situation – which is neither comfortable nor desired by this population itself, but rather open, fluid, and full of social and economic opportunities – is the increasing ability to straddle divergent positions, statuses, and activities. Social, political, economic, and cultural boundaries reveal, for the past as for today, the division of space and the willingness to protect. But at the same time, they give a central place to ambiguous statuses, which are able to transgress those very boundaries. Certain studies show how marginal groups can be mediators who contribute to the functioning of the state (by offering access to imports, contact with people from the outside, assumption of certain functions of state, etc.) and who participate unconsciously and involuntarily in state formation. These practices of straddling constitute the basis of politics. They explain how margins and boundaries are often created and constructed or sometimes exacerbated

44 On economic aspect and especially transborder trade, see Karine Bennafla, "Entre Afrique noire et monde arabe: Nouvelles tendances des échanges informels tchadiens," *Revue Tiers Monde* 152, 10/12 (1997): 879–95, and "La fin des territoires nationaux?," *Politique Africaine* 73 (March 1999): 24–49; Fariba Adelkhah, "Le retour de Sindbad: L'Iran dans le Golfe," *Les Études du CERI*, no. 53 (May 1999). On political aspects and especially violence, see Christian Geffray, *La cause des armes au Mozambique: Anthropologie d'une guerre civile* (Paris: Karthala, 1990); Roland Marchal, "Les mooryann de Mogadiscio: Formes de la violence dans un espace urbain en guerre," *Cahiers d'Études Africaines* 130, XXXIII-2 (1993): 295–320; Karen Barkey, *Bandits and Bureaucrats: The Ottoman Route to State Centralization* (Ithaca, N.Y.: Cornell University Press, 1994); Rémy Bazenguissa, "Milices politiques et bandes armées à Brazzaville: Enquête sur la violence politique et sociale des jeunes déclassés," *Les Études du CERI* 13 (April 1996); Roland Marchal and Christine Messiant, *Les chemins de la guerre et de la paix: Fins de conflit en Afrique orientale et australe* (Paris: Karthala, 1997); Luis Martinez, *La guerre civile en Algérie* (Paris: Karthala, 1998), translated as *The Civil War in Algeria* (London and New York: Hurst and Columbia University Press, 2000); Stephen Ellis, *The Mask of Anarchy* (London: Hurst, 1999).

45 On the past, see Clancy-Smith, "The Maghrib and the Mediterranean World," and Fernand Braudel, *La Méditerranée et le monde méditerranéen à l'époque de Philippe II* (Paris: Armand Colin, 1966), vol. 2, and *Civilisation matérielle, économie et capitalisme, XV–XVIII siècle*, 3 vols. (Paris: Armand Colin, 1979). On the current situation, see Alain Tarrius, *Economies souterraines: Le comptoir maghrébin de Marseille* (Toulouse: L'Aube, 1995); Hibou, *L'Afrique est-elle protectionniste?* and "Les enjeux de l'ouverture au Maroc," and Roitman, *Fiscal Disobedience*.

46 Gavin Kitching, *Class and Economic Change in Kenya: The Making of a Petite Bourgeoisie, 1905–1970* (New Haven, Conn.: Yale University Press, 1980); Bayart, *The State in Africa*; Achille Mbembe, "Crise de légitimité, restauration autoritaire et déliquescence de l'État," in Peter Geschiere and Peter Konings, eds., *Itinéraires d'accumulation au Cameroun* (Paris: Karthala-ASC, 1993), pp. 345–74, and *On Postcolony* (University of California Press, 2001).

and accentuated. In Morocco, for instance, historians have shown how the division between the Makhzen and the Siba was, above all, a fact of central power.[47] This division – or this boundary, which was itself porous and moving – was the expression of a distinct mode of government. The boundary between submission and dissidence, between the center and the margins, could also be fictive. Governing according to the margins was a manner of governing at the least cost and controlling what was largely a fabricated dissidence:[48] In fact, the tribes from outside constituted a political reservoir.

In any case, positions on the boundaries and borderline behavior expose the multiple points of the exercise of power and modes of governing. They allow us to disturb the image of the well-defined and stable state and its coherent practices. In that sense, this volume offers another interpretation of boundaries not as margins or peripheries but as reflections of the center and, in particular, the materialization, the understanding, and the significance of state practices. To govern is to play on the dynamics of passage from one space to another; it is the transgression of boundaries.

Therefore, boundaries among groups, affiliations, domains, logics, norms, and referents can be seen as separators, demarcations, or points from which one thing becomes another. They are barriers, but they can also serve as points of exchange, mediation, and fusion.

In his chapter, Kasaba illustrates how the frontiers of the Ottoman Empire were less obstacles, or places of separation, than spaces of connection. This entailed connections between Jews and Muslims, Christians and Muslims, the Empire and Europe, the Empire and Asia, and so on. For economists, this idea is rather banal since borders are, above all, the site for the establishment of relations between differences, which give rise to exchange. Difference, not homogeneity, is what makes for the richness of exchange. Borders create opportunities; they are not simply sites of separation or obstacle points. Frontier regions are sites of negotiation, as was suggested by the North African case cited above.

The idea of checkpoints developed by Migdal in his Introduction is thus both didactic and enriching. Checkpoints can be thought of as the sites or groups of practices that separate and create difference: techniques of surveillance such as passport and visa controls, as well as manners of dressing, speaking, and consuming. The remarks above on the mediating and central nature of boundaries and margins suggest that checkpoints can also be the sites and groups of practices that allow for fluidity and cohabitation, making possible the compatibility of the different registers that work to merge spaces and to blur differences. An analysis of goodwill practices is, in this regard, quite revealing. Certainly, these practices and the sites of the exercise of power associated with them generate difference, especially by underscoring

[47] Dakhlia, *Le divan des rois.*
[48] Tozy, *Monarchie et islam politique.*

the particular role of the private versus the public realm, or the religious sphere over the secular sphere. However, on closer inspection, we see that these practices and these sites are also founded on the blurring of such oppositions.

As Christine Messiant has shown in a remarkable study of the Angolan case, the Fondation Eduardo Dos Santos (FESA) was – all at once – a product of the general system of clientelist political domination, a sign of the strengthening of presidential power, an instance of the privatization of state functions, an example of the goodwill practices of the president, an expression of civil society, a palliative to inconsistent public interventions, and a factor in the aggravation of the demise of state institutions, among other things.[49] The FESA illustrates how such institutions play the role of a crossroads: as a system of extraction or taxation, which targeted both private and public enterprises and foreign and national economic operators, by persuasion or by coercion; through its various interventions, which were both statist (expenditures for health, education, and infrastructure) and clientelist (festivities in honor of the president); and through the effects of such interventions, which both complemented and substituted for public actions, thus contributing to the demise of the state apparatus. It was not only a site of intersection between allegedly contradictory logics, but also a site where the blurring of boundaries, differences, and oppositions took place.

A similar analysis can be made for the case of Tunisia, which harbors the Fonds de Solidarité National (National Solidarity Fund), better known by its postal bank account number: 26.26.[50] The latter was created by the president, but as a private entity. No public agency controls these funds, and the only titleholder is the president himself. While the Fonds de Solidarité National acts for the "public," it does so, ultimately, for the private glory of the president. Donations by citizens are voluntary and privately enacted, but those who dare not to contribute are subject to pressures and public interventions (fiscal audits, problems in professional activities). These interventions of 26.26 underscore the lacunae of the state, but at the same time, this part of the administrative apparatus works for the state, furnishing information, personnel, and infrastructure. In Morocco, the Mohamed V Foundation and

49 Christine Messiant, "La FESA: À Propos de l'investissement de la société civile par le pouvoir angolais," *Politique africaine* 73 (March 1999): 82–102. FESA is a foundation that was created by the President of the Republic. Through it, private funds are used for the personal charity works of the president, who thus acts in both a private capacity and a public manner (as President of the Republic and President of the MPLA). Funds derive from "donations" (or taxes) from major private companies, such as foreign oil firms, major public entreprises, and the state itself. They are used for health programs, the construction of schools, and infrastructure, as well as for clientelism and in order to appropriate domestic and international resources.

50 Béatrice Hibou, "Les marges de manœuvre d'un 'bon élève économique': La Tunisie de Ben Ali," *Les Études du CERI*, no. 60 (December 1999).

the Fonds Hassan II (Hassan II Fund) seem to indicate a similar logic, although the repressive dimension is less evident. Such situations are also found in other sites and groups of practices that are seemingly opposed, such as the former *waqf* in Muslim states or, today, the charity institutions in Somalia and Sudan[51] and the Foundation for the Disinherited in Iran,[52] which also demonstrates the blurring of frontiers between the religious and the secular.

All these examples demonstrate, on the one hand, the blurring of boundaries between public status (presidential or royal) and private status (of the "patron") and the blurring between public and private aims. On the other hand, they also indicate the complexity of interrelationships between each of these poles and their associated referents, which are supposed to be opposed and antagonistic. They illustrate, then, the final significance of the frontier: a heterotopy, to take up Foucault's vocabulary, or the frontier as a heteronomous space. This is the point made by Kemp's contribution to this volume: Boundaries are spaces in which different forms of logic bloom; frontier zones and those who live on frontiers are subject to the intensification of state power through centralization, territorialization, and surveillance. But the Palestinians were constituted both as a dangerous population and as citizens. Their status as citizens allows them to create a civil society, to participate in Israeli political life, and to find a basis for autonomy. At the same time, they are excluded from the ethno-nationalist project of the state, being summoned to prove their loyalty to a state that cannot be loyal to them since the very definition of the state is "a Jewish state."

Not only boundaries – between public and private or legal and illegal, as well as among spaces, practices, and different referents – are fluid, and not only boundaries are heteronomous spaces. The practices of straddling, articulation, and accommodation that take place *within* them and the multiplicity of forms (property, modes of regulation, legitimacy, intervention, concepts) also characterize political situations. Concretely speaking, what the political and cultural practices presented in this book show us is the plurality of mixed forms that blur referents and boundaries, the multiplicity of principles of legitimacy that characterize both past and contemporary processes of "globalization."

[51] Roland Marchal, "Des contresens possibles de la globalisation," *Politique africaine* 73 (March 1999): 68–81.

[52] Adelkhah, *Being Modern in Iran* 2000, chap. 3, and "Les Iraniens de Californie: Si la République islamique n'existait pas . . . ," *Les Études du CERI* 75 (May 2001).

Index

Lightning Source UK Ltd.
Milton Keynes UK
UKOW01f0906190816

281050UK00001B/77/P

9 780521 068499